Fodor's 05

BELIZE & GUATEMALA

Where to Stay and Eat for All Budgets

Must-See Sights and Local Secrets

Ratings You Can Trust

Fodor's Travel Publications New York, Toronto, London, Sydney, Auckland
www.fodors.com

FODOR'S BELIZE & GUATEMALA 2005
Editors: Carissa Bluestone, Pamela Lee

Editorial Production: Jacinta O'Halloran
Editorial Contributors: Gregory Benchwick, Lan Sluder
Maps: David Lindroth *cartographer;* Bob Blake and Rebecca Baer, *map editors*
Design: Fabrizio La Rocca, *creative director;* Guido Caroti, *art director;* Moon Sun Kim, *cover designer;* Melanie Marin, *senior picture editor*
Production/Manufacturing: Angela L. McLean
Cover Photo: (Coffee canoe, Guatemala): Bo Zaunders/Corbis

ISBN 1-4000-1426-3

ISSN 1522-6123

SPECIAL SALES
This book is available for special discounts for bulk purchases for sales promotions or premiums. Special editions, including personalized covers, excerpts of existing books, and corporate imprints, can be created in large quantities for special needs. For more information, write to Special Markets/Premium Sales, 1745 Broadway, MD 6-2, New York, New York 10019, or e-mail specialmarkets@randomhouse.com.

AN IMPORTANT TIP & AN INVITATION
Although all prices, opening times, and other details in this book are based on information supplied to us at press time, changes occur all the time in the travel world, and Fodor's cannot accept responsibility for facts that become outdated or for inadvertent errors or omissions. So **always confirm information when it matters,** especially if you're making a detour to visit a specific place. Your experiences—positive and negative—matter to us. If we have missed or misstated something, **please write to us.** We follow up on all suggestions. Contact the Belize & Guatemala editor at editors@fodors.com or c/o Fodor's at 1745 Broadway, New York, New York 10019.

PRINTED IN THE UNITED STATES OF AMERICA

10 9 8 7 6 5 4 3 2 1

DESTINATION BELIZE & GUATEMALA

A mere sliver on the Caribbean, Belize extends beyond the boundaries of land, incorporating cayes, atolls, and reefs into its surreal landscape. Guatemala is, in the words of poet Pablo Neruda, the "sweet waist" of Central America, with highlands full of invigorating mountain air and lowland fields of sugarcane that seem to expand, then to melt away, in the dreamlike heat. In Belize you can spend your mornings at a sandbar, snorkeling and feeding manta rays, and your evenings just gaping at the stars. In Guatemala, the center of the Maya heartland, you can explore incomparable ancient ruins, graceful colonial churches, and colorful highland markets. Each country is a destination in its own right, worthy of lengthy exploration, but together they form the ultimate trip, in which you can commune with the angelfish of Belize's spectacular Barrier Reef one day, and peer into pools of boiling lava from the rim of Guatemala's Volcán Pacayá the next. Have a fabulous trip!

Tim Jarrell, Publisher

CONTENTS

Maps

CloseUps

ABOUT THIS BOOK

	The best source for travel advice is a like-minded friend who's just been where you're headed. But with or without that friend, you'll be in great shape to find your way around your destination once you learn to find your way around your Fodor's guide.
SELECTION	Our goal is to cover the best properties, sights, and activities in their category, as well as the most interesting communities to visit. We make a point of including local food-lovers' hot spots as well as neighborhood options, and we avoid all that's touristy unless it's really worth your time. You can go on the assumption that everything in this book is recommended wholeheartedly by our writers and editors. Flip to **On the Road with Fodor's** to learn more about who they are. It goes without saying that no property pays to be included.
RATINGS	Orange stars ★ denote sights and properties that our editors and writers consider the very best in the area covered by the entire book. These, the best of the best, are listed in the **Fodor's Choice** section in the front of the book. Black stars ★ highlight the sights and properties we deem **Highly Recommended,** the don't-miss sights within any region. In cities, sights pinpointed with numbered map bullets ❶ in the margins tend to be more important than those without bullets.
SPECIAL SPOTS	**Pleasures & Pastimes** and chapter title pages focus on experiences that reveal the spirit of the destination. Also watch for **Off the Beaten Path** sights. Some are out of the way, some are quirky, and all are worth while. When the munchies hit, look for **Need a Break?** suggestions.
TIME IT RIGHT	Check **On the Calendar** up front and chapters' **Timing** sections for weather and crowd overviews and best days and times to visit.
SEE IT ALL	Use Fodor's exclusive **Great Itineraries** as a model for your trip. Either follow those that begin the book, or mix regional itineraries from several chapters. In cities, **Good Walks** guide you to important sights in each neighborhood; ⚑ indicates the starting points of walks and itineraries in the text and on the map.
BUDGET WELL	Hotel and restaurant price categories from **¢ to $$$$** are defined in the opening pages of each chapter—expect to find a balanced selection for every budget. For attractions, we always give standard adult admission fees; reductions are usually available for children, students, and senior citizens.
BASIC INFO	**Smart Travel Tips** lists travel essentials for the entire area covered by the book; city- and region-specific basics end each chapter. To find the best way to get around, see the transportation section; see individual modes of travel ("Car Travel," "Train Travel") for details.
ON THE MAPS	**Maps** throughout the book show you what's where and help you find your way around. Black and orange numbered bullets ❶ ❶ in the text correlate to bullets on maps.

BACKGROUND

We give background information within the chapters in the course of explaining sights as well as in **CloseUp** boxes and in **Understanding Belize & Guatemala** at the end of the book. To get in the mood, review **Books & Movies.** The **Spanish vocabulary** can be invaluable.

FIND IT FAST

Within the book, chapters are arranged by country. Chapters are divided into small regions, within which towns are covered in logical geographical order; attractive routes and interesting places between towns are flagged as **En Route.** Heads at the top of each page help you find what you need within a chapter.

DON'T FORGET

Restaurants are open for lunch and dinner daily unless we state otherwise; we mention dress only when there's a specific requirement and reservations only when they're essential or not accepted—it's always best to book ahead. Unless we note otherwise, **hotels** have private baths, phone, TVs, and air-conditioning and operate on the European Plan (a.k.a. EP, meaning without meals). We always list facilities but not whether you'll be charged extra to use them, so when pricing accommodations, find out what's included.

SYMBOLS

Many Listings

- ★ Fodor's Choice
- ★ Highly recommended
- Ruins
- ✉ Physical address
- Directions
- Mailing address
- ☎ Telephone
- Fax
- On the Web
- E-mail
- Admission fee
- Open/closed times
- Start of walk/itinerary
- Ⓜ Metro stations
- Credit cards

Outdoors

- Camping

Hotels & Restaurants

- Hotel
- Number of rooms
- Facilities
- Meal plans
- ✕ Restaurant
- Reservations
- Dress code
- Smoking
- BYOB
- Hotel with restaurant that warrants a visit

Other

- Family-friendly
- Contact information
- ⇨ See also
- Branch address
- ☞ Take note

ON THE ROAD WITH FODOR'S

A trip takes you out of yourself. Concerns of life at home completely disappear, driven away by more immediate thoughts—about, say, what marvels will beguile the next day, or where you'll have dinner. That's where Fodor's comes in. We make sure that you know all your options, so that you don't miss something that's around the next bend just because you didn't know it was there. Because the best memories of your trip might well have nothing to do with what you came to the region to see, we guide you to sights large and small all over the region. You might set out to laze on a beach or hike around Mayan ruins, but back at home you find yourself unable to forget caving in Belize or white-water rafting in Guatemala. With Fodor's at your side, serendipitous discoveries are never far away.

Our success in showing you every corner of these two remarkable countries is a credit to our extraordinary writers. Although there's no substitute for travel advice from a good friend who knows your style, our contributors are the next best thing—the kind of people you would poll for travel advice if you knew them.

Freelance writer **Gregory Benchwick** first fell in love with Latin America when he travelled via chicken bus from Costa Rica to Belize in 1995. Returning to Latin America in 1999, this time to Chile, Gregory first glimpsed the rugged, enchanting, and often inhospitable landscape of El Norte Chico and El Norte Grande, which he wrote about for *Fodor's Chile.* A former editor of the *Bolivian Times,* Gregory has written extensively about travel in Latin America. Gregory updated the Guatemala chapter for this editon.

Belize First magazine editor and publisher **Lan Sluder** has been banging around that country since 1991. In addition to authoring *San Pedro Cool, Adapter Kit: Belize,* and other books on Belize, he has written about the country for *Caribbean Travel & Life,* the *Bangkok Post,* and Canada's *Globe & Mail,* among other publications. Lan updated Belize, Smart Travel Tips, and Understanding Belize & Guatemala for this edition.

Central America

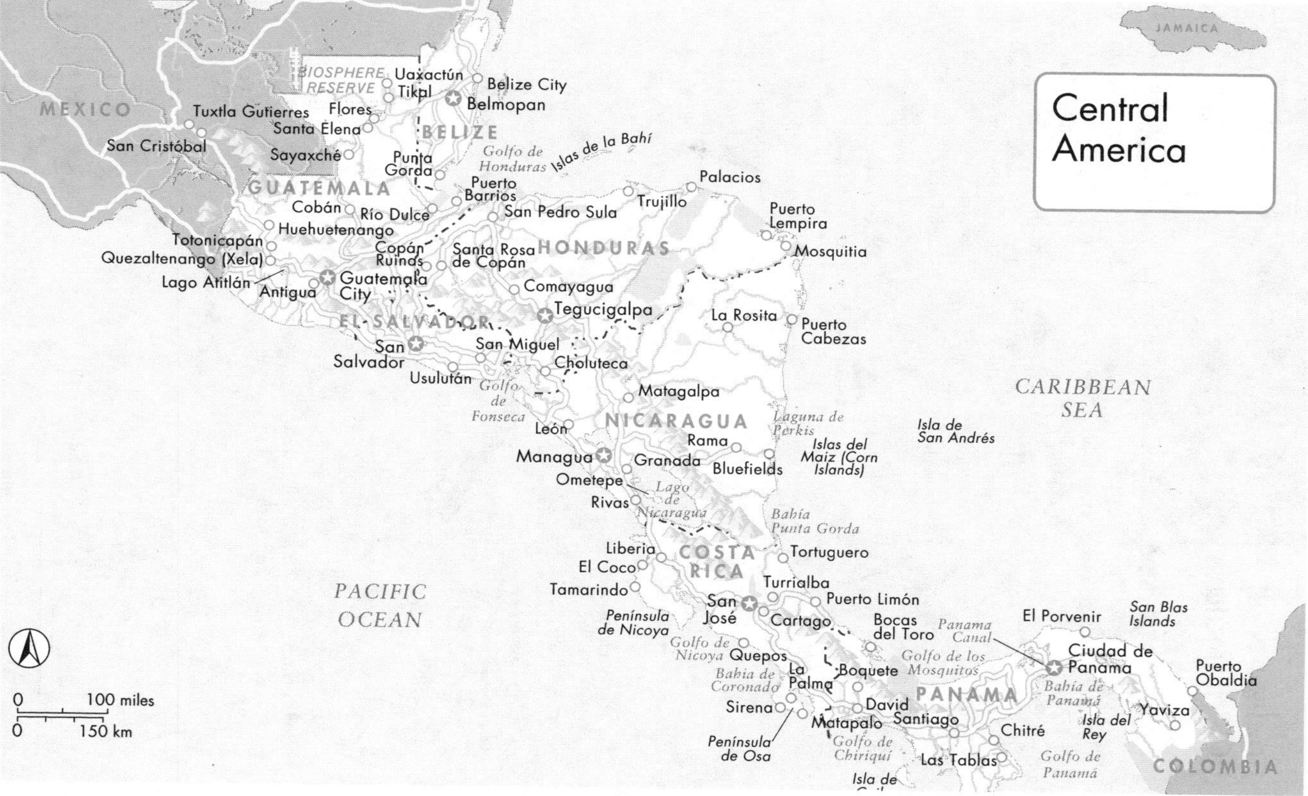

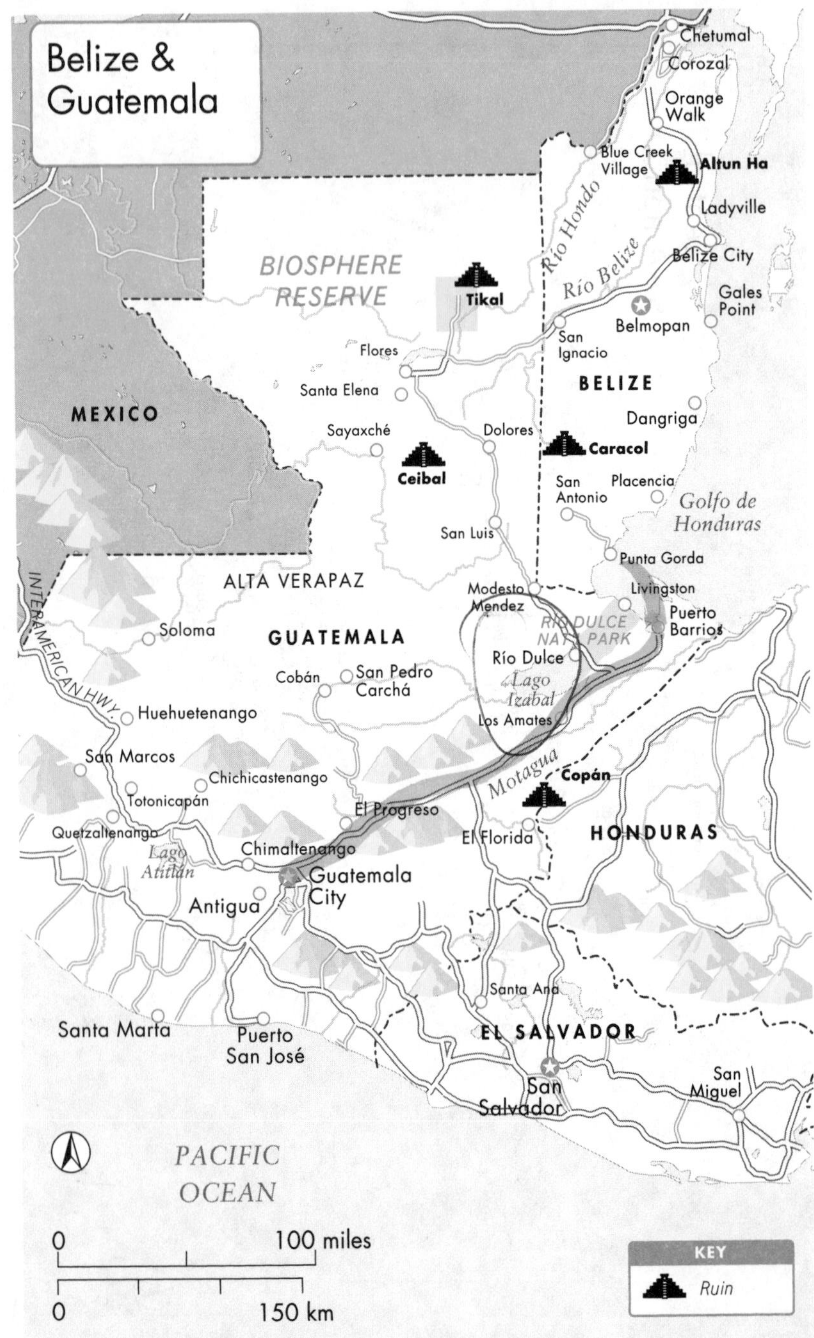
Belize & Guatemala
Chetumal
Corozal
Orange Walk
Blue Creek Village
Altun Ha
Ladyville
Belize City
Río Hondo
Río Belize
BIOSPHERE RESERVE
Tikal
Gales Point
Belmopan
San Ignacio
Flores
Santa Elena
BELIZE
MEXICO
Dangriga
Sayaxché
Dolores
Caracol
Ceibal
San Antonio
Placencia
Golfo de Honduras
San Luis
Punta Gorda
ALTA VERAPAZ
Modesto Mendez
Livingston
Puerto Barrios
RÍO DULCE NAT. PARK
INTERAMERICAN HWY.
Soloma
GUATEMALA
Río Dulce
Cobán
San Pedro Carchá
Lago Izabal
Huehuetenango
Los Amates
San Marcos
Motagua
Copán
Chichicastenango
Totonicapán
El Progreso
HONDURAS
Quetzaltenango
El Florida
Chimaltenango
Lago Atitlán
Guatemala City
Antigua
Santa Ana
Santa Marta
Puerto San José
EL SALVADOR
San Salvador
San Miguel
PACIFIC OCEAN
0
100 miles
0
150 km
KEY
Ruin

WHAT'S WHERE

Although they sit side by side, Belize and Guatemala could hardly be more different. Belize has always had more in common with the islands of the Caribbean Sea than with the rest of Central America. Its astounding stands of coral have made it a world-class diving destination, second only to Australia's Great Barrier Reef. Travelers who come here usually have only three things in mind: sun, sand, and surf.

Guatemala also has a short coastline on the Caribbean, as well as a much longer one on the Pacific, but most of its population lives in the towns and villages of the highlands. The lively outdoor markets show just how little these communities have changed over the centuries. Guatemala has long been a popular destination for backpackers seeking out the mysteries of the Mayan temples.

1 Belize

Wedged between Guatemala and the Yucatán Peninsula, Belize is a sliver of land on the Caribbean Sea. Along its coastline are 400 cayes, some no larger than a tennis court. In the Maya Mountains—the central highlands that form the watershed for Belize's thousands of streams and rivers—there is dense rain forest; in the north, savannas and fields of sugarcane. Because it has the lowest population density of any Central American nation—El Salvador, though a smaller country, has 10 times the population—most of this green interior is still the province of scarlet macaws, tapirs, kinkajous, pumas, and howler monkeys. Even reduced to vapid statistics—550 species of birds, some 300 varieties of orchids, hundreds of butterfly species—the sheer variety of Belize's wildlife is breathtaking. The same goes for its nearly 600 Mayan ruins, which range from the metropolitan splendor of Caracol to the humble burial mounds sprinkled throughout the countryside.

2 Guatemala

Belize may have the beaches, but Guatemala has just about everything else—misty cloud forests, tremendous mountain ranges, smoldering volcanoes, and rain forests of massive mahogany trees draped with mosses, bromeliads, and rare orchids. In the highlands around Lago Atitlán are sleepy villages that come to life each week with vibrant markets. Here you'll find Antigua, the colonial capital filled with quaint cobblestone streets, crumbling monasteries, and the country's finest restaurants and hotels. Take a white-water rafting trip to the Pacific coast, or go boating in the Atlantic Lowlands. Water sports are popular on the Atlantic coast, which spices things up with its distinctive Caribbean flavor. Everywhere are traces of the Maya, especially in El Petén, where the stately pyramids of Tikal rise from the steamy jungle.

GREAT ITINERARIES

Belize and Guatemala are so diverse, and transportation so capricious or simply downright slow, that seeing both countries in depth would take many weeks, and even then you could only hope to hit the highlights. These itineraries, though necessarily limited in scope, still provide you with the best possible mix of reef, rain forest, history, and culture.

Highlights of Belize & Guatemala

10 to 14 days

This itinerary gives you the top sights in both countries in two weeks or less.

ANTIGUA, GUATEMALA **2 days.** Fly into **Guatemala City.** Go immediately to the colonial city of **Antigua.** In this ancient city of cobblestone streets, you're instantly transported back hundreds of years, when the Spanish ruled. Spend a couple of days touring the convents, monasteries, and churches and absorbing the atmosphere of this touristy but charming town. Then, well-fed and well-rested from a stay in a colonial mansion, you'll be ready to tackle the Highlands.

WESTERN HIGHLANDS, GUATEMALA **2 to 3 days.** Start in the heart of the Highlands, with a night in **Panajachel.** In the morning take a launch to the lakeside village of **Santiago Atitlán,** home to one of the largest indigenous communities in Guatemala, and then continue to **Xelajú.** After that, head to the renowned market in the colonial village of **Chichicastenango.**

FLORES & TIKAL, GUATEMALA **2 days.** Return to **Guatemala City** and fly to **Flores,** the pastel-painted town on Lago Petén Itzá. You can stay in this delightful little town, visiting **Tikal,** the most amazing Mayan site in the region, on day trips or stay at Tikal in one of its overpriced but convenient lodges. Even if you're not an early riser, try to get to Tikal early in the morning to take in the sunrise from the top of one of the pyramids. If you have time, see some of the other of the hundreds of Mayan ruins in the Petén such as **Uaxactún** or **Nakún.**

SAN IGNACIO, BELIZE **2 to 3 days.** From Flores, take a van or bus to **San Ignacio,** also known as El Cayo, crossing the border at Melchor/Benque Viejo. If you're on a budget, you can stay in town at an inexpensive hotel. If you have more money to burn, stay at one of the jungle lodges outside of town. While in the San Ignacio area, see **Xunantunich** and **Cahal Pech** ruins, and if you have more time, do a day tour to **Caracol,** a classic Mayan site that in its heyday rivaled Tikal. En route you can visit waterfalls, the Rio Frio cave and perhaps picnic beside the Macal River. You'll also want to see a butterfly farm—Green Hills is the best—or do a canoe trip on the Macal or Mopan River. Don't miss **Actun Tunichil Muknal cave,** one of the highlights of any trip to Belize.

AMBERGRIS CAYE, BELIZE **2 to 4 days.** Fly, or take a bus or shuttle van to **Belize City** (if by bus or van, make a stop at the Belize Zoo), then fly or take a water taxi to **San Pedro.** Snorkel Hol Chan Marine Reserve, including Shark-Ray Alley. Take a day trip to dive or snorkel the Blue Hole at Lighthouse Reef atoll. Relax on the beach, or take a tour to

Lamanai ruins. If you're a golfer, spend a day at Caye Chapel. Return to Belize City by plane or water taxi, and fly home from the international airport.

Caribbean Adventure

12 to 18 days

This itinerary provides the best of the Caribbean coast and cayes, with just a touch of inland adventure.

BELIZE CITY **1 day.** Fly into the international airport near Belize City and spend the night in this Creole city, which, while very different from most of the rest of Belize, has a certain raffish charm. You might even see the ghost of Graham Greene.

AMBERGRIS CAYE **3 to 4 days.** Fly or take a water taxi to **San Pedro.** Enjoy the best restaurants in Belize on this Caribbean resort island. Snorkel Hol Chan Marine Reserve including Shark-Ray Alley. Take a day trip to dive or snorkel the Blue Hole at Lighthouse Reef atoll. Relax on the beach or spend a day golfing at Caye Chapel. Return to Belize City by plane or water taxi.

COROZAL TOWN **1 to 2 days.** Fly or take a water taxi from San Pedro to **Corozal Town,** the northernmost town in Belize. Alternatively, you can return to Belize City and get a rental car to drive the two hours to Corozal. There's not a lot to see or do here, but the setting on the Bay of Chetumal is beautiful, and the town is safe, friendly, and inexpensive. Alternatively, if you want to experience more of mainland Belize and see Mayan ruins, fly or bus to **San Ignacio** or to Flores and Tikal.

CAYES AND ATOLLS **3 to 5 days.** Return by bus or rental car to **Belize City.** Head out for a few days of diving, fishing, or simply beachcombing on one of Belize's three atolls—Lighthouse, Turneffe, or Glovers—or on one of the many beautiful islands on the barrier reef, such as **Tobacco Caye** or **South Water Caye.** Which you choose depends on your wallet and also on how much time you have, as some remote island lodges require 5- or 7-day stays, especially during high-season. Most lodges provide transportation from either Belize City or Dangriga.

PLACENCIA OR HOPKINS, BELIZE **2 days.** Return to Belize City or Dangriga, then fly or go by bus to **Placencia** or **Hopkins.** Hopkins is a small Garifuna seaside village, and Placencia is a little bit of the South Pacific on the southern Belize coast. Both have very good beaches. From either, visit **Cockscomb Preserve.** If you're very lucky, you may see a jaguar.

PUNTA GORDA, BELIZE **2 days.** Fly or take a bus down the Southern Highway to **Punta Gorda** (PG), the southernmost town in Belize. Absorb the outpost atmosphere, take a tour of the Mayan villages near town, and see Belize's rain forest.

ATLANTIC/CARIBBEAN LOWLANDS, GUATEMALA **2 days.** Take a water taxi from PG to the Garifuna village of **Livingston.** This is the Banana Belt of Guatemala, immortalized in the "Banana Trilogy," three books written in the 1950s by Nobel Prize–winning author Miguel Ángel Asturia. From Livingston, take a boat trip up the **Rio Dulce,** one of the most beautiful boat trips in the region.

Return to Punta Gorda, fly to Belize City, and depart from the international airport. Alternatively, go overland or fly to Guatemala City.

Heart of the Mayan Empire

11 to 15 days

This itinerary lets you see the great Mayan sites in Belize and Guatemala.

NORTHERN BELIZE **3 to 4 days.** Fly into the international airport near **Belize City** and spend the night in town. Rent a car and drive north to see some of the Mayan ruins in northern Belize—Altun Ha, Lamanai, Cerros, and Santa Rita. Spend one night each at **Crooked Tree Wildlife Sanctuary, Lamanai,** and **Corozal Town.**

SOUTHERN BELIZE **2 to 3 days.** Return to Belize City and fly or go by bus or rental car to **Punta Gorda.** Use PG as a base to visit the ruins of **Lubaantun** and **Nim Li Punit** (both can be seen in the same afternoon), and to see how the Maya live today in **Toledo.**

WESTERN BELIZE **3 to 4 days.** If driving or going by bus, go directly to **San Ignacio.** Otherwise, return to Belize City and fly to the city. Visit **Caracol,** (the most important site in Belize), Cahal Pech, El Pilar, and Xunantunich. Also take in Actun Tunichil Muknal cave, Barton Creek cave, or Che Chem Ha cave, all of which contain Mayan relics.

FLORES & TIKAL, GUATEMALA **3 to 4 days.** Fly or go by bus or van to **Flores.** Visit **Tikal,** the Angkor Wat of Central America, on a day trip, or stay at Tikal in one of the lodges there. Try to get to Tikal early in the morning to take in the sunrise from the top of one of the pyramids. See some of the other of the hundreds of Mayan ruins in the Petén such as **Uaxactún** (full-day trip) and **Yaxhá** (half-day trip). Return by air to Belize City to fly home.

WHEN TO GO

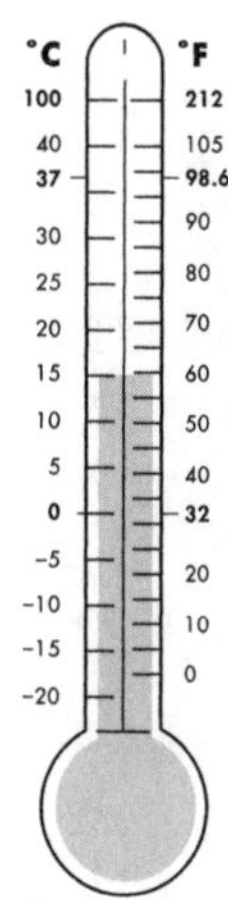

The Central American climate has two basic seasons. The rainy season, which in Spanish-speaking areas is *invierno* (winter), lasts from around June through November; the dry season, which is called *verano* (summer), runs from December through May. However, by "dry season" Belizeans usually mean the months in late spring, before seasonal rains begin in June, when temperatures inland may reach 38°C (100°F).

If you want to escape crowds and high prices and don't mind getting a little wet, visit in the rainy season. Though some restaurants may close and hotels may offer limited facilities, reservations are easy to get, even at top establishments, and you'll have the Mayan ruins and beaches to yourself. Note that Guatemala's busiest time of the year is around Holy Week, from Palm Sunday to Easter Sunday, and that hotels in Antigua, Panajachel, and Chichicastenango fill up months ahead of time. The busiest time in Belize is the Christmas–New Year's period, followed by Easter, but mid-November through April is the high season in Belize.

Climate

Belize's Caribbean coasts get sweltering, humid weather with soaring temperatures, while Guatemala's mountains in the Western Highlands can have downright chilly evenings. Central America's rainy season is marked by sporadic downpours that occur without warning; rainfall is generally heavier in the afternoon than in the morning, so you may want to do the majority of your sightseeing and shopping in the morning, leaving the afternoon flexible. In Belize only in the far south can the rainy season really be called rainy; the Toledo district gets 160 inches or more of rain annually. However, northern Belize gets about the same amount of rain annually as Atlanta, Georgia, and on the cayes rain usually comes in brief squalls, after which the sun comes out. The wet season on the cayes is often accompanied by lashing northerly winds known in Creole as Joe North. In a bad year Joe North can turn into Hurricane Hattie. Hurricane season in the western Caribbean is June through November, but historically storms usually hit September through early November.

Central America's tropical temperatures generally hover between 21°C and 29°C (70°F and 85°F). It's the high humidity that'll make you sweat. Remember to drink plenty of bottled water to avoid dehydration.

The following are average daily maximum and minimum temperatures for cities in Belize and Guatemala.

Forecasts **Weather Channel Connection** ☎ 900/932–8437, 95¢ per minute from a Touch-Tone phone.

BELMOPAN, BELIZE

Jan.	81F	27C	May	87F	31C	Sept.	87F	31C
	67	19		75	24		74	23
Feb.	82F	28C	June	87F	31C	Oct.	86F	30C
	69	21		75	24		72	22
Mar.	84F	29C	July	87F	31C	Nov.	83F	28C
	71	22		75	24		68	20
Apr.	86F	30C	Aug.	88F	31C	Dec.	81F	27C
	74	23		75	24		73	23

GUATEMALA CITY, GUATEMALA

Jan.	73F	23C	May	84F	29C	Sept.	79F	26C
	52	11		60	16		60	16
Feb.	77F	25C	June	81F	27C	Oct.	76F	24C
	54	12		61	16		60	16
Mar.	81F	27C	July	78F	26C	Nov.	74F	24C
	57	14		60	16		57	14
Apr.	82F	28C	Aug.	79F	26C	Dec.	72F	22C
	58	14		60	16		55	13

ON THE CALENDAR

The top seasonal events for both countries are listed below, and any one of them could provide the stuff of lasting memories. If you want your visit to coincide with one of these occasions, be sure to plan well in advance. Guatemala's festivals are particularly lively and colorful.

WINTER

Dec.	In Guatemala, Cobán's **International Orchid Festival** is held in early December in the main square.
	The charming Guatemalan village of Chichicastenango marks the **Día de Santo Tomás** on December 13. During the festivities men wear elegant silver costumes and carry staffs topped by a magnificent sun medallion.

SPRING

Mar.	**Baron Bliss Day,** celebrated on March 19, is when Belize City locals give three cheers for Baron Henry Edward Ernest Victor Bliss, a wealthy English sportsman who offered Belize an immense estate in return for a holiday devoted to sailing and fishing.
Apr.	The celebrations on **Good Friday** show off Guatemala at its most festive. Processions of costumed disciples weave their way through flower-carpeted streets, leaving behind a trail of incense.
May	In Belize, Crooked Tree celebrates the local cash crop with the annual **Cashew Festival.** Held the first weekend of the month, the festival includes sale of jams, jellies, juices, preserves, and other delicacies produced here.On May 24 the country celebrates **Commonwealth Day,** which commemorates the birthday of Queen Elizabeth II, with a bicycle race from Belize City to San Ignacio.
	Every year on the second Sunday in May the Guatemalan city of Cobán fills up with runners and spectators for the 21-km (13-mi) **International Cobán Half Marathon,** which is run over and around the area's beautiful green hillsides. About 2,800 runners from around the world participate annually.

SUMMER

June	The **Día de San Pedro,** a three-day festival honoring St. Peter, is celebrated in San Pedro, Belize. The early morning boat parade is worth a trip here.
	Lobster Festivals are held in Belize's Caye Caulker and Placencia to celebrate the beginning of the lobster-fishing season (June 15). The dates of the festivals vary from year to year.
July	Celebrated in Cobán, **Rabin Ajau** is a traditional festival that runs July 21–26. The week culminates with the crowning of the "daughter of the king."

Aug.	The Belizean village of San Pedro Columbia observes the **Día de San Luis Rey** on August 5 with religious ceremonies and dancing. The **San Pedro Costa Maya Festival,** held in mid-August, is a four-day multicultural bash that takes over Ambergris Caye, Belize.
	The Guatemalan village of San Felipe de Jesús, just north of Antigua, celebrates the **Día de San Felipe** on August 30.
FALL	
Sept.	The **Battle of St. George's Caye** celebrates the David-and-Goliath defeat of the Spanish navy by a motley crew of British settlers, buccaneers, and liberated slaves. This week of merrymaking in Belize begins September 10.
	Guatemalans nationwide celebrate their **Independence Day** on September 15 with traditional music, dances, and costumes.
	September 21 is **National Independence Day** in Belize, honoring the country's independence from Great Britain in 1981.
	In southern Belize, the village of San Antonio holds a colorful Mayan celebration that culminates in the **Feast of St. Luis** on September 25.
Oct.	Todos Santos Cuchumatán is the most frequently visited village in Guatemala, especially during **Festival de Todos Santos.** The longest festival in Guatemala, it begins each year on October 21. The high point of the celebration is a horse race with the competitors riding bareback.
	The **Festival de San Simón** is held in the village of Zunil each year on October 28, the date that the statue of this cigar-smoking deity, also known as Maximón, takes up residence in a new household.
Nov.	On **All Saints' Day,** also known as Day of the Dead, celebrated November 1, huge kites are flown in the cemetery of Santiago Sacatepéquez, near Guatemala City.
	Garífuna Settlement Day marks the arrival of Black Carib settlers, known as Garífunas, from the West Indies in 1823. Processions and traditional dancing are held throughout Belize, especially in Dangriga, but also in Hopkins and elsewhere.

PLEASURES & PASTIMES

Archaeological Treasures The ancient Mayan empire once occupied much of present-day Guatemala and extended east into Belize, north into Mexico, and south into Honduras and El Salvador. The empire crumbled in the middle of the 16th century, but it still left one of the richest cultural and archaeological legacies in the world. Only a fraction of the thousands of Mayan ruins have been excavated from the jungle that over the centuries has swallowed the splendid temples and sprawling cities. Of the many sites in the northernmost reaches of El Petén, Tikal is the most majestic; a visit to the top of one of the temples is an unforgettable experience. Evidence of the Maya is everywhere in the area, from the harder-to-reach pillars in the jungle at Aguateca to the caves at Actun Tunichil Muknal.

Bird-Watching Belize and Guatemala will make a bird-watcher out of anyone. Those who make it their business to memorize their field guide will have to share their binoculars with one and all when the toucans at Tikal fly from tree to tree. If you're a skilled birder in search of the hard-to-find motmot, you can make a beeline for Belize's Cayo or head off the beaten path to Guatemala's Lago Izabal. Guatemala's Biotopo del Quetzal is the place to see the bird whose plumage is as green as emeralds.

Nature's Bounty Central America has a nearly unfathomable array of flora and fauna. The rain forests are home to howler monkeys, which have a roar that will doubtless wake you up in the morning. Forge farther into the jungle and you'll encounter ocelots, pumas, or even the elusive jaguar. To preserve its natural wonders, Belize has created a well-run system of national parks, nature reserves, and wildlife sanctuaries. Guatemala has set up protected areas known as *biotopos* that, despite chronic underfunding, aim to preserve the country's natural resources as well as its archaeological heritage. Many of the protected areas in both countries are in remote locations that are difficult to reach; some are accessible only by all-terrain vehicles or only by boat.

Underwater Adventures It's no secret that Belize's Barrier Reef, a coral necklace stretching the length of the country, offers some of the world's best diving. The reef is not only the longest in the western and northern hemispheres, but also the most spectacular: graceful sea fans and great chunks of staghorn coral make a visit here an exhilarating experience. Although the diving is excellent almost anywhere along the reef, the very best is around the many coral atolls farther out to sea. Extremely popular are Turneffe Island and Lighthouse Reef, the latter the site of the famous Blue Hole. But you'll be amazed at what you can see without a tank. Snorkelers will see moray eels at Hol Chan Marine Reserve and nurse sharks at Shark-Ray Alley.

FODOR'S CHOICE

Fodor'sChoice ★

The sights, restaurants, hotels, and other travel experiences on these pages are our editors' top picks—our Fodor's Choices. They're the best of their type in the area covered by the book—not to be missed and always worth your time. In the destination chapters that follow, you will find all the details.

LODGING

$$$$ **Casa Palopó, Santa Catarina Palopó.** Lago Atitlán's best B&B has outstanding volcano views and gorgeous, brightly painted suites.

$$$$ **Caye Chapel Island Resort, Caye Chapel.** Luxurious villas, a country club setting, and a challenging 18-hole seaside golf course—enough said.

$$$$ **Cayo Espanto, near Ambergris Caye.** Everything's over-the-top at this private island, where your meals are served in your villa by the sea, and your every whim is catered to by your personal butler. The tab? Merely a small fortune.

$$$$ **Chan Chich Lodge, Gallon Jug.** Built atop the plaza of a Mayan temple, this lodge is so close to nature that your neighbors are howler monkeys and toucans.

$$$$ **Posada del Angel, Antigua.** This inn may be the most charming in Central America. The rooms are spacious and luxurious, with lovely corner fireplaces to keep out the chill.

$$$$ **Turtle Inn, Placencia.** Francis Ford Coppola's new beach resort, created with art and building materials from Bali (personally selected by the director), is the most exotic lodging in Belize.

$$$–$$$$ **Blancaneaux Lodge, Mountain Pine Ridge.** At Francis Ford Coppola's Belize hideaway you can stay in luxurious riverfront cabanas or splurge for the director's own villa.

$$$ **Mayan Inn, Chichicastenango.** This inn is a must-see, even if you don't stay the night. The plethora of antiques and intricate woodwork make this as much a museum as a place to hang your hat.

$$$ **Ni'tun Ecolodge, San Andrés.** This cluster of thatch-roof cabins is hidden in the forest on the shores of Guatemala's Lago Petén Itzá.

$–$$$ **The Lodge at Chaa Creek, The Cayo.** The seclusion of the jungle and the conviviality of candlelighted dinners make Chaa Creek the queen of the jungle resorts.

BUDGET LODGING

$$ **Posada de Santiago, Santiago Atitlán.** Sandwiched between two volcanoes on the shores of a lagoon, this hotel brings you every modern convenience while preserving a traditional Indian-village environment.

$	**Hotel La Posada, Cobán.** You won't be able to resist the lovely café on the porch of this simple colonial inn off Cobán's main square. Equally hard to resist is a nap in one of the hammocks.
¢	**Casa Rosada, Livingston.** Rough it in style in your own waterfront bungalow in this Guatemalan town.

RESTAURANTS

$$$$	**Capricorn, Ambergris Caye.** You'll have to take a water taxi to this romantic oceanside eatery, but the excellent seafood makes it worth the trip.
$$–$$$$	**Jake's, Guatemala City.** The best wine list in Central America is only one of the draws here.
$$–$$$$	**Welten, Antigua.** The handmade pasta, topped with inspired sauces and organic vegetables, couldn't be more satisfying. Enjoy your meal on the plant-filled patio, where orchids cascade from above.
$$	**Casa Picasso, Ambergris Caye.** Inspired tapas and pasta go together well with Picasso-inspired paintings by Belizean artists.

BUDGET RESTAURANTS

$–$$	**Café Kelá, Corozal Town.** Who would have thought you could get French crepes—and great pizza—in provincial Corozal Town?
¢–$	**El Bistro, Panajachel, Guatemala.** Enjoy homemade Italian pastas on the shores of Lago Atitlán as hummingbirds attend to flowering vines.
¢–$	**Las Puertas, Flores, Guatemala.** Six sets of swinging doors give Las Puertas its name. Fresh ingredients and smoothies full of just-picked fruit give this popular spot its lasting appeal.

ARCHAEOLOGICAL SITES

Actun Tunichil Muknal, Belize. Some of the country's most interesting Mayan sites are underground, as is this cavern on Roaring Creek near Belmopan. The "Cave of the Stone Sepulcher" holds remarkable artifacts and well-preserved skeletons of human sacrifices.

Caracol, Belize. The most spectacular Mayan site in Belize, Caracol has the remains of five plazas and 32 large structures covering nearly a square mile.

Lamanai, Belize. Nearly 60 Maya structures are spread over this 950-acre reserve, including a massive temple that is the largest Preclassic building in the country.

Quiriguá, Guatemala. This important erstwhile trading center is renowned for its massive stelae, the largest in the Maya world.

Tikal, Guatemala. Guatemala's most famous ruin is the embodiment of the extraordinary accomplishments of the Maya. The vast array of awesome temples and the intricate acropolis once formed a part of a teeming metropolis.

OUTDOOR ACTIVITIES

Canoeing or hiking through El Boqueran, El Estor, Guatemala. Float down this limestone canyon's crystalline river or delve into its many nooks and crannies, including bat-filled caves.

Diving or snorkeling at night, Hol Chan Marine Reserve, Belize. If you're a strong swimmer, this is a special treat. Nocturnal animals, including long-legged spider crabs, casually go about their business in water that sparkles from bioluminescence.

Looking for dolphins, Río Dulce. You will probably only get to see these magical mammals from a canoe, but the paddling will be well worth it as you float quietly between banks of jungle foliage, with egrets and iguanas perched overhead.

Sea kayaking, Glovers Atoll. Explore the remote atoll's 82 square mi of lagoons and patch reefs, about as far as you can get from the confines of civilization.

Soaking in the clear water pools, Semuc Champey. Here the beautiful white water of the Río Cahabón momentarily comes to a pause at a land bridge: the universe's intention, it seems, is serene soaking for the weary traveler.

Watching the sun rise atop a temple, Tikal. Imagine that you're Maya royalty—or an intrepid archaeologist—as the emerging rays wake the jungle into its noisy daily activity.

SMART TRAVEL TIPS

The organizations in this section can provide information to supplement this guide; contact them for up-to-the-minute details, and consult the A to Z sections that appear in each chapter for facts on the various topics as they relate to each country. Happy landings!

AIR TRAVEL

CARRIERS

American, Continental, Delta, TACA, and US Airways fly to Belize from the United States. The major departure gateways are Houston, with daily nonstop service to Belize City on Taca and Continental; Charlotte, with daily nonstop service on US Airways; and Miami, with daily nonstop service on American. Delta has a weekly nonstop flight from Atlanta; Continental has a weekly nonstop flight from Newark. TACA also flies to Belize City from several other U.S. cities with a change of planes in San Salvador, El Salvador.

Guatemala is served by American via Miami or Dallas, Continental via Houston, Iberia via Miami, Mexicana via Mexico City, Taca via Miami or Dallas, and United via Los Angeles. From New York the only nonstop flights are on TACA. From London, Iberia flies direct to Guatemala City via Madrid.

Whereas Guatemala uses regular 727 airplanes for domestic travel between the capital and Flores, Puerto Barrios, Río Dulce, and Huehuetenango, domestic planes in Belize are single- or twin-engine island hoppers. The main carriers are Tropic Air and Maya Island Air, both of which fly to San Pedro, on Ambergris Caye, and Caye Caulker, as well as Corozal, Dangriga, Placencia, Punta Gorda, and Flores, Guatemala. Domestic flights to and from the municipal airport are between BZ$96 and BZ$380 round-trip, except for those flights arranged on Javier Flying Service, which will take you pretty much anywhere for around BZ$340 per hour—flights to Chan Chich Lodge, Blancaneaux Lodge, and Lamanai Outpost Lodge are available.

Major Airlines Aeroméxico ☎ 800/237-6639 🌐 www.aeromexico.com. American ☎ 800/433-7300 🌐 www.aa.com. Continental ☎ 800/525-0280 🌐 www.continental.com. Iberia ☎ 800/772-4642 🌐 www.iberia.com. Mexicana ☎ 800/531-7921 🌐 www.mexicana.com. TACA ☎ 800/535-8780 🌐 www.grupotaca.com. US Airways ☎ 800/428-4322 🌐 www.usairways.com.

Belizean Airlines Javier Flying Service ☎ 223/5360 🖷 223/1731 🌐 www.javiersflying.bz. Maya Island Air ☎ 223/1140, 800/225-6732 in U.S. 🖷 223/0576 🌐 www.mayaislandair.com. Tropic Air ☎ 226/2012, 800/422-3435 in U.S. 🖷 226/2338 🌐 www.tropicair.com.

Guatemalan Airlines Aeroquetzal ☎ 334-7689. Aerovias ☎ 332-5686. Inter Airline ☎ 361-2144. Tikal Jets ☎ 334-5568 🌐 www.tikaljets.com.

CHECK-IN & BOARDING

Always **find out your carrier's check-in policy.** Plan to arrive at the airport about two hours before your scheduled departure time for domestic flights and 2½ to 3 hours before international flights. You may need to arrive earlier if you're flying from one of the busier airports or during peak air-traffic times. To avoid delays at airport-security checkpoints, try not to wear any metal. Jewelry, belt and other buckles, steel-toe shoes, barrettes, and underwire bras are among the items that can set off detectors.

Assuming that not everyone with a ticket will show up, airlines routinely overbook planes. When everyone does, airlines ask for volunteers to give up their seats. In return, these volunteers usually get a several-hundred-dollar flight voucher, which can be used toward the purchase of another ticket, and are rebooked on the next flight out. If there are not enough volunteers, the airline must choose who will be denied boarding. The first to get bumped are passengers who checked in late and those flying on discounted tickets, so get to the gate and check in as early as possible, especially during peak periods.

Always **bring a government-issued photo ID** to the airport; even when it's not required, a passport is best.

CUTTING COSTS

The least expensive airfares to Belize and Guatemala are priced for round-trip travel and must usually be purchased in advance. Airlines generally allow you to change your return date for a fee; most low-fare tickets, however, are nonrefundable.

Airfares to Belize are often twice or more the cost of a ticket to Mexican destinations such as Cancún or Cozumel. If you have the time, **consider flying into Mexico and taking a bus to Belize.** From the Yucatán a first-class or deluxe bus costs BZ$40 or less and takes between five and six hours to Chetumal, Mexico, a border town where you can transfer to a Belize bus. (If you fly into Cozumel, you'll first have to take a ferry to Playa del Carmen.)

You'll save up to 45% on flights within Belize if you **fly to and from the municipal airport near downtown Belize City,** rather than to or from the international airport north of the city in Ladyville. For example, a one-way flight from municipal to San Pedro is BZ$52, but is almost twice that from the international hub—and usually it's on exactly the same plane, which stops at both airports.

It's smart to call a number of airlines and check the Internet; when you are quoted a good price, book it on the spot—the same fare may not be available the next day, or even the next hour. Always check different routings and look into using alternate airports. Also, price off-peak flights, which may be significantly less expensive than others. Travel agents, especially low-fare specialists (⇨ Discounts & Deals), are helpful.

Consolidators are another good source. They buy tickets for scheduled flights at reduced rates from the airlines, then sell them at prices that beat the best fare available directly from the airlines. (Many also offer reduced car-rental and hotel rates.) Sometimes you can even get your money back if you need to return the ticket. Carefully read the fine print detailing penalties for changes and cancellations, purchase the ticket with a credit card, and confirm your consolidator reservation with the airline.

Consolidators **AirlineConsolidator.com** ☎ 888/468-5385 🌐 www.airlineconsolidator.com, for international tickets. **Best Fares** ☎ 800/880-1234 or 800/576-8255 🌐 www.bestfares.com; $59.90 annual membership. **Cheap Tickets** ☎ 800/377-1000 or 800/652-4327 🌐 www.cheaptickets.com. **Expedia** ☎ 800/397-3342 or 404/728-8787 🌐 www.expedia.com. **Hotwire** ☎ 866/468-9473 or 920/330-9418 🌐 www.hotwire.com. **Now Voyager Travel** ✉ 45 W. 21st St., Suite 5A New York, NY 10010 ☎ 212/459-1616 🖷 212/243-2711 🌐 www.nowvoyagertravel.com. **Onetravel.com** 🌐 www.onetravel.com. **Orbitz** ☎ 888/656-4546 🌐 www.orbitz.com. **Priceline.com** 🌐 www.priceline.com. **Travelocity** ☎ 888/709-5983, 877/282-2925 in Canada, 0870/876-3876 in U.K. 🌐 www.travelocity.com.

FLYING TIMES

To Belize City it's roughly 2 hours from Miami and 2½ hours from Charlotte and Houston.

To Guatemala City from Dallas or Houston the flying time is 2 hours; from Miami, 2½ hours; from Los Angeles, 7 hours; from New York or Chicago, 5½ hours; from Toronto via Miami or Mexico City, about 7 hours.

RECONFIRMING

Check the status of your flight before you leave for the airport. You can do this on your carrier's Web site, by linking to a flight-status checker (many Web booking services offer these), or by calling your carrier or travel agent. Always confirm international flights at least 72 hours ahead of the scheduled departure time.

AIRPORTS

International flights to Belize arrive at the Philip Goldson International Airport in Ladyville, 15 km (9 mi) north of Belize City, or at the Belize Municipal Airstrip. Domestic airports (which consist of landing strips with one-room check-in buildings nearby) are in Belize City, Caye Caulker, Corozal, Dangriga, Independence, Placencia, Punta Gorda, San Ignacio, and San Pedro.

The international airports in Guatemala are Aeropuerto Internacional La Aurora, in Guatemala City, and the smaller Aeropuerto Internacional Santa Elena, in El Petén.

Belize **Belize Municipal Airstrip** ✉ Belize City ☎ No phone. **Philip Goldson International Airport** ✉ Ladyville ☎ 225/2014.

Guatemala **Aeropuerto Internacional La Aurora** ✉ Guatemala City ☎ 332-6084 or 332-6085. **Aeropuerto Internacional Santa Elena** ✉ El Petén ☎ 950-1289.

BIKE TRAVEL

In Belize, the lightly traveled rural byways are good for biking, although the rough roads mean you should be prepared for lots of flats. Mountain Pine Ridge, with hardly any traffic on the miles of old logging roads, is an ideal spot for mountain biking. Bicycle racing has become an important sport in Belize, and you often see teams training.

Mountain biking is growing in popularity in Guatemala, particularly in highland towns like Antigua and Huehuetenango. Here the rolling hills, beautiful scenery, and decent (but not too crowded) roadways make for excellent two-wheel excursions. Road biking is less advisable, primarily because Guatemala's narrow highways can barely accommodate the growing number of cars and trucks as it is.

BIKES IN FLIGHT

Most airlines accommodate bikes as luggage, provided they are dismantled and boxed; check with individual airlines about packing requirements. Some airlines sell bike boxes, which are often free at bike shops, for about $20 (bike bags can be considerably more expensive). International travelers often can substitute a bike for a piece of checked luggage at no charge; otherwise, the cost is about $100. Most U.S. and Canadian airlines charge $40–$80 each way.

BIKE RENTALS

In Belize you can rent mountain bikes in the Cayo and road bikes in the resort areas of Ambergris Caye and Placencia. In Guatemala bike-rental shops are in all the good biking towns: Antigua, Panajachel, and Huehuetenango. Plenty of ecolodges and hotels throughout the country also rent bikes or lend them to guests free of charge: mind you, these are not always in the best of shape.

BOAT & FERRY TRAVEL

Since Belize has about 325 km (200 mi) of coastline and some 400 islands dotting the Caribbean, water taxis and small ferries are a primary form of transportation. There is scheduled ferry service six or more times a day from Belize City to Ambergris Caye, Caye Caulker, and Caye Chapel, as well as between those cayes. One-way fare from Belize City to Ambergris Caye is BZ$28, and the trip takes 1¼ hours. To Caye Caulker the fare is BZ$18, and the trip takes 45 minutes. A ferry runs daily between Corozal Town and San Pedro. The fair is BZ$40 one-way, and the trip takes 1½ hours. To reach the more remote cayes, you're basically left to your own devices, unless you're staying at a hotel where such transfers are arranged for you. The resorts on the atolls run their own flights or boats, but these are not available to the general public.

If you are headed to Honduras, ferries run once a week from Placencia and Dangriga, in Belize, to Puerto Cortes, in Honduras, for BZ$100 each way. *Lanchas* (private motor boats) shuttle passengers between Livingston, Guatemala, and Omoa, Honduras, every Tuesday and Friday. The boats leave Livingston at 7:30 and depart Omoa for the return trip at noon. The trip takes 2–3 hours and costs Q240.

For boat travel between Belize and Guatemala, water taxi service is available daily at 9 AM from Punta Gorda, in Belize, to Puerto Barrios and Livingston, in Guatemala, for BZ$20–BZ$25 each way. They return in the afternoon at 2 PM. A boat leaves Puerto Barrios for Punta Gorda on Tuesday and Friday at 7 AM and takes 2½ hours. Lanchas depart around 8–9 and 1–2; the trip takes 50 minutes.

Note that life jackets are typically not provided on boats and that the seas can be rough. Postpone your trip if the weather looks bad, and don't be shy about waiting for another boat if the one offered looks unseaworthy or overcrowded.

BUSINESS HOURS

BANKS & OFFICES

Belize has three local banks, Alliance Bank, Atlantic Bank, and Belize Bank, and two international banks, First International Bank (formerly Barclays) and ScotiaBank (formerly called Bank of Nova Scotia). Hours vary, but the branches are typically open Monday–Thursday 8–1 and Friday 8–1 and 3–6. The Belize Bank branch at Philip Goldson International Airport is open 8:30–4 daily.

In Guatemala most banks are open 9–4 but sometimes stay open until 7 PM. Major banks, such as Bancafe, Banco Industrial, and Banco Occidente, will exchange traveler's checks.

MUSEUMS & SIGHTS

It's a good idea to plan your visit to Belize's museums and archaeological sites for early in the day, as many of them, including popular attractions like Cahal Pech and Xunantunich, close at 4 or 4:30. Many have abbreviated hours on weekends, closing as early as noon.

In Guatemala many museums are closed Monday. Most are open normal business hours, but some close for a few hours in the afternoon. Tikal is open daily 8–6.

SHOPS

Belize is a very laid-back place that requires a certain amount of flexibility when browsing around stores. Shops operate according to the whim of the owner but are generally open 8–noon and 2–8. Larger stores and supermarkets in Belize City do not close at lunch. Some shops and businesses are open a half day on Wednesday and Saturday. On Friday many shops close early for the weekend. In tourist areas such as San Pedro, some shops are open late, until 8 or 9 PM. On Sunday Belize takes it easy—few shops are open.

In Guatemala shops are generally open 10–7, with many closing for a 1–3 lunch break.

BUS TRAVEL

Belize has frequent and inexpensive bus service on the Northern and Western highways, as well as reasonable service in the south along the Hummingbird, Manatee, and Southern highways. Elsewhere, service is spotty. There is no municipal bus service in Belize City, although most of Belize's private bus companies have their main terminals in Belize City. In Belize, because of many mergers, the main bus line is Novelo's, which also owns Southern Transport and Northern Transport. Together, these companies dominate bus service on main routes around the country. Other companies have a handful of buses on limited routes.

In Guatemala brightly colored buses are the transportation of choice for locals and visitors alike. They can get you just about anywhere cheaply and quickly, making them great for short trips. They aren't as convenient for longer journeys, as you'll probably have to change buses once or twice along the way. The down side is that buses can be extremely crowded. Always be prepared for a tight squeeze—this means three to a two-person seat.

Large bags are typically stowed on top—this may make you nervous, but thefts are not common. Except for occasional pick-pocketings, incidents involving foreign travelers on public buses are rare. Drivers and their assistants, called *cobradors* or *ayudantes,* are often a bit gruff but really know their stuff. They can tell you if you're on the right bus and remind you when and where to get off. To be sure you aren't forgotten, **try to sit near the driver.**

From Guatemala City Autobuses de Oriente has service to the Atlantic Lowlands, Las Verapaces, and El Petén. Transgalgos travels to the Western Highlands. Between Guatemala City and Antigua, Transportes Turísticos Atitrans and Turansa are both reputable companies. Línea Dorada offers direct bus service between Guatemala City and Santa Elena and Flores.

Belize Companies **Novelo's** ✉ W. Collet Canal, Belize City ☎ 227/2025. **Southern Transport** ✉ 3 Havana St., Dangriga ☎ 522/2160.

Guatemala Companies **Autobuses de Oriente** ✉ Guatemala City ☎ 238-3894. **Línea Dorada** ✉ Calle Principal, Santa Elena; Calle de la Playa, Flores ☎ 232-9658. **Transgalgos** ✉ Guatemala City ☎ 253-4868.

CLASSES

Expect to ride on old U.S. school buses or retired North American Greyhound buses. On some routes of Belize there are a few express buses with air-conditioning and other comforts. These cost a few dollars more.

In Guatemala inexpensive public buses, also of the converted school bus variety, crisscross the entire country, but they can be slow and extremely crowded. Popular destinations, such as Santa Elena and Río Dulce, are serviced by Pullman buses, which are as well equipped as American bus lines and are considerably more comfortable. Your hotel or Inguat office can make bus travel recommendations and arrangements for you.

FARES & SCHEDULES

Belizean buses are cheap, running about BZ$2–BZ$28 for trips between towns. In Belize most buses on main routes run according to more-or-less reliable schedules; on lesser-traveled routes the schedules may not mean much.

In Guatemala fares on public buses are a bargain at Q2–Q24. Public buses follow loose schedules, sometimes delaying departures until buses fill up. Be aware that on some routes the last bus of the day isn't always a sure thing. Always ask before waiting around.

PAYING

The main terminals in Belize City and some larger towns have ticket windows where you pay in advance and secure a reserved seat. If you board at other points, you pay the driver's assistant and take any available seat.

In Guatemala you pay the bus driver as you board. On intercity buses a fare collector will pass through the bus periodically to take your fare. These fare collectors have an amazing ability to keep track of all riders who have not paid on a jam-packed bus.

Advance-purchase bus tickets and reservations are usually unnecessary for routes within Belize and Guatemala. Arrive at bus terminals about a half hour before your departure.

SHUTTLE TRAVEL

Belize has minivans that shuttle riders between Belize City and San Ignacio. Aguada

Hotel, Santa Elena, has a daily shuttle that costs BZ$60 per person. Línea Dorada runs vans between Belize City and Flores, Guatemala, for BZ$50, and between Belize City and Chetumal for BZ$70 (plus border crossing fees).

Shuttles in Guatemala are private minivans that hold up to eight passengers. They are faster and more comfortable than public buses and maintain a fairly reliable schedule. Advance reservations are usually required. Shuttles can be arranged at the airport, at travel agencies, and at most hotels. Popular routes, like those between Guatemala City, Antigua, Chichicastenango, Panajachel, and Xelajú, run 3–5 times daily; other routes may have less frequent departures. Prices run $7–$35. Atitrans and Servicios Turísticos Atitlán are two reputable companies that operate shuttles throughout the country.

Belize Companies **Aguada Hotel** ☎ 804/3609. **Línea Dorada** ☎ 926/3649.

Guatemala Companies **Atitrans** ☎ 832-1381 or 363-0178. **Servicios Turísticos Atitlán** ☎ 832-1493 or 762-2075.

CAMERAS & PHOTOGRAPHY

With their incredibly varied landscapes, Belize and Guatemala are a photographer's dream. Frothy waves in a turquoise sea and palm-lined crescents of beach are relatively easy to capture on film if you don't let the brightness of the sun on sand and water fool your light meter. You must compensate or else work early or late in the day when the light isn't as brilliant and contrast isn't such a problem. Do **invest in a telephoto lens** if you intend to photograph wildlife: even standard zoom lenses won't capture a satisfying amount of detail. Remember to **bring high-speed film** to compensate for low light in the jungle. The thick tree canopy blocks out more light than you realize.

It's best to **always ask permission before taking pictures of indigenous people,** particularly in market areas and rural villages. Although many are more than happy to comply, others may find it disrespectful, invasive, or even threatening. In Guatemala's smaller towns children may offer to pose for a picture in exchange for a small tip. Or if you snap a candid shot of a child, you may be asked for a few quetzales. This is off-putting to some, but others realize it's a small price for a priceless memento. A nice alternative is to bring an instant camera; the photos are a great gift for youngsters who very likely have never seen a picture of themselves.

Casual photographers should **consider using inexpensive disposable cameras** to reduce the risks inherent in traveling with expensive equipment. One-use cameras with underwater functions make your snorkeling and diving adventures more memorable.

The *Kodak Guide to Shooting Great Travel Pictures* (available at bookstores everywhere) is loaded with tips.

Photo Help **Kodak Information Center** ☎ 800/242-2424 www.kodak.com.

EQUIPMENT PRECAUTIONS

In Belize sand and high humidity are enemies of your camera equipment. To be on the safe side, **pack your gear in plastic bags** to protect it from the elements. Always **keep film, videotapes, and computer disks out of the sun. Don't pack film and equipment in checked luggage,** where it is much more susceptible to damage. X-ray machines used for viewing checked luggage are becoming much more powerful and therefore are much more likely to ruin your film. Remember to **ask for hand inspection of film,** which becomes clouded after repeated exposure to airport X-ray machines. Carry an extra supply of batteries, and **be prepared to turn on your camera, camcorder, or laptop** to prove to airport security personnel that the device is real.

FILM & DEVELOPING

In Belize there are photofinishing services in most major towns, and in Belize City and San Pedro you'll have no trouble locating one-hour photo labs. Guatemala has reliable and affordable photo-development shops, especially in big cities and tourist destinations. Many offer one-hour developing at no extra cost.

CAR RENTAL

Philip Goldson International Airport, near Belize City and Aeropuerto Internacional

La Aurora, Guatemala City, are where you'll find most major car-rental agencies, as well as several local operators. In Belize, prices vary from company to company, but all are high by U.S. standards (BZ$120–BZ$260 per day). For instance, the cost of renting a four-wheel-drive Suzuki Jimny from Budget, including unlimited mileage, is about BZ$150 per day; the weekly rate, about BZ$900, is cheaper. Off-season rates are lower. Some hotels include transportation as part of your room rate. A few resorts have rental cars for about BZ$150–BZ$200 per day.

For serious safaris **rent a four-wheel-drive vehicle,** particularly a Land Rover or an Isuzu Trooper or similar. But because unpaved roads, mudslides in rainy season, and a general off-the-beaten-path landscape are status quo here, it will be comforting to have a four-wheel-drive vehicle no matter where you are going. Note that most Belize agencies do not permit you to take their vehicles over the border into Guatemala or Mexico.

Renting cars has never really caught on in Guatemala, which, given the state of many of the roads, is understandable. However, a car can be an asset to your trip. You don't have to worry about unreliable bus schedules, you have a lot more control over your itinerary and the pace of your trip, and you can head off to explore on a whim. If you do rent a car, **consider a *doble-tracción* (four-wheel-drive) vehicle,** which can manage poorly maintained or unpaved roads. Always **look for guarded lots or hotels with private parking** to prevent theft or damage.

Major Agencies **Alamo** ☎ 800/522-9696 🌐 www.alamo.com. **Avis** ☎ 800/331-1084, 800/879-2847 in Canada, 0870/606-0100 in U.K., 02/9353-9000 in Australia, 09/526-2847 in New Zealand 🌐 www.avis.com. **Budget** ☎ 800/527-0700, 0870/156-5656 in U.K. 🌐 www.budget.com. **Dollar** ☎ 800/800-6000, 0800/085-4578 in U.K. 🌐 www.dollar.com. **Hertz** ☎ 800/654-3001, 800/263-0600 in Canada, 0870/844-8844 in U.K., 02/9669-2444 in Australia, 09/256-8690 in New Zealand 🌐 www.hertz.com. **National Car Rental** ☎ 800/227-7368, 0870/600-6666 in U.K. 🌐 www.nationalcar.com.

INSURANCE

When driving a rented car you are generally responsible for any damage to or loss of the vehicle. You also may be liable for any property damage or personal injury that you may cause while driving. Before you rent, see what coverage you already have under the terms of your personal auto-insurance policy and credit cards.

REQUIREMENTS & RESTRICTIONS

In Belize and Guatemala rental-car companies routinely accept without question driver's licenses from the United States, Canada, and most other countries. Most car-rental agencies require a major credit card for a deposit, and some require you be over 25.

SURCHARGES

Before you pick up a car in one city and leave it in another, ask about drop-off charges or one-way service fees, which can be substantial. Also inquire about early-return policies; some rental agencies charge extra if you return the car before the time specified in your contract while others give you a refund for the days not used. To avoid a hefty refueling fee, fill the tank just before you turn in the car, but be aware that gas stations near the rental outlet may overcharge. It's almost never a deal to buy the tank of gas that's in the car when you rent it; the understanding is that you'll return it empty, but some fuel usually remains.

CAR TRAVEL

EMERGENCY SERVICES

When renting a car, ask the rental agency what it does if your car breaks down in a remote area. Most in Belize send a driver with a replacement vehicle or a mechanic to fix the car. For help in Guatemala, your best bet is to call the National Police or Tourist Police. In either country **consider renting a cellular phone** in case you need assistance along the way.

Guatemalan National Police ☎ 110. **Guatemalan Tourist Police** ☎ 832-0532 Ext. 35 or 832-0533 Ext. 35.

GASOLINE

Modern, U.S.-style gas stations—Texaco, Esso, and Shell brands, some of them with convenience stores and 24-hour service—are found in Belize City and in most major towns. In more remote areas, especially in the southern part of the country, **fill up the tank whenever you see a service station.** Premium unleaded gas costs about BZ$7.75 a gallon. Diesel fuel is about one-third less. Attendants who pump gas for you do not expect a tip.

You will find that prices at Guatemala's service stations are as high as in Belize. At most gas stations an attendant will pump the gas and make change. Plan to **use cash,** as credit cards are rarely accepted.

ROAD CONDITIONS

The four main roads in Belize—the Western Highway, Northern Highway, Hummingbird Highway, and Southern Highway—are now fully paved, except for a short stretch of the Southern Highway that is expected to be paved by mid-2004. These two-lane roads are generally in good condition. Aside from these major thoroughfares, expect to find the surfaces of the dirt, gravel, and limestone roads anywhere from fairly smooth to incredibly rough. Always call ahead during the rainy season, as a few unpaved roads may be impassable.

Immense improvements have been made to Guatemala's ravaged roads. A highway from Río Dulce to Tikal has dramatically reduced travel time along this popular route. It still has no guard rails, however, so it isn't for the squeamish. Roads in remote areas are frequently poorly paved, rife with potholes, and treacherous in the rainy season. Always pick a four-wheel-drive vehicle for travel off the beaten path. You'll generally find signs pointing to large towns, but routes to smaller towns may not be clearly marked. Look for intersections where people seem to be waiting for a bus—that's a good sign that there's an important turnoff nearby.

ROAD MAPS

The best road map to Belize is the *Belize Traveller's Map* (ITMB, Vancouver), which was last updated in 2001. It's a good idea to buy this map before your trip, as it is not always readily available in Belize. *Emory King's Driver's Guide to Beautiful Belize,* updated annually and available in Belize, is a mile-by-mile guide to most roads in Belize. Guatemala's tourism agency and all major car-rental companies have maps of Guatemala.

RULES OF THE ROAD

Drivers in Belize and Guatemala stick to the right. Seat belts are required, and the law is now enforced. There are few speed-limit signs, and police sometimes ignore speeders, though enforcement of all traffic laws is becoming more routine. As you approach small towns, watch out for "sleeping policemen," a local name for speed bumps. Belize has about a dozen traffic lights in the entire country, and only Belize City has anything approaching a traffic jam. Belizean drivers aren't always as skilled as they think they are, and drunk drivers can be a problem.

Guatemala's highways are an adventure, especially when they run along the edges of cliffs soaring high above a valley. Trucks and buses drive unbelievably fast along these routes; if you don't feel comfortable keeping up the pace, pull over periodically to let them pass. The narrow roads mean you can be stuck motionless on the road for an hour while a construction crew stands around a hole in the ground. **Always allow extra travel time** for such unpredictable events, making sure to **bring along snacks and drinks.** Otherwise, if you observe the rules you follow at home, you'll likely do just fine. Just don't expect everyone else to follow them.

CHILDREN IN BELIZE & GUATEMALA

The people of Central America love children, and having yours along may prove to be your special ticket to meeting the locals. Children are welcomed in most hotels and restaurants, especially on weekends, when families go out for lunch in droves. If you are renting a car, don't forget to arrange for a car seat when you reserve. For general advice about traveling with children, consult *Fodor's FYI: Travel with Your Baby* (available in bookstores everywhere).

FLYING

If your children are two or older, ask about children's airfares. As a general rule, infants under two not occupying a seat fly at greatly reduced fares or even for free. But if you want to guarantee a seat for an infant, you have to pay full fare. Consider flying during off-peak days and times; most airlines will grant an infant a seat without a ticket if there are available seats. Experts agree that it's a good idea to use safety seats aloft for children weighing less than 40 pounds. Airlines set their own policies: if you use a safety seat, U.S. carriers usually require that the child be ticketed, even if he or she is young enough to ride free, because the seats must be strapped into regular seats. And even if you pay the full adult fare for the seat, it may be worth it, especially on longer trips. Do **check your airline's policy about using safety seats during takeoff and landing.** Safety seats are not allowed everywhere in the plane, so get your seat assignments as early as possible.

When reserving, request children's meals or a freestanding bassinet (not available at all airlines) if you need them. But note that bulkhead seats, where you must sit to use the bassinet, may lack an overhead bin or storage space on the floor.

LODGING

Considering a kid-friendly hotel? Kids traveling in Belize will see monkeys and parrots at Banana Bank Ranch, outside Belmopan, and Lamanai Outpost Lodge, in Lamanai. Villas at Banyan Bay, on Ambergris Caye, has family-friendly two-bedroom condos, a big pool, and a nice beach. In Guatemala the Posada de Don Rodrigo, overlooking Lago Atitlán in Panajachel, has a pool with a huge waterslide.

Many hotels in Belize and Guatemala allow young children to stay in their parents' room at no extra charge, but many charge children older than age 11 or 12 as extra adults; be sure to **find out the cutoff age for children's discounts.**

SIGHTS & ATTRACTIONS

Kids love Belize, especially those who enjoy the beach and water activities. Among the top attractions are the Belize Zoo, Belize's six butterfly farms, and the many Mayan sites where kids can clamber up and down ancient temples. Children may enjoy taking a guided nature tour to see howler monkeys, crocodiles, snakes, and tarantulas in the wild. In Guatemala consider taking the kids to the Reserva Natural Atitlán, in Panajachel, which has winding tree-lined paths, suspension footbridges, waterfalls, a spider monkey lookout, a butterfly terrarium, and a beach. Climbing Volcán Pacayá, an active volcano near Antigua, is a thrilling and accessible hike for those over 10, and the ruins of Tikal will make history come alive for kids all ages. Places that are especially appealing to children are indicated by a rubber-duckie icon (🐤) in the margin.

SUPPLIES & EQUIPMENT

Baby formula and diapers are available in Belize and Guatemala, but prices are higher than those in the United States. Pasteurized milk is sold in some groceries, and canned or boxed milk is widely available.

COMPUTERS ON THE ROAD

If you're traveling in Belize with a laptop, be aware that the power supply may be uneven, and most hotels do not have built-in current stabilizers. At remote lodges power is often from generators. **Ask about electrical surges** before plugging in your computer.

Electricity is a little more reliable in Guatemala, especially in the larger cities. In either country keep your disks out of the sun and avoid excessive heat for both your computer and disks.

CONSUMER PROTECTION

Whether you're shopping for gifts or purchasing travel services, **pay with a major credit card** whenever possible, so you can cancel payment or get reimbursed if there's a problem (and you can provide documentation). If you're doing business with a particular company for the first time, contact your local Better Business Bureau and the attorney general's offices in your state and (for U.S. businesses) the company's home state as well. Have any complaints been filed? Finally, if you're buying a package or tour, always consider travel insurance that includes default coverage (⇨ Insurance).

CRUISE TRAVEL

Cruising is an increasingly popular way to see Belize. The government says that each year more than 500,000 passengers visit Belize by boat. There are many choices, so look into several companies before you decide a ship is right for you. Many choose a small ship, one holding fewer than 200 passengers, because it can visit small cayes and atolls such as Turneffe Atoll, Goff Caye, Tobacco Caye, and West Snake Caye, along with resort areas such as Ambergris Caye and Placencia. If you prefer, you can opt for a large cruise ship, which carries thousands of passengers and provide all the amenities of a resort. These big boats dock in Belize City. Because of shallow water near shore, passengers are brought ashore in small boats called tenders. Once in Belize, you can snorkel around the islands, explore Mayan ruins, or wander around the historic parts of Belize City.

To learn how to plan, choose, and book a cruise-ship voyage, consult *Fodor's FYI: Plan & Enjoy Your Cruise* (available in bookstores everywhere).

Cruise Lines **American Canadian Caribbean Line** ☎ 800/556-7450 🌐 www.accl-smallships.com. **Carnival Cruise Lines** ☎ 888/227-6482 🌐 www.carnival.com. **Celebrity Cruises** ☎ 800/722-5941 🌐 www.celebritycruises.com. **Holland America** ☎ 877/724-5425 🌐 www.hollandamerica.com. **Norwegian Cruise Line** ☎ 800/327-7030 🌐 www.ncl.com. **Royal Caribbean International** ☎ 800/398-9819 🌐 www.royalcaribbean.com. **Windstar Cruises** ☎ 800/258-7245 🌐 www.windstarcruises.com.

CUSTOMS & DUTIES

When shopping abroad, keep receipts for all purchases. Upon reentering the country, **be ready to show customs officials what you've bought.** Pack purchases together in an easily accessible place. If you think a duty is incorrect, appeal the assessment. If you object to the way your clearance was handled, note the inspector's badge number. In either case, first ask to see a supervisor. If the problem isn't resolved, write to the appropriate authorities, beginning with the port director at your point of entry.

IN BELIZE

Duty-free allowances for visitors entering Belize include 1 liter of liquor and one carton of cigarettes. All electronic and electrical appliances, cameras, jewelry, or other items of value must be declared at the point of entry. You should have no trouble bringing a laptop computer into Belize. Firearms of any type and spearguns are prohibited. As a result of concerns over mad-cow disease, beef imports from the United States currently are prohibited.

To take home fresh seafood of any kind from Belize, you must first obtain a permit from the Fisheries Department. There is a 20-pound limit. The export of Mayan artifacts is strictly prohibited.

Fisheries Department ☎ 223/2623.

IN GUATEMALA

Visitors may enter Guatemala duty-free with a camera, up to six rolls of film, any clothes and articles needed while traveling, 500 grams of tobacco, 3 liters of alcoholic beverages, 2 bottles of perfume, and 2 kg of candy. Unless you bring in a lot of merchandise, customs officers probably won't even check your luggage, although a laptop may attract some attention.

It's illegal to export most Mayan artifacts. If you plan on buying such goods, do so only at reputable stores, and keep the receipt. You may not take fruits or vegetables out of Guatemala.

IN AUSTRALIA

Australian residents who are 18 or older may bring home A$400 worth of souvenirs and gifts (including jewelry), 250 cigarettes or 250 grams of cigars or other tobacco products, and 1,125 ml of alcohol (including wine, beer, and spirits). Residents under 18 may bring back A$200 worth of goods. Members of the same family traveling together may pool their allowances. Prohibited items include meat products. Seeds, plants, and fruits need to be declared upon arrival.

Australian Customs Service ✉ Regional Director, Box 8, Sydney, NSW 2001 ☎ 02/9213-2000 or 1300/363263, 02/9364-7222 or 1800/020-504 quarantine-inquiry line 02/9213-4043 www.customs.gov.au.

IN CANADA

Canadian residents who have been out of Canada for at least seven days may bring in C$750 worth of goods duty-free. If you've been away fewer than seven days but more than 48 hours, the duty-free allowance drops to C$200. If your trip lasts 24 to 48 hours, the allowance is C$50. You may not pool allowances with family members. Goods claimed under the C$750 exemption may follow you by mail; those claimed under the lesser exemptions must accompany you. Alcohol and tobacco products may be included in the seven-day and 48-hour exemptions but not in the 24-hour exemption. If you meet the age requirements of the province or territory through which you reenter Canada, you may bring in, duty-free, 1.5 liters of wine *or* 1.14 liters (40 imperial ounces) of liquor *or* 24 12-ounce cans or bottles of beer or ale. Also, if you meet the local age requirement for tobacco products, you may bring in, duty-free, 200 cigarettes and 50 cigars. Check ahead of time with the Canada Customs and Revenue Agency or the Department of Agriculture for policies regarding meat products, seeds, plants, and fruits.

You may send an unlimited number of gifts (only one gift per recipient, however) worth up to C$60 each duty-free to Canada. Label the package UNSOLICITED GIFT—VALUE UNDER $60. Alcohol and tobacco are excluded.

Canada Customs and Revenue Agency 2265 St. Laurent Blvd., Ottawa, Ontario K1G 4K3 800/461-9999 in Canada, 204/983-3500, 506/636-5064 www.ccra.gc.ca.

IN NEW ZEALAND

All homeward-bound residents may bring back NZ$700 worth of souvenirs and gifts; passengers may not pool their allowances, and children can claim only the concession on goods intended for their own use. For those 17 or older, the duty-free allowance also includes 4.5 liters of wine or beer; one 1,125-ml bottle of spirits; and either 200 cigarettes, 250 grams of tobacco, 50 cigars, *or* a combination of the three up to 250 grams. Meat products, seeds, plants, and fruits must be declared upon arrival to the Agricultural Services Department.

New Zealand Customs Head office: The Customhouse, 17-21 Whitmore St., Box 2218, Wellington 09/300-5399 or 0800/428-786 www.customs.govt.nz.

IN THE U.K.

From countries outside the European Union, you may bring home, duty-free, 200 cigarettes, 50 cigars, 100 cigarillos, or 250 grams of tobacco; 1 liter of spirits or 2 liters of fortified or sparkling wine or liqueurs; 2 liters of still table wine; 60 ml of perfume; 250 ml of toilet water; plus £145 worth of other goods, including gifts and souvenirs. Prohibited items include meat and dairy products, seeds, plants, and fruits.

HM Customs and Excise Portcullis House, 21 Cowbridge Rd. E, Cardiff CF11 9SS 0845/010-9000 or 0208/929-0152 advice service, 0208/929-6731 or 0208/910-3602 complaints www.hmce.gov.uk.

IN THE U.S.

U.S. residents who have been out of the country for at least 48 hours may bring home $600 worth of foreign goods duty-free, as long as they have not used the $600 allowance or any part of it in the past 30 days. This allowance, lower than the standard $800 exemption, applies to the 24 countries in the Caribbean Basin Initiative (CBI)—including Belize and Guatemala. If you visit a CBI country and a non-CBI country, you may bring in $800 worth of goods duty-free, but no more than $600 may be from a CBI country.

U.S. residents 21 and older may bring back 2 liters of alcohol duty-free, as long as one of the liters was produced in a CBI country. In addition, regardless of your age, you are allowed 200 cigarettes and 100 non-Cuban cigars. Antiques, which U.S. Customs and Border Protection defines as objects more than 100 years old, enter duty-free, as do original works of art done entirely by hand, including paintings, drawings, and sculptures. This doesn't apply to folk art or handicrafts, which are in general dutiable. You may also send packages home duty-free, with a limit of one parcel per addressee per day (except alcohol or tobacco products or perfume worth more than $5). You can mail up to $200 worth of goods for personal use; label the package PERSONAL USE and attach a list of its contents and their retail value. If the package contains your used personal belongings, mark it PERSONAL GOODS RETURNED to avoid paying duties. You may send up to $100 worth of goods as a gift; mark the package UNSOLICITED GIFT. Mailed items do not affect your duty-free allowance on your return.

U.S. Customs and Border Protection ✉ For inquiries and equipment registration, 1300 Pennsylvania Ave. NW, Washington, DC 20229 🌐 www.cbp.gov ☎ 877/287-8667, 202/354-1000 ✉ For complaints, Customer Satisfaction Unit, 1300 Pennsylvania Ave. NW, Room 5.2C, Washington, DC 20229.

DISABILITIES & ACCESSIBILITY

Wheelchair accessibility in Central America is extremely limited. Few laws require accessibility for those with disabilities. However, there is a growing awareness of the needs of people with disabilities, and the friendly, helpful attitude of the people goes some way toward making up for the lack of provisions. Exploring Central America's attractions usually involves walking down steep trails, muddy paths, or cobblestone streets. In Belize boats and small planes with no accommodations for those with mobility problems are used to get to the cayes and other remote areas. Airplanes often lack jetways, meaning passengers must walk down steps to get off the plane. Because the docks cannot accommodate larger vessels, cruise-ship passengers are brought to shore in small boats that are difficult to get into without assistance. Buses are not equipped to carry wheelchairs, so wheelchair users should hire a van to get around.

Local Resources In Belize, **Central American Information Center** ✉ Box 50211, San Diego, CA 92105 ☎ 619/262-6489. In Guatemala, **Inguat** ✉ 7 Av. 1-17, Zona 4 ☎ 331-1339 or 331-1333.

RESERVATIONS

When discussing accessibility with an operator or reservations agent, ask hard questions. Are there any stairs, inside *or* out? Are there grab bars next to the toilet *and* in the shower/tub? How wide is the doorway to the room? To the bathroom? For the most extensive facilities meeting the latest legal specifications, opt for newer accommodations. If you reserve through a toll-free number, consider also calling the hotel's local number to confirm the information from the central reservations office. Get confirmation in writing when you can.

SIGHTS & ATTRACTIONS

Few sights in Guatemala were designed with travelers in wheelchairs in mind, and fewer still have been renovated to meet that need. Newer destinations may have the necessary facilities and accommodations, but don't count on it—it's best to call ahead or get a recommendation from someone who has visited the property.

DISCOUNTS & DEALS

Be a smart shopper and compare all your options before making decisions. A plane ticket bought with a promotional coupon from travel clubs, coupon books, and direct-mail offers or purchased on the Internet may not be cheaper than the least expensive fare from a discount ticket agency. And always keep in mind that what you get is just as important as what you save.

DISCOUNT RESERVATIONS

Many of the hotels in Belize and Guatemala—including some budget ones—have Web sites. Discounts, typically 10%–20%, are often available for reservations made online.

To save money, look into discount reservations services with Web sites and toll-free numbers, which use their buying power to get a better price on hotels, airline tickets (⇨ Air Travel), even car rentals. When booking a room, always **call the hotel's local toll-free number** (if one is available) rather than the central reservations number—you'll often get a better price. Always ask about special packages or corporate rates.

When shopping for the best deal on hotels and car rentals, look for guaranteed exchange rates, which protect you against a falling dollar. With your rate locked in, you won't pay more, even if the price goes up in the local currency.

Airline Tickets **Air 4 Less** ☎ 800/AIR4LESS; low-fare specialist.

Hotel Rooms **Accommodations Express** ☎ 800/444-7666 or 800/277-1064 🌐 www.acex.net. **Turbotrip.com** ☎ 800/473-7829 🌐 www.turbotrip.com.

PACKAGE DEALS

Don't confuse packages and guided tours. When you buy a package, you travel on your own, just as though you had planned the trip yourself. Fly–drive packages, which combine airfare and car rental, are often a good deal. In cities, ask the local visitor's bureau about hotel and local transportation packages that include tickets to major museum exhibits or other special events.

DIVING

Belize offers some of the best scuba diving in the world. There are scores of dive sites, though few are accessible from the beach. The cayes and atolls offer world-class diving experiences. The water throughout the Caribbean is crystal clear, often to 200 feet, and the quantity and variety of marine life are astounding.

Resorts often offer guests introductory scuba instruction in a pool, followed by a shallow dive; some hotels have on-site dive shops. All shops offer instruction and certification according to the standards set by either the National Association of Underwater Instructors (NAUI) or the Professional Association of Diving Instructors (PADI). They also have a variety of day and night dives to wrecks, reefs, and underwater walls.

Don't fly within 24 hours after scuba diving.

Organizations **NAUI Worldwide** Box 89789, 1232 Tech Blvd., Tampa, FL 33619 ☎ 800/553-6284 or 813/628-6284 🌐 www.naui.org. **PADI** ✉ 30151 Tomas St., Rancho Santa Margarita, CA 92688 ☎ 800/729-7234 or 949/858-7234 🌐 www.padi.com ✉ 3771 Jacombs Rd., Bldg. C, #535, Richmond, British Columbia, Canada V6V 2L9 ☎ 604/273-0277 or 800/565-8130 ✉ Unit 7, St. Philip's Central, Albert Rd., St. Philip's, Bristol, United Kingdom BS2 0PD ☎ 0117/300-7234 ✉ Unit 3, 4 Skyline Pl., French's Forest, New South Wales, Australia 2086 ☎ 2/9451-2300

EATING & DRINKING

Belize has no unique cuisine, but a gastronomic gumbo of Mexican, Caribbean, Maya, Garífuna, English, and other cuisines provides a tasty variety of dining choices. Belize also has restaurants serving French, Thai, Indian, Chinese, and even Sri Lankan food. On the coast and cayes, seafood—especially lobster, conch, and locally caught fish such as snapper and grouper—is fresh, inexpensive, and delicious. Try creole specialties such as cowfoot soup (yes, made with real cow's feet), "boil up" (a stew of fish, potatoes, plantains, cassava and other vegetables, and eggs), and the ubiquitous "stew chicken" with rice and beans. Many creole dishes are seasoned with red or black *recado,* a paste made from annatto seeds and other spices. In border areas, enjoy mestizo favorites such as *escabeche* (onion soup), *salbutes* (fried corn tortillas with chicken and a topping of tomatoes, onions, and peppers), or *garnaches* (fried tortillas with refried beans, cabbage, and cheese). In Dangriga, Punta Gorda, and other Garífuna areas, try dishes such as *sere lasus* (fish soup with plantain balls) or cassava dumplings. In most areas of Belize you can chow down on American classics like fried chicken, pork chops, and T-bone steaks.

In general, Guatemala does not have a distinguished national cuisine; most top restaurants serve European or American fare. The classic Guatemalan dish is tasty but unremarkable: it has eggs, cheese, refried black beans, meat (either sliced beef or the sausage called *chorizo*), and Guatemala's thick corn tortillas. There are a few standouts, though, including *róbalo,* a common and delicious fish called snook elsewhere; ceviche, chilled marinated seafood flavored with lime or tomato broth; and a few dishes not seen on North American menus, such as *tepisquintle,* (the world's largest rodent) and *sopa de tortuga* (turtle soup). Street vendors typically sell fried chicken and french fries, or *churrosquitos* (sliced beef or chorizo served with pickled cabbage and tortillas). *Huevos motuleños* (layers of fried eggs served on a crispy tortilla with cheese, beans, hot sauce, and sometimes ham) make an amazing breakfast. Vegetarians in both Belize and Guatemala may be "beaned out" after a week or so, although *ensalada aguacate* (avocado salad), *pan de banana* (banana bread), and flan (a crème caramel dessert) never get dull.

Only the most expensive restaurants in Belize and Guatemala accept credit cards and traveler's checks. The restaurants that we list (all of which are indicated by a ✕ symbol) are the cream of the crop in each price category. Properties indicated by a ✕🏨 are lodging establishments whose restaurant warrants a special trip.

MEALTIMES

In Belize breakfast is usually served from around 7 to 9, lunch from 11 to 2, and dinner from 6 to 9. Few restaurants are open late. Remember that small restaurants in Belize may open or close at the whim of the owner. Off-season, restaurants may close early if it looks as if there are no more guests coming, and some restaurants close completely for a month or two, usually in September and October.

In Guatemala lunch is the biggest meal, or at least the longest, running from noon to 2 or 3. Breakfast starts at 7, and dinner is not long after sundown. Restaurants in major tourist areas may stay open later, but most places are all but deserted by 9.

Unless otherwise noted, the restaurants listed in this guide are open daily for both lunch and dinner.

RESERVATIONS & DRESS

Reservations are always a good idea; we mention them only when they're essential or not accepted. Book as far ahead as you can, and reconfirm as soon as you arrive. (Large parties should always call ahead to check the reservations policy.) We mention dress only when men are required to wear a jacket or a jacket and tie.

WINE, BEER & SPIRITS

Although many restaurants in Belize serve terrific tropical mixed drinks, few offer wine. The beer you'll see in Belize most often is Belikin. The lager is also available in a premium version that is sold mostly in more expensive bars and restaurants. The richer Belikin Stout and the milder Lighthouse are also available. Both Belikin and Lighthouse are from Bowen & Bowen brewery, the same brewery that makes the local version of Guinness Stout. American and other imported beers are available in some grocery stores, but prices are high. Due to restrictive import laws, the fine beers of neighboring Mexico and Guatemala are rarely available in Belize. Several Belize companies manufacture liquors, primarily rum but also gin and vodka. Traveller's One Barrel Rum is a particularly good choice, spicing up drinks with a hint of vanilla flavor. Imported wines are available in supermarkets and better restaurants, but at about twice the price of the same wines in the United States. The drinking age in Belize is 18, although IDs are rarely checked.

Guatemala has no real wine market to speak of, but restaurants catering to tourists often have excellent imported bottles. The national beer, called Cabro, is decent, while Gallo is as good as any brand in the United States. Imported liquor and local spirits distilled from sugarcane can be found most everywhere. The official drinking age in Guatemala is 20.

ECOTOURISM

Central America is the original ecotourism destination; as a result, you'll see the term used liberally everywhere. For lodging it can be used to describe a deluxe private cabaña on a tidy beach or a hut in the middle of nowhere with pit toilets. It may also point to environmental conservation efforts by parks or tour companies that are conscious of natural resources and their role in not depleting them. Or it may mean just the opposite. Wildlife parks, butterfly farms, cloud forests, and Mayan ruins are some of the incredible ecodestinations in this area. And mountain biking, bird-watching, jungle hiking, scuba diving, cave tubing, fishing, and white-water rafting are just some of the eco-activities.

You can do your part to protect the natural heritage of Belize and Guatemala by being an ecologically sensitive traveler. Where possible, choose green hotels, those that have taken care to protect the environment and that have energy-efficient cooking, lighting, and cooling systems, and that recycle and dispose of waste responsibly. Be culturally sensitive, as both countries have highly diverse populations, each with different cultural attitudes and perspectives. Also, try to do business with companies that hire local people for positions at all levels, and where possible choose local restaurants and hotels over chain properties. When diving or snorkeling, avoid touching or breaking coral, and don't take part in swim-with-dolphins or swim-with-manatees tours as most naturalists say these programs disturb the animals. Also, use ecofriendly sunscreen. On caving or hiking trips, take nothing but photographs and leave nothing of yours behind. When visiting Maya sites, never remove anything, not even a tiny shard of pottery.

For the most part Belize and Guatemala have reaped the benefits of the growing tourism industry, drawing in much-needed capital to bolster national coffers. The costs of tourism are less obvious, however. Among other effects, indigenous communities are undermined by increasingly tourist-oriented economies—cultivating a plot of land may no longer support a family, but selling knickknacks in the streets just might. There is no easy solution to this dilemma, and balancing the advantages of tourism against its drawbacks is, and will remain, a constant struggle for these nations. The long-term effects are as much dependent on the attitudes and behavior of visitors as they are on prudent national policies.

ELECTRICITY

You won't need a converter or adapter as the electrical current in Belize and Guatemala is 110 volts, the same as in the United States. Outlets in both countries take U.S.-style plugs. In a few remote areas lodges and hotels may generate their own electricity. After the generators are turned off at night, light comes only from kerosene lanterns or your flashlight.

ENGLISH-LANGUAGE MEDIA

BOOKS

Because of shipping costs, books are more expensive in Belize than in North America or Europe. Almost every major tourist destination in Guatemala has one or two stores with used paperbacks in English. Some are willing to trade or lend books. Guatemala City and Antigua are the only places in the country where you will find a significant selection of new books.

NEWSPAPERS & MAGAZINES

Belize has no daily newspapers, but it has a number of brash weeklies. As in most countries, crime and politics make the front pages, often in sensational headlines. The *Reporter,* published in Belize City, is the best independent newspaper. For visitors the chatty *San Pedro Sun,* one of two weeklies on Ambergris Caye, is a good source of information, as is the monthly *Placencia Breeze* in Placencia.

The U.S. travel magazine *Belize First* also has an online edition www.belizefirst.com. Both the print and electronic editions are good sources for cultural, dining, lodging, and service information.

The monthly Guatemalan journal *Revue* has a few articles on local trends. *Lugares y Destinos* is a free bilingual guide produced by the Guatemalan Tourist Commission. *Destination Guatemala* and *Central America Guide* are detailed visitor guides available in most upscale hotels.

The international chain hotels usually have fairly current editions of a few major U.S. and European publications, typically *USA Today,* the *Economist,* and *Newsweek.*

RADIO & TELEVISION

Belize's most informative television news is on Channel 5, which also offers its daily news summaries on the Web (🌐 www.channel5belize.com). Many hotels have cable or satellite TV, with 50 or more channels from the United States and Mexico. Love-FM Radio (95.1) is the nation's leading radio station, playing standards and soft rock.

Cable TV is a popular amenity in Guatemalan hotels. You can expect HBO, Showtime, ESPN, TNT, the Discovery Channel, MTV (a Spanish variation), and one or two feeds from regional stations in the United States (usually from Denver, curiously). Radio stations generally play a mix of American pop, rock, and Latin favorites.

ETIQUETTE & BEHAVIOR

Belizeans and *Chapins* (a nickname for Guatemalans) are incredibly kind and friendly. You will let them know the same is true about you if you **always greet someone with a "good morning," or "buenos días,"** before asking for directions, inquiring about a table in a restaurant, and when entering a store or museum. It will set a positive tone for the conversation, and you'll be received much more warmly.

Don't be tempted to take pictures inside churches. (You'll probably spot clueless tourists snapping away during services, ignorant to the angry looks from worshippers.) **Do not take pictures of indigenous people without first asking their permission**; is customary to thank them by offering a small amount of money.

With the exception of luxury buses and shuttles, the seats on Guatemalan buses are expected to fit three abreast. Always **make room for others on buses.** It's perfectly fine to step into the aisle to let someone take a middle or window seat. In Guatemala it is acceptable to make a quick hiss or whistle to get someone's attention—you may find that you even take up the habit yourself, particularly with waiters. You also may hear men catcall women in this way, which unfortunately is not considered terribly rude either.

BUSINESS ETIQUETTE

Business dress in Belize is casual. Men rarely wear suits and ties, and even the prime minister appears at functions in a white shirt open at the neck. The business environment is more formal in Guatemala, where suits for men are more the norm. Women can wear blouses and skirts.

GAY & LESBIAN TRAVEL

Although many tour operators book trips for gays to Belize and Guatemala, it cannot be said that the countries welcome gays with open arms. In fact Belize has a law that went on the books in 1992 banning gay travelers from entering the country. There have been some signs of progress, however. A few years later the country invited a cruise ship full of gay men that had been turned away from the Cayman Islands to visit Belize instead.

As most are very religious, Belizeans have a very conservative view toward gay people. There are no openly gay or lesbian clubs or bars. Likewise, Guatemala frowns on gay life. There is a handful of gay clubs in Guatemala City, like Pandora's Box, which has been around forever.

Gay- & Lesbian-Friendly Travel Agencies **Different Roads Travel** ✉ 8383 Wilshire Blvd., Suite 520, Beverly Hills, CA 90211 ☎ 323/651-5557 or 800/429-8747 (Ext. 14 for both) 🖷 323/651-5454 ✉ lgernert@tzell.com. **Kennedy Travel** ✉ 130 W. 42nd St., Suite 401, New York, NY 10036 ☎ 212/840-8659, 800/237-7433 🖷 212/730-2269 🌐 www.kennedytravel.com. **Now, Voyager** ✉ 4406 18th St., San Francisco, CA 94114 ☎ 415/626-1169 or 800/255-6951 🖷 415/626-8626 🌐 www.nowvoyager.com. **Skylink Travel and Tour/Flying Dutchmen Travel** ✉ 1455 N. Dutton Ave., Suite A, Santa Rosa, CA 95401 ☎ 707/546-9888 or 800/225-5759 🖷 707/636-0951, serving lesbian travelers.

HEALTH

Belize has a high standard of health and hygiene. You can drink the water in Belize City, on Ambergris Caye, and in most other areas you are likely to visit. In remote villages, however, water may come from shallow wells or cisterns and may not be safe to drink. In Guatemala it's best to **drink only bottled water,** called *agua purificada* in Spanish. It is available even at the smallest stores and is much cheaper than in North America.

HIV/AIDS is an increasing concern in Central America, especially in Belize, where the incidence is the highest in the region.

FOOD & DRINK

The major health risk in Belize and Guatemala is traveler's diarrhea, caused by eating contaminated fruit or vegetables or drinking contaminated water. **Skip uncooked foods and unpasteurized milk and milk products. In Guatemala avoid iced beverages.** Ask for your drinks *sin hielo,* meaning "without ice." In Belize most resort areas have ice that is perfectly safe. Mild cases of traveler's diarrhea may respond to Pepto-Bismol or Imodium (known generically as loperamide). Both can be purchased over the counter in both countries, but you should bring along your own stash in case you are not near a pharmacy. Drink plenty of purified water or tea—chamomile is a good folk remedy. In severe cases rehydrate yourself with a salt-sugar solution: ½ teaspoon salt (*sal*) and 4 tablespoons sugar (*azúcar*) per quart of water.

MEDICAL PLANS

No one plans to get sick while traveling, but it happens, so consider signing up with a medical-assistance company. Members get doctor referrals, emergency evacuation or repatriation, hotlines for medical consultation, cash for emergencies, and other assistance.

Medical-Assistance Companies **International SOS Assistance** www.internationalsos.com 8 Neshaminy Interplex, Suite 207, Trevose, PA 19053 ☎ 215/245-4707 or 800/523-6586 📠 215/244-9617 Landmark House, Hammersmith Bridge Rd., 6th fl., London, W6 9DP ☎ 20/8762-8008 📠 20/8748-7744 12 Chemin Riantbosson, 1217 Meyrin 1, Geneva, Switzerland ☎ 22/785-6464 📠 22/785-6424 331 N. Bridge Rd., 17-00, Odeon Towers, Singapore 188720 ☎ 6338-7800 📠 6338-7611.

OVER-THE-COUNTER REMEDIES

Most medicines requiring a doctor's prescription in your home country also require one in Belize, although drugstores often sell prescription antibiotics and painkillers without asking to see a prescription. In Belize private physicians often own an associated pharmacy, so they sell you the medicine they prescribe. In Guatemala, *farmacias* (drugstores) sell a wide range of medications over the counter, including some drugs that would require a prescription in the United States. Ask for what you want with the generic name. Some pharmacies are open 24 hours and deliver directly to hotels. Most hotel proprietors will direct you to such services.

PESTS & OTHER HAZARDS

Along the Caribbean coasts of Belize and Guatemala, sand fleas (also known as sand flies or no-see-ums) are common on many beaches and in swampy areas. They can infect their victims with leishmaniasis, a disease that in its cutaneous form may cause the skin to develop sores that can sometimes leave scars. In very rare cases the visceral form of leishmaniasis can be fatal if untreated. Always **use a strong insect repellent** containing a high concentration of DEET. Some say that slathering on Avon's Skin So Soft or a citronella product called Naturapel can also deter sand fleas.

The botfly, or beef worm, is one of the most unpleasant of Central American pests. Botfly eggs, deposited under your skin by a mosquito, can grow into larvae. To rid yourself of your unwanted pals, see your doctor. Virtually all honeybees in Belize and Guatemala have mixed with African bees. The sting of these creatures is no worse than that of regular bees, but they are much more aggressive. If attacked by these bees, try to get inside a building or vehicle or under water.

If you're a light sleeper, you might want to **pack ear plugs.** Monkeys howling throughout the night and birds chirping at the crack of dawn are only charming on the first night of your nature excursion.

SHOTS & MEDICATIONS

According to the U.S. Centers for Disease Control and Prevention, there is a limited risk of malaria, hepatitis A and B, dengue fever, typhoid fever, and rabies in Central America. In most urban or easily accessible areas you need not worry. However, if you plan to spend a lot of time in the jungles, rain forests, or other remote regions, or if you want to stay for more than six weeks, **check with the CDC's International Travelers Hotline.**

In areas where malaria and dengue are prevalent, **sleep under mosquito nets.** Pack your own—it's the only way to be sure there are no tears. Always **wear clothing that covers your arms and legs,** apply strong repellent, and spray for flying insects in living and sleeping areas. You might **consider taking antimalarial pills**; Chloroquine is sold as Aralen™ in Central America, and mefloquine is marketed as Lariam. There is no vaccine for dengue.

Rabies is always a concern when you get bitten by a stray dog or a wild animal; scrub the wound under clean running water with soap or iodine—or, failing those, some local rum—and get antirabies shots immediately.

Anyone traveling anywhere should consider having up-to-date shots for tetanus and hepatitis A and B. Children traveling to Central America should have current inoculations against measles, mumps, rubella, hepatitis, and polio.

Health Warnings **National Centers for Disease Control and Prevention** (CDC) ✉ Office of Health Communication, National Center for Infectious Diseases, Division of Quarantine, Travelers' Health, 1600 Clifton Rd. NE, Atlanta, GA 30333 ☎ 877/394-8747 international travelers' health line, 800/311-3435 other inquiries, 404/498-1600 Division of Quarantine 📠 888/232-3299 🌐 www.cdc.gov/travel. **World Health Organization** (WHO) 🌐 www.who.int.

INSURANCE

The most useful travel-insurance plan is a comprehensive policy that includes coverage for trip cancellation and interruption, default, trip delay, and medical expenses (with a waiver for preexisting conditions).

Without insurance you'll lose all or most of your money if you cancel your trip, regardless of the reason. Default insurance covers you if your tour operator, airline, or cruise line goes out of business—the chances of which have been increasing. Trip-delay covers expenses that arise because of bad weather or mechanical delays. Study the fine print when comparing policies.

If you're traveling internationally, a key component of travel insurance is coverage for medical bills incurred if you get sick on the road. Such expenses aren't generally covered by Medicare or private policies. U.K. residents can buy a travel-insurance policy valid for most vacations taken during the year in which it's purchased (but check preexisting-condition coverage). British and Australian citizens need extra medical coverage when traveling overseas.

Always **buy travel policies directly from the insurance company**; if you buy them from a cruise line, airline, or tour operator that goes out of business you probably won't be covered for the agency or operator's default, a major risk. Before making any purchase, review your existing health and home-owner's policies to find what they cover away from home.

Travel Insurers In the U.S.: **Access America** ✉ 2805 N. Parham Rd., Richmond, VA 23294 ☎ 800/284-8300 📠 804/673-1491 or 800/346-9265 🌐 www.accessamerica.com. **Travel Guard International** ✉ 1145 Clark St., Stevens Point, WI 54481 ☎ 715/345-0505 or 800/826-1300 📠 800/955-8785 🌐 www.travelguard.com.

In the U.K.: **Association of British Insurers** ✉ 51 Gresham St., London EC2V 7HQ ☎ 020/7600-3333 📠 020/7696-8999 🌐 www.abi.org.uk. In Canada: **RBC Insurance** ✉ 6880 Financial Dr., Mississauga, Ontario L5N 7Y5 ☎ 800/668-4342 or 905/816-2400 📠 905/813-4704 🌐 www.rbcinsurance.com.

In Australia: **Insurance Council of Australia** ✉ Insurance Enquiries and Complaints, Level 12, Box 561, Collins St. W, Melbourne, VIC 8007 ☎ 1300/780808 or 03/9629-4109 📠 03/9621-2060 🌐 www.iecltd.com.au. In New Zealand: **Insurance Council of New Zealand** ✉ Level 7, 111-115 Customhouse Quay, Box 474, Wellington ☎ 04/472-5230 📠 04/473-3011 🌐 www.icnz.org.nz.

LANGUAGE

English is Belize's official language. Spanish is widely spoken, especially in northern and western Belize. Several Maya dialects and the Garífuna language are also spoken. Creole, which uses versions of English words and a West African–influenced grammar and syntax, is spoken by many Belizeans, especially around Belize City.

In Guatemala Spanish is spoken by the majority of the population. Wherever tourist traffic is heavy, you'll also find English speakers. You'll have considerably less luck in places off the beaten path. In addition, many Guatemalans will answer "yes" even if they don't understand your question, so as not to appear unkind or unhelpful. To minimize such confusion, try posing questions as "Where is so-and-so?" rather than "Is so-and-so this way?"

LANGUAGES FOR TRAVELERS

It's a great idea to learn a few phrases of Spanish if you are traveling to Guatemala or other countries in Latin America. A phrase book and language-tape set can help get you started. Pick up *Fodor's Spanish for Travelers,* available at bookstores everywhere.

LODGING

In Belize you'll likely stay in one of four types of lodging: a traditional hotel, a jungle lodge, a beach resort, or a lodge on a remote caye. Traditional hotels, usually found in Belize City and in larger towns, run the gamut from basic budget places to international-style hotels such as the Radisson Fort George in Belize City. Jungle lodges are concentrated in the Cayo and Orange Walk districts, but they can be found most anywhere. Jungle lodges need not be spartan; most have electricity (though the generator may shut down at night), a number have pools, and a few even have air-conditioning. The typical jungle lodge has a thatch roof and may remind you of a traditional Mayan house. Beach hotels also come in various levels of luxury, from basic seaside cabins on Caye Caulker to deluxe resorts such as the Inn at Robert's Grove and Turtle Inn, on the Placencia Peninsula, Victoria House on Ambergris Caye, or Kanantik near Hopkins. On Ambergris Caye many resorts are "condotels"—small condominium complexes whose individually owned units are managed like a hotel. Lodging choices on remote cayes appeal to the diving and fishing crowd. Amenities vary greatly, from cabins with outdoor baths to simple cottages with chemical toilets to comfortable villas with air-conditioning. Regardless of the kind of lodging, you'll almost invariably stay at a small place of 2–25 rooms where the owners manage the property. Thus, Belize accommodations usually reflect the personalities of their owners, for better or worse.

Although hotels in Belize have published rates, in the off-season you may be able to negotiate a better rate, especially if you are staying more than one or two nights. Walk-in rates are usually lower than prebooked rates, and rooms booked direct on the Internet may be lower than those booked through agents. Despite the global travel slowdown following 9/11, tourism in Belize is booming. This means that Belize hotels have been able to raise rates a little and, especially at peak times, the more popular hotels may be fully booked.

Guatemala now has lodging options that go well beyond the needs of the backpacker, in the forms of reliable international hotels, classy colonial charmers, and rustic retreats with local flair. International chain hotels like Radisson, Marriott, and Camino Real have rooms and facilities equal to those at home. The only thing lacking in this type of lodging is a sense of place, of something uniquely Guatemalan. Fortunately, you don't have to sacrifice hot water or room service for a touch of culture—Antigua has colonial class and modern amenities at the Hotel Santo Domingo, Posada del Ángel, Mesón Panza Verde, and others. Add to the list Casa Palopó, near Panajachel; the Mayan Inn, in Chichicastenango, and the Mansión San Carlos, in Guatemala City. For something a little cheaper and out of the way, the Posada Santiago and the Casa del Mundo, both overlooking Lago Atitlán, offer comfort and culture in utter isolation. Hammocks with remarkable views beat television sets every time.

The lodgings we list are the cream of the crop in each price category. We always list the facilities that are available—but we don't specify whether they cost extra: when pricing accommodations, always ask what's included and what costs extra.

Assume that hotels operate on the European Plan (EP, with no meals) unless we specify that they use the Continental Plan (CP, with a Continental breakfast), Breakfast Plan (BP, with a full breakfast), Modified American Plan (MAP, with breakfast and dinner), or the Full American Plan (FAP, with all meals).

CAMPING

If you don't mind a few mosquito bites, you can camp in Belize. It's generally prohibited in the national parks and preserves but it's allowed at Cockscomb Preserve, at

Half Moon Caye National Monument, and in the Mountain Pine Ridge Reserve at Augustine Village. A number of hotels and lodges in the Cayo, including Clarissa Falls, Trek Stop, and Ian Anderson's Caves Branch Adventure Camp, permit camping. Chaa Creek has a safari camp and permanent campsites on platforms. There are only a few RV campgrounds with hookups in Belize—two are in Corozal District, in northern Belize, the Lagoon Campground and Caribbean Village—but some hotels in rural areas allow those with RVs or trailers to park on their property.

Camping is very popular among the backpacker crowd in Guatemala, and there are campgrounds on the outskirts of Antigua, Xelajú, Santiago Atitlán, and San Pedro Atitlán. Very large cities and very small towns are less likely to have such sites. Travel agencies that arrange outdoor adventures, from climbing volcanoes to mountain biking and white-water rafting, are usually the most informed about camping options in the area, either independently or as part of a trek. In some cases they can rent equipment as well.

HOSTELS

No matter what your age, you can **save on lodging costs by staying at hostels.** In some 4,500 locations in more than 70 countries around the world, Hostelling International (HI), the umbrella group for a number of national youth-hostel associations, offers single-sex dorm-style beds and, at many hostels, rooms for couples and family accommodations. The Belize Tourist Board discourages hostel accommodations, but hostel-type budget hotels are available on Caye Caulker and Ambergris Caye and in Belize City, Punta Gorda, San Ignacio, and elsewhere.

Membership in any HI national hostel association, open to travelers of all ages, allows you to stay in HI-affiliated hostels at member rates; one-year membership is about $28 for adults (C$35 for a two-year minimum membership in Canada, £14 in the U.K., A$52 in Australia, and NZ$40 in New Zealand); hostels charge about $10–$30 per night. Members have priority if the hostel is full; they're also eligible for discounts around the world, even on rail and bus travel in some countries.

Organizations **Hostelling International–USA** ✉ 8401 Colesville Rd., Suite 600, Silver Spring, MD 20910 ☎ 301/495-1240 📠 301/495-6697 🌐 www.hiusa.org. **Hostelling International–Canada** ✉ 205 Catherine St., Suite 400, Ottawa, Ontario K2P 1C3 ☎ 613/237-7884 or 800/663-5777 📠 613/237-7868 🌐 www.hihostels.ca. **YHA England and Wales** ✉ Trevelyan House, Dimple Rd., Matlock, Derbyshire DE4 3YH, U.K. ☎ 0870/870-8808, 0870/770-8868, or 0162/959-2600 📠 0870/770-6127 🌐 www.yha.org.uk. **YHA Australia** ✉ 422 Kent St., Sydney, NSW 2001 ☎ 02/9261-1111 📠 02/9261-1969 🌐 www.yha.com.au. **YHA New Zealand** ✉ Level 1, Moorhouse City, 166 Moorhouse Ave., Box 436, Christchurch ☎ 03/379-9970 or 0800/278-299 📠 03/365-4476 🌐 www.yha.org.nz.

MAIL & SHIPPING

When sending mail to Central America, be sure to include the town and the district, the country name, and the words *Central America* in the address. Belizean mail service is excellent, except to and from remote villages. The stamps, mostly of wildlife, are so beautiful that some people save them as souvenirs. An airmail letter to the United States takes about a week. From Guatemala letters to the United States take one to two weeks, slightly longer to get to Canada and the United Kingdom.

OVERNIGHT SERVICES

If you have to send something fast, use DHL, which is expensive but does the job right. It has offices in Belize City and Guatemala City.

Major Services **DHL** ✉ 38 New Rd., Belize City ☎ 223/4350 ✉ 12 Calle 5-12, Zona 10, Guatemala City ☎ 332-3023.

POSTAL RATES

In Belize an airmail letter to the United States is BZ60¢, a postcard BZ30¢. If your mail is headed to Europe, the cost is BZ75¢ for a letter, BZ40¢ for a postcard.

A letter or postcard from Guatemala to anywhere in the Americas costs Q3; to Europe, Asia, and the Pacific it's Q6.

RECEIVING MAIL

In Belize City you can receive mail addressed to you at the main post office, where it will be kept for at least a month. Bring a passport or other ID to pick it up. The post office is open Monday–Thursday 8–5 and Friday 8–4:30. American Express handles mail for cardholders free of charge. In Guatemala travelers can receive mail addressed to "poste restante" at the main post office in Guatemala City. Those who have charge cards or traveler's checks can use the American Express office in the capital.

MONEY MATTERS

There are two ways of looking at prices in Belize: the country is either one of the cheapest in the Caribbean or it's one of the most expensive in Central America. A good hotel room for two will cost you upwards of BZ$200; a budget one, as little as BZ$20. A meal in one of the more upscale restaurants will cost BZ$50–BZ$75 for one, but you can eat lobster and salad in a seafood shack for as little as BZ$20–BZ$30 or the classic creole dish of stew chicken and rice and beans for BZ$8. Prices are highest in Belize City and Ambergris Caye.

Guatemala can be remarkably inexpensive, especially when you are traveling in the villages of the highlands. Prices for rooms at first-class hotels and meals at the best restaurants, however, approach those in developed countries. Trips into remote parts of the jungle and specialty travel like river rafting and deep-sea fishing are also relatively expensive.

Prices throughout this guide are given for adults. Substantially reduced fees are almost always available for children, students, and senior citizens. For information on taxes, *see* Taxes, *below.*

ATMS

Most Belizean banks have automatic teller machines, but except for offices of two banks, Belize Bank and First Caribbean International Bank (formerly Barclays), the machines don't accept foreign cards. Belize Bank's ATMs—at 12 offices around the country—do accept ATM cards on the CIRRUS and PLUS network. First Caribbean ATMs in Dangriga, Belmopan, and Belize City (usually) also accept non-Belize ATM cards. Still, **don't expect to use ATMs to get most of your cash.** When traveling in northern Belize, you can cross into Mexico and make a withdrawal from one of the many ATM machines in Chetumal, but you will get your dough in pesos that will have to be exchanged for U.S. or Belize dollars.

In Guatemala ATMs that accept foreign cards are easy to find. Banks bearing a CREDOMATIC symbol accept most ATM cards. Before your trip, **make sure your secret code has no more than four digits.** Most ATMs in Guatemala do not accept cards with five or more digits. You can easily change yours at your local bank.

Although ATM transaction fees may be higher abroad than at home, ATM rates are excellent because they are based on wholesale rates offered only by major banks. You won't do as well at exchange booths in airports or rail and bus stations, in hotels, in restaurants, or in stores.

CREDIT CARDS

In Belize and Guatemala MasterCard and Visa are widely accepted, American Express a little less so, and Discover hardly at all. It's a good idea to **bring more than one credit card,** as some establishments accept only one or two types. Hotels and shops in Belize sometimes levy a surcharge for credit card use, usually 4 or 5% but ranging from 2% to 10%. A few in Guatemala also add a surcharge. If you use a credit card, ask if there is a surcharge.

Throughout this guide, the following abbreviations are used: **AE,** American Express; **D,** Discover; **DC,** Diners Club; **MC,** MasterCard; and **V,** Visa.

CURRENCY

Belize dollars are the currency used in the Caribbean nation. There are 5-, 10-, 25-, and 50-cent coins, as well as a coin valued at BZ$1. Bills are in 1, 2, 5, 10, 20, 50, and 100 denominations. For many years the Belizean dollar (BZ$) has been pegged to the U.S. dollar at a rate of BZ$2 per US$1, although private moneychangers may give slightly different rates.

Most prices for tourists are quoted in U.S. dollars, but restaurants and smaller hotels tend to use Belize dollars. Because misunderstandings can occur, **always ask which currency is being used.**

The quetzal, named after Guatemala's national bird, is divided into 100 centavos. There are 1-, 5-, 10-, and 25-centavo coins, and a 1 quetzal coin. Bills come in denominations of ½, 1, 5, 10, 20, 50, and 100 quetzales. At this writing the exchange rate is 8 quetzales to the U.S. dollar.

CURRENCY EXCHANGE

Because U.S. dollars are gladly accepted everywhere, there's little need to exchange yours for Belize dollars. If you're not from the United States, it's best to convert your cash to U.S. currency before arriving in Belize. Other currencies, including Canadian dollars, are not widely accepted in Belize, and you'll have a hard time finding a place that will exchange your money. When paying in U.S. dollars, you may get change in Belize or in U.S. currency, or in both.

Moneychangers at the Mexican and Guatemalan borders operate on a free-market system and pay a rate depending on the demand for U.S. dollars, sometimes as high as BZ$2.20 to US$1. Authorized money changer offices, mainly in Belize City and larger towns, may offer a little more than 2 to 1, typically 2.05 to 1, though this rate varies depending on demand for U.S. dollars. Banks generally exchange at BZ$1.98 to US$1 or less.

When leaving Belize, you can exchange Belizean currency back to U.S. dollars (up to BZ$200). The Belize dollar is difficult, if not impossible, to exchange outside Belize. In this guide all prices are quoted in Belize dollars. The best place to exchange Belize dollars for Mexican pesos is in Corozal, where the exchange rate is quite good. At the Guatemala border near Benque Viejo del Carmen, you can exchange Belizean or U.S. dollars for quetzales—moneychangers will approach you on the Belize side.

In Guatemala, U.S. currency is almost never turned away in shops and restaurants. You can exchange cash on the street in the area around the central post office for slightly more than the official rate, but you run the risk of being shortchanged.

Exchange Services **International Currency Express** ✉ 427 N. Camden Dr., Suite F, Beverly Hills, CA 90210 ☎ 888/278-6628 orders 📠 310/278-6410 🌐 www.foreignmoney.com. **Travel Ex Currency Services** ☎ 800/287-7362 orders and retail locations 🌐 www.travelex.com.

TRAVELER'S CHECKS

In Belize, traveler's checks are widely accepted, though you must have your passport to cash them. **Do not write in the name of the individual or business** to whom you're giving the check, as this will delay its processing by the local banks. Traveler's checks are not as widely accepted in Guatemala, especially not in villages and small towns.

PACKING

Baggage carts are scarce at Central American airports, and international luggage limits are increasingly tight. Whatever you do, **pack light**—casual, comfortable, hand-washable clothing. T-shirts and shorts are acceptable near the beach, while more conservative attire is appropriate in smaller towns. Long-sleeve shirts and long pants will protect your skin from the relentless sun and ferocious mosquitoes. Always **bring along a hat** to block the sun from your face and neck. If you're heading into the Cayo, the mountains, or the highlands, especially during the winter months, bring a light sweater or jacket, as nights and early mornings can be chilly. Sturdy sneakers or hiking shoes or boots with rubber soles are essential. A pair of sandals (preferably ones that can be worn in the water) are indispensable, too.

Be sure to bring along insect repellent, sunscreen, sunglasses. An umbrella is handy in the rainy season. Other items you'll be glad you brought along include a box of tissues, a plastic water bottle, and a flashlight (for occasional power outages, streets without proper lighting, or caves). A mosquito net is a good idea if you're staying at places with no screens in the windows (or no windows at all). Snorkelers should consider bringing their own equipment if there's room in the suitcase. Last, but not least, **bring your favorite brand of condoms and tam-**

pons. You won't find either easily or in familiar brands.

In your carry-on luggage, pack an extra pair of eyeglasses or contact lenses and enough of any medication you take to last a few days longer than the entire trip. You may also ask your doctor to write a spare prescription using the drug's generic name, as brand names may vary from country to country. In luggage to be checked, **never pack prescription drugs, valuables, or undeveloped film.** And don't forget to carry with you the addresses of offices that handle refunds of lost traveler's checks. Check *Fodor's How to Pack* (available at online retailers and bookstores everywhere) for more tips.

To avoid customs and security delays, carry medications in their original packaging. Don't pack any sharp objects in your carry-on luggage, including knives of any size or material, scissors, nail clippers, and corkscrews, or anything else that might arouse suspicion.

To avoid having your checked luggage chosen for hand inspection, don't cram bags full. The U.S. Transportation Security Administration suggests packing shoes on top and placing personal items you don't want touched in clear plastic bags.

CHECKING LUGGAGE

You're allowed to carry aboard one bag and one personal article, such as a purse or a laptop computer. Make sure what you carry on fits under your seat or in the overhead bin. Get to the gate early, so you can board as soon as possible, before the overhead bins fill up.

Baggage allowances vary by carrier, destination, and ticket class. On international flights, you're usually allowed to check two bags weighing up to 70 pounds (32 kilograms) each, although a few airlines allow checked bags of up to 88 pounds (40 kilograms) in first class. Some international carriers don't allow more than 66 pounds (30 kilograms) per bag in business class and 44 pounds (20 kilograms) in economy. On domestic flights, the limit is usually 50 to 70 pounds (23 to 32 kilograms) per bag. In general, carry-on bags shouldn't exceed 40 pounds (18 kilograms). Most airlines won't accept bags that weigh more than 100 pounds (45 kilograms) on domestic or international flights. Expect to pay a fee for baggage that exceeds weight limits. Check baggage restrictions with your carrier before you pack.

Before departure, itemize your bags' contents and their worth, and label the bags with your name, address, and phone number. (If you use your home address, cover it so potential thieves can't see it readily.) Include a label inside each bag and **pack a copy of your itinerary.** At check-in, make sure each bag is correctly tagged with the destination airport's three-letter code. Because some checked bags will be opened for hand inspection, the U.S. Transportation Security Administration recommends that you leave luggage unlocked or use the plastic locks offered at check-in. TSA screeners place an inspection notice inside searched bags, which are resealed with a special lock.

If your bag has been searched and contents are missing or damaged, file a claim with the TSA Consumer Response Center as soon as possible. If your bags arrive damaged or fail to arrive at all, file a written report with the airline before leaving the airport.

PASSPORTS & VISAS

When traveling internationally, carry your passport even if you don't need one (it's always the best form of ID) and **make two photocopies of the data page** (one for someone at home and another for you, carried separately from your passport). If you lose your passport, promptly call the nearest embassy or consulate and the local police.

U.S. passport applications for children under age 14 require consent from both parents or legal guardians; both parents must appear together to sign the application. If only one parent appears, he or she must submit a written statement from the other parent authorizing passport issuance for the child. A parent with sole authority must present evidence of it when applying; acceptable documentation includes the child's certified birth certificate listing only the applying parent, a court order specifically permitting this parent's travel with the child, or a death certificate for the nonapplying parent. Application forms and instructions are available on the Web site of the U.S. State Department's Bureau of Consular Affairs (travel.state.gov).

ENTERING BELIZE & GUATEMALA

To enter Belize, only a passport, valid for at least six months after entry, is necessary for citizens of Australia, Canada, Great Britain, New Zealand, and the United States—no visa is required. If, upon arrival, the customs official asks how long you expect to stay, give the longest period you might stay—you may legally stay in each country for up to 30 days—otherwise the official may endorse your passport with a shorter period. In Belize you can renew your entry permits for up to six months for a fee of BZ$25 per month. Technically, if you are staying for more than 90 days, you need to have an AIDS test, but at present this rule isn't being generally enforced. If you're young and entering Belize by land from Mexico or Guatemala, you may be asked to prove that you have enough money to cover your stay (a valid credit card is usually sufficient). You are supposed to have US$50 a day, although this requirement is rarely enforced. If you enter Guatemala by land, you may need a multiple-entry visa, available at the Guatemalan consulate in your home country.

RESTROOMS

You won't find many public restrooms in Belize, but hotels and restaurants usually have clean, modern restrooms with American-style—indeed American-made—toilets. Hot-water showers in Belize often are the on-demand type, powered by butane gas.

Restrooms in Guatemala use Western-style toilets, although bathroom tissue generally should not be flushed but discarded in a basket beside the toilet.

SAFETY

While traveling in Central America, use common sense. Wherever you go, **don't wear expensive clothing, don't wear flashy jewelry or watches,** and **don't handle money in public.** It's a good idea to keep your money in a pocket rather than a wallet, which is easier to steal. On buses and in crowded areas, hold purses or handbags close to your body; thieves use knives to slice the bottom of a bag and catch the contents as they fall out. **Keep cameras in a secure camera bag,** preferably one with a chain or wire embedded in the strap. Always **remain alert for pickpockets,** especially in the larger cities.

There is considerable crime in Belize City, but it rarely involves visitors. When it does, Belize has a particularly rapid justice system for such crimes, meaning that the offender often gets a trial within hours and, if convicted, can be sent to prison ("the Hattieville Ramada") the same day. Tourist police patrol Fort George and other areas where visitors convene. Police are particularly in evidence when cruise ships are in port. If you avoid walking alone at night (except in well-lighted parts of the Fort George area), you should have no problems. If you're returning to your hotel after dark, use a taxi. If you have to ring the bell to enter the hotel, ask the driver to wait until you are safely inside. Outside Belize City, and possibly the rougher parts of Dangriga and Orange Walk Town, you'll find Belize to be safe and friendly.

Pickpockets are probably the most common threat in Guatemala. They typically work in pairs or in threes; one will distract or disrupt you in some way, while another slips a hand into your pocket or backpack during the commotion. This typically happens in a crowded market or street corner, especially if your hands are full with your luggage or purchases. They are so skilled, you often won't realize you've been robbed until later. If you know you'll be passing through a crowded area (entering or leaving the bus terminal, for example), **carry only the money you'll need** and stow the rest in your money belt. If you have a home base, just bring along a day pack—you'll be significantly less vulnerable without a lot of stuff.

In the last three years there have been sporadic incidents in Belize near border areas with Guatemala. In two or three cases masked men believed to be from Guatemala held up tourist vehicles near San Ignacio in western Belize, especially around the archaeological site of El Pilar. Several other Guatemala–Belize border incidents also have taken place in recent years, including in late 2001 the killing of three machete-wielding Guatemalan farmers by Belize Defence Forces soldiers near San Ignacio. In 2000 a water taxi returning from Puerto Barrios, Guatemala, to Punta Gorda, Belize, was hijacked by Guatemalan nationals who shot and killed six people. Given the hundreds of thousands of visitors to Belize, however, these incidents are isolated, and the vast majority of travelers never experience any crime in Belize.

LOCAL SCAMS

Most Central Americans are extremely honest and trustworthy. It's not uncommon for a vendor to chase you down if you accidentally leave without your change. That said, most organized scams arise with tours and packages, in which you're sold a ticket that turns out to be bogus. **Arrange all travel through a legitimate agency,** and always get a receipt. If a problem does arise, the tourist boards may be able to help mediate the conflict.

WOMEN IN BELIZE & GUATEMALA

If you carry a purse, choose one with a zipper and a thick strap that you can drape across your body; adjust the length so that the purse sits in front of you at or above hip level. Store only enough money in the purse to cover casual spending. Distribute the rest of your cash and any valuables (including credit cards and your passport) between a deep front pocket, an inside jacket or vest pocket, and a hidden money pouch. Do not reach for that money pouch in public.

Many women travel alone or in small groups in Belize without any problems. Machismo is not as much an issue in the former British Honduras as it is in neighboring countries. Unfortunately, Guatemala has been the site of some disturbing assaults on women. These have occurred on buses, usually late at night in remote areas. Always **avoid traveling alone at night.** There's very little crime outside the major cities, but it does happen. In 2001 two Dutch women were raped while hiking along the shore of Lago Atitlán. Hiring a guide through the local tourist office or through a respectable tour agency can help to avoid such situations.

The most common complaint by women is catcalling, which is typically more of an annoyance than a threat. Most women, locals and foreigners alike, try to brush it off.

SHOPPING

Belize does not have the rich artistic tradition of neighboring Guatemala, Honduras, and Mexico. Gift shops offer the usual collection of off-color T-shirts and gaudy knicknacks. However, there are handicrafts, furniture, music (punta rock), foods and drinks, and other items that make good souvenirs from Belize. Rum, Belikin beer, Marie Sharp's hot sauces and jams, coffee from Gallon Jug, colorful Belize postage stamps, and high-quality chairs and other furniture made from tropical hardwoods are all reasonably priced.

For souvenir seekers, Guatemala's handicrafts, called *artesanía* or *típica,* always draw the most attention, particularly the handwoven tapestries, carved wooden masks, hand-blown glass, and traditional clothing such as women's colorful *huipiles.* Such goods are beautiful and inexpensive, and they're sold throughout the country. Miniature wooden or ceramic frames make great little keepsakes, as do small hand-painted wooden jewelry boxes or masks. More exclusive items include jade carvings and jewelry, antiques, and particularly complex weavings, especially those made of silk instead of cotton, and are best purchased in Guatemala City, Antigua, and, to a lesser extent, Xelajú.

WATCH OUT

The sale of some items contributes to the destruction of the natural environment, so **avoid items made from coral** and turtle or tortoise shells. **Never purchase items pil-**

fered from archaeological sites, particularly stone carvings. They may be confiscated when you leave the country, and perhaps worse, your souvenir shopping aids in the destruction of irreplaceable historical and cultural relics. The export of Mayan artifacts is strictly prohibited.

SIGHTSEEING TOURS

In Belize all tourist guides are required to take a series of training courses and must be licensed by the government. If in doubt about the credibility of a guide, ask to see a license.

A guide's license in Guatemala means little. Here, nothing beats a personal recommendation. Ask other travelers first, and your hotel second. Otherwise, stick to the established agencies to avoid getting cheated. Tikal is an exception: official guides wear a "Carnet de Guía de Turismo" (Tourist Guide ID) and can be hired at the visitor center. Many hotels also arrange guided tours to the ruins and surrounding sights.

STUDENTS IN BELIZE & GUATEMALA

Central America is a fantastic place for students and those on a budget. You can live well on Q100 (US$12) a day in Guatemala. Belize is more expensive; expect to shell out BZ$50–BZ$90 (US$25–US$45) a day. There are few hostels as such, but Guatemala and Belize are packed with cheap lodging possibilities. Any option near the bus station is usually affordable. One of the cheapest ways to spend the night, of course, is camping, and as long as you have your own tent or hammock, it's easy to set up camp in many areas (always ask for permission, of course). To get good tips and advice on traveling within a budget, look for informational bulletin boards and talk to other backpackers.

IDs & Services **STA Travel** ✉ 10 Downing St., New York, NY 10014 ☎ 212/627–3111, 800/777–0112 24-hr service center 🖷 212/627–3387 🌐 www.sta.com. **Travel Cuts** ✉ 187 College St., Toronto, Ontario M5T 1P7, Canada ☎ 800/592–2887 in U.S., 416/979–2406 or 866/246–9762 in Canada 🖷 416/979–8167 🌐 www.travelcuts.com.

TAXES

The Belizean government levies a hotel tax of 7% (expected to increase to 9% in 2005) and an airport-departure tax of BZ$70, which must be paid in either U.S. or Belize dollars when you leave the country. Some international airlines flying to Belize now include the US$35 exit fee in the price of the ticket. An on-land border fee is BZ$30, plus a conservation tax of BZ$7.50, and is charged at the Guatemalan and Mexican borders, even for day trips. In this case you can **ask that your conservation tax be applied toward your airport-departure tax** as credit. For most consumer goods and services, including restaurant meals, tours, rental cars, and diving, there is an 9% sales tax.

Most Guatemalan hotels and some tourist restaurants charge an additional 10% tourist tax. The airport-departure tax is US$20.

VALUE-ADDED TAX

The unpopular Belize value-added tax has been repealed. Guatemalan stores, restaurants, and hotels charge a 10% V.A.T.

TELEPHONES

AREA & COUNTRY CODES

The country code for Belize is 501; for Guatemala, 502. The country code is 1 for the United States, 61 for Australia, 64 for New Zealand, and 44 for the United Kingdom.

CELLULAR PHONES

You can rent a cell phone in Belize starting at BZ$10 a day. Check at the Belize Telecommunications Ltd. office at the international airport, across the parking lot near the rental car offices. Car rental companies in Belize also rent cell phones, as do some shops in San Pedro and Belize City. It is also possible use your own cell phone in Belize, but you will have to have it reprogrammed. This costs about BZ$100 and can be done at the BTL office at the international airport. Overall, though, it's easier to just rent a cell phone. Once you rent the phone, you'll need to buy a BTL phone card to activate it and pay for outgoing calls (incoming calls are not charged). These phone cards are available in denominations of BZ$10 to BZ$50. In Guatemala you can rent a phone, not to mention a car, from Avis.

DIRECTORY & OPERATOR ASSISTANCE

To obtain directory information for Belize from the United States, dial 412/555–1515. For Guatemalan operator assistance (in Spanish) dial 121; for information (in Spanish) dial 124.

INTERNATIONAL CALLS

When calling a Belize number from abroad, dial the international long distance code of 011, the country code of 501, the area code, and the seven-digit number, in that order. When calling from another city in Belize, dial 0, then the area code and the number.

For numbers in Guatemala, you don't need to dial an area code when calling from abroad or from within the country.

LONG-DISTANCE SERVICES

AT&T, MCI, and Sprint access codes make calling long-distance relatively convenient, but you may find the local access number blocked in many hotel rooms. First ask the hotel operator to connect you. If the hotel operator balks, ask for an international operator, or dial the international operator yourself. One way to improve your odds of getting connected to your long-distance carrier is to travel with more than one company's calling card (a hotel may block Sprint, for example, but not MCI). If all else fails, call from a pay phone.

Belize Access Codes **AT&T** ☎ 811 from pay phones, 555 from hotels. **MCI** ☎ 815 from pay phones, 557 from hotels. **Sprint** ☎ 812 from pay phones, 556 from hotels.

Guatemala Access Codes **AT&T** ☎ 190. **MCI** ☎ 189. **Sprint** ☎ 195.

PHONE CARDS

In Belize you can buy phone cards from any BTL office or at many shops for amounts ranging from BZ$5 to BZ$50. Guatemala's public pay phones use prepaid calling cards, which you can purchase at small markets, pharmacies, and Telgua offices. Ask for a *tarjeta telefónica.*They come in denominations of Q20, Q30, and Q100; calls within Guatemala cost 15–50 centavos per minute.

PUBLIC PHONES

Belize has a good nationwide phone system. There are pay phones on the street in the larger towns. All pay phones in Belize now require a prepaid phone card. Local calls cost 25¢; calls to other districts cost BZ$1.

In Guatemala it's easier to make local calls from your hotel. Telgua is the national phone company, and every decent-size town has a Telgua office, most of which are open daily 7 AM–midnight. You usually have to wait to submit your number to the cashier and then wait again to be called to use a phone. Do not use the black, red, or blue wall-mounted phones with signs that read FREE COLLECT CALL. They charge a whopping $10 per minute and have a five-minute minimum.

TIME

Belize and Guatemala time is the same as U.S. central standard time. Daylight saving time is not observed.

TIPPING

Belize restaurants rarely add a service charge, so in better restaurants you should tip 10%–15% of the total bill. At inexpensive restaurants leave small change or tip 10%. Many hotels and resorts add a service charge of 10% to bills, so at these places additional tips are not necessary. In general, Belizeans tend not to expect tips, though this is changing with increased tourism. It's not customary to tip taxi drivers.

In Guatemala restaurant bills do not typically include gratuities; 10% is customary. Bellhops and maids expect tips only in the expensive hotels. Guards who show you around ruins and locals who help you find hotels or give you little tours should also be tipped.

TOURS & PACKAGES

Because everything is prearranged on a prepackaged tour or independent vacation, you spend less time planning—and often get it all at a good price.

BOOKING WITH AN AGENT

Travel agents are excellent resources. But it's a good idea to collect brochures from several agencies, as some agents' suggestions may be influenced by relationships with tour and package firms that reward them for volume sales. If you have a special interest, find an agent with expertise in that area; the American Society of Travel Agents (ASTA; ⇨ Travel Agencies) has a database of specialists worldwide. You can log on to the group's Web site to find an ASTA travel agent in your neighborhood.

Make sure your travel agent knows the accommodations and other services of the place being recommended. Ask about the hotel's location, room size, beds, and whether it has a pool, room service, or programs for children, if you care about these. Has your agent been there in person or sent others whom you can contact?

Do some homework on your own, too: local tourism boards can provide information about lesser-known and small-niche operators, some of which may sell only direct.

BUYER BEWARE

Each year consumers are stranded or lose their money when tour operators—even large ones with excellent reputations—go out of business. So check out the operator. Ask several travel agents about its reputation, and try to **book with a company that has a consumer-protection program.** (Look for information in the company's brochure.) In the United States, members of the United States Tour Operators Association are required to set aside funds ($1 million) to help eligible customers cover payments and travel arrangements in the event that the company defaults. It's also a good idea to choose a company that participates in the American Society of Travel Agents' Tour Operator Program; ASTA will act as mediator in any disputes between you and your tour operator.

Remember that the more your package or tour includes, the better you can predict the ultimate cost of your vacation. Make sure you know exactly what is covered, and beware of hidden costs. Are taxes, tips, and transfers included? Entertainment and excursions? These can add up.

Tour-Operator Recommendations **American Society of Travel Agents** (⇨ Travel Agencies). **National Tour Association** (NTA) ✉ 546 E. Main St., Lexington, KY 40508 ☎ 859/226-4444 or 800/682-8886 ⎙ 859/226-4404 ⊕ www.ntaonline.com. **United States Tour Operators Association** (USTOA) ✉ 275 Madison Ave., Suite 2014, New York, NY 10016 ☎ 212/599-6599 ⎙ 212/599-6744 ⊕ www.ustoa.com.

PACKAGES

Like group tours, independent vacation packages are available from major tour operators and airlines. The companies listed below offer vacation packages in a broad price range.

Air/Hotel **Tropical Travel** ☎ 800/365-6232.

From the U.K. **Journey Latin America** ☎ 0208/747-8315 ⎙ 0208/742-1312. **South American Experience** ☎ 0207/976-5511 ⎙ 0207/976-6908.

THEME TRIPS

Adventure **Adventure Center** ✉ 1311 63rd St., #200, Emeryville, CA 94608 ☎ 510/654-1879 or 800/227-8747 ⎙ 510/654-4200 ⊕ www.adventurecenter.com. **American Wilderness Experience** ✉ Box 1486, Boulder, CO 80306 ☎ 800/444-0099 ⎙ 303/444-3999 ⊕ www.gorptravel.com. **Himalayan Travel** ✉ 110 Prospect St., Stamford, CT 06901 ☎ 203/359-3711 or 800/225-2380 ⎙ 203/359-3669 ⊕ www.gorp.com/himtravel/htm. **International Expeditions** ✉ One Environs Park, Helena, AL 35080 ☎ 205/428-1714 or 800/633-4734 ⎙ 205/428-1714 ⊕ www.internationalexpeditions.com. **International Zoological Expeditions** ✉ 210 Washington St., Sherborn, MA 01770 ☎ 503/655-1461 or 800/543-5343 ⎙ 503/655-4445 ⊕ www.ize2belize.com. **Mountain Travel-Sobek** ✉ 6420 Fairmount Ave., El Cerrito, CA 94530 ☎ 510/527-8100 or 888/687-6235 ⎙ 510/525-7710 ✎ info@mtsobek.com ⊕ www.mtsobek.com. **Slickrock Adventures** ✉ Box 1400, Moab, UT 84532 ☎ 800/390-5715 ⎙ 435/259-6996 ⊕ www.slickrock.com. **Wilderness Travel** ✉ 1102 9th St., Berkeley, CA 94710 ☎ 510/558-2488 or 800/368-2794 ⊕ www.wildernesstravel.com.

Art & Archaeology **Archaeological Conservancy** ✉ 5301 Central Ave. NE, #1218, Albuquerque, NM 87108 ☎ 505/266-1540 ⎙ 505/266-0311 ⊕ www.gorp.com/archcons. **Far Horizons Archaeological & Cultural Trips** ✉ Box 91900, Albuquerque, NM 87199 ☎ 505/343-9400 or 800/552-4575 📠 505/343-8076 🌐 www.farhorizon.com. **Meetings and Incentives in Latin America (MILA)** ✉ 100 S. Greenleaf Ave., Gurnee, IL 60031 ☎ 847/249-2111 or 800/367-7378 📠 847/249-2772 🌐 www.milatours.com or www.mayapath.com. **Sanborn's Viva Tours** ✉ 2015 S. 10th St., Box 519, McAllen, TX 78505 ☎ 956/682-9872 or 800/395-8482 📠 210/682-0016 🌐 www.sanborns.com.

Bird-Watching **Victor Emanuel Nature Tours** ✉ Box 33008, Austin, TX 78764 ☎ 512/328-5221 or 800/328-8368 📠 512/328-2919 🌐 www.ventbird.com.

Fishing **Artmarina** ✉ 1390 S. Dixie Hwy, Suite 2221, Miami, FL 33146 ☎ 305/663-3553 📠 305/666-6445 ✉ fish@artmarina.com 🌐 www.artmarina.com. **Fishing International** ✉ Box 2132, Santa Rosa, CA 95405 ☎ 707/542-4242 or 800/950-4242 📠 707/546-3474 ✉ fishint@wco.com 🌐 www.fishinginternational.com. **Rod & Reel Adventures** ✉ 566 Thomson La., Copperopolis, CA 95228 ☎ 209/785-0444 or 800/356-6982 📠 209/785-0447 🌐 www.rodreeladventures.com.

Scuba Diving & Snorkeling **Go Diving** ✉ 5610 Rowland Rd. #100, Minnetonka, MN 55343 ☎ 612/931-9101 or 800/328-5285 📠 612/931-0209. **Rothschild Dive Safaris** ✉ 900 West End Ave., #1B, New York, NY 10025 ☎ 212/662-4858 or 800/359-0747 📠 212/749-6172. **Scuba Diving & Snorkeling Worldwide** ✉ Box 471899, San Francisco, CA 94147 ☎ 415/922-5807 📠 415/922-5662. **Tropical Adventures** ✉ 111 2nd Ave. N, Seattle, WA 98109 ☎ 206/441-3483 or 800/247-3483 📠 206/441-5431.

Hiking/Trekking/Walking **Backroads** ✉ 801 Cedar St., Berkeley, CA 94710 ☎ 510/527-1555 or 800/462-2848 📠 510/527-1444. **Country Walkers** ✉ Box 180, Waterbury, VT 05676-0180 ☎ 802/244-1387 or 800/464-9255 📠 802/244-5661. **Quetzalventures** ✉ 4 Calle Poniente 38, Antigua, Guatemala ☎ 406-8709 or 406-8710 🌐 www.quetzalventures.com.

Yacht Charters **Ocean Voyages** ✉ 1709 Bridgeway, Sausalito, CA 94965 ☎ 415/332-4681 📠 415/332-7460. **TMM (Belize) Ltd.** ✉ Coconut Dr., San Pedro, Belize ☎ 226/3016 📠 226/3072 🌐 www.sailtmm.com/Belize/beaut2.htm.

TRAVEL AGENCIES

A good travel agent puts your needs first. Look for an agency that has been in business at least five years, emphasizes customer service, and has someone on staff who specializes in your destination. In addition, **make sure the agency belongs to a professional trade organization.** The American Society of Travel Agents (ASTA)—the largest and most influential in the field with more than 20,000 members in some 140 countries—maintains and enforces a strict code of ethics and will step in to help mediate any agent-client disputes involving ASTA members if necessary. ASTA (whose motto is "Without a travel agent, you're on your own") also maintains a Web site that includes a directory of agents. (If a travel agency is also acting as your tour operator, *see* Buyer Beware *in* Tours & Packages.)

Local Agent Referrals **American Society of Travel Agents** (ASTA) ✉ 1101 King St., Suite 200, Alexandria, VA 22314 ☎ 703/739-2782 or 800/965-2782 24-hr hotline 📠 703/684-8319 🌐 www.astanet.com. **Association of British Travel Agents** ✉ 68-71 Newman St., London W1T 3AH ☎ 020/7637-2444 📠 020/7637-0713 🌐 www.abta.com. **Association of Canadian Travel Agencies** ✉ 130 Albert St., Suite 1705, Ottawa, Ontario K1P 5G4 ☎ 613/237-3657 📠 613/237-7052 🌐 www.acta.ca. **Australian Federation of Travel Agents** ✉ Level 3, 309 Pitt St., Sydney, NSW 2000 ☎ 02/9264-3299 or 1300/363-416 📠 02/9264-1085 🌐 www.afta.com.au. **Travel Agents' Association of New Zealand** ✉ Level 5, Tourism and Travel House, 79 Boulcott St., Box 1888, Wellington 6001 ☎ 04/499-0104 📠 04/499-0786 🌐 www.taanz.org.nz.

VISITOR INFORMATION

Learn more about foreign destinations by checking government-issued travel advisories and country information. For a broader picture, consider information from more than one country.

Tourist Information **Belize Tourist Board** ✉ New Central Bank Bldg., Level 2, Gabourel La., Belize City, Belize ☎ 223/1913, 800-624-0686 in U.S. 📠 223/1943 🌐 www.travelbelize.org. **Inguat** ✉ 7a Av. 1-17, Zona 4, Guatemala City, Guatemala ☎ 331-1333 📠 331-4416 🌐 www.guatemala.travel.com.gt.

In the U.K. **Belize High Commission** ✉ 10 Harcourt House, 19A Cavendish Sq., London W1M 9AD ☎ 0207/499-9725. **Guatemalan Embassy** ✉ 13 Fawcett St., London SW10 9HN ☎ 0207/351-3042.

In the U.S. **Belizean Embassy** ✉ 2535 Massachusetts Ave., NW, Washington, DC 20008 ☎ 202/332-9636 📠 202/332-6888. **Guatemalan Embassy**

✉ 2220 R St., NW, Washington, DC 20008 ☎ 800/464-8281 📠 561/241-7687.

Government Advisories **U.S. Department of State** ✉ Overseas Citizens Services Office, 2100 Pennsylvania Ave. NW, 4th fl., Washington, DC 20520 ☎ 202/647-5225 interactive hotline or 888/407-4747 🌐 www.travel.state.gov. **Consular Affairs Bureau of Canada** ☎ 800/267-6788 or 613/944-6788 🌐 www.voyage.gc.ca. **U.K. Foreign and Commonwealth Office** ✉ Travel Advice Unit, Consular Division, Old Admiralty Bldg., London SW1A 2PA ☎ 0870/606-0290 or 020/7008-1500 🌐 www.fco.gov.uk/travel. **Australian Department of Foreign Affairs and Trade** ☎ 300/139-281 travel advice, 02/6261-1299 Consular Travel Advice Faxback Service 🌐 www.dfat.gov.au. **New Zealand Ministry of Foreign Affairs and Trade** ☎ 04/439-8000 🌐 www.mft.govt.nz.

WEB SITES

Do check out the World Wide Web when planning your trip. You'll find everything from weather forecasts to virtual tours of famous cities. Be sure to visit Fodors.com (🌐 www.fodors.com), a complete travel-planning site. You can research prices and book plane tickets, hotel rooms, rental cars, vacation packages, and more. In addition, you can post your pressing questions in the Travel Talk section. Other planning tools include a currency converter and weather reports, and there are loads of links to travel resources.

For information on Belize, visit: 🌐 www.travelbelize.org or 🌐 www.belizefirst.com (at this site, Lan Sluder, a contributor to this guide and the author of four books on Belize, offers to answer any reasonable question about Belize by e-mail, usually within 48 hours). Another informative site is 🌐 www.belizenet.com, which has a forum about Belize. For destination-specific information check out, among others, 🌐 www.ambergriscaye.com for Ambergris Caye; 🌐 www.gocayecaulker.com for Caye Caulker; 🌐 www.belizex.com for the Cayo district; 🌐 www.placencia.com for Placencia; 🌐 www.hopkinsbelize.com for the Hopkins area; and 🌐 www.corozal.com or 🌐 www.belizenorth.com for northern Belize.

For general information on Guatemala, go to 🌐 www.guatemala.travel.com.gt or 🌐 www.travel-guatemala.org.gt. For information on Lago Atitlán destinations, also see 🌐 www.atitlan.com, or for Río Dulce go to 🌐 www.mayaparadise.com.

BELIZE

1

BEST WAY TO HONOR COUSTEAU
A pilgrimage dive to the Blue Hole ⇨*p.39*

BEST BREATH OF FRESH AIR
The forests of Mountain Pine Ridge ⇨*p.63*

BIGGEST BLOCK PARTY
Dangriga's Settlement Day Festival ⇨*p.69*

MAYAN MOTHER LODE
Caracol, Belize's grandest ruins ⇨*p.66*

BEST PLACE TO GO BAREFOOT
Laid-back beach town Placencia ⇨*p.78*

BEST DIGS FOR DIVERS
Turneffe Island Lodge ⇨*p.39*

LOUDEST SANCTUARY
A howler monkey haven, outside of Belize City ⇨*p.16*

Updated by
Lan Sluder

A SLIVER OF LAND wedged between Guatemala and the Caribbean Sea, Belize is only 109 km (68 mi) wide at its broadest point. Yet, within its diminutive borders Belize probably has the greatest variety of flora and fauna of any country its size in the world.

In the Maya Mountains, the central highlands that form the watershed for thousands of streams and rivers, there's dense rain forest; in the north there are savannas and vast fields of sugarcane. Most of the interior remains uninhabited because Belizeans are by temperament and tradition town dwellers. Additionally, Belize has the lowest population density of any country in Central America—El Salvador, the only smaller country, has 10 times as many people.

Less than an hour's flight from the mainland is the Barrier Reef, a great wall of coral stretching the entire length of the coast. Dotting the reef are over 400 cayes, and farther out to sea are three coral atolls—all great for diving and snorkeling. Some of the cayes are no more than Robinson Crusoe islets of white coral sand and mangroves, inhabited by frigate birds, pelicans, and the occasional fisherman, who spends a few days diving for conch and lobster, sleeping under a sheet of canvas strung between two trees. Others, like Ambergris Caye, are becoming increasingly popular, and accompanying the crowds is an ample supply of bars, restaurants, and inns.

The name Belize is a conundrum. According to *Encyclopaedia Britannica,* it derives from *belix,* an ancient Maya word meaning "muddy water." Anyone who's seen the Belize River swollen by heavy rains can vouch for the aptness of this description. Others trace the name's origin to the French word *balise* (beacon), though no one can explain why a French word would have caught on in a region once dominated by the English. (For years Belize was known as British Honduras.) Perhaps nothing more than a drinker's tale, another theory connects Belize to the Maya word *belikin* (road to the east), which happens to be the name of the national beer. Some say Belize is a corruption of Wallace, the name of a Scottish buccaneer who founded a colony in 1620; still others say the pirate wasn't Wallace but Willis, that he wasn't Scottish but English, and that he founded a colony not in 1620, but in 1638. We'll never know if Wallace and Willis were one and the same, or how a *w* could become a *b* and an *a* slip to an *e*. But what's in a name, anyway? Grab a Belikin and come up with a few theories of your own.

There was indeed a pirate named Wallace, a onetime lieutenant of Sir Walter Raleigh who later served as Tortuga's governor. Perhaps it was liquor or lucre that turned Governor Wallace into pirate Wallace. Sometime between 1638 and 1662 he and 80 fellow renegades washed up near St. George's Caye, and proceeded to live for years off the booty from cloak-and-dagger raids on passing ships. The two stout men on Belize's flag are not pirates, however, but a pair of woodcutters standing beneath a logwood tree. Under them is a Latin inscription: *sub umbra floreat*—"In the shade of this tree we flourish." What's most remarkable about the men is that one is black, the other white—a celebration of Belize's historic and emblematic racial mixture.

GREAT ITINERARIES

If you have 2–4 days

If your international flight arrives early enough, say by 4:30 PM, head directly to one of the cayes. Otherwise, spend your first night in **Belize City** and take a morning flight or ferry to **Ambergris Caye.** Spend a few days poking around San Pedro, the island's main town, and exploring the nearby Barrier Reef. If you fancy a laid-back tropical paradise with fewer tourists and less development, travel to the southern town of **Placencia,** where you can also dive and snorkel.

If you have 5–6 days

It's said that Belize is the only country where you can scuba dive before breakfast and hike in the rain forest after lunch, but to do this you have to plan carefully. Head first to **Ambergris Caye** for a few days of fun in the sun. If you would like to extend your underwater adventures, move on to one of the remote coral atolls such as **Turneffe Atoll** or **Lighthouse Reef Atoll.** For the jungle experience, head to **San Ignacio,** in the Cayo district, and take excursions from one of the lodges in the area. From here you can canoe down the Macal River, hike through the rain forest, or explore the Mayan ruins at **Xunantunich** or **Caracol.**

If you have 7–10 days

If you have more than a week, it's worth spending a bit more time around **Belize City.** For Mayan ruins put **Altun Ha** or **Lamanai** on your list. If it's nature you want, visit the **Crooked Tree Wildlife Sanctuary** and **Community Baboon Sanctuary.** Fly to **Ambergris Caye** for two or three days of diving and sunbathing; then fly back to Belize City and head for the resorts around **San Ignacio** to see the rain forests that make Belize a naturalist's paradise. Finally, head south to **Placencia** or **Hopkins** for a luscious last few days of snorkeling and relaxing under palm trees. Or if you've had enough beach time, explore Belize's least-visited spots, **Punta Gorda,** in the far south, or **Corozal,** in the north.

Belize's white population descends from the English buccaneers and subsequent settlers of what was first known as the Honduran Bay Settlement. They worked under grueling conditions in the jungles and forests to export logwood to England, where it was prized as a textile dye. As the craftsmen of Europe learned of mahogany's value, the loggers were joined by many more.

Most of the black population descends from slaves brought from Jamaica to work in the logging industry. By the early 18th century people of African descent came to outnumber those of British origin in Belize. But rather than fight each other, whites and blacks eventually united to defeat a common enemy.

That enemy appeared in 1798, in the form of a fleet of 31 ships. After more than a century of trying to uproot this upstart colony from its backyard, the Spanish had come to exterminate it. Residents had a total of one sloop, some fishing boats, and seven rafts, but their maritime knowledge enabled them to defeat the invaders in two hours. That was the last Spanish attempt to forcibly dislodge the settlement, though bitter wrangles over British Honduras's right to exist continued for nearly a century.

In the 19th century Belize's early settlers were joined by mestizos (people of mixed Indian and European heritage) and Garífunas (Caribbean people). Later came Mennonites fleeing persecution in Europe. All these groups, like Belize's most recent refugees—people from Hong Kong unwilling to live under communist rule—found in this tiny country a tolerant and amiable home.

In many ways a landlocked island, Belize has more in common with Trinidad or St. Kitts than with Guatemala or El Salvador. English, the official language here, aligns the nation with the British Caribbean ("tea" refers to about any meal, for example, just as it does in the West Indies and cockney London). Only in a few aspects is Belize like its Central American neighbors: Spanish is widely spoken in the north and west, while Mayan dialects are heard mainly in the south. Moreover, half of the population is Roman Catholic while only 6% is Anglican.

Belize officially became an independent nation on September 21, 1981, 110 years after becoming a British Crown colony. The British, who at the request of the Belizean government had maintained a small military presence since independence, finally pulled out in 1994, but relations between the two countries remain close. Belize's defense force is still trained by the Brits; and Harrier jump jets, which used to inspire gasps from arriving tourists by flying backward over the airport, are still on call in case Guatemala should try to reassert its claim to what it once called its 13th province. At the same time, initiatives like Mundo Maya—an effort by Central American states to coordinate tourism to Mayan sites—are paving the way for greater regional cooperation.

If you're intent on finding a sprawling beach resort or a golfer's paradise, look elsewhere. On the other hand, if you want to take a night dive through a tunnel of living coral, explore a jungle resounding with the call of howler monkeys, or clamber on ancient Mayan ruins, the "adventure coast"—as Belize is rightly called—won't disappoint. Experiencing the assortment of colorful birds and animals that live here is just one of this easygoing country's rich gifts. Clever Belize will probably remain a nature lover's haven for decades to come.

EXPLORING BELIZE

Although it's no longer the capital, Belize City remains the country's transportation hub. From here you can reach the Mayan ruins in the north; the mountainous Cayo district in the west; the villages along the coast to the south, and the cayes and atolls in the Caribbean. The majority of travelers, having heard the (somewhat exaggerated) rumors about Belize City crime, choose to move on quickly. You may want set up a base near San Ignacio or Belmopan to explore the western part of the country, in Placencia or Hopkins to explore the country's southern coast, in Corozal Town to check out the north, or even on Ambergris Caye or Caye Caulker, from which you can make day trips to the mainland.

Beaches Most of the mainland coast is fringed with mangrove swamps and therefore has few beaches. The few that do exist aren't spectacular. This changes dramatically on the islands off the coast, particularly Ambergris Caye. The beaches aren't expansive—generally a small strip of sand at the water's edge—but their white coral sand, palm trees, and mint-green water assure you that you're in the Caribbean. The best beach on the mainland is in Placencia, in the south. The Hopkins–Sittee Point area also has a good beach.

Caving Belize is riddled with hundreds of caves, many of them unexplored in modern times. The most easily visited are those in Cayo, in Western Belize. Near San Ignacio are the caves at Barton Creek. Near Belmopan is Footprint Cave, where you can spend hours floating through underground rivers on an inner tube. Also in the area is Actun Tunichil Muknal, with its wealth of Mayan artifacts. The remote Chiquibul system along the Guatemala border contains Cebeda, thought to be the country's largest cave. You don't need a guide to visit open caverns such as Rio Frio, but others require an experienced guide.

Fishing Some of the world's most exciting sportfishing lies off Belize's coast and cayes. Fly-fishing is excellent on the shallow flats between the mainland and the reef, giving anglers a rare opportunity to achieve the "grand slam" of tarpon, bonefish, permit and snook in one day. Farther out to sea, sailfish, wahoo, and marlin abound. Several specialty resorts and fishing camps, such as Turneffe Flats, El Pescador, and the Lillpat Sittee River Lodge, cater to the angler, but most hotels can help you organize excellent fishing trips.

Scuba Diving & Snorkeling The Barrier Reef, a coral necklace of 320 km (198 mi) stretching from the Yucatán Peninsula to the tip of Guatemala, is the longest in the western hemisphere. If you include the three coral atolls farther out to sea—Lighthouse Reef, Glover's Reef, and the Turneffe Islands—Belize has more than 560 km (347 mi) of reef waiting to be explored. That's more than Bonaire, Cozumel, and all the Caymans put together.

The cast of aquatic characters here is endless. One moment you can come upon an enormous spotted eagle ray, its needlelike tail streaming out behind; the next you may find the feisty little damselfish, a bolt of blue no bigger than your little finger. There are bloated blowfish hovering in their holes like nightclub bouncers; lean and mean barracuda patrolling the depths; and queen angelfish that shimmy through the water with the puckered lips and haughty self-assurance of a supermodel.

Wildlife Within this tiny country you'll find animals like scarlet macaws, tapirs, jaguars, kinkajous, mountain lions, and howler monkeys, making Belize one of the best places on earth to experience up close the color and variety of tropical wildlife. Most hotels can book you a wildlife tour, and many jungle lodges, especially in Cayo, have their own guides to lead you into the wild.

About the Restaurants

Although it's not among the world's greatest, Belizean food is one of Central America's best cuisines. Staples include tasty treats—like the fry-jack, a beignetlike dough fried to a golden crisp and served at breakfast—rice and beans, fried chicken, and tasty creole "stew chicken." Added to these are such acquired tastes as iguana, known as "bush chicken" or "bamboo chicken;" gibnut, a small rodent dubbed the "royal rat" after Queen Elizabeth dined on it during a state visit; and oddities of the British culinary heritage, like bread-and-butter pudding and cow-foot soup. With the world's second-largest coral reef running along its coastline, Belize whips up some of the Caribbean's tastiest seafood. Belizean chefs have learned to prepare fish for a lighter northern palate (not everything's deep fried), and at their best dishes like grilled red snapper in a papaya-pineapple sauce, shrimp coated with coconut, or blackened shark steak squirted with fresh lime can be sublime. Meals are washed down with delicious fresh-squeezed juices, like lime, watermelon, and mango. However, you may decide that the national drink of Belize is orange Fanta or Belikin beer.

The best restaurants are usually in hotels and resorts and bear comparison with good, though not first-class, eateries in North America or Europe. Ambergris Caye is Belize's fine dining center with several excellent restaurants, such as Capricorn, Casa Picasso, and Blue Water Grill. An increasing number of restaurants are carrying substantial wine lists, although the import taxes are high, so you may pay more than you'd like. Be careful not to judge a restaurant by the way it looks; some of the best cooking comes from the humblest-looking cabanas. When in doubt, follow your nose.

Belize is a casual place and demands little in the way of a dress code. A few expensive restaurants and clubs in Belize City prefer but don't require a jacket for men. On the cayes, you won't even need shoes at most restaurants. Reservations are advisable: cooks buy ingredients for evening meals based on the number of guests expected.

About the Hotels

Chain hotels are the exception rather than the rule in Belize. Here you'll find smaller establishments shaped by the personalities of their owners, most of whom are American or British. Because of the salt and humidity, operating a hotel in the tropics is an art in itself, the closest thing to keeping house on a ship's deck. Without constant maintenance, things start to rust, the thatch (a frequently used natural building material from either the bay palm or cohune palm) leaks, and the charms of paradise quickly fade.

Rooms tend to be more expensive in Belize than elsewhere in Central America. The priciest places are in Belize City and Ambergris Caye, but they also offer more for your money because there's more competition. Hardest to find are good accommodations at moderate prices. Lodgings tend to leap from spartan to luxurious, with the middle ground occupied by grand hotels that have fallen on hard times or small ones that are overcharging. Budget travelers, however, have a wide selection.

WHAT IT COSTS In Belize Dollars					
	$$$$	$$$	$$	$	¢
RESTAURANTS	over BZ$35	BZ$25–BZ$35	BZ$15–BZ$25	BZ$8–BZ$15	under BZ$8
HOTELS	over BZ$400	BZ$300–$400	BZ$200–$300	BZ$100–$200	under BZ$100

Restaurant prices are per person for a main course at dinner. Hotel prices are for two people in a standard double room, including tax and service.

Timing

Belize is a year-round destination, but some seasons are preferable to others. The dry season, from February or March to May or June, can be the least attractive time for inland trips, with dusty roads and wilting vegetation, but this is a good time to visit the coast. The rainy season is June through September, extending in some areas through November. The wet weather varies dramatically depending on where you are: the deep south gets as much as 160 inches of rain each year, but the rest of the country gets a lot less. Moreover, the rain is not continuous; sudden thunderstorms are followed by sun. On the cayes the wet season can be accompanied by lashing winds, known as "Joe North." Perhaps owing to global climate changes, the wet and dry seasons have become less predictable in recent years. In summer 2003, for example, most of the country was dry; seasonal rains didn't begin in earnest until October and November, and winter 2003–2004 was wetter than normal.

The western Caribbean's hurricane season is from June through November. Hurricanes have been relatively rare in Belize—usually one every decade—but two big storms slammed the country in as many years. In September 2000 Hurricane Keith struck Ambergris and Caulker, killing three and causing more than BZ$400 million in damage. In October 2001 Hurricane Iris came ashore near Placencia, killing more than 20 (including 17 Americans staying in a dive boat) and leaving some 13,000 people in the country's southern region temporarily homeless. Thanks to relief and rebuilding efforts, as well as Mother Nature's healing green thumb, today you will notice few if any effects of the storms.

Scuba enthusiasts can dive all year, but the water is clearest from April to June. Between November and February cold fronts from North America can push southward, producing blustery winds known as "northers" that bring rain and rough weather and tend to churn up the sea, reducing visibility. Water temperatures rarely stray from 27°C (80°F), so many people dive without a wet suit.

BELIZE CITY

From the air you realize how small Belize City is—with a population of about 50,000, it's more of a town than a city. Few of the ramshackle buildings here are taller than the palm trees. After a couple of miles, streets simply give way to a largely uninhabited country where animals outnumber people.

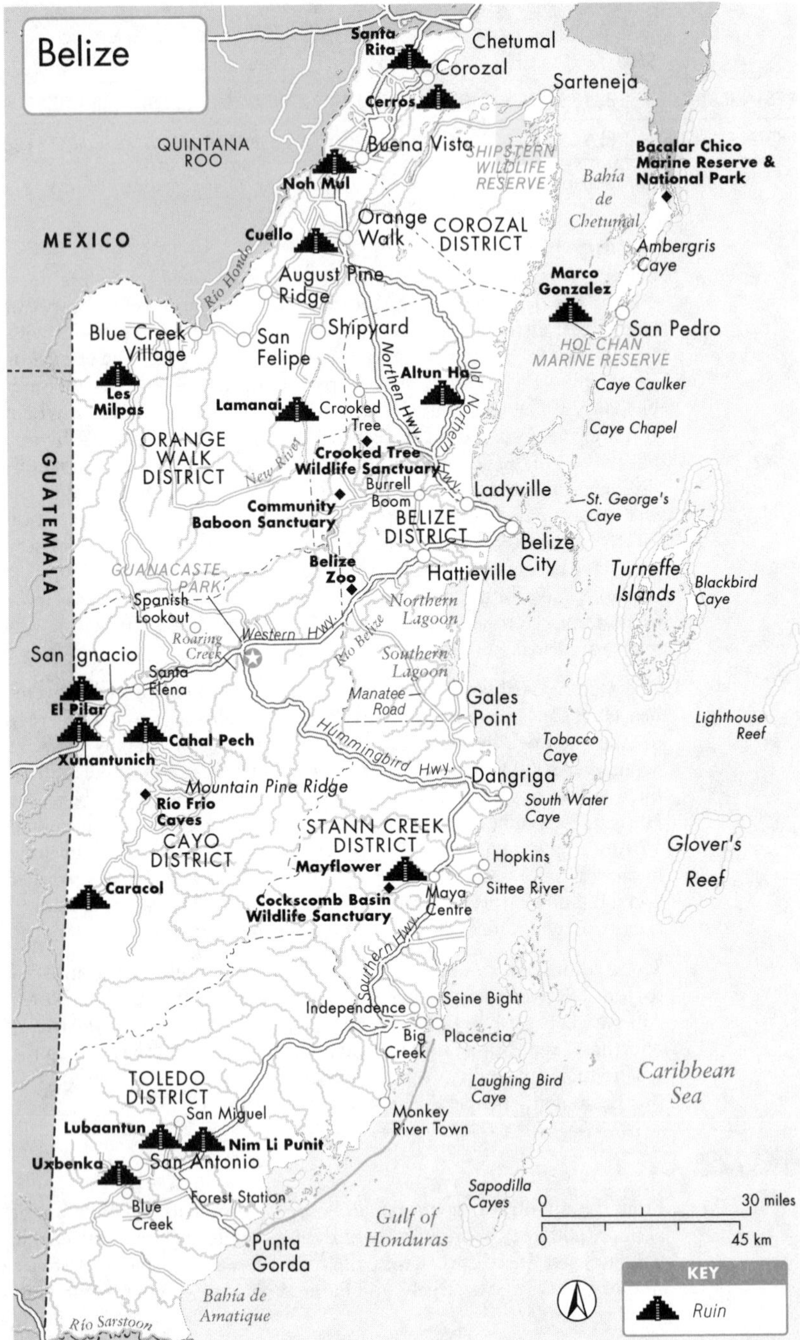
Belize
Chetumal
Santa Rita
Corozal
Sarteneja
Cerros
QUINTANA ROO
Buena Vista
SHIPSTERN WILDLIFE RESERVE
Bacalar Chico Marine Reserve & National Park
Bahía de Chetumal
Noh Mul
MEXICO
Cuello
Orange Walk
COROZAL DISTRICT
Ambergris Caye
Río Hondo
August Pine Ridge
Marco Gonzalez
Blue Creek Village
San Felipe
Shipyard
San Pedro
HOL CHAN MARINE RESERVE
Northern Hwy.
Old Northern Hwy.
Altun Ha
Les Milpas
Lamanai
Crooked Tree
Caye Caulker
Caye Chapel
ORANGE WALK DISTRICT
New River
Crooked Tree Wildlife Sanctuary
GUATEMALA
Burrell Boom
Ladyville
St. George's Caye
Community Baboon Sanctuary
BELIZE DISTRICT
Belize City
Belize Zoo
Hattieville
Turneffe Islands
Blackbird Caye
GUANACASTE PARK
Spanish Lookout
Northern Lagoon
Roaring Creek
Western Hwy.
Río Belize
San Ignacio
Southern Lagoon
Santa Elena
El Pilar
Manatee Road
Gales Point
Lighthouse Reef
Cahal Pech
Hummingbird Hwy.
Tobacco Caye
Xunantunich
Dangriga
Mountain Pine Ridge
Río Frio Caves
South Water Caye
STANN CREEK DISTRICT
CAYO DISTRICT
Glover's Reef
Hopkins
Mayflower
Caracol
Sittee River
Maya Centre
Cockscomb Basin Wildlife Sanctuary
Southern Hwy.
Seine Bight
Independence
Placencia
Big Creek
Caribbean Sea
TOLEDO DISTRICT
Laughing Bird Caye
San Miguel
Monkey River Town
Lubaantun
Nim Li Punit
Uxbenka
San Antonio
Forest Station
Sapodilla Cayes
Blue Creek
Gulf of Honduras
0
30 miles
0
45 km
Punta Gorda
KEY
Ruin
Bahía de Amatique
Río Sarstoon

Perhaps because of its strange history, Belize was one of Pax Britannia's most neglected colonies. The British, who were usually generous in such matters, left little of either great beauty or interest in their former colony's capital—no parks or gardens, no university, no museums. One of the clichés about Belize City is that the most exciting thing that happens here is the opening of the rusty swing bridge on Haulover Creek.

In 1961 the city was almost annihilated by Hurricane Hattie, and authorities decided to move Belize's capital to Belmopan, robbing Belize City of its reason for being. Thus began a long, dark night that caused even more damage than Hurricane Hattie. Press accounts of street crime made Belize City sound like south-central Los Angeles, though it wasn't ever as bad. In the mid-1990s both the government and private sector began a concerted effort to stop the hemorrhage of travelers, and thus money, away from the city. In 1995 a Tourism Police Unit was created to help cut down on crime, and officers on foot patrol are now a familiar sight. To make getting around the city easier, roads were resurfaced and traffic lights were installed. A new waterfront walkway was built along Eve Street.

At the turn of the millennium other changes were underway. More and more colonial buildings were restored, making the Fort George area an increasingly pleasant place to stay. Late 2001 saw the unveiling of a new cruise-ship terminal and shopping area called Fort Point Tourist Village, and plans are afoot for Carnival Cruise Lines to build a larger terminal. Though shallow water in the harbor means passengers must be brought ashore in tenders, the city now gets more than half a million cruise-ship passengers annually, creating new tourism jobs but raising concern that the fragile ecology of reef and rain forest could be damaged. There's still a lot of work to be done, but Belize City *is* slowly recreating itself.

Numbers in the margin correspond to points of interest on the Belize City map.

Exploring Belize City

If you're prepared to go beyond a cursory excursion, Belize City will repay your curiosity. Belizeans are natural city dwellers, and there's an infectious sociability on streets like Albert and Queen, the main shopping strips. The finest British colonial houses—graceful white buildings with wraparound verandas, painted shutters, and fussy Victorian woodwork—are on the North Shore, near the Radisson Fort George, the most pleasant part of the city in which to stroll.

a good walk

Start your tour of Belize City at the **Swing Bridge** ① ⚑, which crosses the Haulover River. If for some reason you're here at 5:30 AM or 5:30 PM weekdays, you can watch it in action. Near the Swing Bridge on North Front Street is the **Marine Terminal** ② from which you can take water taxis to the cayes. Also here is the Coastal Zone Museum, which has displays on the Barrier Reef, and the Marine Museum, which has displays about the country's maritime history. Walk southeast along the water on Front Street to reach the **Fort George Lighthouse** ③; get a view of the bustling city harbor just over the promontory. Walk north on Marine Parade and behold the Radisson Fort George Hotel, guarded by white-helmeted attendants. Next door is the Chateau Caribbean, a seaside colonial mansion that was once a private hospital. It adjoins Memorial Park, a tranquil respite with welcome sea breezes. You can stop at the Tourist Village for a bathroom break (they're spotless), a little gift shopping, or a snack. Farther inland are most of the embassies, housed in well-preserved mansions; the impressive U.S. Embassy is on Gabourel Lane just south of Queen Street. While on Gabourel Lane, stop in at the **Museum of Belize** 4, a small space in the Central Bank Building complex with an eclectic collection of Belizeana.

South of the Swing Bridge on Regent Street are some beautiful buildings, including a cement reconstruction of the original wooden courthouse here, which burned down in 1926. Along the Southern Foreshore is a cultural center called the **Bliss Institute** 5. The center overlooks the harbor and hosts arts events. At the end of Regent Street is **St. John's Cathedral** 6, built by slaves with bricks that served as ballast in the hulls of ships arriving from Europe. One block southwest lies Yarborough Cemetery, where the inscriptions on the headstones once hinted at tales of deceit, murder, and derring-do, though you'd be hard-pressed to find any legible inscriptions after the passing of a century. Nearby is the **House of Culture** 7, the former residence of Belize's governor-general.

TIMING The demeanor of Belize City with its narrow, sun-burned streets and ramshackle houses changes little from day to day, or season to season. The exception is Sunday, when the city becomes almost a ghost town, and summer, when the flame trees with their fire-orange blossoms add a vibrant color to the town.

Belize City is fairly compact, so this walk should take only a few hours.

Sights to See

5 **Bliss Institute.** This building, overlooking the harbor from Haulover Creek's south bank, houses the National Arts Council and hosts cultural events throughout the year. There are a drama series in April, the Children's Festival of the Arts in May, dance festivals in June and July, and musical and cultural performances during September's monthlong independence celebration. Mayan artifacts from Caracol are on display in the entryway. ✉ *2 Southern Foreshore, between Church and Bishop Sts.* ☎ *227/2110* ⏲ *Weekdays 8:30–noon and 1–5.*

3 **Fort George Lighthouse.** Towering over the entrance to Belize Harbor, this lighthouse stands guard on the tip of Fort George Point. It was designed and funded by the country's greatest benefactor, Baron Bliss, to whom a memorial stands nearby. The lighthouse is for photo ops only—you can't enter it. ✉ *Fort St.*

7 **House of Culture.** Formerly called Government House, the city's finest colonial structure is said to have been designed by the illustrious British architect Sir Christopher Wren. Built in 1812 it was once the residence of the governor general, the queen's representative in Belize. Following Hurricane Hattie, he and the rest of the government moved to Belmopan,

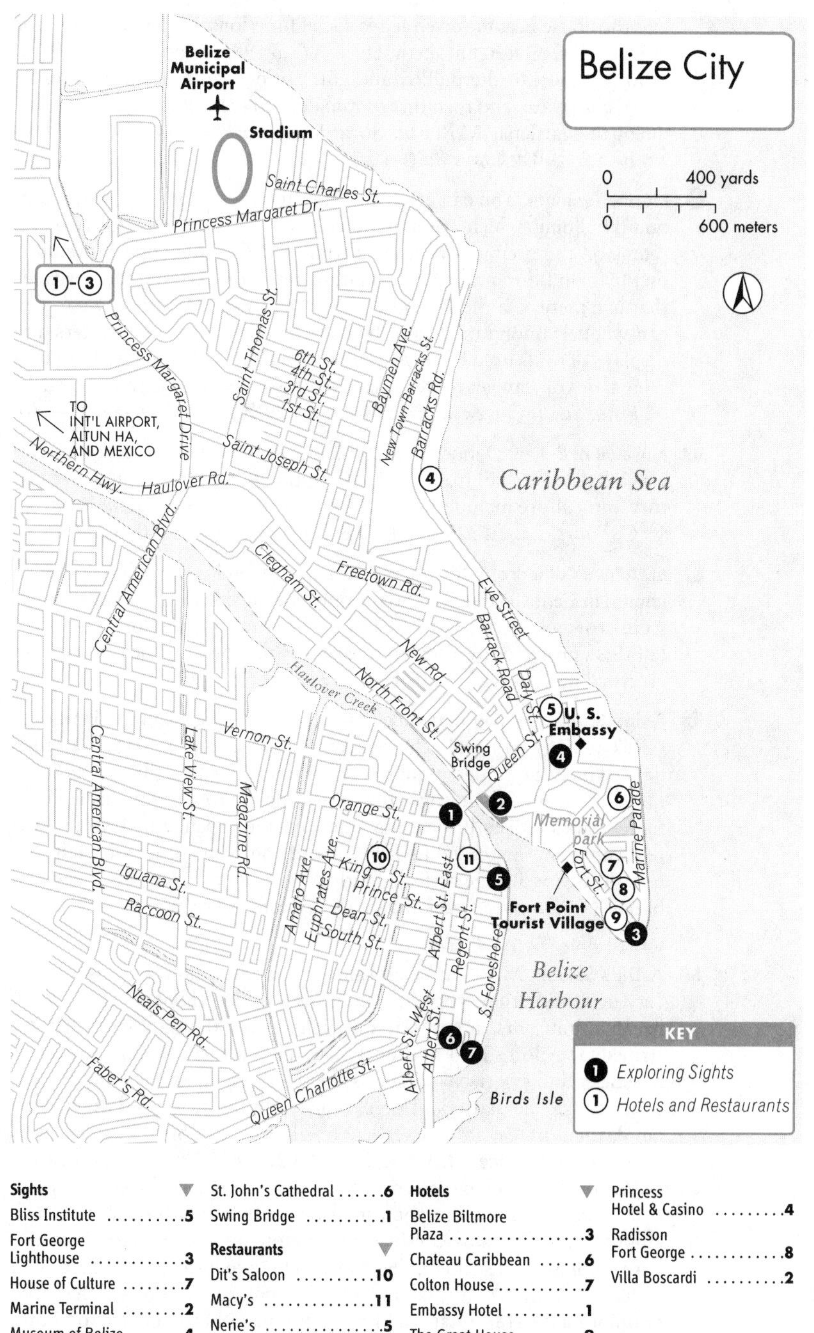

Sights

Bliss Institute 5
Fort George Lighthouse 3
House of Culture 7
Marine Terminal 2
Museum of Belize 4
St. John's Cathedral 6
Swing Bridge 1

Restaurants

Dit's Saloon 10
Macy's 11
Nerie's 5

Hotels

Belize Biltmore Plaza 3
Chateau Caribbean 6
Colton House 7
Embassy Hotel 1
The Great House 9
Princess Hotel & Casino 4
Radisson Fort George 8
Villa Boscardi 2

and the house became a venue for social functions and a guesthouse for visiting VIPs. (Queen Elizabeth stayed here in 1985, Prince Philip in 1988.) Now it's open to the public, and you can peruse its archival records, silver, glassware, and furniture or mingle with the tropical birds that frequent the gardens. ✉ *Regent St. at Southern Foreshore* ☎ *227/3050* 🎫 *BZ$5* ⏲ *Weekdays 8:30–4:30.*

❷ **Marine Terminal.** You can catch a boat to the cayes from this white clapboard building, which was a firehouse in the 1920s. Browse the two museums on the premises while you wait. The **Coastal Zone Museum** is on the main floor and has information about the reef and the creatures that live there. On the second floor is the **Marine Museum,** where you can wander among models of boats that have sailed these waters and displays of tools used by shipwrights. One ticket gets you into both museums, or you can get in free if you've booked passage on a ferry. ✉ *10 N. Front St., at Queen St.* ☎ *223/1969* 🎫 *BZ$4* ⏲ *Mon.–Sat. 8–4:30.*

❹ **Museum of Belize.** Debuting in 2002, this small but interesting museum was a Belize City jail from the 1850s until 1993. Displays on Belize history and culture include ancient Mayan artifacts and an actual jail cell. ✉ *Gabourel La.* ☎ *223/4524* 🎫 *BZ$10* ⏲ *Tues.–Fri. 10–6, Sat. 10–3.*

❻ **St. John's Cathedral.** On Albert Street's south end is the oldest Anglican church in Central America and the only one outside England where kings were crowned. From 1815 to 1845 four kings of the Mosquito Coast (a British protectorate along the coast of Honduras and Nicaragua) were crowned here. ✉ *Albert St.* ☎ *227/2137.*

⚑ ❶ **Swing Bridge.** As you may have guessed, the bridge spanning Haulover Creek actually swings. Each weekday at 5:30 AM and 5:30 PM, four men hand-winch the bridge a quarter-revolution so waiting boats can continue upstream (when it was the only bridge in town, this snarled traffic for blocks). The bridge, made in England, opened in 1923; it was renovated and upgraded in 1999. It's the only one of its kind left. Before the Swing Bridge arrived, cattle were "hauled over" the creek in a barge. ✉ *Haulover Creek where Queen and Albert Sts. meet.*

Where to Stay & Eat

¢–$$ ✕ **Dit's Saloon.** More café-cum-saloon than restaurant, Dit's is a Belize City institution that specializes in beans and rice. (Like many older Belizean restaurants, it's got a sink right in the dining room.) Cheery striped tablecloths lend this local place a homey feel. Among the must-try sticky and sweet baked goods are the three-milks cake and the coconut tarts. The platters of eggs, beans, and toast, washed down with ample mugs of tea, are an excellent breakfast value. Sip on the delicious fresh-squeezed juices. ✉ *50 King St.* ☎ *227/3330* 💳 *No credit cards.*

¢–$$ ✕ **Macy's.** Stewed iguana, known locally as bamboo chicken, is available on request here, but you can also try armadillo, brocket deer, and gibnut. Macy, the Jamaican-born proprietor, says iguana is tough to prepare—it has to be scalded, then washed in lime juice and vinegar—but delicious to eat. On display are a letter from the bishop of Belize congratulating the staff on its catering feats and a photo of Harrison Ford, who commandeered the table by the door during the making of *The Mosquito Coast.* ✉ *18 Bishop St.* ☎ *207/3419* ▭ *No credit cards.*

¢–$$ ✕ **Nerie's.** Always packed with locals, Nerie's is the *vox populi* of dining in Belize City. Many traditional dishes are on the menu here, including fry jacks for breakfast and cow-foot soup and *garifuna sere* (fish soup with coconut milk) for lunch. Stew chicken with rice, beans, and a soft drink will only set you back BZ$10. ✉ *Queen and Daly Sts.* ☎ *223/4028* ✉ *124 Freetown Rd.* ☎ *224/5199* ▭ *No credit cards.*

★ $$$ ✕ **Radisson Fort George.** Porters in white pith helmets perpetuate a sense of British colonialism at Belize City's finest hotel. Lush red and ocher fabrics, faux-leopard carpets, and reproduction rattan and hardwood antiques recreate the British raj of the 1880s. There are panoramic views of the sea through tinted glass from rooms in the six-story tower, while those in the executive wing across the road overlook the river and one of the hotel's two pools. Dining options include the expensive Stonegrill Restaurant or the coffeeshop, Le Petit Café. The Baymen's Tavern is one of the city's popular upscale watering holes. ✉ *2 Marine Parade* ☎ *227/7400, 800/333–3333 in U.S.* 📠 *227/3820* 🌐 *www.radissonbelize.com* *102 rooms* *Restaurant, room service, in-room data ports, some in-room safes, minibars, cable TV, 2 pools, gym, dive shop, marina, fishing, bar, shops, laundry service, business services, meeting rooms, car rental, travel services, no-smoking rooms* ▭ *AE, MC, V.*

$$–$$$ ✕ **Princess Hotel & Casino.** Big-time gambling arrived in Belize when its first Las Vegas–style casino opened at this sprawling hotel, the largest in Belize, in 2000. Though it's not quite the MGM Grand, the casino has tables for black jack, poker, craps, roulette, and more than 400 machines. Belize's only movie theater and bowling alley are also here. Alas, the rooms and service aren't as exciting as the gaming, though they all have views of the harbor and four of the suites have balconies. ✉ *Kings Park* ☎ *223/2670* 📠 *223/2660* 🌐 *www.princessbelize.com* *179 rooms, 5 suites* *Restaurant, room service, cable TV, pool, gym, hair salon, dive shop, marina, fishing, bowling, bar, casino, theater, laundry service, business services, meeting rooms, car rental, travel services, no-smoking rooms* ▭ *AE, MC, V.*

★ $$ ✕ **The Great House.** Among Fort George's most stunning sights is the grand colonial facade of this large wooden house. Owner Steve Maestre converted his home into an outstanding inn with one of the city's best restaurants. The large rooms have polished pine floors. There are wraparound veranda where you can relax while taking in the sea breeze. On the ground floor a tiny gallery of shops leads to the Smoky Mermaid, where amiable servers deliver Caribbean-influenced seafood dishes, inventive pasta, and savory barbecues in a large courtyard shaded by breadfruit and sapodilla trees. ✉ *13 Cork St.* ☎ *223/3400* 📠 *223/3444* 🌐 *www.greathousebelize.com* *16 rooms* *Restaurant, fans, in-room fax, in-room safes, refrigerators, cable TV, shops, laundry service, car rental, travel services* ▭ *AE, DC, MC, V.*

$–$$ ✕ **Belize Biltmore Plaza.** Previously in deterioration, this hotel is staging a comeback with many improvements to its pool, grounds, and rooms. "Deluxe premier" rooms, with new carpets and mattresses, are worth the extra cost. The Victorian Room (BZ$20–BZ$50), which serves entrées like stew chicken and New York strip, is now a popular lunch spot for local businesspeople. ✉ *Mile 3½, Northern Hwy.* ☎ *223/2302* 🖷 *223/2301* 🌐 *www.belizebiltmore.com* *80 rooms* *Restaurant, room service, cable TV, pool, 2 bars, shops, laundry service, business services, meeting rooms, travel services* 💳 *AE, MC, V.*

$ **Chateau Caribbean.** Bright Caribbean colors enliven the rooms in this colonial-style hotel, where some scenes in the 1980 movie, *The Dogs of War,* were filmed. Suites have balconies overlooking the harbor. As this is Belize, don't expect everything to work perfectly—your room's louvered windows might not close, defeating the air-conditioning. The second-floor restaurant has ocean views, and a menu with an unusual combination of Chinese and Caribbean dishes: you can have grilled snapper with rice and beans while your dining companion tries the sweet-and-sour pork. ✉ *6 Marine Parade* ☎ *223/0800* 🖷 *223/0900* 🌐 *www.chateaucaribbean.com* *20 rooms* *Restaurant, room service, cable TV, bar, laundry service, meeting rooms* 💳 *AE, MC, V.*

$ **Villa Boscardi.** If you're edgy about Belize City, this B&B in the northern suburbs might be your cup of herbal tea. Franco and Francoise Boscardi (he's Italian, she's Belgian) opened their quiet residential area home to guests. Its four rooms are bright, sunny, and stylish, with hints of both Europe and Belize in their decor. A detached bungalow in the back has a refrigerator and coffeemaker. An evening shuttle to downtown restaurants is included in the rate; airport pick-up is BZ$20, half the regular taxi fare. ✉ *6043 Manatee Dr., turn toward sea off Northern Hwy. at Golding Ave., then left on 2nd lane to 5th house on right* ☎🖷 *223/1691* 🌐 *www.villaboscardi.com* *4 rooms, 1 cottage* *Fans, some refrigerators, cable TV, airport shuttle, car rental* 💳 *AE, MC, V* *CP.*

¢–$ **Embassy Hotel.** Just across the parking lot from the international airport, this is lodging for people in transit. Although there's little charm and some rooms look onto shabbier regions, it's safe, clean, and convenient. Not completely devoid of charm, it has a sunny roof deck where you can relax in a hammock or challenge a friend to a game of table tennis. Staying longer? Consider the one-bedroom apartments. The hotel will store your luggage or dive gear for a fee of about BZ$2 a day. *Philip S. W. Goldson International Airport* ☎ *225/3333* 🖷 *225/2267* 🌐 *www.embassyhotelbelize.com* *40 rooms, 7 suites, 8 apartments* *Restaurant, bar, travel services* 💳 *MC, V.*

Sports & the Outdoors

Belize Dive Connection (✉ 2 Marine Parade, Belize City ☎ 223/4526 🖷 227/8808) runs trips from the Radisson Fort George dock. Dive trips to Hol Chan Marine Reserve near Ambergris Caye cost around BZ$180 per person.

Sea Sports Belize (✉ 83 N. Front St., Belize City ☎ 223/5505) will take you to Caves Branch River for cave tubing (BZ$205), the Belize River for canoeing (BZ$205), Goff's Caye for snorkeling (BZ$173), or Turneffe Atoll for diving (from BZ$280).

Shopping

Fort Point Tourist Village (✉ At Fort George cruise ship docks, east of Swing Bridge ☎ 223/7008) is packed with day-trippers when cruise ships are in port and nearly deserted at other times. It has around 30 gift shops, clean restrooms, a cybercafé, a car rental kiosk, restaurants, and other services. **National Handicraft Center** (✉ 2 South Park St. ☎ 223/3636) has Belizean souvenir items, including hand-carved figurines, handmade furniture, pottery, and woven baskets. Belize's premier art gallery, **Image Factory** (✉ 91 N. Front St. ☎ 223/4151), is run by a nonprofit foundation, has exhibitions that change monthly, and a store selling pieces by more than 20 Belizean artists.

To stock up on picnic supplies, head to **Brodies** (✉ Mile 2½, Northern Hwy. ☎ 223/5587). **Save-U Supermarket** (✉ Sancas Plaza at Northern Hwy. and Central American Blvd. ☎ 223/1291) is a good place for groceries, liquor, and sundries.

Side Trips from Belize City

Belize Zoo

★ Turn a sharp corner on the jungle trail, and suddenly you're face to face with a black jaguar, the largest cat in the western hemisphere. The big cat growls a deep rumbling threat. You jump back, thankful that a strong but inconspicuous fence separates you and the jaguar.

One of the smallest, but arguably one of the best, zoos in the world, the Belize Zoo packs a lot into 29 acres. Containing more than 125 native species, the zoo has self-guided tours through several Belizean ecosystems—rain forest, lagoons, and riverine forest. Along with the rare black jaguar and the spotted jaguar, you'll see the country's four other wild cats: the puma, margay, ocelot, and jaguarondi. Perhaps the zoo's most famous resident is April, a Baird's tapir. This relative of the horse and rhino is known to locals as the mountain cow, and is also Belize's national animal.

The zoo owes its existence to the dedication and drive of one gutsy woman, Sharon Matola. An American who came to Belize as part of a film crew, Matola stayed on to care for some of the semi-tame animals used in the production. She opened the zoo in 1983 and in 1991 it moved to its present location. She's also an active environmentalist.

Besides touring the zoo, you can also hike or canoe through the adjacent 84-acre Tropical Education Center. The center is involved in a green-iguana breeding project. Dormitory accommodations, with outdoor toilets, are available at the center for BZ$30 per person; spiffier cabins go for BZ$65–$70. Overnighters can take a nocturnal zoo tour for BZ$20. ✉ *48 km (30 mi) west of Belize City* ☎ *220/8004* 🌐 *www.belizezoo.org* 🎫 *BZ$15* ⏲ *Daily 9–4:30.*

Community Baboon Sanctuary

One of Belize's most fascinating wildlife conservation projects is the Community Baboon Sanctuary, which is actually a haven for black howler monkeys. Spanning a 32-km (20-mi) stretch of the Belize River, the reserve was established in 1985 by a group of local farmers. The howler monkey—an agile bundle of black fur with a deafening roar—was then zealously hunted throughout Central America and was facing extinction. Today the sanctuary is home to nearly 1,000 black howler monkeys, as well as numerous species of birds and mammals. Thanks to ongoing conservation efforts, you can see the howler monkeys in a number of other areas, including at Lamanai in northern Belize, along the Macal and Belize rivers in western Belize, and near Monkey River in southern Belize. Exploring the Community Baboon Sanctuary is easy thanks to about 5 km (3 mi) of trails that start near a small museum and visitor center. ✉ *50 km (31 mi) west of Belize City* ☎ *220/2181* 🎫 *BZ$10* ⏲ *Daily 8–5.*

Crooked Tree Wildlife Sanctuary

A paradise for animal lovers, this wildlife sanctuary encompasses a chain of inland waterways covering about 3,000 acres. Traveling through by canoe, you're likely to see iguanas, crocodiles, coatis, and turtles. The sanctuary's most prestigious visitor, however, is the jabiru stork. With a wingspan up to 9 feet, it's the largest flying bird in the Americas. For birders the best time to come is in the dry season, roughly from February to early June, when lowered water levels cause birds to group together to find water and food, making them easy to spot. Snowy egrets, snail kites, ospreys, and black-collared hawks, as well as two types of duck—Muscovy and black-bellied whistling—and all five species of kingfisher native to Belize can be spotted.

One of Belize's oldest inland villages, Crooked Tree, is at the reserve's center. With a population of about 800, most of Creole origin, the community has a church, school, and one of the surest signs of a former British territory: a cricket pitch. An excellent village guide is **Sam Tillett** (✉ Crooked Tree Village ☎ 220/7026). Expect to pay about BZ$20 an hour for guide services. ✉ *Turn west off Northern Hwy. at Mile 30.8, then drive 3 km (2 mi)* ☎ *223/4987 for Belize Audubon Society* 🎫 *BZ$8.*

WHERE TO STAY & EAT

$ **Bird's Eye View Lodge.** This two-story concrete hotel, though covered with vines and flowers, seems out of place at a lagoon's edge. You'll find, however, that the friendly and welcoming service inside is consistent with Belize's down-home reputation. You can pick from spic-and-span private rooms or a bed in the dorm-style room. The hotel's small and appealing dining room serves filling creole fare (BZ$8–BZ$18). ✉ *Crooked Tree* ☎ *225/7027* ✉ *birdseye@btl.net* *10 rooms, 1 dorm-style room* *Restaurant, fans, lake, boating, horseback riding, laundry service; no a/c in some rooms, no room phones, no room TVs* 💳 *AE, MC, V.*

¢–$ **Nature Resort.** You're guaranteed to see (and hear) plenty of howler monkeys at this small, Belizean-owned lodge on the Belize River. Dr. Roy

Young and family provide simple, clean accommodations convenient to the Baboon Sanctuary. The resort rents canoes and horses for exploring the area. ✉ *Bermudian Landing Village near Baboon Sanctuary visitor center* ☎ *610/1378* *5 cabanas; 6 rooms, 2 with shared baths* *Restaurant, fans, boating, horseback riding; no a/c in some rooms, no room phones, no room TVs* *MC, V.*

Belize City A to Z

AIR TRAVEL

Philip S. W. Goldson International Airport is near Ladyville, 14 km (9 mi) north of the city. In addition to international flights, a domestic terminal has flights to Ambergris Caye and Caye Caulker and the coastal towns of Dangriga, Placencia, and Punta Gorda. Taxis to town cost BZ$40. The Belize City Municipal Airport, on the seafront about 2 km (1 mi) north of the city center, also has flights to these destinations. Fares from the municipal airport are about 10%–45% cheaper than similar flights departing from the international airport.

BUS TRAVEL TO & FROM BELIZE CITY

Belize City is the hub of the country's fairly extensive bus network, so there's regular service to most regions and to the Guatemalan and Mexican borders. Novelo's and its subsidiaries, Northern Transport and Southern Transport, are the dominant carriers in the country.

Novelo's ✉ W. Collet Canal, Belize City ☎ 227/2025.

BUS TRAVEL WITHIN BELIZE CITY

There's no point-to-point bus service within Belize City. If you're headed for another part of the city a taxi is your best option. Don't walk around the city at night except in the Fort George area.

CAR RENTAL

Most international rental-car agencies have locations at Philip S. W. Goldson International Airport as well as in Belize City. Branches at the airport are usually closed Sunday. Avis has a branch at Belize City Municipal Airport as well.

Budget's got the best service in town and has a fleet of low-mileage vehicles. Some locally owned companies, such as Crystal Auto Rental and Lewis Car Rental, are less expensive than the international chains and offer service that's almost as good, but their vehicles may have higher mileage.

Local Agencies **Avis** ✉ Municipal Airport, Belize City ☎ 223/4619 ✉ Philip S. W. Goldson International Airport, Ladyville ☎ 225/2385. **Budget** ✉ Mile 2 ½, Northern Hwy., Belize City ☎ 223/2435 ✉ Philip S. W. Goldson International Airport, Ladyville ☎ 223/2435. **Crystal Auto Rental** ✉ Northern Hwy., Mile 4¾, Belize City ☎ 223/1600 ✉ Philip S. W. Goldson International Airport, Ladyville ☎ 223/1600. **Hertz** ✉ 11A Cork St., Belize City ☎ 223/5395 ✉ Philip S. W. Goldson International Airport, Ladyville ☎ 223/5395. **Lewis Auto Rental** ✉ 16 Woods St., Belize City ☎ 227/4193. **Thrifty** ✉ Central American Blvd. and Fabers Rd., Belize City ☎ 207/1271 ✉ Philip S. W. Goldson International Airport, Ladyville ☎ 225/2436.

CAR TRAVEL

There are only two highways to Belize City: the Northern Highway, which leads from the Mexican border, 165 km (102 mi) away, and the Western Highway, which runs 131 km (81 mi) from Guatemala. Both are paved and in good condition. Signs guide you to nearby destinations such as the Belize Zoo.

Finding your way around the city itself, however, is rather difficult. The downtown area's narrow one-way streets, usually without identifying signs, often end abruptly due to construction work or an inconveniently located river. Give your nerves a break and explore the city by taxi or on foot in safer sections like the Fort George area.

EMERGENCIES

Karl Heusner Memorial, a public hospital, and Belize Medical Associates, a private facility, both have 24-hour emergency rooms. Brodie's Pharmacy, at Market Square and on the Northern Highway, is open daily (hours vary). Community Drug, with several locations in Belize City, is open daily, and its Farmers Market location is open daily 8–8 including holidays.

See Dr. Osbert Usher if you need to see a dentist on short notice.

Doctors & Dentists **Osbert Usher** ✉ 16 Magazine Rd. ☎ 227/3415.

Hospitals **Belize Medical Associates** ✉ 5791 St. Thomas St. ☎ 223/0303. **Karl Heusner Memorial** ✉ Princess Margaret Dr. ☎ 223/1548.

Pharmacies **Brodie's Pharmacy** ✉ Regent St. at Market Sq. ✉ Northern Hwy., Mile 2 ½. **Community Drug** ✉ Farmers' Market ✉ 18 Albert St.

MAIL & SHIPPING

The main post office is inside the historic Paslow Building, just north of the Swing Bridge. It's open weekdays 8–noon and 1–4:30. Mail service from Belize City to the United States and other countries is generally fast and reliable (airmail to the United States usually takes about five days). For faster service use DHL and FedEx; both have offices in Belize City.

Overnight Services **DHL** ✉ 38 New Rd. ☎ 223/4350. **Federal Express** ✉ 32 Albert St. ☎ 227/3507.

Post Offices **Main Post Office** ✉ N. Front St. at Queen St. ☎ 223/2201.

MONEY MATTERS

U.S. dollars are accepted everywhere in Belize, but if you need to exchange another currency, you can do so at one of the five banks in Belize City: Alliance Bank, Atlantic Bank, Belize Bank, First Caribbean International Bank (formerly Barclays), and ScotiaBank. Most banks have their main offices on Albert Street in downtown Belize City, with smaller branches scattered around the city. Expect to be charged a 1%–2% fee if you exchange U.S. dollars.

Though most banks in Belize City have ATMs, many machines won't accept cards issued outside Belize—or, if they do, they're frequently on the fritz. The ATMs of Belize Bank are your best bet. With about a dozen locations in Belize City, San Pedro, San Ignacio, Corozal

Town, Belmopan, Dangriga and Punta Gorda, Belize Bank accepts foreign ATM cards on the CIRRUS and PLUS networks. First Caribbean branches in Belize City, Dangriga, and Belmopan work with non-Belize ATM cards, but these machines are often out of order. Try not to depend on ATMs for all your cash. Most banks offer cash advances on cards issued by Visa and MasterCard for a fee ranging from BZ$5 to BZ$30.

Banks **Alliance Bank** ✉ Princess Margaret Dr. ☎ 223/5698. **Atlantic Bank** ✉ Freetown Rd. ☎ 223/4123. **Belize Bank** ✉ 60 Market Sq. ☎ 227/7132. **First Caribbean International Bank** ✉ 21 Albert St. ☎ 227/7211. **ScotiaBank** ✉ Albert St. ☎ 227/7027.

SAFETY

Belize City earned a reputation for street crime in the early '90s, but the government has made great progress in cleaning up the problem. Still, the crime rate in Belize City is comparable to that of a large American metropolis's distressed inner city area. Take the same precautions you'd take in any city—don't wear expensive jewelry or watches, avoid handling money in public, and leave valuables in a safe. On buses and in crowded areas hold purses and backpacks close to your body. Check with the staff at your hotel before venturing into any unfamiliar areas, particularly at night.

TAXIS

Cabs cost BZ$5 for one person between any two points in the city, plus BZ$1 for each additional person. Outside the city you're charged by the distance you travel. Traveling between the International Airport and any point in the city (including the businesses and hotels along the Northern Highway) is BZ$40. There are no meters, so be sure to agree on a price before you leave. You can find taxis at Market Square or by the Swing Bridge. For pick-up, call Cinderella Plaza Taxi or Plaza Taxi Service.

Cinderella Plaza Taxi ☎ 223/0371. **Plaza Taxi Service** ☎ 223/3340.

TOURS

S&L Travel and Tours is an established tour operator, with daily trips to Lamanai, Xunantunich and Altun Ha Mayan sites, Belize Zoo, the Mountain Pine Ridge, and the Sibun River for cave tubing. Belize Trips's Katie Valk, a transplanted New Yorker, can organize a custom trip to almost anyplace in the country. With her hotel connections she can even get you a room when everything seems booked. Keep in mind that many Belize City tour operators now focus more on the booming cruise ship market, which brings customers by the thousands, than on individual needs.

Belize Trips ✉ Box 1108, Belize City ☎ 223/0376 🌐 www.belize-trips.com. **SL Travel and Tours** ✉ 91 N. Front St. ☎ 227/7593 🌐 www.sltravelbelize.com.

VISITOR INFORMATION

The Belize Tourist Board, in the New Central Bank Building, is open weekdays 8–noon and 1–5.

Belize Tourist Board ✉ New Central Bank Bldg., Level 2, Gabourel La., Box 325, Belize City ☎ 223/1913 or 800/624-0686 📠 223/1943 🌐 www.travelbelize.org.

THE CAYES & ATOLLS

Imagine heading back to shore after a day of snorkeling, the white prow of your boat pointing up towards the billowing clouds, the sky's base darkening to deep lilac, spray from the green water pouring over you like warm rain. To the left San Pedro's pastel buildings huddle among the palm trees like a detail from a Paul Klee canvas. To the right the surf breaks in a white seam along the reef.

You can experience such adventures off the coast of Belize, where more than 400 cayes (pronounced "keys," as in the Florida Keys) dot the Caribbean Sea like punctuation marks in a long, liquid sentence. Most cayes lie inside the Barrier Reef, which allowed them to develop undisturbed by tides and winds that would otherwise have swept them away. The vast majority are uninhabited but for pelicans, brown- and red-footed boobies, and some creatures curiously named wish-willies (a kind of iguana). Island names are evocative and often humorous: there are Wee Wee Caye, Laughing Bird Caye, and—why ask why?—Bread and Butter Caye. Names can suggest the company you should expect: Mosquito Caye, Sandfly Caye, and Crawl Caye, which is supposedly infested with boa constrictors. Several, like Cockney Range or Baker's Rendezvous, simply express the whimsy or nostalgia of early British settlers. The battle for control of the high seas spilled over into nomenclature. English names took precedence following the 1798 Spanish rout at the Battle of St. George's Caye: Turneffe, for Terre Nef; Lighthouse Reef, for Quattro Cayos; Glover's Reef, for Longorif.

Farther out to sea, between 48 km and 96 km (30 mi and 60 mi) off the coast, are the atolls, which are impossibly beautiful when viewed from the air. At their center the water is mint green: the white sandy bottom reflects the light upward and is flecked with patches of mangrove and rust-color sediment. Around the atoll's fringe the surf breaks in a white circle before the color changes abruptly to ultramarine as the water plunges to 3,000 feet.

The origin of Belize's atolls remains a mystery, but evidence suggests that unlike the Pacific atolls, which formed by accretion around the rims of submerged volcanoes, these grew from the bottom up, as vast pagodas of coral accumulated over millions of years on top of limestone fault blocks. The Maya were perhaps the first humans to discover the atolls, using them as stopovers on their trading routes. Piles of seashells and rocks, known as "shell maidens," probably placed as markers, have been found on the Turneffe Islands.

Scuba Diving

Dive destinations are often divided into two broad categories—the reef and the atolls. Most reef diving is done on Belize's northern section, particularly off Ambergris Caye. Here the reef is just a few hundred yards from shore, making access to dive sites extremely easy: the journey by boat takes as little as 10 minutes. Coast and coral are farther apart as you head south, which means a greater dependence on weather. On Ambergris Caye you might be stuck in your hotel during a morning storm, but you'll still have a good chance of getting out in the afternoon. Most dive shops are attached to hotels, where the quality of dive masters, equipment, and facilities can vary considerably.

Many resorts have diving courses. A one-day basic familiarization course costs between BZ$250 and BZ$350. A four-day PADI certification course costs BZ$700–BZ$800. One popular variant is a referral course, where the academic and pool training is done at home, but not the required dives. The cost for two days is about BZ$500.

For a truly dramatic experience, head to the atolls for some of the world's greatest diving opportunities. One caveat: most atolls are far removed from the accommodations. If you're staying on Ambergris Caye, Glover's Reef is out of the question for a day trip by boat. Even with perfect weather—which it often isn't in winter—a trip to Lighthouse Reef takes between two and three hours. Turneffe is more accessible, though it's still a long and costly day trip, and you're unlikely to reach the atoll's southern tip, which has the best diving.

If you're determined to dive the atolls, you can stay at an island resort or a live-aboard dive boat. The resorts are marvelous hangouts for those desiring a real castaway experience. You could go stir crazy, however, if you're interested in nightlife. You might also find yourself significantly poorer at trip's end. A live-aboard can be great fun, weather permitting, but the cost (BZ$2,600–BZ$4,800 per person) is about the same as staying in a resort. The Belize government levies a cruising tax of BZ$30 per week per diver.

The ***Belize Aggressor III*** (✉ Box 1470, Morgan City, LA 70381 ☎ 985/385–2628, 800/348–2628 in U.S. and Canada 📠 985/384–0817 🌐 www.aggressor.com) is an orderly operation run by a khaki-clad crew of five, who can accommodate up to 18 passengers. It uses a 120-foot luxury cruiser powered by twin 500-horsepower engines and equipped with ultramodern communication systems. The exhaustive schedule involves five single-tank dives a day, including one at night. Staterooms are spacious double-berth cabins brightened with sky-blue fabrics, light-wood trim, and multiple windows instead of small portholes. All have private baths, TVs and VCRs, plus individual climate controls. Weeklong tours depart from the dock at the Radisson Fort George in Belize City. The boat makes scheduled stops at all three atolls, but most dives are on Lighthouse Reef's southeast corner.

The ***Nekton Pilot*** (✉ 520 S.E. 32nd St., Fort Lauderdale, FL 33316 ☎ 954/463–9324 or 800/899–6753 📠 954/463–8938 🌐 www.nektoncruises.com) operates in winter and spring months. The 80-foot craft's twin hull makes it appear like it's walking across the water on four big feet. Based on the same technology that allows oil platforms to operate in the rough waters of the North Sea, the design is supposed to provide more stability and reduce the chance of seasickness. Up to 32 divers can stay in outside cabins. On board there are a sundeck and hot tub. Most itineraries include visits to all three of Belize's atolls, with the opportunity for four or five dives daily, plus a night dive.

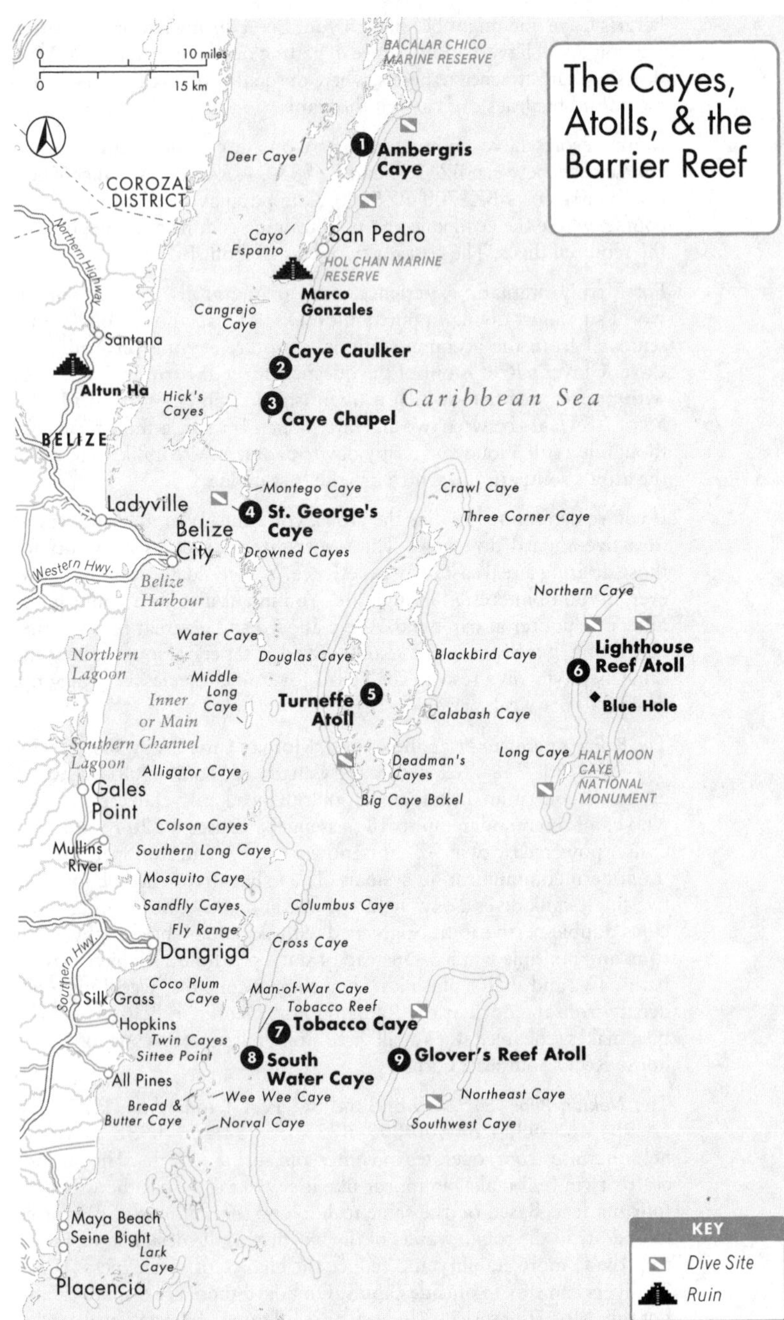

The Cayes, Atolls, & the Barrier Reef
0
10 miles
0
15 km
BACALAR CHICO MARINE RESERVE
COROZAL DISTRICT
Northern Highway
Deer Caye
1 Ambergris Caye
Cayo Espanto
San Pedro
HOL CHAN MARINE RESERVE
Marco Gonzales
Cangrejo Caye
Santana
2 Caye Caulker
Altun Ha
Hick's Cayes
3 Caye Chapel
Caribbean Sea
BELIZE
Montego Caye
Crawl Caye
Ladyville
4 St. George's Caye
Three Corner Caye
Belize City
Drowned Cayes
Western Hwy.
Belize Harbour
Northern Caye
Water Caye
Lighthouse Reef Atoll
Northern Lagoon
Douglas Caye
Blackbird Caye
6
Middle Long Caye
Inner or Main
5 Turneffe Atoll
Blue Hole
Calabash Caye
Southern Channel Lagoon
Long Caye
HALF MOON CAYE NATIONAL MONUMENT
Alligator Caye
Deadman's Cayes
Gales Point
Big Caye Bokel
Colson Cayes
Mullins River
Southern Long Caye
Mosquito Caye
Sandfly Cayes
Columbus Caye
Fly Range
Dangriga
Cross Caye
Southern Hwy.
Coco Plum Caye
Man-of-War Caye
Silk Grass
Tobacco Reef
Hopkins
7 Tobacco Caye
Twin Cayes
Sittee Point
8 South Water Caye
9 Glover's Reef Atoll
All Pines
Wee Wee Caye
Northeast Caye
Bread & Butter Caye
Norval Caye
Southwest Caye
Maya Beach
Seine Bight
Lark Caye
Placencia
Laughing Bird Caye Marine Reserve
KEY
Dive Site
Ruin

Numbers in the margin correspond to points of interest on the Cayes, Atolls, & the Barrier Reef map.

Ambergris Caye

1 *56 km (35 mi) northeast of Belize City.*

At 40 km (25 mi) long and 7 km (4½ mi) wide, Ambergris is the queen of the cayes. On early maps it was often referred to as Costa de Ambar, or the Amber Coast, a name supposedly derived from the blackish substance secreted by sperm whales—ambergris—that washes up on the beaches. However, no proof exists that ambergris was ever found here.

A few years ago, when you flew into the caye's main town, San Pedro, your plane's wingtips would have nearly brushed the laundry hanging in people's backyards. And once you landed, you could walk from one end of town to the other in 10 minutes. Today you need a bike just to get from one end of the airstrip to the other. Every year there are more cars, more souvenir shops, and more tourists. Ambergris will never be like Cancún, but it's the most developed—some would say overdeveloped—of the cayes. Still, only one street is paved (the rest are sand), transportation is most commonly by golf cart and bike or by foot, and the tallest building is just three stories.

At its core, the town remains unchanged: a couple of rows of brightly painted wooden houses flanked by the ocean on one side and the lagoon on the other. Old men lean over their balconies in the evenings to watch the world go by, and many people stroll down the roads barefoot. Stores and restaurants still have names like Lily's, Celi's, or Lee's. With a population of around 4,400, San Pedro is a small, friendly, and prosperous village. It has one of the country's highest literacy rates and an admirable level of awareness about the reef's fragility.

Tourism slowed temporarily in 2000 when Hurricane Keith slammed the island with 140 mph winds. The storm killed three people on the caye and caused millions of dollars in damage. Today there are no traces of the storm's aftermath: the hotels and other businesses quickly reopened, and even the palm trees have recovered. Because the winds came from the west, beaches actually accreted sand. Hurricane Iris, which followed in 2001, did severe damage to parts of southern Belize, but had absolutely no effect on Ambergris Caye.

Development on Ambergris continues relentlessly, but the far north of the island remains pristine, or close to it. At the top of the caye, butting up against Mexico, **Bacalar Chico Marine & Nature Reserve** spans 105 square km (41 square mi) of land, reef, and sea. Here you may cross paths with white-tail deer, ocelots, saltwater crocodiles, and, according to some reports, pumas and jaguars. A small visitor center opened in 2003. There are excellent diving, snorkeling, and fishing opportunities, especially off Rocky Point. You'll need a boat and a guide to take you here. An all-day snorkel trip to Bacalar Chico costs around BZ$170. ⊠ *North end of Ambergris Caye* 🎫 *BZ$5.*

Fodor's Choice ★ The reef's focal point is the **Hol Chan Marine Reserve** (Maya for "little channel"), 6 km (4 mi) from San Pedro at the southern tip of Ambergris. It's a 20-minute boat ride from the island. Hol Chan is a break in the reef about 100 feet wide and 20 feet–35 feet deep, through which tremendous volumes of water pass with the tides. The 13-square-km (5-square-mi) park has a miniature Blue Hole, a 12-foot-deep cave whose entrance often attracts the fairy basslet, an iridescent purple-and-yellow fish frequently seen here. The reserve is also home to a large moray eel population.

Varying in depth from 50 feet to 100 feet, Hol Chan's canyons lie between buttresses of coral running perpendicular to the reef, separated by white, sandy channels. Some sides are very steep; others are gently rolling undulations. Occasionally, you may find tunnel-like passageways from one canyon to the next. Not knowing what's in the next "valley" as you come over the hill can be pretty exciting. Because fishing is off-limits here, divers can see abundant marine life, including spotted eagle rays. There are throngs of squirrel fish, butterfly fish, parrot fish, and queen angelfish, as well as Nassau groupers, barracuda, and large shoals of yellowtail snappers.

Shark-Ray Alley is a sandbar where you can snorkel alongside nurse sharks and rays (who gather here to be fed) and even larger numbers of day-trippers. Sliding into the water is a feat of personal bravery—the sight of sharks and rays brushing past is spectacular yet daunting. A night dive here is a special treat: bioluminescence causes the water to light up, and many nocturnal animals emerge, such as octopus and spider crab. Because of the strong current you'll need above-average swimming skills, especially at night. ✉ *Southern tip of Ambergris Caye* 🎫 *BZ$10.*

Where to Stay & Eat

One of your biggest decisions in Ambergris Caye will be choosing a place to stay. There are three basic options: in or near the town of San Pedro, in the South Beach or South End area beyond town, or on North Ambergris, beyond the channel. Access to restaurants, bars, and other activities is easiest in and around San Pedro. Accommodations in town are generally simple and reasonably priced (BZ$30–BZ$250), but rooms on the main streets can be noisy, not so much from cars as from late-night revelers. San Pedro also has several small bistros where fish arrives at your table fresh from the ocean, and sometimes you'll find yourself eating with your feet in the sand. Newer, more upscale hotels are at the town's north and south edges. For silence and sand, head out of town for resort-style accommodations. For privacy and a sense of escape, consider the South End, which is a golf cart ride away, or the even more remote North Ambergris, which is reached mainly by water taxi.

Whether you arrive in San Pedro by air or by ferry from Belize City, you'll be met by a small crowd of friendly, but pushy cab drivers touting cheap lodging deals. Note that hotels pay these drivers a commission, which is reflected in the hotel rate. For the best rates call the hotel directly upon your arrival. During the off-season (May–October), hotels offer walk-in rates that are up to a third less than advertised rates.

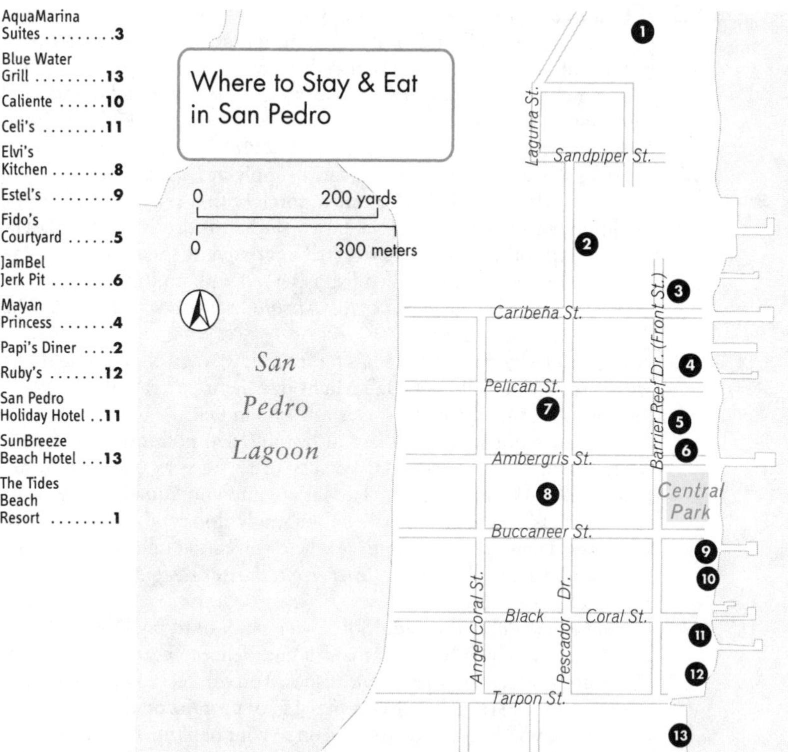

SAN PEDRO
$$–$$$$ ✕ **Blue Water Grill.** Close to the beach and perpetually busy, this restaurant's seats are on a raised, covered deck with views of the barrier reef a few hundred yards away. The emphasis here is on seafood, but there's wood-fired pizza, and Tuesday is sushi night. The coconut shrimp is great. ✉ *Beachfront at SunBreeze Hotel* ☎ *226/3347* ▭ *AE, MC, V.*

$$–$$$$ ✕ **Caliente.** Come here for a seat where you can catch sea breezes, and dig into spicy Mexican dishes with a Caribbean twist, such as margarita shrimp or *caracol al mojo de ajo* (grilled conch with garlic sauce). The local expat community often congregates here for lunch and a few piña coladas. ✉ *Beachfront, Barrier Reef Dr. in Spindrift Hotel* ☎ *226/2170* ▭ *MC,V* ⏲ *Closed Mon.*

★ $$–$$$$ ✕ **Elvi's Kitchen.** Initially, Elvi Staines sold burgers from the window of her house in 1974. Soon she added a few tables on the sand under a flamboyant tree. A quarter century later the tree remains (cut back to fit inside the roof), but everything else is changed. Enter through massive mahogany doors and you'll be tended to by a staff of a couple dozen. The burgers are still good, but Elvi's now specializes in upmarket dishes such as shrimp in watermelon sauce or crab claws with garlic butter. For dessert, don't pass on the coconut pie. ✉ *Pescador Dr.* ☎ *226/2176* ▭ *AE, MC, V* ⏲ *Closed Sun.*

$–$$$ ✕ **Fido's Courtyard.** Sooner or later you're sure to end up at Fido's, sipping something cold and contemplating the ocean views. This casual restaurant and bar is one of San Pedro's most popular places, serving fish-and-chips and pizza. It's open every day for lunch and dinner, and some nights, depending on the season, there's live music. ✉ *Beachfront, Barrier Reef Dr., just north of Catholic church* ☎ *226/3176.*

$–$$$ ✕ **Papi's Diner.** Atmosphere is in short supply at Papi's, as are views of the sea. Little more than a screened porch with a few wooden tables, the unpretentious diner is tucked away at San Pedro's north end. The seafood and other dishes are expertly prepared at some of the town's most reasonable prices. Grilled fish is served with multiple side dishes. ✉ *Pescador Dr., at north end of town behind Seven Seas Resort* ☎ *226/2047* ▭ *No credit cards.*

$–$$ ✕ **Estel's Dine by the Sea.** Estella's father-in-law was a World War II flier with a squadron called Di Nah Might (his flight jacket is displayed on the wall). Not surprisingly, this is one of San Pedro's best places for a hearty American-style breakfast of bacon, fried potatoes, and freshly squeezed juice. Later in the day you can order burgers, Mexican meals, and excellent seafood dishes. The little white-and-aqua building is on the beach, as you might infer from the sandy floor and porthole-shape windows. There's a terrace outside where you can sit under a thatch umbrella and watch pelicans. ✉ *Beachfront, Barrier Reef Dr.* ☎ *226/2019* ▭ *No credit cards.*

¢–$$ ✕ **JamBel Jerk Pit.** In the middle of town next door to Big Daddy's is this casual eatery, which blends Jamaican and Belizean cuisines (hence the name) to produce spicy jerk-style dishes. You can relax in the main dining room, where reggae is always playing, or upstairs on the roof, where it's often so windy you need to hang on to your napkin. The ocean views make it worth the trouble. ✉ *Barrier Reef Dr.at Central Park and Big Daddy's* ☎ *226/3303* ▭ *AE, MC, V.*

¢–$ ✕🏨 **Ruby's.** No wonder budget-minded travelers flock to this clean, simple hotel on the beach: air-conditioned rooms with private baths and balconies facing the ocean go for BZ$100. Try the breakfast burritos at the hotel's little restaurant, which opens at 5 for the fishing and diving crowd. On the other side of the island, a 15-room branch recently opened with even lower rates, but the original seafront location is the way to go. ✉ *Beachfront, south end of Barrier Reef Dr., at Tarpon St.* ☎ *226/2063* 🖷 *226/2434* 🌐 *www.ambergriscaye.com/rubys* ⇨ *23 rooms, 21 with bath* ♁ *Restaurant, beach, fishing; no a/c in some rooms, no room phones, no room TVs* ▭ *MC, V.*

$$$ 🏨 **AquaMarina Suites.** On the water at the north end, this suites hotel is within walking distance of everything in town, but is more luxurious than most hotels found there. Although the suites are on the small side, they're handsomely furnished in light, tropical colors and have queen-size beds, kitchens with mahogany cabinets, and private balconies with gorgeous views of the water. Note that the pool is tiny and the beach is busy, with a fair amount of walk-by and boat traffic. ✉ *Beachfront, Barrier Reef Dr.* ☎ *226/4675* 🖷 *226/3414* 🌐 *www.aquamarinasuites.com* ⇨ *14 suites* ♁ *Kitchens, cable TV, pool, beach, bar, shop, travel services* ▭ *AE, MC, V.*

$$–$$$ **SunBreeze Beach Hotel.** This mid-size resort across from the airstrip at the town's southern edge, has large rooms that surround a plant-filled courtyard. Five deluxe rooms have whirlpool baths; all are equipped for guests with disabilities. There's a small beach area (with a seawall, though), a shaded pool, and a dive shop. The island's only paved street, a short strip of cobblestone put down in 1999, is outside the front door. *Coconut Dr. 226/2191 or 800/688–0191 in U.S. and Canada 226/2346 www.sunbreeze.net 39 rooms Restaurant, some refrigerators, cable TV, pool, beach, dive shop, dock, shops, laundry service, meeting rooms, travel services AE, MC, V.*

$$ **Mayan Princess.** Sitting pretty in the middle of town, this pink hotel has rattan furniture covered with pastel-color fabrics. Sliding doors open onto verandas, where you can eat meals prepared in your well-equipped kitchenette. In the low season—and sometimes even the high season—room prices drop dramatically. It doesn't hurt to ask for a deal when making reservations. *Beachfront, Barrier Reef Dr. 226/2778 226/2784 www.mayanprincesshotel.com 23 apartments Fans, kitchenettes, cable TV, beach, travel services AE, MC, V.*

$$ **San Pedro Holiday Hotel.** Trimmed in cheery pink and white colors, this spic-and-span quartet of colonial-style houses is in the center of San Pedro. All rooms have polished wood floors, and many have views of the small in-town beach. Celi's Restaurant on the first floor has casual beachfront dining. *Beachfront, Barrier Reef Dr. 226/2014 226/2295 www.sanpedroholiday.com 14 rooms, 1 suite, 1 apartment Restaurant, fans, some refrigerators, beach, dive shop, windsurfing, bar, shops, laundry service, travel services; no room phones, no TV in some rooms AE, MC, V.*

$$ **The Tides Beach Resort.** If diving is your reason for being, and you don't want to spend a ton of money, you couldn't do better than this hotel, owned by Patojo Paz, one of the island's most experienced dive masters, and his wife. The three-story wood-frame structure recalls a time before everyone built with reinforced concrete. Top picks here are the second and third floor oceanfront rooms, which have balconies overlooking the beach. The hotel is north of town, but you can walk along the beach to San Pedro's bars and restaurants. *Beachfront, Boca del Rio Dr., north of town 226/2283 226/3797 www.ambergriscaye.com/tides 8 rooms Fans, some refrigerators, beach, pool, dive shop, dock, bar, laundry service; no room phones, no TV in some rooms MC, V CP.*

NORTH OF SAN PEDRO

$$$$ Fodor's Choice ★ **Capricorn.** Almost from the day it opened, this small seaside bistro has been considered the island's best restaurant. New owners took over in 2003, but you can still rely on favorites like rosemary focaccia, beef medallion with grilled lobster, and seafood crepes. For dessert there's equally dreamy tropical treats such as coconut ice cream. You need to take a water taxi here (BZ$10 per person each way), but once you've settled on the veranda, just steps from the sea, you'll be glad you made the trip. There are three little cabanas for those who don't want to leave. *5 km (3 mi) north of San Pedro 226/2809 Reservations essential AE, MC, V.*

$$$–$$$$ **Rendezvous Restaurant & Winery.** Next door to Journey's End resort is Belize's only Thai–French restaurant. Start off with the *som tum* (shredded papaya) and *cho cho* (a local squash) in a tangy sauce with peanuts, coriander, and dried shrimp. Follow with chicken in spicy red curry sauce, and then the chocolate truffle cake with Belizean *wongla* (sesame seed) candy. The owners, who have lived and worked in Thailand and Singapore, also produce and bottle their own wines using imported grape concentrate. Rent the honeymoon suite above the restaurant if you can't bear the water-taxi ride (BZ$10 per person each way) back to your hotel. ✉ *8 km (5 mi) north of San Pedro* ☎📠 *226/3426* 💳 *AE, MC, V.*

$$–$$$ ✕ **Sweet Basil.** Sweet Basil is the place to pick up the goods for a picnic. You'll have to ride your bike or golf cart up Pescador Drive to the "cut" (a cross-caye channel), where a hand-pulled ferry will take you and your vehicle across for BZ$5. Look for the pink-and-blue house a quarter of a mile on, where you can relax on the upstairs veranda and gnosh on some of Belize's scarcer commodities, like lox, prosciutto, and imported cheese. ✉ *Tres Cocos area, North Ambergris* ☎ *226/3870* 💳 *MC, V* ⊙ *Closed Mon.*

★ **$$$$** ✕🏨 **Mata Chica.** Casitas in shades of mango, banana, and blueberry offset by brilliant white sand give this resort a Gauguin-like quality. Inside, the fabric, artwork, and tiles echo these brilliant colors. For extra space, choose a two-bedroom villa or the 5,000-square-foot "Beach Mansion." Delectable though pricey seafood is served at Mambo. Formerly in the fashion business, Nadia Taricco and her husband, Philippe Berthome, brought with them a guest list that has included such stars as Mick Jagger, but you'll feel special even if your 15 minutes haven't arrived yet. The beach here is postcard pretty so you might not mind that there's no pool. ✉ *8 km (5 mi) north of San Pedro* ☎ *220/5010* 📠 *220/5012* 🌐 *www.matachica.com* *12 casitas, 2 villas, 1 beach house* *Restaurant, fans, spa, beach, snorkeling, boating, fishing, bar, laundry service, travel services; no room phones, no room TVs, no kids under 10* 💳 *AE, MC, V.*

$$$$ 🏨 **Captain Morgan's Retreat.** Featured prominently on *Temptation Island*, this resort hasn't been shy about touting its turn on the reality show. But instead of scantily clad beauties, here you'll find a long, quiet stretch of sand lined with thatch-roof cabanas. Newer condos have a sitting room and kitchen. The pool surrounded by a hardwood deck offers an alternative to a dip in the ocean, which isn't at its best here. Despite the attractive setting, the staff has a high turnover rate, making for unreliable service, and the rates aren't much of a bargain either. ✉ *6 km (4 mi) north of San Pedro* ☎ *226/2567, 888/653–9090 in U.S.* 📠 *307/587–8914* 🌐 *www.ambergriscaye.com/captmorgan* *14 cabanas, 12 condos* *Restaurant, fans, pool, beach, dive shop, dock, bicycles, volleyball, bar, laundry service, travel services; no TV in some rooms* 💳 *AE, DC, MC, V.*

$$$$ 🏨 **El Pescador.** Nearly every place on Ambergris Caye claims that it offers fishing trips, but this hotel has the best angling resources. Loosely described as a "fishing camp," the main lodge is actually a handsome colonial house with comfortable, if not luxurious, rooms with mahogany floors. Adjoining the lodge are deluxe two- and three-bedroom villas (with prices to match). You can enjoy a fine meal, served family style in the dining room, or a drink on the veranda. Most guests arrive as part of a fishing package; prices start at BZ$2,080 per person for three nights. ✉ *5 km (3 mi) north of San Pedro* ☎ *226/2398* 📠 *226/2977* 🌐 *www.elpescador.com* *13 rooms, 4 villas* *Dining room, fans, kitchens, 2 pools, beach, dock, boating, fishing, bar, shop, laundry service, travel services; no TV in some rooms* ▭ *MC, V* *FAP.*

$$$$ **Portofino.** Even if you're not a newlywed, try the honeymoon suite at this tranquil North Ambergris resort. Inside a thatch cabana, the 800-square-foot suite has the island's best sea views and a private whirlpool. The other cabanas have four-poster bamboo beds draped with linen mosquito nets (although mosquitoes are rarely a problem). Two "tree house" suites are perched on wooden stilts above the sand. ✉ *10 km (6 mi) north of San Pedro* ☎ *220/5096* 📠 *226/4272* 🌐 *www.portofinobelize.com* *8 rooms, 3 suites* *Restaurant, room service, fans, minibars, beach, snorkeling, boating, fishing, bar, laundry service, travel services; no room phones, no room TVs* ▭ *AE, MC, V* *CP.*

$$$–$$$$ **Playa Blanca.** Run by British expatriate Gary "Gaz" Cooper, a well-known dive operator in San Pedro, Playa Blanca feels like a private home. Stay in a beach cabana or in the pièce de résistance: a 2,200-square-foot suite with three bedrooms, two baths, and stunning views of the water. Packages include dives in the area. ✉ *8 km (5 mi) north of San Pedro* ☎ *226/4455* 🌐 *www.playablancabelize.com* *3 suites* *Fans, kitchens, refrigerators, pool, beach, dive shop, snorkeling, windsurfing, boating, fishing, bar* ▭ *MC, V.*

$$ **Salamander Hideaway.** Far north on the caye, this new resort appeals to those who seek peace and quiet. There are five simple thatch cabanas on the beach, and three two-level jungle cabanas in the back. If you like watersports, there's free access to kayaks, windsurfers, snorkel equipment, and small sailboats. This far north, the reef is close enough to shore that you can kayak out for snorkeling. Salamander is an "ecocentric" resort, with solar and wind power; the spa is housed in a Native American teepee. ✉ *18 km (11 mi) north of San Pedro* ☎ *602/1713* 🌐 *www.salamanderbelize.com* *8 cabanas* *Restaurant, fans, beach, spa, dive shop, snorkeling, windsurfing, boating, fishing, bar; no a/c, no room TVs* ▭ *MC, V.*

SOUTH OF SAN PEDRO

$–$$$ **Jade Garden.** Classic Cantonese dishes have a Caribbean twist at this restaurant. You'll find fish chow mein and conch kebabs on the menu, alongside American-style 12-ounce T-bone steaks and Belizean-style pork chops. The attractive restaurant fills the top two floors of a white colonial-style building just outside town. It's outfitted with handsome rattan furniture and pastel tablecloths, making this one of the caye's more comfortable restaurants. ✉ *Coconut Dr., ¼ mi south of airstrip* ☎ *226/2126* ▭ *AE, MC, V.*

$$ Fodor's Choice ★ **Casa Picasso.** Belizean artists created the Picasso-inspired art on the walls of this Spanish-influence restaurant, which specializes in tapas like *gamas a la plancha* (sauteed shrimp with red pepper). Lasagna and other pasta dishes are also served, along with freshly baked rustic Italian bread. The restaurant has the island's largest selection of desserts, including a tangy key lime pie. ✉ *Sting Ray St., off Coconut Dr., on lagoon side* ☎ *226/4507* ▭ *AE, MC, V.*

★ $$$$ **Villas at Banyan Bay.** Enjoy little luxuries like a whirlpool bath in your room? This complex about 3 km (2 mi) south of town will suit you splendidly. Buildings with red-tile roofs house stylishly furnished two-bedroom condos with verandas overlooking the sea. You won't feel cramped here—these are some of the island's largest and most luxe apartments. Cathedral ceilings in the main living area sport a stunning array of tropical hardwoods. The kid-friendly pool is one of the island's largest, and Mar de Tumbo tops the short list of the island's best beaches. Rico's Bar & Grill has a beautiful setting on the water. ✉ *Coconut Dr., 3 km (2 mi) south of San Pedro* ☎ *226/3739* 🖷 *226/2766* 🌐 *www.banyanbay.com* *42 apartments* *Restaurant, fans, in-room hot tubs, kitchens, cable TV, pool, beach, dive shop, dock, bar, laundry service, travel services* 💳 *AE, MC, V.*

★ $$–$$$$ **Banana Beach Resort.** Thanks to its friendly staff's accommodating attitude, not always evident in Belize, this resort has one of the island's highest guest occupancy rates. Owner Tim Jeffers doubled the hotel's size in 2002. The original section, built around an interior courtyard, has one-bedroom suites; the units on the second and third floor, just steps from the sea, are worth the extra money. The newer section has regular rooms at bargain prices, plus deluxe "flex suites" that expand from one to four bedrooms, depending on your needs. A new restaurant, El Divino (named after a beloved staffer who passed away), is the island's only steak house and martini bar. ✉ *Coconut Dr., 3¼ km (2 mi) south of San Pedro* ☎ *226/3890* 🖷 *226/3891* 🌐 *www.bananabeach.com* *24 rooms, 42 suites* *Restaurant, fans, some kitchens, cable TV, 2 pools, beach, dive shop, dock, boating, shops, laundry service, Internet, travel services, no smoking rooms* 💳 *AE, D, MC, V* *CP.*

$$$$ Fodor's Choice ★ **Cayo Espanto.** On a tiny private island west of Ambergris Caye, this luxury resort has a staff-to-guest ratio of two to one. Each villa comes complete with a splash pool, Egyptian cotton linens, and a personal butler. Several villas have walls that literally fold back to let in the Caribbean sun. As a guest, you meet with the chef to plan your day's meals, which are delivered to your own waterside table. For all this personal care you'll pay a small fortune. ✉ *5 km (3 mi) west of Ambergris Caye* *Box 90, San Pedro* ☎ *888/666–4282 in U.S.* ☎🖷 *221/3001* 🌐 *www.aprivateisland.com* *5 villas* *Dining room, room service, fans, cable TV, 4 pools, beach, dock, snorkeling, boating, fishing, laundry service, travel services* 💳 *AE, MC, V* *FAP.*

$$$–$$$$ **Ramon's Village Resort.** One of the first resorts on the cayes, Ramon's has grown into one of its largest, but still retains its thatch-and-sand atmosphere. Just a five-minute stroll from town, the resort attracts a younger crowd who take their margaritas by the pool. Ramon's has a well-regarded dive operation, sending out guests in seven dive boats. A small artificial reef near the 420-foot pier brings fish to snorkelers, and its 500-foot beach is among San Pedro's best. The hotel also manages a collection of cottages across the street called Steve and Becky's Cute Little Hotel. ✉ *Coconut Dr.* ☎ *226/2071, 800/624–4315 in U.S.* 🖷 *226/2214* 🌐 *www.ramons.com* *61 rooms, 8 cottages* *Restaurant, room service, fans, some kitchens, some refrigerators, cable TV, pool,*

beach, dive shop, dock, snorkeling, boating, fishing, bar, shop, laundry service, travel services; no TVs in some rooms ▭ *AE, MC, V.*

★ **$$$–$$$$** **Victoria House.** With its bougainvillea-filled gardens, this property 3 km (2 mi) south of San Pedro has the style and seclusion of a diplomatic residence. In the white colonial-style house with airy verandas and tile walkways are three ample suites with mahogany furnishings, steps from a gorgeous pool. Newly upgraded stone-and-thatch casitas are arranged around a palm shaded lawn. In 2003 Victoria House took over two adjacent beach houses, including a five-bedroom villa. Try dishes like shrimp salpicón or seafood bouillabaisse in the main restaurant or opt for the more casual Admiral Nelson's Bar. ✉ *Coconut Dr., 3 km (2 mi) south of San Pedro* ☎ *226/2067, 800/247–5159 in U.S.* 📠 *404/373–3885* 🌐 *www.victoria-house.com* *12 rooms, 10 casitas, 3 suites, 3 villas* *Restaurant, fans, kitchens, pool, beach, dive shop, dock, snorkeling, windsurfing, boating, fishing, bar, laundry service, travel services; no TV, no phones* ▭ *AE, D, MC, V.*

$$$–$$$$ **Xanadu Island Resort.** It's billed as the "world's first monolithic dome resort," a description that might appeal only to engineers. Happily, these domes look nicer than they sound and the result is a structure that can withstand winds up to 300 mph. There's a melange of one-, two- and three-bedroom units. All are attractively furnished in earth tones and have modern amenities. There are a nice little stretch of beach and a 350-foot pier. You also get free access to bikes, canoes, and kayaks. ✉ *Coconut Dr., 2 km (1 mi) south of San Pedro* ☎ *226/2814* 📠 *226/3409* 🌐 *www.xanaduresort-belize.com* *16 suites* *Fans, kitchens, cable TV, pool, beach, dock, snorkeling, bicycles, Internet, travel services, no-smoking rooms* ▭ *AE, MC, V.*

$ **Changes In Latitudes.** Out front, the sign depicting an igloo melting beneath a tropical sun is an in-joke about Canadian owner Lori Reed's move south to run this little B&B. The tranquil inn is near San Pedro's restaurants and bars, but isn't on the beach. Although they're all on the small side, the rooms are clean and have louvered windows to allow breezes in. The three garden-side rooms get the most light. A full breakfast is served in the common room, but you can prepare your own meals or store beer upstairs in the fridge. Ask Lori about recommended local restaurants and tours. ✉ *Coconut Dr., ¼ mi south of San Pedro* ☎📠 *226/2986* 🌐 *www.ambergriscaye.com/latitudes* *6 rooms* *Fans, laundry service, travel services; no room phones, no room TVs* ▭ *AE, MC, V* *BP.*

¢ **Pedro's Backpacker Inn.** Gregarious British expat Peter Lawrence opened the island's only hostel-style accommodations in 2003. A single bed and shared bath in this white frame house on stilts go for BZ$25, or you can get a bed, barbecue dinner, and a Belikin beer for BZ$40. ✉ *Princess Dr., south of San Pedro* ☎ *226/3825* 🌐 *www.backpackersbelize.com* *20 rooms* *Fans; no a/c, no room phones, no room TVs* ▭ *MC, V.*

CONDOTELS In addition to the Villas at Banyan Bay, Xanadu, Mayan Princess, and Banana Beach Resort, there are several small island condos with units for daily or weekly rental. They usually lack a restaurant, bar, or pool, but they're all beachside with large rooms and fully equipped kitchens.

Most have cable TV, fans, and air-conditioning. Because they're usually individually owned—the nonresident owners let local managers rent them out when they're not on vacation here—you won't find any cookie-cutter decor.

Belizean Reef Suites (✉ Coconut Dr. ☎ 226/2582 🌐 www.AmbergrisCaye.com/bzreef) is a six-unit oceanfront condo south of town. There's no pool, but you can soak up the sun on a small beach. **Belizean Shores** (☎ 226/3000 🌐 www.belizeanshores.com), about 7 km (4 mi) north of San Pedro, has 12 buildings with sea views, and a large, beautiful pool. **Corona del Mar** (☎ 226/2055), aka Woody's Wharf, is a laid-back group of affordable apartments and rooms south of town. **Belize Tradewinds Paradise Villas** (☎ 226/2822, 800/451–7776 in U.S. 🌐 www.tradewindsparadisevillas.com) owns and manages 12 attractive one- and two-bedroom condos at the Paradise Villas complex at the town's north edge. The 12-unit **The Palms** (☎ 226/3322 🌐 www.belizepalms.com) has an idyllic location at the town's southern edge. **White Sands Cove** (☎ 800/887–2054 in U.S. 🌐 www.whitesandscove.com) is a group of 16 condos about 5¾ km (3½ mi) north of San Pedro. **Sunset Beach Resort** (☎ 226/2373 🌐 www.ambergriscaye.com/sunsetbeach), about 4 km (2½ mi) south of town, has large three-bedroom units and a pool.

VACATION HOMES Ambergris Caye has dozens of homes that can be rented on a weekly basis. These range from simple two-bedroom cottages that go for BZ$1,000–BZ$2,000 a week to luxurious four- or five-bedroom villas, which might rent for BZ$5,000–BZ$10,000 or more weekly. In most cases credit cards are not accepted. **Caye Management** (☎ 226/3077 🌐 www.cayemanagement.com) is the island's oldest and largest rental management company.

Sports & the Outdoors

BOATING Belize will never rival the British Virgin Islands for sailing. The shallow water kicks up a lot of chop, and hidden coral heads and tidal currents are dangerous for even those familiar with the area. When you charter a boat you have to stay inside the barrier reef, but there's a lot of beautiful territory to explore. **Tortola Marine Management** (✉ Coconut Dr. ☎ 226/3026 📠 226/3072 🌐 www.sailtmm.com), which has a small fleet of catamarans (35 feet–47 feet) and one monohull, is the best boating outfit. Rates vary, depending on boat type and time of year, but range from BZ$3,700 to more than BZ$16,000 a week, not including provisions, cruising fee (BZ$30 per person), and incidentals. Skippers and cooks are each an additional BZ$200 per day. Split among three to eight people, the prices are competitive with hotel rates.

SCUBA DIVING Sensing a future in tourism, the people of Ambergris Caye were the first to cater to those hoping to witness Belize's undersea world. Ambergris Caye is superior in number of dive shops, experience of dive masters, and range of equipment and facilities. San Pedro even has a hyperbaric chamber and an on-site doctor to tend divers with the bends, financed by contributions from all the dive shops.

Most dive masters are former fishermen, who began diving on the side and ended up doing it full time. The best have an intimate knowledge of the reef and a superb eye for coral and marine life. They're ecologically aware, comprehending that the reef's destruction will be a tragic event in itself, as well as deprive them of a way to support their families. A group of dive masters fastened a network of buoys to the bedrock to prevent further destruction of the coral; boats and kayaks can tie up to the buoys instead of anchoring on the coral. In bad weather one anchor dragged across the bottom can destroy more coral than 1,000 divers.

Speedboats take divers to their destinations. Power generally comes from two hefty outboards mounted on the back, and with the throttle open it's an exhilarating ride. Sit in the middle if you don't want to get splashed. Many boats are constructed from solid mahogany. As they're the major investment of the dive companies, the boats are lovingly maintained.

Dives off Ambergris are usually single tank at depths of 50 feet–80 feet, allowing about 35 minutes of bottom time. Most companies offer two single-tank dives per day, one in the morning and one in the afternoon. Snorkeling generally costs BZ$40–BZ$60 per person for two or three hours or BZ$90–BZ$200 for a day trip, including lunch. Diving trips run BZ$70–BZ$80 for a single-tank dive, BZ$100–BZ$130 for a double-tank dive, and BZ$340–BZ$400 for day trips with dives to Turneffe Atoll or Lighthouse Reef.

Ambergris Divers (✉ Coconut Dr., San Pedro, Ambergris Caye ☎ 226/2634 📠 226/4263 🌐 www.ambergrisdivers.com) offers a range of local and atoll dive and snorkel trips. **Amigos del Mar** (✉ Off Barrier Reef Dr., near Mayan Princess Hotel ☎ 226/2706 🌐 amigosdive.com) is perhaps the island's most consistently recommended dive operation. It offers a range of local dives as well as trips to Turneffe Atoll and Lighthouse Reef in a fast 42-foot dive boat. The well-regarded and exclusive **Gaz Cooper's Dive Belize** (✉ 5 mi north of town at Playa Blanca Resort ☎ 226/3202 🌐 www.divebelize.com) boasts that it has the island's smallest dive operation.

Nightlife

With live music most nights, **Barefoot Iguana** (✉ Coconut Dr., ¾ km south of town) is the island's loudest bar. Known for its burgers, **BC's Beach Bar** (✉ South of SunBreeze Hotel) is a popular oceanfront bar that hosts all-you-can-eat barbecues on Sunday afternoon. **Big Daddy's** (✉ Barrier Reef Dr., north side of Central Park) is the scene of all the action in downtown San Pedro. Since it's right on the water, there's a beachside barbecue some nights. The music and real boozing don't get started until late, usually around 11. Across the street from Big Daddy's is **Jaguar's Temple** (✉ Barrier Reef Dr.), a popular San Pedro dance club.

Shopping

At **Belizean Arts** (✉ Fido's Courtyard off Barrier Reef Dr. ☎ 226/3019) you'll find works by local painters including Walter Castillo and Pen Cayetano. Also on display are handicrafts from the region, including hand-painted animal figures from Mexico, masks and fabrics from Guatemala, and brilliantly colored tropical fish made of coconut wood. About 3 km (2 mi) south of town, **Hummingbird Rattan** (✉ Coconut Dr. at Mar de Tumbo ☎ 226/2960) sells high-quality wood and rattan furniture made in Belize. The owner of **Sea Gal Boutique** (✉ Barrier Reef Dr., in Holiday Hotel ☎ 226/2431) has an artist's eye for beauty: everything here is stunning, even the T-shirts. **Island Supermarket** (✉ Coconut Dr., south of town ☎ 226/2972) has the largest selection of groceries, liquor, and beer.

Caye Caulker

❷ *8 km (5 mi) south of Ambergris Caye, 29 km (18 mi) northeast of Belize City.*

For many years Caye Caulker had a reputation as a haven for belligerent British "squaddies" (soldiers) and backpackers in search of cheap digs. Yet, its more charming aspects are breaking through as more upscale lodgings open up in town. Flowers outnumber cars ten to one (golf carts, bicycles, and bare feet are the preferred means of transportation).

As you might guess from all the NO SHIRT, NO SHOES, NO PROBLEM signs at the bars, the living is relatively easy here. This is the kind of place where most of the listings in the telephone directory give addresses like "near football field." However, Caye Corker, as it's often called in Belize, isn't immune to change. A public pier opened in 2003, many hotels are adding air-conditioning (though none has a pool yet), and the island now has three cybercafés and several upmarket restaurants; there are even a couple of condos.

A plethora of dive and snorkel operators offer reef tours (some of them are "cowboys"—unaffiliated and unreliable—so make sure you use a reputable company). Plan on spending about BZ$30–BZ$50 for a snorkeling trip around the island or to Hol Chan Marine Reserve. If you run out of money, don't worry. One of the island's newer amenities is a bank.

Where to Stay & Eat

$–$$$ ✕ **CocoPlum Gardens.** It's a bit of a hike to this little restaurant at the island's south end, but a shuttle will pick you up on Front Street near the basketball court. It's worth the effort—enjoy wholesome breads, fresh-made granola, and other all-natural foods, all in a lovely garden setting (the owners also operate a nursery). While you're here, browse the small gallery and gift shop with Belizean-made crafts. ✉ *South end of island, near airstrip* ☎ *226/0226* ▭ *MC, V* ⊙ *Closed Fri. and Sat. No lunch.*

$–$$$ ✕ **Habaneros.** On the front door is a hand-painted drawing of a habanero pepper plant, but you shouldn't feel threatened—not everything here is super spicy. When you taste the Snapper Santa Fe or the Brazilian pork, you'll know why this is considered the best restaurant between San Pedro and Belize City. ✉ *Front St.* ☎ *226/0486* ▭ *AE, MC, V.*

$–$$ ✕ **Rasta Pasta.** This is the third reincarnation of Rasta Pasta in Belize: the first, in San Pedro, lost its lease, and the second, in Placencia, was destroyed by Hurricane Iris. The third time's a charm, though, and people line up salivating for owner Maralyn Gill's conch fritters, chicken tostadas, giant English muffins, and scrumptious coconut macaroons. ✉ *Front St.* ☎ *206/0356* ▭ *MC, V* ⊙ *Closed Wed.*

"ROOTS" BELIZEANS

IF YOU SPEND MUCH TIME talking with Belizeans, sooner or later conversation will turn to " roots." It's not a vegetable, but a term referring to people born in Belize who share a certain set of values. Usually, but not always, it connotes ordinary folk, not wealthy Belizeans. These are Belizeans who ride the bus instead of driving a new Ford Explorer.

"Being roots Belizean is a way of life, a mindset, and a unique set of values," says Wendy Auxillou, a second-generation Belizean who lives on Caye Caulker.

Roots Belizeans enjoy the simple pleasures of life: talking with friends they run into on the streets of Belize City; skipping work or school to swim in the sea, river, or lagoon; sitting on a veranda on a hot afternoon; fishing in an old wooden skiff; raising chickens in the back yard for Sunday dinner. More recently, it's going to a local restaurant or bar for karaoke, as Belizeans have developed a genuine affection for the pasttime.

Roots is about community involvement. Children are often looked after by aunts and grannies, as well as neighbors. Misbehaving children might find themselves answereing to a slew of adults in addition to their parents.

It's going to the market and eating boiled corn, dukunu (boiled cornbread), garnaches (crispy tortillas topped with beans and rice), and Belizean-style hot dogs, which are wrapped in bacon and grilled with onions. It's buying bananas 20 for a dollar. It's enjoying the smell and taste of all the local fruits, like tambran, grocea, a dozen different kinds of mangoes, sapodilla, mamie, hicama, watermelon, pineapple, guava, and papaya. It's about going to restaurants with local flavor, like Caladium in Belmopan, Nerie's in Belize City, Clarissa Falls near the Cayo, and Victor's near Orange Walk Town.

"It's about eating johnny cakes or plucking chickens with your neighbor, just because," says one Belizean.

Some claim that the original and perhaps only roots Belizeans are Creoles, descendents of the rough-and-ready Baymen and freed African slaves. Others argue that anybody can be a roots Belizean, that there are roots Mestizos, roots Maya, even roots Mennonites.

— Lan Sluder

1

$–$$ ✕ **The Sandbox.** Whether outside under the palms or indoors under the lazily turning ceiling fans, you'll always have your feet in the sand here. The names of regulars are carved on the backs of the chairs. Open from 7 AM to 10 PM, the Sandbox serves lobster omelet for breakfast, ceviche or seafood salad for lunch, and red snapper in mango sauce for dinner. The chowders are also very good. Prices are reasonable, and portions are large. At night the bar gets very lively. ⊠ *Front St. near public pier* ☎ *226/0200* ▭ *AE, MC, V.*

¢–$ ✕ **Cindy's.** Get your morning latte fix here. Add a mango *licquado* (a smoothie with fruit and yogurt) and a fresh-baked muffin, and you've got the freshest breakfast on the island. Almost everything on the menu is organic, vegan, or both. If you're out of reading material, Cindy's also has a lending library. The café opens from around 7 AM to 1:30 PM. ⊠ *Front St.* ☎ *226/0093* ▭ *No credit cards* ⊗ *No dinner.*

★ $$ **Iguana Reef Inn.** Far and away Caye Caulker's most upmarket lodging, Iguana Reef has just about everything but a concierge. The suites are colorfully furnished with handmade furniture and local artwork and have air-conditioning, which is unusual for the island. Upstairs suites have vaulted ceilings with skylights. The latest addition is a thatch-roof bar. Because the inn is on the island's lee side, you have the benefit of sunset views from your veranda, but you're not on the beach. Co-owner James Dombrowski has a lot of information about the island. ⊠ *Near end of Middle St., next to soccer field* ☎ *226/0213* 🖷 *226/0087* ⊕ *www.iguanareefinn.com* *12 suites* *Fans, refrigerators, snorkeling, fishing, bar, travel services; no room phones, no room TVs, no kids under 10* ▭ *AE, MC, V.*

¢–$$ **De Real Macaw.** De Real Macaw represents the "new Caulker" trend in hotels here: better service, bigger rooms, more amenities like air-conditioning and cable TV, and all at a good value. You have a choice of six rooms or two larger apartment suites. ⊠ *Front St. at the north end* ☎ *226/0459* 🖷 *226/0497* ⊕ *www.derealmacaw.com* *6 rooms, 2 suites* *Fans, refrigerators, cable TV, beach, laundry service; no a/c in some rooms, no phones in some rooms* ▭ *D, MC, V.*

$ **Chocolate's.** Chocolate is a seventysomething Belizean who rents out one of Caye Caulker's best rooms—a romantic retreat with a four-poster bed, vaulted mahogany ceiling with fan, and a screened-in veranda that looks out to the sea. The tile bath has a gigantic shower (terry cloth robes are nearby). Chocolate helped pioneer manatee-watching trips to Goff Caye and is notable for his dedication to conservation. ⊠ *At north end of island, near the Split* ☎ *226/0151* *1 room* *Fans, refrigerator, snorkeling, shop; no a/c, no room phone, no room TV* ▭ *MC, V.*

$ **Lazy Iguana B&B.** This B&B may be the tallest structure on any of the cayes. The views of the sunsets from the fourth-level rooftop terrace are terrific, though the hotel's location on the island's back side means you need to swat an occasional mosquito while you watch. The rooms are furnished with attractive wicker and tropical hardwood furniture. Feel free to make yourself at home in the common room, which has TV and Internet access—owner Mo Miller says no shoes are required. ⊠ *South of main public pier on back side near airstrip* ☎ *226/0350* 🖷 *226/0320* ⊕ *www.lazyiguana.net* *4 rooms* *Fans, no-smoking rooms; no room phones, no room TVs, no kids under 10* ▭ *MC, V* *CP.*

★ ¢–$ **Treetops.** Owners Terry and Doris Creasey (he's British, she's German) bring international flair to this seaside guesthouse, which is so well run and such a good value that it's almost always full. One room has an East African theme, with authentic masks and spears, and another has art from Malaysia and Indonesia. Two third-floor suites, Sunset and Sunrise, each have a king-size bed and private balcony with a view of the water. *Caye Caulker 226/0240 226/0115 www.treetopsbelize.com 4 rooms, 2 with bath, 2 suites Fans, refrigerators, cable TV, beach, snorkeling, laundry service, travel services; no a/c in some rooms, no phones in some rooms, no kids under 12, no smoking MC, V.*

¢ **Trends Beachfront Hotel.** One of the first things you see when you arrive at the island's pier is this little hotel, painted tropical pink and green. Thanks to its location and bright rooms, it's usually booked full. TVs are available on request. At this writing, the equally popular Seaside Cabanas next door, which was destroyed in a fire in 2003, was set to reopen in mid-2004. *Near Front St. at public dock 226/0094 226/0097 www.trendsbze.com 6 rooms, 1 cabana Fans, refrigerator; no a/c, no room phones, no TVs in some rooms MC, V.*

Sports & the Outdoors

If you're looking for someone to take you out to the reef, **Frenchie's Diving Services** (Front St. north of the public pier 226/0234) is a respected local operator. For trips to the Blue Hole and local dives, **Paradise Down** (Front St. north of the public pier 226/0437) has three well-equipped dive boats.

Shopping

Annie's Boutique (North end of island, near the Split at Chocolate's 226/0151) has some of Belize's best clothing for women and children. Here you'll find dresses and sarongs made with fabrics from Bali, unique silver jewelry, and Guatemalan bags. **Galleria Hicaco** (Front St. 226/0178) has Belizean arts and crafts, including jewelry, dolls, carvings, and pottery.

Caye Chapel

3 *2 km (½ mi) south of Caye Caulker, 10 km (6 mi) south of Ambergris Caye.*

Not since the days of British colonialism has Belize had a real 18-hole golf course. But for traveling golfers, a course opened in 1999 on Caye Chapel, a privately owned 265-acre island. It's a beautiful par-72 course, playing to more than 7,000 yards, flat but long, with four par-5 holes. Challenges include brisk prevailing winds and an occasional crocodile. This is Belize's best course (a smaller 9-hole public course is near Belmopan at Roaring River Golf Club). If you're not staying at the Caye Chapel Island Resort, which grants guests full access, you can still play for BZ$400 per person, including lunch, club, and cart rental.

Where to Stay & Eat

$$$$ Fodor'sChoice ★ **Caye Chapel Island Resort.** Designed as a corporate retreat, this resort accommodates anyone who's got the cash. The expansive villas, which stand at imperial attention along the seafront, are similar to what you might see in exclusive gated communities in Boca Raton, Florida. Inside

you'll find every luxury—whirlpool baths, expansive wet bars, and kitchens with the latest German appliances. A dozen "budget" casitas, though anything but, have a price tag that's significantly less than the villas. Rates include all meals and unlimited golf. The golf course's clubhouse has a restaurant with indoor and open-air dining and stunning views of the sea. ✉ *Caye Chapel* ☎ *226/8250* 🖷 *226–8201* 🌐 *www.belizegolf.cc* *8 villas, 12 casitas* *Restaurant, fans, some in-room hot tubs, kitchens, cable TV, tennis courts, 18-hole golf course, pool, gym, beach, dive shop, dock, boating, marina, fishing, basketball, bar, laundry service, airstrip, Internet, travel services; no smoking* 💳 *AE, D, MC, V* 🍽 *FAP.*

St. George's Caye

❹ *15 km (9 mi) northeast of Belize City.*

Just a stone's throw from Belize City, this small caye is steeped in history. The state of Belize had its origins here, as St. George's Caye held the original British settlement's first capital. In 1798 the island was the site of a decisive battle with the Spanish. Islanders had only one sloop, while the Spanish had 31 ships. Their knowledge of the sea, however, helped them to defeat the invaders in two hours.

Getting to St. George's Caye couldn't be easier, as the boat trip from Belize City takes little more than 20 minutes. Some Belize City residents weekend in their private cottages here. Although St. George's Caye has great places to dive, many serious scuba enthusiasts choose to head out to the more pristine atolls.

Where to Stay & Eat

$$$$ **St. George's Lodge.** In colonial days this long-established resort was a British favorite because of its proximity to Belize City. Today divers favor St. George's Caye, undoubtedly because of the diving program led by Fred Good. You have a choice of basic rooms in the main building or thatch cottages by the water. Electricity comes from the lodge's own windmills, and the shower water is heated by the sun. The restaurant serves homemade bread and soups and grilled snapper or grouper, and coffee is delivered to your door in the morning. Weekly dive packages start at around BZ$3,425 per person, including meals. ✉ *1604 Maple St., Nokomis, FL 34275* ☎ *220/4444, 800/678–6871 in U.S.* 🖷 *941/488–3953* 🌐 *www.gooddiving.com* *10 rooms, 6 cabanas* *Restaurant, fans, beach, dive shop, snorkeling, travel services; no a/c, no room phones, no room TVs* 💳 *AE, MC, V* 🍽 *FAP.*

Turneffe Atoll

❺ *40 km (25 mi) east of Belize City.*

This chain of tiny islands and mangrove swamps makes up an atoll the size of Barbados. The largest of the three atolls, Turneffe, is the closest to Belize City. It's one of the best spots for diving, thanks to several steep drop-offs. Only an hour from Lighthouse Reef and 45 minutes from the northern edge of Glover's Reef, Turneffe is a good base for exploring all of the atolls.

The best-known attraction, and probably Belize's most exciting wall dive, is the **Elbow,** at Turneffe's southernmost tip. You may encounter eagle rays swimming nearby. As many as 50 might flutter together, forming a rippling herd. This is generally considered an advanced dive because of the strong currents, which sweep you toward the deep water beyond the reef.

Though it's most famous for its spectacular wall dives, the atoll has dives for every level. The leeward side, where the reef is wide and gently sloping, is good for shallower dives and snorkeling; you'll see large concentrations of tube sponges, soft corals such as forked sea feathers and sea fans, and plenty of fish. Also on the atoll's western side is the wreck of the *Sayonara.* No doubloons to scoop up here—it was a small passenger and cargo boat that sank in 1985—but it's good for wreck dive practice.

Where to Stay & Eat

$$$$ **Turneffe Flats.** The sound of the surf is the only thing you'll hear at these smart blue-and-white beachfront cabins. The rooms, fitted with elegant hardwoods, are a far cry from the bare-bones fishing camp that occupied this site in the early '80s. You can dive here—a Pro 48 dive boat is on standby and the reef is only 200 yards from shore—but the ubiquitous fishing-pole racks suggest that snook, bonefish, and permit are still the dominant lure. You pay a pretty penny to indulge your passion, however—a weekly fishing package for two is around BZ$12,700. ✉ *Northern Bogue* ✉ *Box 36, Deadwood, SD 57732* ☎ *800/815–1304 or 605/578–1304* 🖷 *605/578–7540* 🌐 *www.tflats.com* *10 rooms* *Dining room, dive shop, snorkeling, fishing; no room phones, no room TVs, no kids under 12* 💳 *D, MC, V* 🍽 *FAP.*

★ **$$$$** **Turneffe Island Lodge.** White dive tanks serving as fence posts and a rusty anchor from an 18th-century British warship set the tone at this south end resort. This was Turneffe Atoll's first dive lodge, and it bagged the best spot a few hundred yards from the legendary Elbow. If you came to Belize for the diving, this is an ideal base. The rooms, in palm-shaded cottages with sea views, have been refurbished without spoiling the cozy feeling created by the varnished hardwood fittings. Seven beachfront cabanas are solid mahogany inside. The two-story colonial-style house holds the bar and the dining room. ✉ *Coco Tree Caye* ☎ *713/313–4670 or 800/874–0118* 🖷 *713/313–4671* 🌐 *www.turneffelodge.com* *12 rooms, 7 cabanas* *Restaurant, fans, dive shop, snorkeling, fishing, bar, travel services; no room phones, no room TVs* 💳 *AE, MC, V* ⊗ *Closed Sept. and Oct.* 🍽 *FAP.*

Lighthouse Reef Atoll

6 *80 km (50 mi) east of Belize City.*

If Robinson Crusoe had been a man of means, he would have repaired here for a break from his desert island. It's the most distant of Belize's atolls, but it's also the most accessible, thanks to an airstrip at Lighthouse Reef Resort.

Lighthouse Reef is about 29 km (18 mi) long and less than 2 km (1 mi) wide and is surrounded by a seemingly endless stretch of coral. Here you'll find two of the country's best dives. From the air, the **Blue Hole,** a breathtaking vertical chute that drops several hundred feet through the reef, looks like a dark blue eye in the center of the shallow lagoon. The Blue Hole was first dived by Jacques Cousteau in 1970 and has since become a diver's pilgrimage site. Just over 1,000 feet wide at the surface and dropping almost vertically to a depth of 412 feet, the Blue Hole is like swimming down a mine shaft. This excitement is reflected in the thousands of stickers reading, "I Dived the Blue Hole."

The best diving on Lighthouse Reef is at **Half Moon Caye.** A classic wall dive, Half Moon Caye begins at 35 feet and drops almost vertically to blue infinity. Floating out over the edge is a bit like free-fall parachuting. Magnificent spurs of coral jut out to the seaward side, looking like small tunnels; they're fascinating to explore and invariably full of fish. An exceptionally varied marine life hovers around this caye. On the gently sloping sand flats behind the coral spurs, a vast colony of garden eels stirs, their heads protruding from the sand like periscopes. Spotted eagle rays, sea turtles, and other underwater wonders frequent the drop-off.

Although difficult to reach and lacking accommodations, **Half Moon Caye National Monument,** Belize's easternmost island, offers one of Belize's greatest wildlife encounters. Part of the Lighthouse Reef system, Half Moon Caye owes its protected status to the presence of the red-footed booby. The bird is here in such numbers that it's hard to believe it has only one other nesting ground in the entire Caribbean (on Tobago Island, off the coast of Venezuela). Some 4,000 of these birds hang their hats on Half Moon Caye, along with iguanas, lizards, and loggerhead turtles. The entire 40-acre island is a nature reserve, so you can either explore the beaches or head into the bush on the narrow nature trail. Above the trees at the island's center is a small viewing platform—at the top you're suddenly in a sea of birds that will doubtless remind you of a certain Alfred Hitchcock movie. Several dive operators and resorts arrange day trips and overnight camping trips to Half Moon Caye.

Where to Stay & Eat

$$$$ **Lighthouse Reef Resort.** A 20-minute flight from Belize's international airport brings you to the beach at Lighthouse Reef Resort. You have a choice of simple cabanas, suites with pine-plank floors, and handsome colonial-style villas with Queen Anne–style furnishings. The setting—palm trees line the water—is breathtaking, and there are superior diving opportunities. Seven-night dive packages, which include 20 meals, 17 dives, and air transfer from Belize City, cost BZ$3,290–BZ$3,925 per person. ✉ *Northern Caye* ☎ *800/423-3114 in U.S.* 🖷 *941/439-2118 in U.S.* 🌐 *www.scuba-dive-belize.com* *11 rooms* *Restaurant, fans, some refrigerators, beach, dive shop, dock, fishing, travel services; no room phones, no room TVs* 💳 *MC, V* *FAP.*

Tobacco Caye

❼ *18 km (11 mi) southeast of Dangriga.*

If you don't want to pay a lot for your place in the sun, Tobacco Caye may be for you. It's a tiny island—barely four acres—but it's right on the reef, so you can wade in and snorkel all you want. All the accommodations here are budget places, basically wood cabins, some not much larger than sheds. A half-dozen hotels vie for space, making the islet seem even smaller than it is. Periodically they get blown away by storms but are rebuilt, usually a little better than they were before. Prices remain fairly low, around BZ$60–BZ$125 a day per person, including meals. A word of caution: hotels can be very casual about reservations. After making reservations months in advance, you may arrive to find that your reservation has been lost and the hotel is fully occupied. Fortunately, it's usually easy to find a room in another hotel. Lana's on the Reef and Gaviota's are the cheapest hotels, with good food but tiny rooms. The island has no shops, bars, or restaurants, except those at the hotels, but there is one dive shop. Boats leave from the Riverside Restaurant in Dangriga for the 30-minute, BZ$30 trip to Tobacco Caye.

Where to Stay & Eat

$$ **Tobacco Caye Lodge.** This cluster of pastel blue cabins is a mere few feet from the turquoise sea. There's a bit more room here for stretching out than at the island's other lodges, as the property extends from the sea to the lagoon. A thatch-roof bar is set away from the cabins, and three simple but filling meals are included in the rate. ⊠ *Tobacco Caye* ☎ *520/5033* 🌐 *www.tclodgebelize.com* *6 cabins* *Fans, beach, snorkeling, fishing, bar; no a/c, no room phones, no room TVs* *MC, V* *FAP.*

$ **Ocean's Edge Lodge.** Nestled beneath coconut palms are these seven rustic, white cabins. The young staff is amiable, and the dining room-cum-lounge has a bar, pool table, board games, small library, and karaoke system. ⊠ *Tobacco Caye* ☎ *614/9633 or 800/967–8184* 🌐 *www2.symet.net/beltex* *7 cabins* *Fans, beach, snorkeling, fishing, bar; no a/c, no room phones, no room TVs* *MC, V* *FAP.*

South Water Caye

8 *23 km (14 mi) southeast of Dangriga.*

The first southern island developed for tourism, tiny South Water Caye has good off-the-beaten-reef diving. The reef is only a short swim from shore. The nearby **Smithsonian Institution's Marine Research Laboratory** (⊠ Carrie Bow Caye) welcomes visitors by appointment; contact the Blue Marlin Lodge for more information.

Where to Stay & Eat

$$$$ **Blue Marlin Lodge.** An excellent base for fishing, snorkeling, and diving trips, this appealing resort is only 50 yards from the reef. Accommodations, which spread out over half the caye, range from thatch-roof cabanas to a trio of aquamarine-color concrete dome buildings. Rooms are so close to the sea that wave sounds may lull you to sleep. The restaurant and bar are great places to swap stories with other travelers. The minimum stay is four days. ⊠ *South Water Caye* ☎ *522/2243, 800/798–1558 in U.S.* *522/2296* 🌐 *www.bluemarlinlodge.com* *16 rooms* *Restaurant, beach, dive shop, billiards, snorkeling, fishing, bar, babysitting, travel services; no a/c in some rooms, no room phones, no room TVs* *MC, V* *FAP.*

$$$–$$$$ **Pelican's Pouch.** Once a convent belonging to the Sisters of Mercy, the colonial-era main house at this peaceful island retreat has five large rooms on the second floor. The dining room, which serves fresh seafood and Belizean-style dishes, is on the ground floor. There are also three cottages, including a honeymoon cottage, Egret's Escape. You're steps from one of Belize's best beaches, where you can swim, snorkel, and fish to your heart's content. ✉ *South Water Caye* ☎ *522/2044* 🖷 *522/2570* 🌐 *www.pelicanbeachbelize.com* *5 rooms, 3 cottages, 1 student dorm* *Restaurant, beach, dive shop, snorkeling, boating, fishing, travel services; no a/c, no room phones, no room TVs* 💳 *AE, MC, V* 🍽 *FAP.*

Glover's Reef Atoll

9 *113 km (70 mi) southeast of Belize City.*

Fodor's Choice ★

Named after the pirate John Glover, this coral necklace strung around a 208-square-km (80-square-mi) lagoon is the southernmost of Belize's three atolls. Visitors to Glover's Reef are charged BZ$5 a day.

Although most of the best dive sites are along the atoll's southeastern side, one exception is **Emerald Forest Reef,** named for its masses of huge green elkhorn coral. Because the reef's most exciting part is only 25 feet down, it's excellent for novice divers. **Long Caye Wall** is an exciting wall with a dramatic drop-off hundreds of feet down. It's a good place to spot turtles, rays, and barracuda.

Southwest Caye Wall is an underwater cliff that falls quickly to 130 feet. It's briefly interrupted by a narrow shelf, then continues its near-vertical descent to 350 feet. This dive gives you the exhilaration of flying in blue space, so it's easy to lose track of how deep you are going. Both ascent and descent require careful monitoring.

Kayaking is another popular sport here; you can paddle out to the atoll's many patch reefs for snorkeling. Most hotels rent kayaks.

Where to Stay & Eat

$$$$ **Isla Marisol.** At Isla Marisol you can sip a cold Belikin in a bar perched at the end of a pier, a hundred feet out in the Caribbean. After a breakfast of mango and johnnycake, you can dive "The Pinnacles," where coral heads rise 40 feet from the ocean floor. After a lobster dinner, wander back to your cabin, a breezy retreat built of tropical hardwoods. Beachcomber packages including meals and transport to the island start at BZ$1,250 per person for three days. ✉ *Southwest Caye* ☎ *520/2056* 🌐 *www.islamarisol.com* *10 cabins* *Fans, beach, dive shop, snorkeling, fishing, bar; no a/c, no room phones, no room TVs* 💳 *AE, MC, V* 🍽 *FAP.*

$ **Glover's Atoll Resort.** This little group of cabins is a lesson in laid-back living. Forget about electricity and running water and surrender to a life of fishing, diving, snorkeling, and swimming. You bring your tackle for boat or shore fishing and your own food supplies, though simple meals and a few basics such as bottled water are sold at the 9-acre island. This is as close as they come to a *Gilligan's Island*–style vacation spot.

✉ Northeast Caye ⓓ Box 563, Belize City ☎ 520/5016 ⊕ www.glovers.com.bz 11 cabins with shared bath, 1 dorm, campground ♨ Dining room, beach, dive shop, snorkeling, fishing; no a/c, no room phones, no room TVs ▭ MC, V.

The Cayes & Atolls A to Z

AIR TRAVEL TO & FROM THE CAYES & ATOLLS

Maya Island Airways and Tropic Air operate flights to Ambergris Caye and Caye Caulker from both the municipal and international airports in Belize City. Each has hourly service every day to Ambergris Caye between about 7:30 AM and 5:30 PM. In high season, additional flights are added to accommodate demand. Round-trip fares for the 20-minute flight are about BZ$104 (municipal) and BZ$186 (international).

The airstrip on Ambergris Caye is at San Pedro's southern edge. You'll always find taxis waiting at the airstrip, and most hotels run shuttles. If you're proceeding on foot, it's about five minutes to the hotels in town. The airstrip on Caye Caulker is at the island's south end. Hotels may send a golf cart to pick you up. Otherwise, you'll find that taxis are available.

There are no scheduled flights to the other cayes, although Lighthouse Reef and Caye Chapel both have airstrips where charter flights can land.

Maya Island Airways ⓓ Box 458, Municipal Airport, Belize City ☎ 223/1140, 800/225-6732 in U.S. ⊕ www.mayaislandair.com. **Tropic Air** ⓓ Box 20, San Pedro ☎ 226/2012, 800/422-3435 in U.S. ⊕ www.tropicair.com.

BOAT & FERRY TRAVEL

A variety of boats connect Belize City with Ambergris Caye. The cost is BZ$28 one-way for the 75-minute trip. The most dependable, operated by the Caye Caulker Water Taxi Association, leave from the Belize Marine Terminal on North Front Street. The speedy open boats depart Belize City at 8, 9, 10:30 AM, noon, 1:30, 3 and 4:30 PM and return from San Pedro at 7, 8, 9:30 AM, and 1, 2:30, 3:30, 5:30 PM. Caye Caulker Water Taxi Association boats take 45 minutes to reach Caye Caulker, and cost BZ$18 each way. Departures are every 90 minutes between 8 AM and 5:30 PM, with return trips departing the Public Pier in Caye Caulker between 6:30 AM and 4 PM (5 PM on Friday, Saturday, and Sunday). Boats can drop you at Caye Chapel as well.

To reach the more remote cayes, you're left to your own devices. You can charter boats in either San Pedro or Belize City, but they're not cheap. The resorts on the atolls run their own flights or boats, but these aren't available to the general public. Ask your hotel if it provides transportation. For the southern cayes, inquire about boats departing from Dangriga. Dangriga's Pelican Beach Hotel sends a boat to its resort on South Water Caye. Several boats make the run from Dangriga to Tobacco Caye for BZ$30 per person one-way. Check at the Riverside Restaurant in Dangriga or ask at your hotel on Tobacco Caye—Captain Buck is the most dependable operator.

Caye Caulker Water Taxi Association ✉ Marine Terminal, N. Front St. at Swing Bridge, Belize City ☎ 223/1969.

EMERGENCIES

For medical care on Ambergris Caye try the Lions Club Clinic or Dr. Giovanni Solarzano or Dr. Lerida Rodriguez. On Caye Caulker, the Caye Caulker Health Center, usually staffed by a volunteer doctor, is open weekdays 8–11:30 and 1–4:30. For dental care or serious ailments you need to go to Belize City.

Doctors **Lerida Rodriguez** ✉ Galleria Bldg., San Pedro ☎ 226/3197. **Giovanni Solarzano** ✉ San Carlos Medical Clinic, San Pedro ☎ 226/2918.

Clinics **Lions Clinic** ✉ Near airstrip, San Pedro ☎ 226/2073. **Caye Caulker Health Center** ✉ Front St. near Lena's Hotel, Caye Caulker ☎ 226/0166.

HEALTH

Visiting Ambergris Caye is like a vacation in Florida—you'll face few health concerns worse than sunburn. San Pedro's water, from a treated municipal water supply, is safe to drink. On Caye Caulker, the water, usually from brackish shallow wells, often smells of sulfur. To be safe, drink only bottled water. On other remote cayes the water usually comes from cisterns. Stick to the bottled stuff. At times, the sandflies on Caye Caulker and some remote cayes can be irksome—apply baby oil or another oily lotion liberally to your feet and ankles to keep them at bay.

MAIL & SHIPPING

On Ambergris Caye the post office in San Pedro is open weekdays 8–noon and 1–5. On Caye Caulker the post office is on Back Street on the south side of town. It's open 9–noon and 2–5 weekdays and 9–noon Saturday.

Post Offices **Caye Caulker** ✉ Back St. ☎ 226/0325. **San Pedro** ✉ Barrier Reef Dr. ☎ 226/2250.

MONEY MATTERS

Atlantic Bank, on Barrier Reef Drive in San Pedro, is open Monday, Tuesday, Thursday, and Friday 8–noon and 1–3, Wednesday 8–1, and Saturday 8:30–noon. Belize Bank, on Barrier Reef Drive in San Pedro, is open Monday–Thursday 8–1 and Friday 8–1 and 3–6. Alliance Bank in San Pedro is open 8–1 Monday–Thursday, and 8–4:30 Friday. There is just one bank on Caye Caulker, Atlantic Bank on Back Street, south of Chan's Market. It's open weekdays 9–1. Although all these banks have ATMs, only the one at Belize Bank in San Pedro accepts cards issued outside Belize, if they are on the CIRRUS or PLUS networks. Cash advances on your Visa or MasterCard are available at these banks.

Atlantic Bank ✉ Barrier Reef Dr., San Pedro ☎ 226/2195 ✉ Back St., Caye Caulker ☎ 226/0207. **Alliance Bank** ✉ Barrier Reef Dr., San Pedro. **Belize Bank** ✉ 49 Barrier Reef Dr., San Pedro ☎ 226/2482.

TOURS

All tour guides in San Pedro and on Caye Caulker should be members of their respective associations—if in doubt, ask to see identification. Among San Pedro's top tour operators are Tanisha Tours, which offers excellent trips to Altun Ha and Lamanai, and SEAduced by Belize, which is unrivaled for its nature and kayak tours. On Caye Caulker,

Chocolate is the best-known guide and tour operator and he and the people he has trained are known for their full-day manatee trips.
Chocolate Tours ✉ Front St., Caye Caulker ☎ 226/0151. **SEAduced by Belize** ✉ Tarpon St., San Pedro ☎ 226/2254. **Tanisha Tours** ✉ San Pedro ☎ 226/2314.

VISITOR INFORMATION

Ambergris Caye, Caye Caulker, and the other cayes are in some ways stepchildren of Belize's official tourist industry. Though these islands draw more visitors than any other area, the Belize Tourist Board and Belize Industry Tourist Association seem to give short shrift to the cayes. There may or may not be an official tourist information office open in San Pedro when you're there, and there isn't one on Caye Caulker. In any case, by far the best source of information on the island is online. Operated by Marty Casado, www.AmbergrisCaye.com has more than 6,000 pages of facts and figures on San Pedro, along with a good bit of information on Caye Caulker and other parts of the country.

NORTHERN & CENTRAL BELIZE

Thanks to Belize's small size, most of the country is accessible from Belize City. The north sees fewer travelers than the Cayo, but it's got some of Belize's most fascinating Mayan sites, as well as several first-class jungle lodges and resorts. As this is sugarcane country, the landscape is mostly flat. Near Orangewalk Town are large Mennonite communities, filled with hardworking farmers. To the northwest near the Guatemala border are big tracts of land, much of it still wild and unsettled, with some of the world's few remaining old-growth mahogany trees. Corozal Town, next door to Mexico, is a place to slow down, relax and enjoy the laid-back atmosphere of a charming small town on the beautiful Bay of Chetumal. Sarteneja village, in the far northeastern part of Corozal District, is a still undiscovered fishing village set at the edge of the sea, near the Shipstern wildlife reserve. Northern Belize gets less rain than anywhere else in Belize, a fact that's reflected in the sunny disposition of the local population, mostly Mayas and Mestizos.

Numbers in the margin correspond to points of interest on the Northern and Central Belize map.

Río Bravo Conservation Area

❶ *3½ hrs west of Belize City.*

Created with the help of distinguished British naturalist Gerald Durrell, the Río Bravo Conservation Area spans 250,000 acres near the spot where Belize, Guatemala, and Mexico meet. The four-hour drive from Belize City takes you through wild lands where you may encounter a troupe of spider monkeys, wildcats, flocks of ocellated turkeys, a dense shower of butterflies—anything but another vehicle.

Within the reserve's borders are more than 60 Mayan sites; many have yet to be explored. The most important is **La Milpa,** Belize's largest site beside Caracol and Lamanai. At its height between 400 and 830, La Milpa was home to almost 50,000 people. The suburbs of this city spread out

some 5 km (3 mi) from the city center, and the entire city encompassed some 78 square km in area. So far, archaeologists have discovered 20 large courtyards and 19 stelae.

Where to Stay & Eat

$$$$ Fodor'sChoice ★ **Chan Chich Lodge.** Perhaps one day the spirit of Smoking Shell or another fierce Mayan ruler will take revenge on Barry Bowen for erecting cabanas amidst a Mayan archaeological site. Until then, this is one of Central America's best jungle lodges. Ex-president Jimmy Carter is among the lodge's many illustrious guests. Guides lead wildlife excursions into the several hundred thousand acres of surrounding bush. Tour options include bird-watching treks (some 350 species have been identified here) and horseback rides to Mayan ruins that remain undisturbed. You're more likely to see an elusive jaguar here than anywhere else outside the Belize Zoo. Each of the thatch-roof cabanas has a wraparound veranda. A gorgeous pool is screened to keep out insects. *Box 37, Belize City 223/4419, 800/451–8017 in U.S. 223–4419 www.chanchich.com 12 cabanas Restaurant, fans, pool, lake, horseback riding, bar, library, shop, laundry service, travel services; no a/c, no room phones, no room TVs AE, MC, V FAP.*

Altun Ha

2 *45 km (28 mi) north of Belize City.*

If you've never experienced an ancient Mayan city, make a trip to Altun Ha. It's not Belize's most dramatic site—Caracol takes that award—but it's the most accessible and thoroughly excavated. People resided here for nearly two millennia; the first inhabitants settled before 900 BC, and their descendants finally abandoned the site around AD 900. At its height the city was home to 10,000 people.

A team from the Royal Ontario Museum first excavated the site in the mid-1960s and found 250 structures spread over more than 1,000 square yards. At Plaza B, in the Temple of the Masonry Altars, archaeologists unearthed the grandest and most valuable piece of Mayan art ever discovered—the head of the sun god Kinich Ahau. Weighing nearly 10 pounds, it was carved from a solid block of green jade. The head is kept in a solid steel vault in the Bank of Belize's central branch. *No phone* *BZ$10* *Daily 9–5.*

Lamanai

3 *About 39 km (24 mi) south of Orange Walk Town.*

Fodor'sChoice ★

Lamanai ("submerged insect" in Maya, often mistranslated as "submerged crocodile") is Belize's longest-occupied Mayan site, inhabited until well after Christopher Columbus discovered the New World in 1492. In fact, archaeologists have found signs of continuous occupation from 1500 BC until AD 1700.

Lamanai's residents carried on a lifestyle that was passed down for millennia, until the Spanish missionaries arrived. You can still see the ruins of the missionaries' church in the nearby village of Indian Church. The same village also has an abandoned 19th-century sugar mill. With its immense drive wheel and steam engine—on which you can still read the name of the manufacturer, Leeds Foundry of New Orleans—swathed in strangler vines and creepers, it's a haunting sight.

In all, 50 or 60 Mayan structures are spread over this 950-acre archaeological reserve. The most impressive is the largest Preclassic structure in Belize—a massive, stepped temple built into the hillside overlooking the river. Many structures at Lamanai have only been superficially excavated. Trees and vines grow from the tops of temples, the sides of one pyramid are covered with vegetation, and another pyramid rises abruptly from the forest floor. There are no tour buses or cold-drink stands here—just ruins and the slowly advancing forest.

There are several ways to get here. One option is to drive on the well-maintained unpaved road from Orange Walk Town. From here head west to Yo Creek, then southwest to San Felipe village, a total of 39 km (24 mi). In San Felipe go straight (the road to Chan Chich turns to the right) for another 19 km (12 mi) to reach the ruins. It's about a 1½-hour drive. The best way to approach the ruins, however, is by boat, which takes just a little longer. Boats leave from the New River Bridge, about 10 km

(6 mi) south of Orange Walk. You can also catch a 15-minute long charter plane from Belize.

On the grounds of the site you'll find a small museum, where caretakers gladly show you a 2,500-year progression of pottery, carvings, and small statues. ✉ *Near Indian Church village, Orange Walk District* 🎫 *BZ$10* ⏲ *Daily 9–5.*

Where to Stay & Eat

$$$ **Lamanai Outpost Lodge.** Perched on a low hillside, this lodge has an expansive view of the New River Lagoon and is home to the Lamanai Field Research Center. Here you'll find resident naturalists, archaeologists, and ornithologists. Even when you sneak off to the bar lounge, the Digger's Roost, you can see archaeological memorabilia. A dock extends 130 feet into the lagoon and is a good place for swimming—keep an eye out for ol' Mr. Croc. Opportunities for bird-watching are extensive with at least 370 species identified near the lodge. The thatch cabanas are amidst lovely gardens and have porches with lagoon views. The Lamanai ruins are within walking distance. ✉ *Indian Church* ☎ *223/3578, 888/733–7864 in U.S.* 🖷 *220/9061* 🌐 *www.lamanai.com* *20 cabins* *Restaurant, fans, refrigerators, lake, boating, bar, library, laundry service, Internet, travel services; no a/c, no room phones, no room TVs* 💳 *AE, MC, V* ⏲ *Closed Sept.*

Corozal

❹ *153 km (95 mi) north of Belize City.*

Originally settled by refugees from the Yucatán during the 19th-century caste wars, Corozal is the last town before you reach Río Hondo, the river separating Belize from Mexico. Though thoroughly ignored by today's travelers, this friendly town is great for a few days of easy living by the turquoise waters of Corozal Bay. It's hard not to fall into the laid-back lifestyle here—a sign at the entrance of Reyes Grocery advertises STRONG RUM, 55 BELIZE DOLLARS A GALLON. The climate is unequivocally appealing, with less rain than almost anywhere else in Belize.

Still, sleepy Corozal is slowly waking up. The Corozal Free Zone, south of the Santa Elena border crossing, is starting to be known as a place where businesses can escape Belize's high import duties and where visitors from Mexico can buy tax-free gas. A casino is planned for the area, but in typically Belizean fashion, the planning process is taking years.

English is the official language, but Spanish is just as common here. The town was largely rebuilt after Hurricane Janet nearly destroyed it in 1955, so it's neat and modern. Many houses are clapboard, built on wooden piles, though a growing clan of expats, especially in the Consejo Shores area north of town, are putting up new houses that wouldn't look out of place in Florida. One of the few remaining colonial-era buildings is a portion of the old fort in the center of town. The history of Corozal, including a graphic depiction of the brutality of colonial rule on the indigenous people, is depicted in a strikingly beautiful mural by Manuel Villamar Reyes on the wall of Town Hall.

In a landmark 1886 building near the market, the **Corozal Cultural Center,** now a museum and tourist information center, once served as a lighthouse. You can still see the spiral staircase and parts of the original beacon. Also on display are hand-blown rum bottles and a traditional Mayan thatch hut. ✉ *Off 1st Ave. at edge of Corozal Bay* ☎ *422–3176* *BZ$3* ⏲ *Tues.–Sat. 9–noon and 1–4:30.*

Not far from Corozal are several Mayan sites. The closest, **Santa Rita,** is a short walk from the town's center. Only a few of its structures have been excavated, so it takes some imagination to picture this settlement, founded in 1500 BC, as one of the district's major trading centers. ✉ *Corozal* ☎ *No phone* *BZ$5* ⏲ *Daily 8–4.*

Cerros, a Late Preclassic center, is south of Corozal on the coast. As at Santa Rita, little has been excavated, but the site, dating from about 2000 BC, includes a ball court, several tombs, and a large temple. The setting, on a peninsula in the Bay of Chetumal, is beautiful. The best way to get here is by boat from Corozal, around BZ$120 to BZ$180 for up to four people. ✉ *Corozal* ☎ *No phone* *BZ$10* ⏲ *Daily 8–4.*

Where to Stay & Eat

$–$$ Fodor'sChoice ★ **Café Kelá.** Corozal is probably the last place you'd expect to find good French food, but this café, with five tables under a cozy palapa near the bay, is proof that in Belize anything is possible. Everything here is delicious, from the savory crepes to grouper sautéed with herbs. And the prices? *Mais oui,* it's hard to spend more than a few dollars per person. The succulent fruit juices are freshly squeezed, and the pizzas are the best in town. ✉ *37 1st Ave., about 2 blocks north of Corozal Cultural Center* ☎ *422/2833* *No credit cards.*

¢–$ **Cactus Plaza.** For a great bargain, grab a seat at the counter or at an outdoor table under a canvas awning and order a plateful of tacos, tostadas, *salbutes* (stuffed tortillas), and other Mexican finger foods. You won't be stuck with a big check: most entrées are under BZ$2. Everything is freshly made and tasty. ✉ *6 6th St. S, 2 blocks west of bay* ☎ *442/0394* *No credit cards.*

$ **Casablanca by the Sea.** It's worth a short trip to Consejo, just to see the hand-carved mahogany doors gracing each room's entrance at this inn. Beverly Temte, an expat from New England, created this appealing, small hotel. The best rooms are the three second-floor suites facing the bay. Other rooms are all on the small side. The first-floor restaurant serves tasty Belizean and American food. ✉ *Consejo, 18 km (8 mi) northeast of Corozal Town* ☎ *423/1018* *423/1003* *www.casablanca-bythesea.com* *7 rooms, 3 suites* *Restaurant, fans, cable TV, dock, bar, meeting rooms, travel services; no room phones* *AE, MC, V.*

$ **Copa Banana.** Opened in 2004, this homelike hotel has five sunny suites carved out of two houses on Corozal Bay. Guests share a kitchen, dining room, and living room. The owners, who run a real estate agency in Corozal, also rent cars. ✉ *409 Corozal Bay Rd.* ☎ *422/0284* *422/2710* *www.copabanana.bz* *5 rooms* *Fans, cable TV, car rental; no room phones* *MC, V.*

$ **Corozal Bay Inn.** With more than an acre of beachfront on Corozal Bay, this inn's property includes the town's only sand beach, created by its owners, who trucked in tons of sand. The serene bayside resort has thatch cabanas in pastel colors and a popular restaurant and bar. ✉ *Almond Dr. off Northern Hwy. at south end of Corozal Town* ☎ *422/2691* 📠 *800-836/9188* 🌐 *www.corozalbayinn.com* *10 cabanas* *Restaurant, refrigerators, cable TV, pool, beach, dock, marina, fishing, bar, Internet, travel services; no room phones* 💳 *MC, V.*

¢ **Hok'ol K'in Guesthouse.** Named after a Yuacatec Maya phrase that welcomes the rising sun, this motel is across the street from Corozal Bay. Guest rooms cool naturally here, thanks to the bay's stiff breezes. Although they're a bit crowded with two queen beds, rooms have verandas with hammocks that grant you extra space. Second-floor rooms have the best views. One room is wheelchair accessible. The restaurant serves breakfast, snacks, and juicy burgers. Inexpensive and intriguing tours, including one to local schools, are available. ✉ *1 block south of the market* ☎ *422/3329* 📠 *422/3569* *maya@btl.net* *9 rooms* *Restaurant, fans, bar, travel services; no a/c, no room phones, no room TVs* 💳 *AE, MC, V.*

Sarteneja

5 *67 km (40 mi) from Corozal.*

Lobster fishing and pineapple farming are the two main industries in this small community of mestizo people. Sarteneja is also a center for building wooden boats. Although it has traditionally had more in common with nearby Mexican villages than with the rest of Belize, Sarteneja has experienced many changes in conjunction with improvements on the road to Orange Walk.

The 81 square km (31 square mi) of tropical forest forming the **Shipstern Wildlife Reserve** are, like the Crooked Tree Wildlife Sanctuary, a paradise for bird-watchers. Look for egrets (there are 13 species here), American coots, keel-billed toucans, flycatchers, warblers, and several species of parrots. Mammals are in healthy supply as well, including peccaries, pumas, jaguars, and raccoons. The butterfly farm next to the visitor center used to export pupae but is now a small education area with some staff left flitting about. For overnight stays cabins on the reserve may be rented for BZ$20 a night. Sarteneja village has a couple of guest houses—ask in the village about availability. ✉ *Sarteneja* ☎ *223/4533* 📠 *223/4985* 🌐 *www.belizeaudubon.org* *BZ$10.*

Northern & Central Belize A to Z

AIR TRAVEL

Tropic Air and Maya Island Air each fly four or five times daily between Ambergris Caye and the airstrip at Corozal, about 3 km (2 mi) south of town off the Northern Highway. The journey takes 20 minutes and costs BZ$70 one-way. There's no direct service to Belize City or other destinations in Belize.

Tropic Air ✉ Northern Hwy. ☎ 226/2012, 800/422-3435 in U.S. **Maya Island Air** ✉ South End ☎ 422/2333, 800/225-6732 in U.S.

BOAT & FERRY TRAVEL

An old sugar barge ferries passengers and cars across the New River from just south of Corozal Town to the road to Copper Bank, Cerros, and the Shipstern peninsula. The Puebla Nuevo ferry is free from 6 AM to 9 PM daily. To get to the ferry from Corozal, take the Northern Highway toward Orange Walk Town to just south of Jal's Travel and Paula's Gift Shop. Turn left and follow the road for 4 km (2½ mi) to the ferry landing.

A daily ferry operates between Corozal Town and Ambergris Caye. The *Thunderbolt* departs from Corozal at the pier near Reunion Park at 7 AM and returns from San Pedro at 3 PM, leaving from the Thunderbolt dock on the back side of the island. Fare is BZ$45 one-way. Thunderbolt has three 250-horsepower outboards, a canopy cover with sliding windows, and bus-style seats.

Boat & Ferry Information **Thunderbolt** ✉ San Pedro Town ☎ 226/2217.

BUS TRAVEL

Novelo's makes the 3½-hour journey between Belize City and Corozal several times a day. The cost is about BZ$12, but it's more for express service. Buses also continue on to Chetumal, Mexico.

Bus Information **Novelo's** ✉ 13 4th Ave., Corozal ☎ 422/3034.

CAR RENTAL

Car-rental agencies in Belize City will deliver vehicles to Corozal for a small fee. Copa Banana hotel also rents cars. Corozal police enthusiastically ticket cars from other parts of Belize for such minor violations as parking the wrong way on a one-way street, so be especially cautious.

CAR TRAVEL

From Belize City Corozal is the last stop on the Northern Highway before you hit Mexico. The 153-km (95-mi) journey will probably take about two hours, unless you're slowed by sugar cane trucks.

EMERGENCIES

For dental and medical care many of Corozal's residents go to Chetumal, Mexico. In Corozal call Dr. John Trummer if you need medical care or Dr. Glenda Major if you require a dentist. The Corozal Hospital, with only limited facilities, is on the Northern Highway.

Doctors & Dentists **John Trummer, M.D.** ✉ Santa Rita Rd. ☎ 422/2129. **Glenda Major, D.D.S.** ✉ 1st St. S ☎ 422/2837.

Hospitals **Corozal Hospital** ✉ Northern Hwy. ☎ 422/2076.

Pharmacies **V-Mart Pharmacy** ✉ 4th Ave. and 1st St. N ☎ 422/2597.

HEALTH

Health and hygiene standards are high in Corozal and in most of northern Belize. Around Cerros and Sarteneja be prepared for lots of mosquitoes, some of which may carry malaria or dengue fever. Bring plenty of strong insect repellent; one with 30% DEET is recommended.

MAIL & SHIPPING

The Corozal post office, on the west side of the main town plaza, is open 8:30–noon and 1–4:30.

Post Offices **Corozal** ✉ 5th Ave. ☎ 422/2462.

MONEY MATTERS

Although American dollars are accepted everywhere in Corozal, money changers at the Mexico border and in Corozal Town exchange Belize dollars for U.S. and Mexican currency, usually for better rates than in banks. The three banks in Corozal have ATMs, but only Belize Bank accepts cards issued outside Belize. Belize Bank's ATMs are on the CIRRUS and PLUS networks. You can also cross the border to Chetumal and use the ATMs there, although you'll get your money in pesos.

Atlantic Bank ✉ 1 Park St. S ☎ 422/3473. **ScotiaBank** ✉ 4th Ave. ☎ 422/2046. **Belize Bank** ✉ 5th Ave. at 1st St. S ☎ 422/2087.

SAFETY

Corozal is one of Belize's safest areas. Petty theft and burglaries aren't uncommon, however, so use common sense when traveling through the area.

TAXIS

To get around Corozal, call the Taxi Association or ask your hotel to arrange for transportation.

Taxi Association ✉ 1st St. S ☎ 422/2035.

TOURS

Stephan Moerman, a French biologist, provides excellent tours of Cerros and other local archaeological sites. Henry Menzies arranges trips to Mexico as well as to sites around Corozal. He'll also meet you in Chetumal and bring you across the border.

Stephan Moerman ✉ 37 1st. Ave. ☎ 422/2833. **Henry Menzies** ✉ Caribbean Village, South End ☎ 422/3415.

VISITOR INFORMATION

Brochures and visitor information are available in the Corozal Cultural Center, on 1st Avenue near the market. The best source of online information about Corozal is 🌐 www.corozal.com, put together by students at a local community college. Another good site is Belize North, 🌐 www.belizenorth.com.

Tourist Information **Corozal Cultural Center** ✉ 1st Ave. ☎ 422/3176.

THE CAYO

When the first jungle lodges opened in the Cayo, not many people thought this wild district on the country's western border would become a tourist magnet. The region was too remote. Today more than half of those touring Belize visit the Cayo sometime during their trip, making this the country's second most popular destination. Comprising more than 5,200 square km (2,000 square mi) and about 53,000 inhabitants, the mountainous region is Belize's largest district.

You'll know you're entering the Cayo a few miles west of Belmopan, Belize's capital. Running along the Belize River for miles, the road winds out of the valley and heads into a series of sharp bends. In a few minutes you'll see cattle grazing on steep hillsides and horses flicking their tails.

Other things change as you enter the Cayo. The Creole people who live along the coast give way to Maya; English is replaced by Spanish as the predominant language; and off the main roads four-wheel-drive vehicles become a necessity. The lost world of the Maya comes alive through majestic, haunting ruins. And the Indiana Jones in you can hike through the jungle, ride horseback, canoe down the Macal or Mopan rivers, and explore incredible caves.

Mountain lions, jaguars and their diminutive cousins the ocelots, even smaller margays, and other wildlife appearing on Belize's currency can be found in the Cayo. Ornithologists in search of the country's 400-plus avian species carry telescopes, cameras, and tape recorders with miniscule microphones, but for most people a pair of binoculars will do. Even if you've never been bird-watching, setting off through the jungle in search of motmots, masked tityras, violaceous trogons, and scaly throated leaftossers as the sun burns off the early morning mist will have you hooked.

National Geographic filmed *Journey to the Underworld* in the Cayo's Caves Branch River area, where fascinating limestone caves are found in lush tropical forests. Many of these caverns, hung with glistening white stalactites, have barely been explored. Resorts such as Caves Branch, Pook's Hill, and Jaguar Paw are arranging more and more expeditions for guests who want to see the caves from an inner tube or a boat. Serious spelunkers can even explore with scuba gear. Before trying either, though, inquire about histoplasmosis, a fungal infection of the lungs that can threaten explorers who venture into caves containing large numbers of bats.

As for lodging, you may be out in the bush, but you won't be roughing it. Some of the country's finest accomodations are in the Cayo, with simple cabanas as well as beautifully landscaped resorts. All place special emphasis on ecotourism, and most are on what might be called "safari strip"—the Western Highway heading from San Ignacio toward Guatemala.

Numbers in the margin correspond to points of interest on the Cayo and the Deep South map.

Belmopan

❶ *80 km (50 mi) southwest of Belize City.*

The best way to see Belize's capital is through the rearview mirror as you head toward the Cayo. The brainchild of Belize's longest-serving prime minister, George Price, Belmopan was conceived as Belize's answer to Brasilia and Canberra—a resplendent, modern capital city. Instead, it's a dreary cluster of concrete office buildings plunked in the middle of nowhere, proving that cities can't be created overnight. Even more distressing, the money that went into this failed project could've been channeled into revamping and transforming the seaside town of Belize City.

Worth a quick visit on the way out of Belmopan is Belize's small nature reserve, **Guanacaste National Park,** named for the huge guanacaste trees

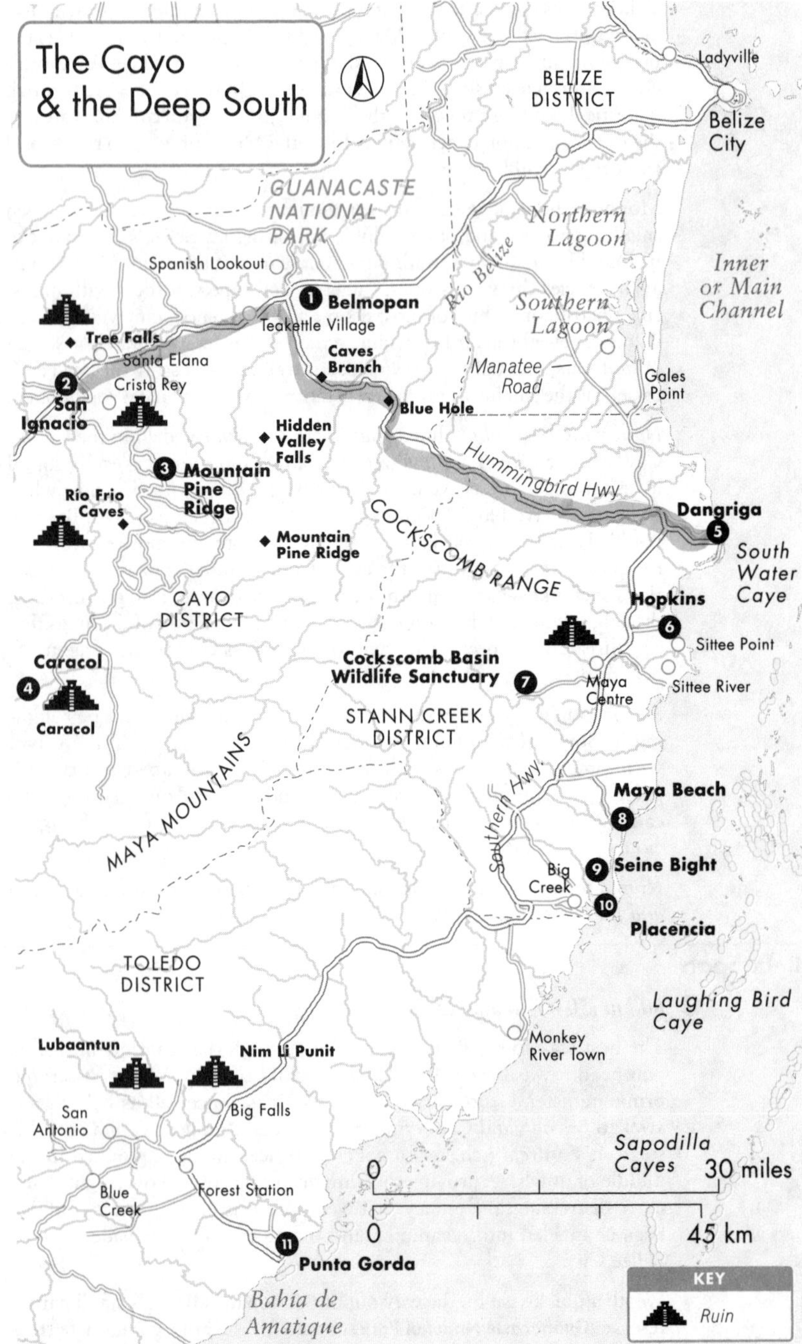
The Cayo & the Deep South
Ladyville
BELIZE DISTRICT
Belize City
GUANACASTE NATIONAL PARK
Northern Lagoon
Inner or Main Channel
Spanish Lookout
Río Belize
1 Belmopan
Southern Lagoon
Teakettle Village
Tree Falls
Santa Elana
Caves Branch
Manatee Road
Gales Point
2 San Ignacio
Cristo Rey
Blue Hole
Hidden Valley Falls
Hummingbird Hwy
3 Mountain Pine Ridge
Río Frio Caves
Dangriga
5
Mountain Pine Ridge
COCKSCOMB RANGE
South Water Caye
Hopkins
CAYO DISTRICT
6
Sittee Point
Caracol
Cockscomb Basin Wildlife Sanctuary
7
Maya Centre
Sittee River
4
Caracol
STANN CREEK DISTRICT
MAYA MOUNTAINS
Southern Hwy.
Maya Beach
8
9 Seine Bight
Big Creek
10
Placencia
TOLEDO DISTRICT
Laughing Bird Caye
Monkey River Town
Lubaantun
Nim Li Punit
Big Falls
San Antonio
Sapodilla Cayes
0
30 miles
Blue Creek
Forest Station
0
45 km
11 Punta Gorda
Bahía de Amatique
KEY
Ruin

that grow here. Also called monkey's ear trees because of their oddly shaped seedpods, the trees tower more than 100 feet. Locals use them for dugout canoes called dorries. The 50-acre park has a rich population of tropical birds, including smoky brown woodpeckers, black-headed trogons, red-lored parrots, and white-breasted wood wrens. You can try one of the eight hourly tours every day, or you can wander around on your own. *Daily, tours every hr 8:30–3:30* *BZ$5.*

The small hilltop village of **Spanish Lookout,** about 19 km (12 mi) north of the Western Highway, is one of the centers of the Mennonite community in Belize. The village's blond-haired, blue-eyed residents may seem out of place in this tropical country, but they're actually responsible for many of Belize's major projects. They built nearly all the area's resorts, and most of the eggs and milk you'll consume during your stay comes from their farms. The women dress in cotton frocks and head scarves, and the men don straw hats, suspenders, and dark trousers. Some still travel in horse-drawn buggies, though many Mennonites around Spanish Lookout have embraced pick-up trucks and modern farming equipment. The cafés and small shops in Spanish Lookout offer a unique opportunity to mingle with these world-wary people, but they don't appreciate being gawked at or photographed any more than you do.

Less than a half hour south of Belmopan, **Blue Hole** is a natural turquoise pool surrounded by mosses and lush vegetation, excellent for a cool dip. The Blue Hole is actually part of an underground river system. On the other side of the hill is St. Herman's Cave, once inhabited by the Maya. A path leads up from the highway, right near the Blue Hole, but it's quite steep and difficult to climb unless the ground is dry. To explore the cave, it's best to wear sturdy shoes and bring a flashlight. Some years ago there were some unfortunate incidents at the site, with tourists robbed and, in one case, sexually assaulted. Subsequently, a full-time attendant has been appointed to patrol the area. *Hummingbird Hwy.* *BZ$8.*

Where to Stay & Eat

$$$ **Jaguar Paw.** Although this lodge is down a long dirt road, it's anything but rustic. Eye-popping Mayan murals, by American painter Pamela Braun, adorn the massive structure's inner walls. Each room has air-conditioning and a theme—the Victorian Room has a country armoire and sheer curtains; the Pioneer Room has a pebble-lined shower and rough-hewn wooden bed. Surrounding all this are 215 acres of jungle containing a zipline and caves, that you (and at times hundreds of day-trippers from cruise ships and Ambergris Caye) can float through on an inner tube. *Off Western Hwy., turn south at Mile 37 and follow dirt road 11 km (7 mi)* *888/775–8645 in U.S.* *www.jaguarpaw.com* *16 rooms* *Restaurant, fans, pool, fishing, hiking, bar, travel services; no room phones, no room TVs* *AE, DC, MC, V.*

★ **$$** **Pook's Hill.** When the lamps are lit each night on the polished rosewood veranda, this low-key jungle lodge, on 300 remote acres, is one of the most pleasant places in the Cayo. The stone-and-thatch cabanas are laid out on a grassy clearing around a small Mayan site. During the day you can swim, ride horses through a 6,800-acre reserve filled with wildlife, or boat up the Roaring River to a series of caves, many of which contain Mayan burial sites. ✉ *At Mile 52 of Western Hwy., head south for 8 km (5 mi)* ☎ *820/2017* 📠 *822/3361* 🌐 *www.pookshillbelize.com* *9 cabanas* *Dining room, hiking, bar; no a/c, no room phones, no room TVs* 💳 *MC, V.*

★ $–$$ **Banana Bank Ranch.** Along the banks of the Belize River is this jungle lodge, which is one of the best spots for families. Equestrians of all skill levels can choose from 50 horses. Owners John and Carolyn Carr (he's a former Montana cowboy, she's a noted artist) arrange trips where you can canoe, among other things. Several domesticated animals live on the 4,000-acre property, including a ravishing jaguar named Tika. The Headquarters is a restored century-old house, which functions as a café and lounge. The thatch cabanas, with their curving walls, are modest but comfortable. ✉ *Off Western Hwy., turn north at Mile 48* ☎ *820/2020* 📠 *820/2026* 🌐 *www.bananabank.com* *7 cabanas, 3 rooms* *Restaurant, fans, pool, horseback riding, bar, travel services; no a/c in some rooms, no room phones, no room TVs* 💳 *MC, V.*

★ ¢–$$ **Caves Branch Adventure Co. & Jungle Camp.** More-intrepid guests at this 58,000-acre private reserve will head to the bunkhouse, while those in search of creature comforts will appreciate the mahogany and bamboo cabanas. Owner Ian Anderson offers more than a dozen wilderness adventures. On the tubing expedition to Footprint Cave you spend hours floating around underground lakes and crawling past stalagmites into dry chambers. Perhaps you'll take lunch where Maya once performed bloodletting rituals. Cold Belikins await you when you return, followed by a delicious dinner. "Bad Ass" expeditions into the jungle last 7 to 9 days. ✉ *19½ km (12 mi) south of Belmopan at Mile 41½ of Hummingbird Hwy.* ☎ *822/2800* 📠 *888/265-4579 in U.S.* 🌐 *www.cavesbranch.com* *4 suites, 10 cabanas, 7 with shared bath, 8 beds in bunkhouse* *Restaurant, fans, hiking, bar, travel services; no a/c, no room phones, no room TVs* 💳 *MC, V.*

San Ignacio

❷ *37 km (23 mi) southwest of Belmopan.*

When you hear the incredible commotion made by grackles in the town square's trees, you'll know you've arrived at San Ignacio, the hub of the Cayo district. San Ignacio is an excellent base for exploring western Belize. Nearby are three Mayan ruins, as well as a few national parks and a cluster of butterfly farms.

With its well-preserved wooden structures, dusty little San Ignacio is a Belizean town where you might wish to linger. Evenings are cool and mosquito free, and the colonial-era streets are lined with a few funky bars and restaurants. It's worth coming at sunset to listen to the eerily beautiful sounds of these iridescent birds.

You can ask to work the crank yourself as you ride a hand-pulled ferry across the Mopan River, near the village of San José Succotz, toward ★ the archaeological site of **Xunantunich** (pronounced *zoo-nan-too-nitch*), which means "stone maiden." As you hike through the profusion of maidenhair ferns to the ruins, you'll encounter numerous butterflies flitting through the air. A magnificent avenue of cohune palms announces your arrival at an important ceremonial center from the Maya Classic Period. Drinks and snacks are available at a visitor center that provides the history of the site. El Castillo, the massive 120-foot-high main pyramid, was built on a leveled hilltop. Though it's not as excavated as Altun Ha, the pyramid has a spectacular 360-degree panorama of the Mopan River valley. On the eastern wall is a reproduction of one of the finest Mayan sculptures in Belize, a frieze decorated with jaguar heads, human faces, and abstract geometric patterns telling the story of the Moon's affair with Morning Light. ✉ *Southwest of San Ignacio* *BZ$10* *Weekdays 8–5, weekends 8–4.*

El Pilar, a less frequented archaeological site, is still being excavated under the direction of Anabel Ford, a professor at the University of California. Excavations of Mayan ruins have traditionally concentrated on public buildings, but at El Pilar the emphasis has been on domestic architecture—everything from reconstructing houses to replanting gardens with crops used by the Maya. El Pilar, occupied from 700 to 1000, shows evidence of sentry posts in some areas, suggesting that this was a community of high-ranking officials surrounded by a hostile population. Two well-marked trails take you around the site. Because the structures haven't been stripped of vegetation, you may feel like you're walking through a series of shady orchards. Don't forget binoculars: in the 5,000-acre nature reserve there's some terrific bird-watching. Behind the main plaza a lookout grants a spectacular view across the jungle to El Pilar's sister city, Pilar Poniente, on the Guatemalan border. Note that several incidents of robbery have occurred at or near this site. ✉ *13 km (8 mi) west of Bullet Tree Falls* *BZ$10* *Daily 8–5.*

Just outside San Ignacio is a third major Mayan ruin, the unfortunately named **Cahal Pech** ("place of the ticks"). It was occupied from around 900 BC to AD 1100. At its peak, in AD 600, Cahal Pech was a medium-size settlement with some three dozen structures huddled around seven plazas. It's thought that it functioned as a guard post, watching over the nearby confluence of the Mopan and Macal rivers. It may be somewhat less compelling than the area's other ruins, but it's no less mysterious, given that these structures mark the presence of a civilization we know so little about. Look for answers at the small museum. ✉ *South of San Ignacio* *BZ$10* *Daily 8–5.*

The **Rainforest Medicine Trail,** founded by Rosita Arvigo and now owned by the Lodge at Chaa Creek, gives you a quick introduction to traditional Mayan medicine. Arvigo met Don Elijio Pantí, a Belizean shaman, and in 1985 became his apprentice by promising to preserve traditional healing practices. The Trail takes you on a short, self-guided walk through the rain forest, giving you a chance to study the symbiotic nature of its plant life. Learn about the healing properties of such indigenous plants as gumbo-limbo and man vine and see some of the endangered medicinal plants that Arvigo and her colleagues rescued. The center has sent about 3,000 species of Belizean plants to the U.S. National Institutes of Health for analysis. The shop here sells Mayan medicinal products like Belly Be Good and Flu Away, as well as Arvigo's excellent books.

✉ *Next to the Lodge at Chaa Creek* ☎ *824/3870* 🎫 *BZ$12 for Rainforest Medicine Trail.*

The **Chaa Creek Natural History Center** is a small but ever expanding museum of Belize's flora and fauna. It has a tiny library and lots of displays on everything from butterflies to snakes (thankfully pickled in jars). Outside is a screened-in blue morpho butterfly breeding center. If you haven't encountered blue morphos in the wild, you can see them up close here and even peer at their slumbering pupae, which resemble jade earrings. Once you're inside the double doors, the blue beauties, which look boringly brown when their wings are closed, flit about or remain perfectly still, sometimes on your shoulder or head, and open and close their wings to a rhythm akin to inhaling and exhaling. Tours are led by a team of naturalists. ✉ *The Lodge at Chaa Creek* ☎ *824/2037* 📠 *824/2501* 🌐 *www.chaacreek.com* 🎫 *BZ$10* ⏲ *Daily 9–4.*

The life's work of Ken duPlooy, an ornithologist who died in 2001, and the personable Judy duPlooy is the 45-acre **Belize Botanical Gardens**, a collection of hundreds of trees, plants, and flowers from all over Central America. Enlightening tours are given by local Maya who can tell you the names of the plants in Maya, Spanish, and English as well as explain their varied medicinal uses. An orchid house holds the duPlooys' collection of 180 orchid species. ✉ *duPlooy's Lodge, San Ignacio, head 7½ km (4¾) mi west on Benque Rd., turn left on Chial Rd.* ☎ *824/3101* 📠 *824/3301* 🌐 *www.duplooys.com* 🎫 *BZ$10.*

Besides thoughtful displays on Cayo flora and fauna, **Tropical Wings**, a little nature center, raises 20 species of butterfly including the blue morpho, owl, giant swallowtail, and monarch varieties. The facility, at the Trek Stop campsite (see below), has a small restaurant and gift shop. ✉ *10 km (6 mi) west of San Ignacio* ☎ *823/2265* 🎫 *BZ$5.*

Where to Stay & Eat

IN SAN IGNACIO

$–$$ ✕ **Sanny's Grill.** Sanny's democratic motto proclaims: PRICES ANYONE CAN AFFORD. With a hot grill and sizzling spices, this restaurant transforms Belizean basics, like chicken or pork chops, beyond standard fare. Try the champagne shrimp or lime-thyme red snapper, along with the tastiest, spiciest rice and beans in the Cayo. Eat them in the casual dining room or out on the covered deck. In a residential area off Benque Road, the place can be hard to find after dark. ✉ *23rd St., heading west of San Ignacio, look for a sign just beyond the Texaco station* ☎ *824/2988* 💳 *No credit cards* ⏲ *No lunch Sun.*

¢–$ ✕ **Eva's.** Not merely a bustling café-bar, this Cayo institution also acts as an Internet café, bulletin board, information center, trading post, and meeting place. In addition to the bacon, eggs, and sandwiches, Eva's serves authentic Belizean fare. Mugs of wickedly strong black tea are always available. Presiding over the colorful chaos is Bob Jones, a garrulous British ex-serviceman, who can divulge information about anything from canoe rental to what to do if you get bitten by a fer-de-lance. ✉ *22 Burns Ave.* ☎ *824/2267* 🌐 *www.evasonline.com* 💳 *No credit cards.*

$$$ 🏨 **Windy Hill Resort.** The cabanas at this lodge all have private verandas and are perched on a low hill across the landscaped grounds. Fur-

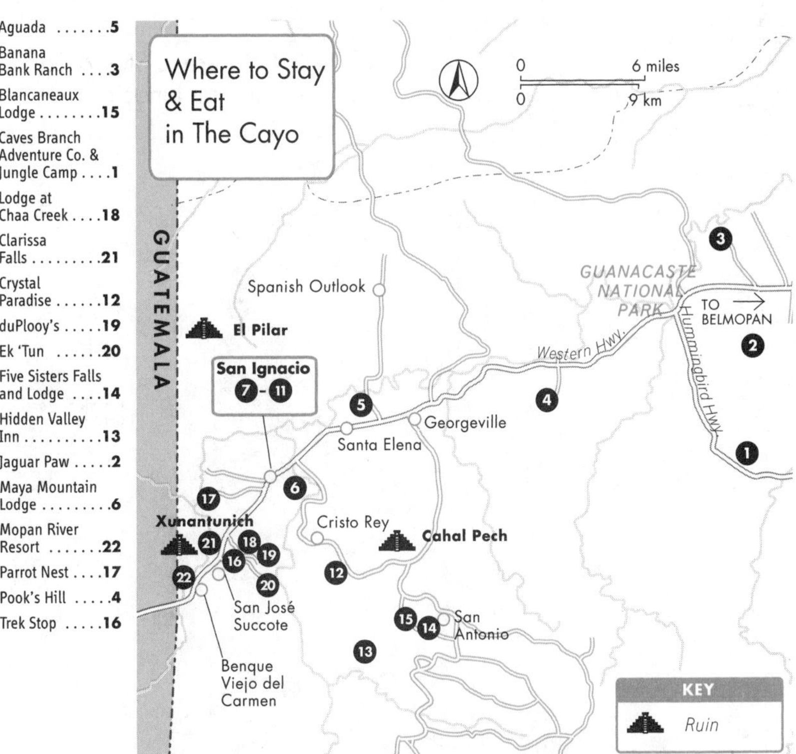

nishings are custom-made from local hardwoods, and decorations include handwoven Guatemalan rugs. Each cabana is cooled by a ceiling fan. The resort is on 100 acres just south of San Ignacio, right beside the highway. It runs many tours to Tikal, Caracol, and other destinations. ✉ *Benque Rd., 1½ km (1 mi) west of San Ignacio* ☎ *824/2017* 🖷 *824/3080* 🌐 *www.windyhillresort.com* *25 cabanas* *Restaurant, cable TV, fans, pool, horseback riding, travel services; no a/c in some rooms, no room phones, no room TVs* 💳 *AE, MC, V.*

$$ **San Ignacio Resort Hotel.** It doesn't look like much from the road, but this hotel has spacious and comfortable rooms with verandas that face the jungle. The Running W restaurant specializes in steak, and the bar is large and often crowded. Birding and other excursions can be arranged by the staff. There's an iguana hatchery on the property and next door is a small casino packed with video poker machines, one-armed bandits, and a few live tables. ✉ *Buena Vista Rd., San Ignacio* ☎ *824/2034* 🖷 *824/2134* 🌐 *www.sanignaciobelize.com* *20 rooms* *Restaurant, cable TV, pool, bar, casino, laundry service, meeting rooms, travel services* 💳 *AE, MC, V.*

¢–$ **Casa Blanca Guest House.** Though it's in the center of San Ignacio, on bustling Burns Avenue, this new hotel is an oasis of quiet and one of Belize's top budget choices. The rooms, with cool white walls and lo-

Casa Blanca Guest House 7
Eva's 8
San Ignacio Resort Hotel 9
Sanny's Grill 11
Windy Hill Resort 10

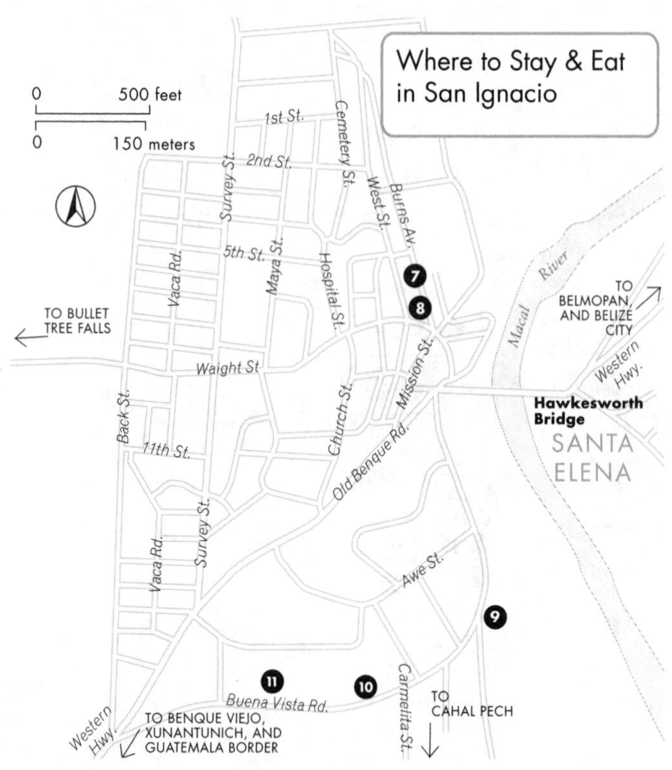

cally made wood furniture, are a big step above typical budget lodging. You can prepare yourself snacks or full meals in the shared kitchen. ✉ *10 Burns Ave., San Ignacio* ☎ *824/2080* ⊕ *www.cayoonline.com/casablanca* *9 rooms* *Fans, travel services; no a/c in some rooms, no room phones, no room TVs* ▭ *MC, V.*

NEAR SAN IGNACIO ¢–$ **Clarissa Falls.** The rumbling low falls are the first and last sounds of the day at Clarissa Falls. It's a well-known place among Belizeans, who come for tasty enchiladas and black bean soup served under an open-air palapa overlooking the Mopan River. Owner Chena Galvez and her sister Anna create the simple, savory food, which the friendly staff serves in copious quantities. This rolling 900-acre expanse of grassy pasture is the Galvez family ranch. Chena has spent her life here and over the years she has built a small colony of homey thatch cabanas. ✉ *Western Hwy., 9 km (5½ mi) west of San Ignacio* ☎ *824/3916* ⊕ *www.clarissafalls.com* *12 cabanas, 11 with bath* *Restaurant, fans, 1-hole golf course, hiking, bar; no a/c, no room phones, no room TVs* ▭ *MC, V.*

★ $$$$ **Mopan River Resort.** Belize's first truly all-inclusive resort has a reasonably priced package. Once you've taken the short ferry trip across the Mopan River to the resort's manicured palm-studded grounds, you're in your own private bit of paradise. The cabanas have traditional facades, but house modern amenities like cable TVs and minibars with gratis soft drinks and beer. Co-owner Pamella Picon is an ordained minister who can marry you in the resort's wedding chapel. ✉ *Benque Viejo del Carmen* ☎ *823/2047* 🖷 *823/3272* 🌐 *www.mopanriverresort.com* *12 cabanas* *Dining room, some kitchens, minibars, refrigerators, cable TV, pool, laundry service, travel services; no a/c, no room phones, no smoking* 💳 *D, MC, V* *AI* *Closed Aug.–Oct.*

★ $$$ **Ek 'Tun.** At Ek 'Tun sapphire blue water gushes from natural mineral springs into a rock-lined pool among towering palms. You're immersed in complete solitude here—you can even skinny-dip, if you like—with only the howler monkeys for company. Arrive by river skiff to the 600-acre grounds, which have giant ceiba trees and flowering shrubs. With only two rustic but lovely thatch-roof cottages, this is more of a bed-and-breakfast in the jungle than a traditional lodge. On the extensive network of trails you can spot orange-breasted falcons and toucans. Excellent meals are served in a stucco-and-thatch dining room overlooking the Macal river. ✉ *On Macal River 20 km (12 mi) upriver from San Ignacio* ☎ *820/3002* 🌐 *www.ektunbelize.com* *2 cabanas* *Dining room, pool, hiking, horseback riding, bar, travel services; no a/c, no room phones, no room TVs, no kids under 18, no smoking in cabanas, no kids under 16* 💳 *MC, V.*

$$–$$$ **duPlooy's.** High above a bend in the Macal River called Big Eddy is this spectacular resort. From the deck, 30 feet above the forest floor, you look straight out to a dramatic sweep of limestone cliffs. From the sandy beach below you can swim and dive off the rocks. On the premises is the 45-acre Belize Botanical Gardens. Bungalows are filled with hardwood furnishings. The two-story cottage has wraparound porches, king-size beds, whirlpool bath, fridge, and great views. There are less expensive rooms in the jungle lodge. The food is terrific, and there's always a vegetarian option. ✉ *San Ignacio, head 7½ km (4¾) mi west on Benque Rd., turn left on Chial Rd.* ☎ *824/3101* 🖷 *824/3301* 🌐 *www.duplooys.com* *4 cabanas, 15 rooms, 7 with shared bath* *Dining room, fans, hiking, horseback riding, laundry service, travel services; no a/c, no room phones, no room TVs, no smoking* 💳 *MC, V.*

$–$$$ Fodor's Choice ★ **The Lodge at Chaa Creek.** Everything about this jungle resort outclasses other lodges. To start, there's the beautiful hardwood furniture, a friendly staff of 70, and a magnificent setting on 330 acres of rolling hills above the Macal River. The whitewashed stone cottages manage to be both extremely simple and elegant. Ideal for honeymooners are the "tree top" suites with whirlpools. For budget travelers there's the Macal River Safari Camp, with small A-frame rooms on individual wooden platforms. The resort's spa is the best in Belize. Additionally, Chaa Creek's tours are among the country's finest. ✉ *West of San Ignacio, drive 7½ km (4¾) mi on Benque Rd., turn left on Chial Rd.* ☎ *824/2037* 🖷 *824/2501* 🌐 *www.chaacreek.com* *20 rooms, 5 suites, 10 casitas* *Restaurant, room service, fans, spa, hiking, horseback riding, laundry service, meeting rooms, travel services; no a/c, no room phones, no room TVs* 💳 *AE, D, MC, V.*

¢–$ **Maya Mountain Lodge.** Designed with the nature lover in mind, this hilltop lodge never aspired toward luxury. Owners Bart and Suzi Mickler designed the nature trails: one passes 150 edible jungle plant species, the other focuses on ornamental plants. In summer they run workshops on ecology, birding, and other subjects. The whitewashed cottages all have private patios. A large wooden building has rooms for budget-conscious guests. The pleasant open-air dining room serves tempting, wholesome food. There's a small above-ground pool, and the grounds are thriving thanks to more than a decade of tender loving care. ✉ *Cristo Rey Rd., 2 km (1 mi) outside San Ignacio* ☎ *824/2164* 🖷 *824/2029* 🌐 *www.mayamountain.com* ⇆ *8 cottages, 6 rooms* ♨ *Restaurant, fans, pool, hiking, laundry service, travel services; no a/c in some rooms, no room phones, no room TVs* ▭ *AE, MC, V.*

¢–$ **Parrot Nest.** Overcome your phobia of high places and stay in one of two tree house rooms at this lodge, which also has four cabins on the ground. All lodgings are spic-and-span, comfy, and very good values. You can canoe in the Mopan River, which surrounds the lodge on three sides. Manager Pat Barbutti does a nice job of making everyone feel welcome; Parrot Nest is often booked solid. For BZ$2 a *collectiva* (collective taxi) takes you here from downtown San Ignacio, and a regular taxi will cost about BZ$15. Yes, you will definitely see parrots here. ✉ *Bullet Tree Falls* 🌐 *www.parrot-nest.com* ⇆ *6 cabins, 5 share baths* ♨ *Restaurant, fans, travel services; no a/c, no room phones, no room TVs* ▭ *MC, V.*

¢ **Aguada.** Jump on an opportunity to stay in this tidy, attractive, and cheap hotel in Santa Elena, a low-key town near San Ignacio. Aguada is so popular that the owners have added more rooms overlooking the pool. There's a friendly restaurant with Belizean dishes and American standards like burgers. In the large common room are a TV and games. The hotel is within walking distance of downtown San Ignacio. A genuine London taxi cab, used for trips around the Cayo, and vans that run to and from the airports in Belize City are also available. ✉ *Santa Elena* ☎ *824/3609* 🌐 *www.aguadahotel.com* ⇆ *14 rooms* ♨ *Restaurant, pool, travel services; no room phones, no room TVs* ▭ *MC, V.*

¢ **The Trek Stop.** After a day out and about, a cold Belikin and filling Mexican and Belizean dishes await you at this cluster of neat-as-a-pin cabins. Tents or just campsites are also available, as is a common kitchen for preparing your own grub. American expats and their Belizean partners opened this spot on top of a hill near San José Succotz in 1998. It's an exceptional find, particularly for budget travelers, as cabin rates are just BZ$20 per person. ✉ *San José Succotz, 9⁶⁄₁₀ km (6 mi) west of San Ignacio* ☎ *823/2265* 🌐 *www.thetrekstop.com* ⇆ *6 cabins without bath* ♨ *Restaurant, bar, travel services; no a/c, no room phones, no room TVs, no smoking* ▭ *MC, V.*

Sports & the Outdoors

CANOEING The Cayo's many rivers, especially the Mopan and Macal, make it an excellent place for canoeing. Most of the larger resorts, like Chaa Creek and duPlooy's, have canoes. In San Ignacio you can rent canoes from **Toni Canoes** (☎ 824/3292), which also organizes guided trips and overnight camping trips.

CAVING
Fodor'sChoice ★
Over the millennia, as dozens of swift-flowing rivers bored through the soft limestone, the Maya Mountains became pitted with miles of caves. The Maya used them as burial sites and, according to one theory, as sub-

terranean waterways that linked the Cayo with communities as far north as the Yucatán. Previously, the caves fell into a 1,000-year slumber, disturbed only by the nightly flutter of bats. In recent years the caves have been rediscovered by spelunkers. First on the scene was Ian Anderson, owner of **Caves Branch Adventure Co. & Jungle Camp** (✉ 19½ km [12 mi] south of Belmopan ☎📠 822/2800 🌐 www.cavesbranch.com). He and his friendly staff of trained guides run exhilarating adventure-themed caving, tubing, and hiking trips from a tiki-torchlighted jungle camp just south of Belmopan. David Simson, of **David's Adventure Tours** (✉ San Ignacio ☎ 824/3674) was the first to do tours of the now-popular Barton Creek Cave. **Mayawalk Adventures** (✉ San Ignacio ☎ 824/3070 🌐 www.mayawalk.com) specializes in tours to the spectacular, and spooky, cave of Actun Tunichil Muknal.

HORSEBACK RIDING

When it comes to horseback riding adventures, the undisputed local experts are found at the lodges of **Mountain Equestrian Trails** (✉ Pine Ridge Rd. ☎ 820/4041 🌐 www.metbelize.com) and Chaa Creek. **Easy Rider** (✉ Collins Ave., San Ignacio ☎ 824/3734) also runs equestrian tours of the Mayan ruins and other points of interest in the region.

Shopping

Among the many small stores in downtown San Ignacio is **Celina's Superstore** (✉ 43 Burns Ave. ☎ 824/2247), which has almost anything you'll need, including picnic supplies, toiletries, booze, and more.

Caesar's Place (✉ Western Hwy., east of San Ignacio ☎ 824/2341) has T-shirts, hammocks, postcards, and jewelry for last-minute shoppers. Don't expect a deal, though.

Mountain Pine Ridge

❸ *27 km (17 mi) south of San Ignacio.*

The Mountain Pine Ridge is the high country of Belize—some 300 square mi (780 square km) of low mountains and rolling hills, an out-of-place ecosystem, covered in part by vast pine forests and crisscrossed with old logging roads. The higher elevations—up to about 3,700 feet—provide cooler temperatures and, of course, outstanding views. Heading southeast from San Ignacio, the road winds up from the Macal Valley through fertile farm country where corn, peanuts, and beans grow in small roadside clearings. A few miles beyond the village of Cristo Rey, the vegetation gets wilder as the road swings away from the river. Cohune palms, trumpet trees, wild papayas, and strangler vines grow in profusion, while here and there a crop of bananas or corn cuts into the hillside. Shortly before the village of **San Antonio,** a plateau with fine views of the Maya Mountains emerges. With its sheep, goats, and orange trees, San Antonio's cluster of brightly painted wooden houses clinging to the hillside at 1,000 feet looks like a tropical version of a Greek hilltop community.

A rugged dome of granite and limestone containing some of the most ancient rocks in Central America, the 780-square-km (300-square-mi) ★ **Mountain Pine Ridge Forest Reserve** is a highlight of any journey to Belize and an adventure to reach. Along with the Cockscomb Basin

Wildlife Sanctuary and the Mayan ruins at Lamanai, it's a sight no visitor should miss.

As you leave the lush tropical forest, the road circles the western slopes of the mountains. Baldy Beacon, at just over 3,000 feet, lies to the east. After lowland Belize's heat and humidity, the cooler air is enormously refreshing. Unfortunately, some of the savanna here is marked by dead trees. A southern pine beetle infestation in 2000 and 2001 killed thousands of acres of mountain pines. The trees are regenerating, however, and new growth pines are already 6 feet to 12 feet tall.

Aside from the pines, you'll also see lilac-color mimosa, St. John's wort, and occasionally a garish red flower known as hotlips. There's also a huge variety of ferns, ranging from the tiny maidenhair fern to giants the size of coconut palms, and a fair selection of Belize's 154 orchid species. Look out for the craboo, a wild tree whose berries are used in a brandy-like liqueur believed to have aphrodisiac properties. Birds love this fruit, so any craboo is a good place to spot orioles and woodpeckers.

There are about 2,400 km (1,500 mi) of roads here, all built by the British army, which, with U.S. and Belize forces, still uses the area for jungle warfare training. (If the military is training in the area, they'll post signs warning you about it.) Some roads have names, but most have numerical monikers, like A10. An improved road to Caracol is being built and may open by 2005. Of course, the best way to see this area is on a mountain bike or your own feet, not bouncing around in an Isuzu Trooper. The village of Augustine is home to the forest reserve's headquarters. It's the only place in the area where you're allowed to camp.

Inside Mountain Pine Ridge Forest Reserve is **Hidden Valley Falls.** Also known as the Thousand Foot Falls (it actually drops nearly 1,600 feet), it's the highest in Central America. A thin plume of spray plummets over the edge of a rock face into an ostensibly bottomless gorge below. The catch is that the viewing area is some distance from the falls. To climb closer requires a major commitment. A shelter, some benches, and a public rest room provide creature comforts. At the nearby **Río On** you can sunbathe on flat granite boulders or dunk yourself into crystal-clear pools and waterfalls.

Just outside the reserve are the **Río Frio Caves.** They're only a few miles down a steep track, but ecologically speaking, these caves are in a different world. In the course of a few hundred yards, you drop from pine savanna to tropical forest. Nothing in Belize illustrates its extraordinary geological diversity so clearly as this startling transition. A river runs right through the center and over the centuries has carved the rock into fantastic shapes. Swallows fill the place, and at night ocelots and margays pad silently across the cold floor in search of slumbering prey. Seen from the dark interior, the light-filled world outside seems more intense and beautiful than ever. Rising vertically through the cave's mouth is a giant hardwood tree, *Pterocarpus officialis*. Its massive paddle-shape roots are anchored in the sandy soil of the riverbank and its green crown strain toward the blue sky.

More than 30,000 pupae are raised annually at the **Green Hills Butterfly Ranch,** the largest and best of Belize's six butterfly farms. For a closer look at the creatures, the facility has about 30 species in a 2,700-square-foot flight area. Jan Meerman, who's published a book on Belize's butterflies, runs the place with Dutch partner Tineke Boomsma. ✉ *Mile 8, Pine Ridge Rd.* ☎ *820/4017* *BZ$10* ⏲ *Daily 8–4.*

The newly established **Elijio Panti National Park,** created in 2001 and named after the famed Guatemala-born herbal healer who died in Cayo in 1996 at the age of 106, is a wonderful addition to Belize's already extensive national parks system. It spans 13,000 acres around the villages of San Antonio, Cristo Rey, and El Progreso. The hope is that eliminating hunting in this park will encourage more wildlife to return to western Belize. So far, the park boundaries are as yet ill-defined, no admission fee is charged, and an official welcome center and other park formalities are absent.

Where to Stay & Eat

$$$–$$$$ Fodor'sChoice ★ **Blancaneaux Lodge.** As you sweep down this upscale resort's hibiscus- and palm-lined drive, past the croquet lawn, you may feel like you're in Beverly Hills. Indeed, the lodge is owned by Francis Ford Coppola. Spread on a hillside above the Privassion River, the villas with their soaring thatch ceilings, Japanese-style tile baths, and screened porches overlooking the river have appeared in *Architectural Digest.* The filmmaker's own villa, one of the Cayo's finest dwellings, is available when he isn't in town. A fleet of Land Rovers takes you to remote Mayan ruins or on shopping trips to Guatemala. Those with their own planes can fly into the resort's landing strip. ✉ *Mountain Pine Ridge* ☎ *824/3878, 800/746–3743 in U.S.* *824/3919* *www.blancaneaux.com* *7 cabanas, 5 villas* *Restaurant, fans, hiking, horseback riding, bar, laundry service, airstrip, travel services; no a/c, no room phones, no room TVs* *AE, MC, V* *CP.*

$–$$ **Five Sisters Falls & Lodge.** With a laid-back and romantic style, this lodge is perched on a steep hill and overlooks the waterfall that gives the place its name. Accommodations are in thatch cabanas with screened porches, as well as in boxy rooms in the main building. A tram will take you down to the river if you're eager to avoid the 286 steps. After your swim, the thatch-roof bar is a great place to unwind. The restaurant, with a beautiful view of the falls, prepares savory Belizean food. ✉ *Near San Antonio* ☎ *800/447–2931 in U.S.* *820/4005* *www.fivesisterslodge.com* *8 cabanas, 7 rooms, 5 with bath* *Restaurant, fans, hiking, bar, meeting room; no a/c, no room phones, no room TVs* *AE, MC, V* *CP.*

★ **$$$** **Hidden Valley Inn.** Rescued from mediocrity by its new owners, a prominent Belize City family, Hidden Valley Inn sits on thousands of acres and has more than a dozen waterfalls. For romantics, a catered champagne lunch can be eaten at your own private waterfall. The cottages have mahogany furnishings, tile floors, and fireplaces. Dinner is served in the Main House, with its vaulted ceilings and four fireplaces. After dinner, sip on coffee grown on the premises. There are excellent birding opportunities here. ✉ *Mountain Pine Ridge* ☎ *822/3320* *822/*

3334 🌐 www.hiddenvalleyinn.com 12 cottages Restaurant, fans, hiking, mountain bikes, horseback riding, bar, laundry service, travel services; no a/c, no room phones, no room TVs AE, MC, V.

$–$$ **Crystal Paradise.** In the village of Cristo Rey, this resort is one of the area's few Belizean-owned family operations. The Tuts, an equal mix of Creole, Maya, and Spanish cultures, have 10 children. Eldest son Jeronie can identify more than 200 bird species and is an expert on medicinal plants. The Tuts offer a good variety of reasonably priced tours, including jungle camping, river excursions, and horseback riding. The simple whitewashed cabanas have Guatemalan bedspreads along with other pleasant touches. ✉ *Cristo Rey Rd., 6¾ km (4 mi) from San Ignacio* ☎ *824/2772 🌐 www.crystalparadise.com 8 cabanas, 12 rooms Restaurant, fans, hiking, horseback riding; no a/c, no room phones, no room TVs MC, V MAP.*

Shopping

The village of San Antonio is home to the **Tanah Art Museum** (✉ San Antonio ☎ 824/3310), run by four sisters with clever hands and great business acumen. Look for the eye-catching slate carvings. At the other end of the village is the Magana family's arts-and-crafts shop, **Magana Zaactunich Art Gallery** (✉ San Antonio ☎ No phone), which specializes in wood carvings.

Caracol

4 *65 km (40 mi) south of San Ignacio, a 3-hr journey by road.*

Fodor's Choice ★

Caracol (Spanish for "snail") is the most spectacular Mayan site in Belize, as well as one of the most impressive in Central America. It was once home to as many as 200,000 people, nearly the population of modern-day Belize. It was a metropolis with five plazas and 32 large structures covering almost a square mile. Once Caracol has been fully excavated it may dwarf even the great city of Tikal, which is only a few dozen miles away. The latest evidence suggests that Caracol won a crushing victory over Tikal in the mid-6th century, a theory that Guatemalan scholars haven't quite accepted. Until a group of *chicleros* (collectors of gum base) stumbled on the site in 1936, Caracol was buried under the jungle of the remote Vaca Plateau. It's hard to believe it could have been lost for centuries, as the great pyramid of Canaa is Belize's tallest structure. The road to Caracol is decent, and it's being improved in 2004 and 2005, but if you want to drive on your own, be sure to inquire about road conditions at the visitor center. ✉ *From Mountain Pine Forest Ridge reserve entrance, head south 23 km (14 mi) to village of Douglas De Silva; turn left and go 58 km (36 mi) BZ$15 ⏲ Daily 8–4.*

The Cayo A to Z

AIRPORTS & TRANSFERS

Most people bound for the Cayo fly into Belize City. Maya Island Air flies between the international airport to an airstrip near San Ignacio. There are three flights daily; a one-way ticket costs BZ$177. Many Cayo hotels and lodges have van transportation from both airports in Belize City for about BZ$300 for up to four people each way. Several hotels in San Ignacio, including Aguada, run shuttles between Belize City and San Ignacio, for around BZ$30 a person. Call ahead for reservations.

Airlines & Contacts **Maya Island Air** ✉ Box 458, Municipal Airport, Belize City ☎ 223/1140, 800/225-6732 in U.S. 🌐 www.mayaislandair.com.

BUS TRAVEL

Novelo's has frequent service between Belize City and San Ignacio. The journey on the Western Highway takes about three hours and costs BZ$8–BZ$12, depending on whether the bus is local or express.

Novelo's ✉ 1 Wyatt St., San Ignacio ☎ 824/2508.

CAR RENTAL

Safe Tours Belize is an esteemed rental agency in Santa Elena, just east of San Ignacio.

Safe Tours Belize ✉ Western Hwy., Santa Elena ☎ 824/3731.

CAR TRAVEL

To get to the Cayo, simply follow the well-maintained, two-lane Western Highway from Belize City. Watch out for "sleeping policemen" (speed bumps) near villages along the route.

EMERGENCIES

In case of emergency, there's the private La Loma Luz Hospital, in Santa Elena, east of San Ignacio, as well as the public hospital, San Ignacio Hospital.

Hospitals **La Loma Luz Hospital** ✉ Western Hwy., Santa Elena ☎ 824/3253. **San Ignacio Hospital** ✉ Western Hwy., San Ignacio ☎ 824/2066.

Hot Lines **Police** ☎ 824/2111.

Pharmacies **The Pharmacy** ✉ 24 West. St., San Ignacio ☎ 824/2510.

HEALTH

Health standards in the Cayo are high. The water in San Ignacio and Santa Elena comes from a treated municipal system, so it's safe to drink. Resorts in the region have their own safe water systems. There are relatively few mosquitoes or other insects in the Cayo, as the porous limestone terrain means that rain doesn't stand in puddles. A few cases of dengue fever and malaria have been reported in the Cayo, however, so you may want to slather yourself with repellent that contains DEET.

MAIL & SHIPPING

The San Ignacio post office is on Hudson Street. It's open weekdays 8–noon and 1–4:30 and Saturday 8–noon.

Post Offices **San Ignacio** ✉ Hudson St., San Ignacio ☎ 824/2049.

MONEY MATTERS

Although American dollars are accepted everywhere, you can exchange money at the border crossing in Benque Viejo del Carmen. Banks in San Ignacio include Atlantic, Belize Bank, and ScotiaBank. They are all downtown on Burns Avenue. All have ATMs, but only Belize Bank accepts cards issued outside the country.

Banks **Atlantic Bank** ✉ 17 Burns Ave., San Ignacio ☎ 824/2596. **Belize Bank** ✉ 16 Burns Ave., San Ignacio ☎ 824/2031. **ScotiaBank** ✉ Burns Ave. at Riverside St., San Ignacio ☎ 824/4190.

SAFETY

Being close to Guatemala's El Petén region, thousands of Cayo visitors take short trips across the border to view the fantastic ruins of Tikal. It's proximity to this tourist attraction is a boon for the Cayo but also a burden, as the poverty-stricken population of northern Guatemala spills over into relatively affluent Belize. On several occasions armed gangs from Guatemala have robbed tourists around San Ignacio, especially near the El Pilar Mayan site. In early 2004 San Ignacio's mayor was briefly kidnapped and robbed by armed Guatemalans. However, nearly all visitors to the Cayo say they feel quite safe. As a visitor, you are unlikely to encounter any problems.

TOURS

Most jungle lodges offer a full range of day trips. The largest and best lodge-affiliated tour operations are Chaa Creek Expeditions and Windy Hill Tour Company. For cave tours, David's Adventure Tours, Mayawalk Adventures, and Caves Branch Adventure Company are the best. Toni's River Adventures is the leading operator for canoe trips.

Chaa Creek Expeditions ✉ 77 Burns Ave., San Ignacio ☎ 824/2037 🌐 www.chaacreek.com. **Caves Branch Adventure Company** ✉ Mile 41½, Hummingbird Hwy., Belmopan ☎ 824/2800 🌐 www.cavesbranch.com. **David's Adventure Tours** ✉ Savannah St., San Ignacio ☎ 824/3674. **Mayawalk Adventures** ✉ 19 Burns Ave., San Ignacio ☎ 824/3070 🌐 www.mayawalk.com. **Windy Hill Tour Company** ✉ Western Hwy., San Ignacio ☎ 824/2017 🌐 www.windyhillresort.com.

VISITOR INFORMATION

There's a Belize Tourist Industry Association office at the Cahal Pech ruins, but the best way to find out what's going on is to stop by Eva's in San Ignacio, a café that doubles as an unofficial visitor center. Owner Bob Jones, a British ex-soldier, knows the Cayo like the back of his hand. You can also contact local tour operators.

Belize Tourist Industry Association ✉ Cahal Pech, San Ignacio ☎ 824/4236. **Eva's** ✉ 22 Burns Ave., San Ignacio ☎ 824/2267.

PLACENCIA & ENVIRONS

As always in Belize, the transition from one landscape to another is swift and startling. When you approach Dangriga, the lush, mountainous terrain of the north gives way to flat plains bristling with orange trees. The Stann Creek Valley is Belize's San Fernando Valley, the place where most of its fruit is grown. Bananas were the original bumper crop here, and banana plantations are still an important industry. Equally startling is the cultural segue: whereas San Ignacio has a Spanish feeling, this area is strongly Afro-Caribbean.

Tourist dollars, the staple of contemporary Belize, have largely slipped past Dangriga, but they're rapidly transforming Placencia, the region's most striking spot. Several years ago there were only three small resorts north of town. Now there are about 20, stretching up to the village of Seine Bight and beyond. The paving of the Southern Highway from Dangriga all the way to Punta Gorda has made the region much more accessible. Off the main highway, however, most roads consist of red dirt and potholes. Real estate sales are a driving force here in Placencia, Hopkins, and elsewhere along the coast. Much of the seafront land north of Placencia has been divided into lots awaiting development; if things continue at this pace, the area will one day rival Ambergris Caye as Belize's top beach destination.

Tourism in Placencia and elsewhere in southern Belize suffered a major blow in October 2001, when Hurricane Iris slammed the region with 140 mph winds and a 10-foot storm surge. The villages of Seine Bight, Placencia, and Monkey River were badly hit, with more than 90% of the homes destroyed or badly damaged. No lives were lost on the peninsula, but at Big Creek 20 people died when a live-aboard dive boat called *Wave Dancer* capsized, throwing passengers and crew into the swirling black waters. After the storm it took several months for water, electricity, and other services to be restored. Many hotels and restaurants were closed for months, and some older places shuttered for good. Nature heals itself quickly in this climate, though, and entrepreneurs have invested heavily in reconstruction and new buildings. Today, almost all signs of the hurricane have vanished.

Numbers in the margin correspond to bullets on the Cayo and the Deep South map.

Dangriga

5 *160 km (99 mi) southeast of Belmopan.*

With a population of 8,800, Dangriga is the largest town in the south and the home of the Garífuna (or Black Caribs, as they're also known). Perhaps the most unusual of the ethnic groups calling Belize home, the Garífuna's story is both bizarre and moving, an odyssey of exile and dispossession in the wake of the confusion wrought in the New World by the Old. The Garífuna are descended from a group of Nigerian slaves who were shipwrecked on the island of St. Vincent in 1635. The Caribs, St. Vincent's indigenous population, fiercely resisted the outsiders at first, but they eventually overcame their distrust.

In the eyes of the British colonial authorities, the new ethnic group that developed after years of intermarriage was an illegitimate and troublesome presence. Worse still, the Garífuna sided with, and were succored by, the French. After nearly two centuries of guerrilla warfare, the British decided that the best way to solve the problem was to deport them en masse. After a circuitous and tragic journey across the Caribbean, during which thousands perished of disease and hunger, the exiles arrived in Belize.

That the Garífuna have preserved their cultural identity testifies to Belize's extraordinary ability to encourage diversity. They have their own religion, a potent mix of ancestor worship and Catholicism; their own

PERMANENT VACATIONS

THAT WELL-TANNED LADY RELAXING *under a palm tree on the beach may not be a tourist after all. She could be an expatriate who decided to chuck it all and move to Belize. Thousands of Americans, Canadians, Europeans, and Asians have already done so or have bought property and plan to move later, perhaps after retirement.*

Attracted by the idea of comparatively low real estate prices, a frost-free climate, and an awesome spectra of activities, many expats are drawn to Belize, especially to Ambergris Caye, Corozal, and the Cayo. Ambergris Caye has an idyllic Caribbean island atmosphere. Corozal Town and its environs have Belize's lowest living costs, and Mexico is right next door. The Cayo appeals to those who want land for growing fruit trees or keeping a few horses.

With houses renting for as little as BZ$400 a month (though some in San Pedro go for 10 times that amount), and land selling at prices last seen in the United States in the 1960s, retirement dollars can stretch very far here. Beachfront building lots go for as little as BZ$100,000 to BZ$150,000—still pricey, but cheap in comparison to oceanfront lots in Florida or California. There are no major restrictions against foreigners owning land in Belize. Moreover, with English as an official language and English Common Law forming the basis of Belize's legal system, Belize is very accommodating to expats.

In late 2001 the government unveiled a program called the Qualified Retired Persons Incentive Program to attract retirees to Belize. In exchange for depositing BZ$4,000 a month in a Belize bank for living expenses, and proving that you have the resources to do so, anyone aged 45 and older can get official residency, along with the right to import household goods, a car, boat, and even an airplane tax-free. The application costs about BZ$1,500 and is relatively painless. After getting Qualified Retired Persons status, you have almost all the rights of a Belize citizen except you can't vote or work for pay. The Belize Tourist Board (BTB) administers the program, and details are available on its Web site, www.travelbelize.org.

The B.T.B. won't disclose exactly how many applications it's received, but they've gotten at least a few thousand so far. It's a wonder that more people haven't applied: 70 million baby boomers in the United States alone are expected to retire over the next 5 to 20 years. Many of them will be looking for alternatives to cold winters and high prices up north.

For those not quite ready to retire, it's still possible to move to Belize, although work permits are difficult to obtain, and salaries are a fraction of those in the United States, Canada, or Western Europe. The best option may be to invest in or start a business in Belize that employs Belizean workers, thus paving the way for a self-employment work permit and fast-track residency.

Of course, Belize isn't for everyone. And Belize, as seen from the perspective of a full-time resident, isn't the same as the Belize that's experienced by vacationers. Expats anywhere face culture shock, and Belize presents some special situations, including lack of high-tech medical care and a higher risk of theft and burglary than back home.

— Lan Sluder

language, which, like Carib, has separate male and female dialects; their own music, a percussion-oriented sound known as punta rock; and their own social structure, which dissuades young people from marrying outside their community. In writer Marcella Lewis, universally known as Auntie Madé, they also had their own poet laureate. In 2002 the United Nations designated the Garífuna as a World Heritage culture.

For the traveler, there's not much to keep you in Dangriga. But for one day each year, November 19, the town cuts loose with a week of Carnival-style celebrations—this is Garífuna Settlement Day, when these proud people celebrate their arrival in Belize and remember their roots.

Where to Stay & Eat

$$$$ **Mama Noots Jungle Resort.** Being environmentally conscious doesn't have to come at the expense of comfort. A combination solar, wind, and hydro system generates this resort's electricity. Most of the produce served in the open-air dining room is grown on the grounds. Rooms, in thatch cabanas or a modern concrete building, have views of the rugged Maya Mountains. Because the resort is *backabush* (in the forest), owners Kevin and Nanette Denny advise guests to bring lightweight "jungle clothing," plus plenty of insect repellent and an adventuresome spirit. Nearby are the Mayflower archaeological site and miles of jungle trails and waterfalls. The Mayflower site includes two minor ceremonial centers, Maintzunun and T'au Witz, which are still mostly covered in bush. Wildlife spotting and birding are excellent here. ✉ *Near Mayflower archaeological site* ☎ *422/3666* 🌐 *www.mamanoots.com* *6 rooms, 1 duplex cabana* *Dining room, fans, hiking, bar, travel services; no a/c, no room phones, no room TVs, no smoking in rooms* *AE, MC, V* *FAP.*

$–$$ **Pelican Beach Resort.** Despite its linoleum floors and thin wood walls, this waterfront hotel outside Dangriga is the best the town has to offer. There's a dock and small beach area, but the water's not appealing for swimming. The staff is knowledgeable and friendly. Most rooms are in a two-story colonial-style building with a veranda. Some have porches with sea views. The restaurant has dependable food and service. The resort has an annex on Southwater Caye, Pelican's Pouch, an hour away by boat. ✉ *Northeast of Dangriga* ☎ *522/2044* *522/2570* 🌐 *www.pelicanbeachbelize.com* *20 rooms* *Restaurant, fans, dock, boating, bar, laundry service, meeting rooms, travel services; no a/c in some rooms, no phones in some rooms, no TV in some rooms* *AE, MC, V.*

Hopkins

6 *17 km (10 mi) south of Dangriga on the Southern Hwy., then 3⅓ km (2 mi) east on a dirt road.*

Hopkins is an intriguing Garífuna village on the coast about halfway between Dangriga and Placencia. Garífuna culture is more accessible here than in Dangriga. Hopkins has the same toast-color beaches as those in Placencia, and a number of new resorts have opened to take advantage of them. Americans, Canadians, and Europeans are snapping up beachfront land here at prices lower than in Placencia or on Ambergris

Caye, but so far only a few vacation homes have been built. If there's a downside to the area, it's the sandflies, which can be vicious.

Where to Stay & Eat

More exotic than Hopkins' resort dining facilities are places, such as **Iris Restaurant** (✉ Hopkins ☎ No phone) or **Innies Restaurant** (✉ Hopkins ☎ No phone), where you dine in tiny rooms or on the porch of someone's home. Try authentic Garífuna cuisine like *sere* (fish in coconut milk) or *bundiga* (green bananas, fish, and spices in coconut milk); they also offer french fries and burgers. You'll have a wonderful time and won't pay more than BZ$20 per meal.

★ $$$$ **Kanantik Reef & Jungle Resort.** At this all-inclusive luxury resort, you can experience the barrier reef without having to make decisions more complicated than whether to have fish or steak for dinner. Here you can frolic on a palm-lined private beach and snorkel, sail, or kayak at your leisure. Kanantik—a Mopan Maya word meaning "to take care"—has air-conditioned cabanas tucked onto 300 acres south of Hopkins. Echoing African themes, the large and luxuriously outfitted cabanas are striking round structures with conical roofs. Everything except motorized fishing and imported liquors is included in the daily rate. ✉ *Off Southern Hwy., between Hopkins and Placencia peninsula* *Box 1482, Belize City* ☎ *520/8048, 800/965–9689 in U.S.* *www.kanantik.com* *25 cabanas* *Dining room, fans, refrigerators, pool, beach, dive shop, dock, snorkeling, boating, fishing, horseback riding, bar, laundry service, airstrip, Internet, travel services; no room TVs, no kids under 14* *MC, V* *AI.*

$$–$$$$ **Jaguar Reef Lodge.** At night, with a row of torches burning on the beach and the thatch-covered dining room glowing in lamplight, this lodge has an East African feel. Nestled on the coast, it has views over the water in one direction and of the green slopes of the Maya Mountains in the other. Inside the whitewashed stone cottages are soaring pitched ceilings with exposed wooden beams. There's a B&B annex on Coco Plum island, so you can do a coast and caye package. For those who aren't excited about swimming in the sea, there's a seaside pool. Meals (dinner is BZ$48) are served in a waterside dining room with indoor and outdoor seating. You'll find the staff here polite and easygoing. ✉ *Hopkins* ☎ *520/7040, 800/289–5756 in U.S.* *www.jaguarreef.com* *8 rooms, 8 suites, 7 duplex cabanas* *Restaurant, fans, refrigerators, pool, beach, gym, dive shop, dock, snorkeling, fishing, bar, laundry service, Internet, travel services; no room phones, no room TVs, no smoking* *MC, V.*

★ $$$–$$$$ **Hamanasi.** From the dirt road the hotel looks inconspicuous, but Hamasani (Garífuna for "almond") is actually among Belize's superior beach and dive resorts. Upon your arrival, you'll notice that the manicured grounds and lobby are all lined with artwork. The "zero effect" pool seems to stretch to infinity. Choose from regular rooms, gorgeous suites with king-size four-poster beds of barba jolote wood, and "tree houses" on stilts. Most people come here for the diving opportunities, but you won't feel out of place if you want to snorkel or just laze around the pool. The restaurant serves delicious seafood. ✉ *Hopkins* ☎ *520/7073, 877/552–3483 in U.S.* *520/7090* *www.hamanasi.com* *8 rooms, 10 suites* *Restaurant, fans, refrigerators, pool,* *beach, dive shop, dock, boating, fishing, bar, Internet, travel services; no room TVs, no room phones, no smoking* ▭ *MC, V.*

$ **Beaches and Dreams.** New hotels are popping up all around the region, but Beaches and Dreams managed to secure one of the area's nicest tan-color stretches of shoreline. This tiny B&B has two octagonal cottages, each with vaulted ceilings, rattan furniture, and a small veranda just a few feet from the sea. The pub-style restaurant serves some of the best food and coldest drinks in Hopkins. Try the seafood-and-fruit kebabs or the Cajun chicken pizza. ✉ *Sittee Point* ☎ *523/7078* 🌐 *www.beachesanddreams.com* *4 rooms* *Restaurant, fans, beach, bar, travel services; no a/c, no room phone, no room TVs* ▭ *MC, V* *CP.*

¢ **Tipple Tree Beya Hotel.** Tiny Tipple Tree Beya Hotel provides a comfortable alternative to the coast's upmarket resorts. Here you can relax on the beach or kick back in a hammock. Run by friendly Patricia Sturman, the inn has three rooms that are simple but immaculately clean, as well as a separate private cabin with a kitchenette. You can even pitch a tent on the beach. Bicycles and kayaks are available for rent. ✉ *Hopkins* ☎ *520/7006* 🌐 *www.tippletree.net* *3 rooms, 1 with shared bath, 1 cabin* *Beach, snorkeling, travel services; no a/c, no room phones, no room TVs* ▭ *MC, V.*

¢–$ **Toucan Sittee.** Neville Collins ran a store in San Ignacio before he retired to this 20-acre farm on the Sittee River, where he grows 60 different kinds of fruit trees including 10 mango varieties. This peaceful retreat has wood cottages on stilts with three rooms and two small apartments. Between relaxing among the ginger plants, you should try the activities that Collins can arrange, such as canoeing, hiking, and bird-watching. Meals (dinners BZ$18) use organic ingredients grown on the farm. There are delicious vegan and vegetarian options. Like all lodges in these parts, this one can get a bit buggy, so bring repellent. ✉ *Sittee River* ☎ *523/7039* 🌐 *www.toucansittee.info* *3 rooms with shared bath, 2 apartments* *Fans, refrigerators, fishing; no a/c, no room phones, no room TVs* ▭ *MC, V.*

Sports & the Outdoors

The best diving operation in the area is at **Hamanasi** (✉ Hopkins ☎ 520/7073 🌐 www.hamanasi.com). Here you'll find the newest equipment and the biggest boats. **Second Nature Divers** (✉ Sittee River ☎ 523/7038) has a good reputation as well.

Shopping

Jaguar Reef Resort (✉ Hopkins ☎ 520/7040) has a fine little gift shop filled with pottery and embroidery as well as Garífuna crafts. The store also carries Marie Sharp's superb hot sauces, New Age music, and drugstore items like sunscreen and the crucial no-see-um repellent.

Cockscomb Basin Wildlife Sanctuary

★ 7 *48 km (30 mi) southwest of Dangriga.*

The mighty jaguar, once the undisputed king of the Central and South American jungles, is now endangered. But it has a haven in the Cockscomb Basin Wildlife Sanctuary, which covers 102,000 acres of lush rain forest in the Cockscomb Range of the Maya Mountains. Thanks to this reserve, as well as other protected areas around the country, Belize has the highest concentration of jaguars in the world.

Jaguars are shy, nocturnal animals that prefer to keep their distance from humans, so the possibility of viewing one in the wild is small. The jaguar, or *el tigre,* as it's known in Spanish, is nature's great loner, a supremely independent creature that shuns even the company of its own kind. Except during a brief mating period and the six short months the female spends with her cubs before turning them loose, jaguars live alone, roaming the rain forest in splendid isolation. At certain times of year, however, jaguars are routinely spotted here. In November 2001 visitors saw jaguars, including mothers with cubs, nearly every day on the road to the visitor center. They had to get up early, though, as the sightings occurred between 5:30 and 6.

In the 1980s seven jaguars were tagged with radio collars in a misguided attempt by an American naturalist to track their movements. Special steel cages were built to catch them because they had smashed several wooden ones to pieces. A jaguar would enter a cage, trip a door behind it, and find itself captive. The captured jaguars were so powerful that in their desperate attempts to escape they threw the 300-pound cages around like matchboxes. They sheared off most of their teeth as they tried to bite through the steel. Within a year all seven had died.

Other conservation efforts have been more successful. Today there are an estimated 25–30 jaguars (8–10 adult males, 9–10 adult females, and the rest young animals) spread over about 400 square km (154 square mi). This is the world's largest jaguar population. In contrast, the jaguar was hunted to extinction in the United States by the late 1940s.

Cockscomb Basin also has native wildlife aside from the jaguars. You might see other cats—pumas, margays, and ocelots—plus coatis, kinkajous, deer, peccaries, and, last but not least, tapirs. Also known as the mountain cow, this shy, curious creature appears to be half horse, half hippo, with a bit of cow and elephant thrown in. Nearly 300 species of birds have been identified in the Cockscomb Basin, including the keel-billed toucan, the king vulture, several hawk species, and the scarlet macaw.

Within the reserve is Belize's best-maintained system of jungle and mountain trails, most of which lead to at least one outstanding swimming hole. The sanctuary also has spectacular views of Victoria Peak and the Cockscomb Range. Bring serious bug spray with you—the reserve is alive with mosquitoes and tiny biting flies called no-see-ums—and wear long-sleeve shirts and long pants. The best times to hike anywhere in Belize are early morning, late afternoon, and early evening, when temperatures are lower and more animals are on the prowl.

You have to register in a thatch building at Maya Centre on the Southern Highway before proceeding several miles to the visitor center. In the same building is a gift shop selling baskets and slate carvings by local Maya craftspeople, at good prices. The road winds through dense vegetation—splendid cahune palms, purple mimosas, orchids, and big-leaf plantains—and as you go higher the marvelous sound of tropical birds, often resembling strange windup toys, grows stronger and stronger. This is definitely four-wheel-drive terrain. You may have to ford several small rivers as well as negotiate deep, muddy ruts. At the end, in a clearing with hibiscus and bougainvillea bushes, you'll find a little office where you can buy maps of the nature trails, along with restrooms, several picnic tables, cabins, and a campground.

Walking along these 12 well-marked nature trails is a good way to get to know the region. Most are loops of 1–2 km (½–1½ mi), so you can do several in a day. The most strenuous trail takes you up a steep hill, from the top of which is a magnificent view of the entire Cockscomb Basin. ✉ *Outside Maya Centre* ☎ *227/7369* 🎫 *BZ$10* ⏲ *Daily 8–5.*

Where to Stay & Eat

You can camp in the reserve for BZ$10 a night per person, or for a little more money you can stay in pleasant new rooms in cabins with solar-generated electricity for BZ$44 per person. Book in Belize City through the Belize Audubon Society (☎ 223/5004).

¢ **Tutzil Nah Cottages.** Gregoria Chun and his family, Mopan Maya people who've lived in this area for generations, provide accommodations in simple thatch cabanas. Meals also are available, and the Chuns provide a range of tours to Cockscomb and Mayan sites. ✉ *Near Maya Centre, Mile 13 ½, Southern Hwy.* ☎ *520/3044* 🌐 *www.mayacenter.com* *5 cabanas* *No a/c, no room phones, no room TVs* ▭ *No credit cards.*

Maya Beach

8 *56 km (35 mi) south of Dangriga.*

Maya Beach is a sleepy beach community at the northernmost part of the Placencia peninsula, about 24½ km (15 mi) from the Southern Highway, just past the "elbow" in the unpaved road locals call Riversdale. If you come here by road from the Southern Highway, you'll get a quick glimpse, through mangroves, of the startlingly blue Caribbean. All the businesses catering to tourists are off the main road (actually, it's the only road) that leads to Placencia. Maya Beach is the latest front in the peninsula's development, with "For Sale" signs dotting the roadside and several new resorts opening or being planned. These new resorts join a small group of laid-back seaside hotels and cabins. If you stay here, you may want to rent a car, as there's no public transportation up and down the peninsula, and taxis are expensive (about BZ$30 to Placencia).

Where to Stay & Eat

$–$$$ ✕ **Mango of Maya Beach.** Owner and chef Chris Duffy, a painter from Connecticut, serves something different every day in her tiny thatch-top restaurant. All the entrées are sophisticated by Belizean standards—field greens with Dijon vinaigrette, lobster scampi, and tropical fruit fondue are often on the menu. Lunch and dinner are served daily, but she appreciates it if you let her know you're coming. ✉ *Maya Beach, 2 km (1 mi) north of Seine Bight, on main road* ☎ *614/7023* ▭ *MC, V.*

$$$$ **Zeboz Caribbean Resort.** Transplant an upscale Texas condo community to Belize, and you might end up with something like Zeboz. The 9-acre

resort opened in 2003 and has about everything you'd expect: tennis courts, an upscale restaurant with a wine cellar, a swimming pool that's among the largest in Belize, and 600 feet of sandy beachfront, with a dock that goes out some 200 feet. Sandfleas can be pesky here. The one-bedroom apartments are spacious and have a whirlpool bath and tile floors. If you don't want to leave, you can buy a condo here, starting at about BZ$300,000. ✉ *Maya Beach, 6½ km (4 mi) north of Seine Bight* ☎ *520/4110, 877/932–6946 in U.S.* 📠 *520/4112* 🌐 *www.zeboz.com* *20 condo apartments* *Restaurant, fans, kitchenettes, beach, pool, tennis, dock, dive shop, fishing, snorkeling, bar, Internet, travel services* 💳 *AE, MC, V.*

$$ **Calico Jack's.** Owner Chester Williams developed a new hurricane-resistant technique, employing foam-filled concrete blocks, to build this small beachfront resort at the peninsula's far north end. Atop the rather odd-looking blocks, decorated with what are supposed to be Mayan glyphs (but which look more like grade-school drawings), rest wood beams and cohune thatch roofs. Whatever your feelings about this resort's appearance, you won't be disappointed by the stunning beach. There are two tempting private docks with thatch palapas and hammocks. ✉ *Maya Beach, 6½ km (4 mi) north of Seine Bight* ☎ *523/8009* 📠 *520/8103* 🌐 *www.calicojacksvillage.com* *9 cabanas* *Restaurant, fans, beach, pool, docks, fishing, snorkeling, bicycles, badminton, bar, Internet, travel services; no a/c in some rooms, no room phones, no room TVs* 💳 *AE, MC, V* 🍽 *CP.*

$$ **Green Parrot.** Families with younger kids will appreciate these Mennonite-built cottages along a beautiful beach as each has a dining area and a fully stocked kitchenette. The sleeping quarters are upstairs in a loftlike space with a pitched wooden roof. One nifty feature is an octagonal wall panel, operated by pulleys, that can be opened for a bedside view of the ocean. Two of the thatch cabanas have outdoor showers. The beachfront restaurant and bar are decorated with high-back chairs of varnished cane that were crafted locally. ✉ *Maya Beach, 6½ km (4 mi) north of Seine Bight* ☎ *523/8009* 📠 *523/2488* 🌐 *www.greenparrot-belize.com* *6 cabins, 2 cabanas* *Restaurant, fans, beach, dock, snorkeling, bar; no a/c, no room phones, no room TVs* 💳 *AE, MC, V* 🍽 *CP.*

$$ **Singing Sands.** The six wood-and-thatch cabanas here are small and simply decorated with Guatemalan needlecrafts. They were relocated after Hurricane Iris and now have better views. Singing Sands has its own 25-foot boat for snorkeling, a dock with a nice area for swimming, and a pool for those who'd rather take a dip in freshwater. ✉ *Maya Beach* ☎ *800/649–3007 in U.S.* 🌐 *www.singingsands.com* *6 cabanas* *Restaurant, fans, refrigerators, pool, beach, dive shop, dock, bar, Internet, travel services; no a/c, no room phones, no room TVs* 💳 *AE, D, MC, V.*

$ **Barnacle Bill's.** If you're the independent type, this property has a pair of wooden bungalows set among palm trees about 60 feet from the surf. Each cottage is on stilts and has a private bath and a kitchen where you can prepare your own meals. There are complimentary bikes and kayaks. ✉ *23 Maya Beach Way* ☎📠 *523/8010* 🌐 *www.gotobelize.com/barnacle* *2 cottages* *Fans, beach, snorkeling, bicycles, fishing; no a/c, no room phones, no room TVs* *MC, V.*

Seine Bight

9 *65½ km (40 mi) south of Dangriga.*

Like Placencia, its creole neighbor to the south, Seine Bight is a small coastal fishing village. It may not be like this for long, though, as Placencia's resorts are stretching north to and through this Garífuna community. The beach is among the best in Belize, even though garbage sometimes mars the view. Hotels do rake and clean their beachfronts, and several community cleanups have been organized in an effort to solve this problem. All the businesses catering to tourists are off the main road (actually, it's the only road) that leads to Placencia. Like Placencia village, Seine Bight was devastated by Hurricane Iris in October 2001, and many of the village's simple wooden homes were destroyed.

Where to Stay & Eat

★ **$$$–$$$$** **Inn at Robert's Grove.** Energetic New Yorkers Bob and Risa Frackman invite you to stay at their place on a palm-lined stretch of beach. You can play tennis and swim in the sea or one of the beachside pools. Their chef packs lunches for boat rides to deserted cayes and serves dinner in the seaside dining room. Such personal attention makes this one of Belize's top beach resorts. Opt for the posh suites, with verandas overlooking the ocean. The hotel has a dive center and a private caye for picnics or overnight trips. ✉ *1 km (½ mi) south of Seine Bight* ☎ *523/3565, 800/565–9757 in U.S.* 📠 *523/3567* 🌐 *www.robertsgrove.com* *20 rooms, 12 suites* *2 restaurants, fans, some refrigerators, cable TV, 2 tennis courts, 2 pools, gym, beach, dive shop, dock, snorkeling, windsurfing, boating, fishing, bars, shop, laundry service, travel services* *AE, MC, V.*

$$–$$$ **Nautical Inn.** The rooms at this inn are in two-tier octagonal buildings, shipped from North Carolina. They've got American-style fixtures, firm mattresses, and glass-wall showers. The pool is one of the nicest on the peninsula. There are canoes as well as a dive boat to transport you to the reef. On Wednesday evening the hotel hosts Garífuna drummers and coconut bowling. ✉ *Seine Bight* ☎ *523/3595, 800/688–0377 in U.S.* 📠 *523/3594* 🌐 *www.nauticalinnbelize.com* *12 rooms* *Restaurant, fans, some refrigerators, cable TV, pool, beach, dive shop, dock* *AE, MC, V.*

Shopping

Painter and writer Lola Delgado moved to Seine Bight from Belize City in the late 1980s. Her workshop, **Lola's Art,** displays her cheerful acrylic paintings of local scenes (BZ$100 and up). She also sells hand-painted cards and some of her husband's wood carvings. Espresso and pastries are available. Open 9 AM–10 PM, the workshop is up a flight of steps in a tiny wooden house off the main street, behind the football field.

Placencia

10 *8 km (5 mi) south of Seine Bight, 85 km (52 mi) south of Dangriga.*

Set in a sheltered half-moon bay with crystal-clear water and almost 5 km (3 mi) of palm-dotted white sand, this fishing village is straight out of a Robert Louis Stevenson novel. Founded by pirates, the community is now inhabited by an extraordinary mélange of peoples. To the west the Cockscomb Range ruffles the tropical sky with its jagged peaks; to the east a line of uninhabited cayes grazes the horizon. From here you can dive along the reef, hike into the jungle, explore the Mayan ruins at Lubantuun, or treat yourself to some of the best sportfishing in the country. Once you arrive, you'll probably just want to lie in a hammock with a good book, perhaps getting up long enough to cool off in the waves.

Placencia is so small that it doesn't even have a main street—it has a concrete path just wide enough for two people. Setting off purposefully from the southern end of town, the path meanders through everyone's backyard, passes wooden cottages on stilts overrun with bougainvillea and festooned with laundry, then, as if it had forgotten where it was headed in the first place, peters out abruptly in a little clearing filled with lovely white morning glories. Stroll along the sidewalk, and you've seen the town. If you don't mind it being a little rough around the edges, you'll be utterly enchanted by this rustic village, where the palm trees rustle, the waves lap the shore, and no one is in a hurry.

Along the path are most of the village's quaint inns and palapa-covered cafés, which serve mainly burgers, rice and beans, and a bit of seafood. With the opening of more and more small resorts up the peninsula, Placencia's restaurants are beginning to compete with those in Ambergris Caye.

In 2001 the eye of Hurricane Iris came ashore right at Placencia. Few homes or hotels were spared, and many of the old frame structures, especially on the sea side, were blown down or washed away forever. Today, however, except for a few vacant lots and some gaps in lines of coconut palms, you wouldn't know that a storm had blown through.

Where to Stay & Eat

$–$$$ ✕ **Pickled Parrot Bar & Grill.** This popular feet-in-the-sand restaurant and bar is in the heart of Placencia. Fresh seafood is the main draw, but owner Wende Bryan also offers pizza on Friday and burgers every day. ✉ *Off main road, behind Wallen's Market* ☎ *523/3330* ▭ *AE, MC, V.*

$$$$ ✕🏨 **Turtle Inn.** Francis Ford Coppola's second hotel in Belize is among

Fodor'sChoice ★

the country's most exotic resorts on one of Placencia's best beaches. Furnishings, art, and most of the construction materials were selected in Bali by Coppola and his wife. The two-bedroom seafront villas have not one or two, but three bathrooms (two Japanese-style ones indoors and one in a walled outdoor garden). Should you need anything, you're as-

Pickled Parrot . . . **6**
Harry's Cozy Cabanas **8**
Kitty's Place **2**
Lydia's Guesthouse **5**
Mariposa Beach Suites . . . **1**
Manatee Inn . . . **4**
Tradewinds **7**
Turtle Inn **3**

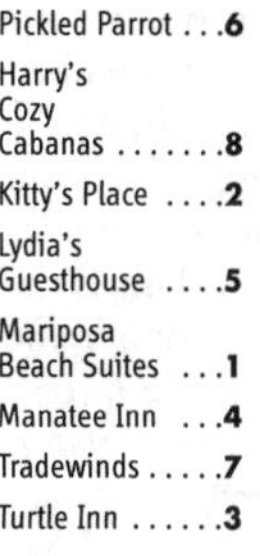

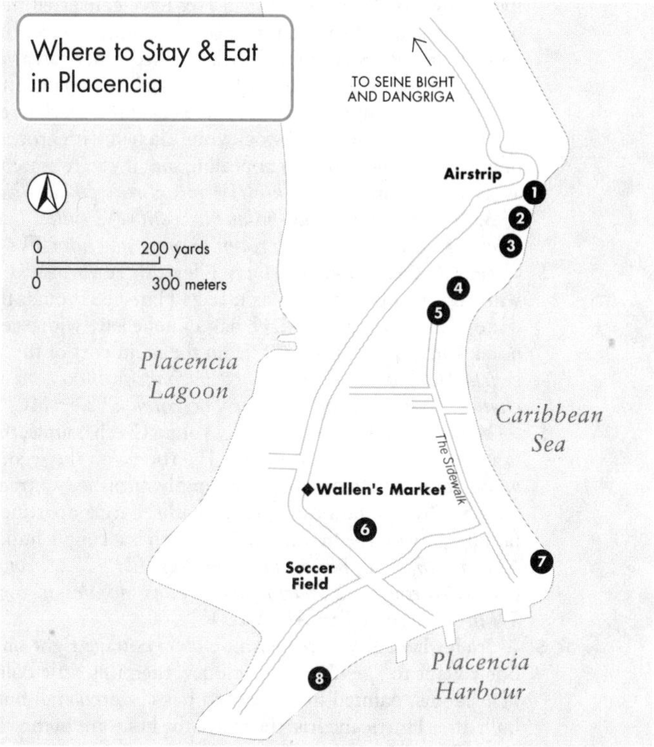

signed a "houseman" with walkie-talkie. The open-air Gaugin Beach Grill is great for pizza (baked in a wood-burning oven), seafood, and Neibaum-Coppola wines. ✉ *Placencia village* ☎ *800/746–3743 in U.S. and Canada* 🌐 *www.blancaneauxlodge.com* ⇨ *12 cabanas* ♨ *Restaurant, fans, pool, beach, dive shop, boating, shop, travel services; no a/c, no room phones, no room TVs* ▭ *AE, MC, V* 🍴 *CP.*

¢–$$$ **Kitty's Place.** Opened in 1987, Kitty's has stood the test of time. It has a barefoot feel that newer places can't duplicate. On one of the peninsula's most beautiful stretches of beach, it offers a mixed bag of accommodations, from single rooms to studios and three prime seafront cottages, now with air-conditioning. The refurbished upstairs restaurant, decorated with Bob Marley posters, is lively and serves mouthwatering local fare. For BZ$600, Kitty will pack you off to French Louie Caye, your own private island for the night. The resort also rents a dozen nearby houses by the week. ✉ *2½ km (1½ mi) north of Placencia* ☎ *523/3227* 📠 *523/3226* 🌐 *www.kittysplace.com* ⇨ *8 rooms, 2 with shared bath, 3 cabanas, 12 rental houses* ♨ *Restaurant, pool, beach, dive shop, boating, shop, Internet, travel services; no a/c in some rooms, no room phones, no TV in some rooms* ▭ *AE, D, MC, V.*

$$ **Mariposa Beach Suites.** Wings painted on posts in the gardenlike grounds signal that you've arrived at Mariposa (Spanish for "butterfly"). Owners Peter and Marcia Fox have converted the ground floor of their beachfront home into a brace of suites, each with a queen bed and kitchen. Pamela Braun, a Belize-based American artist, painted the Mayan decorations on the walls. Out back is a small cottage where you can lounge in your own private palapa near the beach or on the veranda. If you like, the Foxes will stock your kitchen with groceries. This is the opposite of a big resort, an appealing spot if you're searching for a home away from home. ✉ *2½ km (1½ mi) north of Placencia* ☎ *523/4069* 🖷 *523/4076* 🌐 *www.mariposabelize.com* *2 suites, 1 cottage* *Fans, kitchens, beach; no a/c, no room phones, no room TVs* ▭ *MC, V.*

$ **Harry's Cozy Cabanas.** Harry Eiley's three varnished-wood cabanas with screened porches are as nice as Harry is, though they don't have quite as much character. Each has a kitchenette with a refrigerator. The hotel is in a quiet area away from the main part of the village. ✉ *Placencia Harbor* ☎ *523/3155* *harbaks@yahoo.com* *Fans, kitchenettes; no a/c, no room phones, no room TVs* ▭ *MC, V.*

$ **Manatee Inn.** Run by a friendly young Czech couple, the Manatee Inn is a good value for your money. The rooms on the second floor of this wood-frame two-story lodge are simply furnished, extremely clean, and have hardwood floors and private baths. Larger apartments, perfect for families, are on the first floor. The beach is a couple hundred feet away. ✉ *At north end of Placencia village* ☎🖷 *523/4083* 🌐 *www.manateeinn.com* *6 rooms, 2 apartments* *Fans; no a/c, no room phones, no TV in some rooms* ▭ *AE, MC, V.*

★ $ **Tradewinds.** If you're yearning for a cottage right on the beach but don't want to spend a lot of money, then this little colony is for you. Five cabins, painted in Caribbean pastels, are small but pleasant. Rebuilt after Hurricane Iris, they have the best spot in the village, secluded about 20 feet from the sea at the peninsula's south point. ✉ *South Point, Placencia* ☎ *523/3122* *5 cabins* *Fans, refrigerators, beach, snorkeling; no a/c, no room phones, no room TVs* ▭ *MC, V.*

¢ **Lydia's Guesthouse.** For cheap and cheerful, plus friendly and clean, stay at this budget guesthouse in Placencia village. Many guests become regulars, coming back again and again. You can use the refrigerator and basic shared kitchen to prepare your meals. Owner Lydia Villaneuva also manages several nearby rental houses and apartments, if you need more space. ✉ *North end of Placencia village* ☎ *523/3117* 🖷 *523/3354* 🌐 *www.placencia.com/members/lydias.html* *8 rooms, all with shared bath* *Fans; no a/c, no room phones, no room TVs* ▭ *AE, MC, V.*

Sports & the Outdoors

FISHING The fly-fishing on the flats off the cayes east of Placencia is some of Belize's best. You'll encounter plentiful tarpon—they flurry 10 deep in the water at times—as well as permit, bonefish, and snook. Most of the better hotels can arrange guides. If you want a local guide, call **Kevin Modera** (☎ 523/4018 🌐 www.kevinmodera.com). He has great information about fishing in Placencia.

SAILING **The Moorings** (✉ Placencia Harbor, Placencia ☎ 888/952–8420 in U.S.) offers bareboat catamaran charters, with a week's sailing going for around BZ$9,000. **Talisman** (✉ Placencia Harbor, Placencia) is a 52-foot ketch offering day sailing trips for BZ$240 per person or longer trips from BZ$540 to BZ$650 including meals and drinks. **TMM Placencia** (✉ Placencia Harbor, Placencia ☎ 800/633–0155 in U.S.), also in San Pedro, expanded into Placencia in 2003. Rates vary, depending on boat type and time of year, but range from BZ$3,700 to more than BZ$16,000 a week, not including provisions, cruising fee (BZ$30 per person), and incidentals. Skippers and cooks are each an additional BZ$200 per day.

SCUBA DIVING

By the time you get this far south, the reef is as much as 33 km (20 mi) offshore, necessitating boat rides of at least 45 minutes to reach dive sites. Because this part of the reef has fewer cuts and channels, it's also more difficult to get out to the seaward side, where you'll find the best diving. As a result, most of the diving in this region is done from off-shore cayes, which are surrounded by small reefs, usually with gently sloping drop-offs of about 80–100 feet. This isn't the place for spectacular wall dives—you're better off staying in the north or heading out to the atolls. Near Moho Caye, southeast of Placencia, you'll find brilliant red and yellow corals and sponges that rarely appear elsewhere in Belize. Whale sharks, gentle giants of the sea, appear off Placencia, in the Gladden Spit area, in late spring and early summer. You can snorkel or dive with them on day trips (around BZ$160–BZ$300) from Placencia. The best time to see whale sharks is three or four days before and after a full moon April through early June.

Diving costs a little more in Placencia than elsewhere. All-day trips, including two-tank dive, all gear, and lunch, run BZ$150–BZ$200. Snorkeling is about BZ$80–BZ$100 for a trip that lasts almost all day.

Most of the larger resorts, like the Inn at Robert's Grove and Turtle Inn, have good dive shops. Brian Young runs the respected **Seahorse Dive Shop** (☎ 523/3166). For snorkeling trips and gear there's **Ocean Motion** (☎ 523/3363), on the sidewalk in the heart of Placencia village (by the grocery store).

Placencia & Environs A to Z

AIR TRAVEL

Both Tropic Air and Maya Island Air fly to Placencia from Belize City (BZ$118 from the municipal airport, BZ$140 from the international one). There are more than 20 flights daily between Belize City and Placencia. The airstrip is about 3 km (2 mi) north of Placencia's center, so you'll probably want to take a taxi (BZ$10 from the center of town) if your hotel doesn't provide a shuttle.

Maya Island Air ✉ Placencia airstrip ☎ 523/3475 🌐 www.mayaairways.com. **Tropic Air** ✉ Placencia airstrip ☎ 523/3410 🌐 www.tropicair.com.

BUS TRAVEL

For routes north to Belmopan and Dangriga, and south to Punta Gorda, try Southern Transport, a successor to Z-Line. The main bus stop in Placencia is near the Shell station. The bus station in Dangriga is seven blocks south of town on the main road, near the Texaco and Shell stations.

Southern Transport ✉ 3 Havana St., Dangriga ☎ 522/2160.

CAR RENTAL

Budget and other rental agencies in Belize City will deliver a car to Placencia for a fee of around BZ$130.

CAR TRAVEL

To get to Placencia, head southeast from Belmopan on the Hummingbird Highway. Once a potholed nightmare, the thoroughfare is now one of Belize's best roads, as well as its most scenic. On your right rise the jungle-covered Maya Mountains, largely free of signs of human habitation except for the occasional field of corn or beans.

If you want to drive directly from Belize City to Placencia, take the turnoff at Mile 30 on the Western Highway for Dangriga and the south. The 60-km (36-mi) Manatee Road is unpaved—dusty in dry weather, sometimes flooded after rains—but it saves about three-quarters of an hour on the drive south.

The Southern Highway is now beautifully paved from Dangriga south. From the Southern Highway to Placencia most of the 42 km (25 mi) road is unpaved and can be treacherous after rains, even for four-wheel-drive vehicles.

EMERGENCIES

Although Placencia now has a nurse, an acupuncturist, a part-time chiropractor, and a natural healer, for serious medical attention you should go to Dangriga.

Hospitals **Dangriga Regional Hospital** ✉ Stann Creek District Hwy., Dangriga ☎ 522/2078.

HEALTH

Malaria and dengue fever are present in the region's more remote reaches. The water supply in Dangriga isn't dependable, so make sure to drink bottled water. Placencia and Hopkins have safe, treated water.

MAIL & SHIPPING

The Placencia post office is on the second floor of a wooden building at the south end of the sidewalk. It's usually open 8:30–noon and 1–4 weekdays.

Post Offices **Placencia** ✉ South end of sidewalk ☎ 62/3104.

MONEY MATTERS

In Placencia, Atlantic Bank is open weekdays 8–noon. None of the ATMs in town accept foreign-issued cards. Belize Bank in Dangriga has an ATM that (usually) accepts foreign cards on the PLUS and CIRRUS networks. First Caribbean International Bank (formerly Barclays) in Dangriga has an ATM that may accept your card.

Banks **Atlantic Bank** ✉ At end of main road, Placencia ☎ 523/3386. **Belize Bank** ✉ 24 St. Vincent St., Dangriga ☎ 522/2903. **First Caribbean International Bank** ✉ Commerce St., Dangriga ☎ 522/2015.

TAXIS

If you need a ride to the airport in Dangriga, call Neal's Taxi. Fare from downtown to the airstrip at the town's north end costs about BZ$6. Taxis are more expensive in Placencia, given the relatively short distances involved. It's BZ$30 one-way from Placencia to Maya Beach, BZ$10 from Placencia village to the airstrip. Your hotel can arrange a taxi for you.

Neal's Taxi ✉ 1 St. Vincent St., Dangriga ☎ 522/3309.

TOURS

Many tour guides and operators offer dive and snorkel trips to Laughing Bird or other cayes, wildlife tours to Monkey River, and excursions to Maya ruins such as Nim Li Punit or Lubaantun. For the more adventurous traveler, Toadal Adventures has excellent biking, hiking, and kayaking tours.

Toadal Adventures Belize ✉ Point Placencia, Placencia ☎ 253/3207 🌐 www.toadaladventure.com.

1

VISITOR INFORMATION

The Placencia office of the Belize Tourism Industry Association is in a building near the gas station at the village's south end. The agency publishes the *Placencia Breeze,* an informative monthly newspaper. Placencia has a very helpful Web site listing all accommodations, restaurants, and bars, 🌐 www.placencia.com. Hopkins has an interesting Web site put together by locals, 🌐 www.hopkinsbelize.com

Belize Tourism Industry Association ✉ Point Placencia, Placencia ☎ 523/4045.

TOLEDO & THE DEEP SOUTH

For many years ill-maintained roads, spotty communications, and the country's highest annual rainfall—as much as 160 inches—kept Belize's southernmost region off-limits to all but the most adventurous of travelers. The precipitation hasn't changed (you'll need boots and an umbrella in the rainy season), but with improvements to the Southern Highway—all of the highway has been beautifully paved, except for a short stretch near Golden Stream which should be paved by the time you read this—and the opening of new lodges and hotels, the riches of the Toledo district are finally becoming accessible. It's similar to the Cayo district 10 years ago, except that the flora and fauna are even more dramatic.

Toledo is the only part of Belize that has a genuine rain forest, and its canopy of trees conceals a plethora of wildlife, including jaguars, margays, and tapirs, and an assortment of tropical birds. The area's rich Mayan heritage is just being unearthed, including a major site currently being excavated by a team from the National Geographic Foundation. By all accounts, it dwarfs even Caracol.

Toledo doesn't have good beaches: the waters of the Gulf of Honduras are invariably muddy from silt deposited by numerous rivers flowing from the Maya Mountains. But the cayes off the coast are well worth exploring. The closest are the Snake Cayes; farther out are the Sapadilla Cayes, the largest of which is Hunting Caye. A horseshoe-shape bay at the caye's eastern end has beaches of white coral where turtles nest in late summer.

Hurricane Iris swept across Toledo in 2001. It did little damage to Punta Gorda, but it wreaked havoc on the thatch homes of southern

Toledo's Mayan villages, leaving 13,000 people homeless. The storm destroyed an estimated 16,000 acres of bananas, rice, corn, and other crops and blew down tens of thousands of trees, including many mature tropical hardwoods. With government and private help, Toledo residents have rebuilt their homes, and the tropical climate of southern Belize quickly regenerated the vegetation.

Punta Gorda

11 *164 km (102 mi) south of Placencia.*

Most journeys south begin in the region's administrative center, Punta Gorda. Founded in 1867 by immigrants from the United States and settled by missionaries, Punta Gorda once boasted 12 sugar estates, each with its own mill. By 1910, however, the town had almost been swallowed by the jungle. Its fortunes revived after World War II, when Britain built an important military base here, but when that closed in 1994, the linchpin of the local economy was yanked out. With increased tourist dollars, PG (as it's affectionately known) is starting to pick up again, but the town maintains a frontier atmosphere. Don't expect many tourist services. When you ask for ice at your hotel, you may get a blank stare. Restaurant food ranges from fair to truly awful. In keeping with its evangelical origins, many visitors are missionaries who vie for the souls of the Maya by offering them free dentistry or medicine. But on market days, Wednesday and Saturday, the town comes to life with Guatemalan vendors, who pack the downtown area with colorful fruit and vegetable stands.

Where to Stay & Eat

¢–$$ ✕ **Grace's.** An established spot, Grace's has genuine values and serves a hearty plate of beans and rice and other Belizean staples. Get a seat near the entrance and eye the town's street life. This is PG's best place for a full breakfast of eggs, bacon, fry jacks and, of course, beans. For dinner you can always get chicken, but you can usually get fresh fish, too. In the same area and quite popular are Emery's and Earth Runnins, if you tire of Grace's. ✉ *19 Main St.* ☎ *No phone* ▭ *No credit cards.*

$$$ **El Pescador South Resort & Adventure Center.** One of the world's best permit fisheries is in the Gulf of Honduras: bonefish, tarpon, and snook are all plentiful here. Indeed, El Pescador PG (associated with Ambergris Caye's El Pesacador) opened in 2002 to capitalize on the area's fishing opportunities. On 470 acres above the Rio Grande River (take a tram to the bottom), the fishing lodge has awesome views of the sea and jungle. Howler monkeys troop by regularly. After a day on a fishing skiff or exploring the Toledo rain forest, dive into the pool, then sup on fish and fresh vegetables from the lodge's farm. The spacious cottages have vaulted ceilings, tile floors, and ice-cold air-conditioning. ✉ *8 km (5 mi) north of Punta Gorda* *Box 135, Punta Gorda* ☎ *722/0050, 800/242–2017 in U.S.* *722/0051* *www.elpescadorpg.com* *12 cottages* *Dining room, fans, bar, pool, billiards, fishing, shops, travel services; no room phones, no room TVs* ▭ *MC, V.*

$ **Sea Front Inn.** With its pitched roofs and stone-and-wood facade, this four-story hotel may remind you of a ski lodge in the Swiss Alps. Directly overlooking the Gulf of Honduras, with the green humps of the Saddle Back Mountains as a backdrop, its top floors command especially spectacular views. There are a dozen single and double rooms and two suites with kitchenettes. Each is unique, fitted with with Belizean hardwoods. A third-floor restaurant (open only for breakfast) has a roof supported by rosewood tree trunks etched with Mayan carvings. Unfortunately, service here leaves a lot to be desired. ✉ *Front St., Punta Gorda* ☎🖷 *722/2300* 🌐 *www.seafrontinn.com* *12 rooms* *Dining room, fans, cable TV, snorkeling, travel services; no room phones* 💳 *MC, V.*

¢ **Nature's Way Guest House.** In this ramshackle house near the water are an assortment of rooms for travelers on a budget. Like a hostel, it's a meeting place for travelers exploring the frontier or heading on to Guatemala or Honduras. Choose from one of the spartan rooms or a bunk in one of the dorm-style rooms. On the breakfast-only menu are tofu, yogurt, and granola. The owner is glad to share with you his strong opinions on Toledo and just about anything else. ✉ *83 Front St., Punta Gorda* ☎ *722/2119* *17 rooms with shared bath* *Restaurant, travel services; no a/c, no room phones, no room TVs* 💳 *No credit cards.*

¢ **T.E.A.** The Toledo Ecotourism Association arranges stays in one of 10 participating Mayan and Q'eqchí villages. You stay in a simple but clean guest house, then visit Mayan homes for breakfast, lunch, and dinner. The English-speaking staff will arrange vegetarian or special meals. During the day there are walks to the nearby ruins or to waterfalls that empty into shimmering pools. For some this is a rare opportunity to learn about a culture. For others chickens running in and out may be a bit too authentic an experience. ✉ *Front St., Punta Gorda* ☎ *722/2096* 🖷 *722/2199* *ttea@btl.net* *Hiking; no a/c, no room phones, no room TVs* 💳 *No credit cards.*

Sports & the Outdoors

FISHING For bonefish and tarpon head to the estuary flats at the end of the Río Grande. **Fish & Fun** (☎ 722/2670), operated by George Coleman and Ovel Leonardo, runs snorkeling and fly-fishing trips to nearby rivers and the cayes. **El Pescador** (☎ 722/0050, 800/242–2017 in U.S.) can provide good local guides.

SCUBA DIVING This far south the reef has pretty much broken up, but individual cayes have their own small reef systems. The best of the bunch is at the Sapodilla cayes, which have great wall dives. The only drawback is that they are 64 km (40 mi) off the coast: a day's dive trip will cost BZ$350 per person. **Sea Hunt Adventures** (☎ 722/2845) can arrange diving, snorkeling, and fishing trips.

The Maya Heartland

Drive a few miles out of town, and you'll find yourself in the heartland of the Maya people. Half the population of Toledo is Maya, a far higher proportion than any other region, and you'll find the people here are more cohesive and more political than anywhere else in Belize. The Toledo Maya Cultural Council has created an ambitious network of Maya-run guesthouses, and in 1995 it initiated the Mayan Mapping Project. By collating oral history and evidence of ancient Mayan settlements, the project hopes to secure rights to land that the Maya have occupied for centuries, but that the Belizean government have ceded to multinational logging companies.

The Maya divide into two groups: Mopan Maya and Q'eqchí-speaking peoples from the Guatemalan highlands. Most of the latter are recent arrivals, refugees from repression and overpopulation. Each group tends to keep to itself, living in separate villages and preserving unique traditions. The village of **San Antonio,** a market town 56 km (35 mi) west of Punta Gorda, is Toledo's second-largest town. It was settled by people from the Guatemalan village of San Luis, who revere their former patron saint. The village church, built of stones carted off from surrounding Mayan ruins, has a stained-glass window donated by another city with a connection to the saint: St. Louis, Missouri. The people of San Antonio haven't forgotten their ancient heritage, though, and each June 13 they take to the streets for a festival that dates back to pre-Columbian times. Like other parts of Toledo, San Antonio lost many of buildings to Hurricane Iris in 2001.

A little farther west is the Q'eqchí village of **San Pedro Columbia,** a cheerful cluster of brightly painted buildings and thatch houses. One of the most eye-catching is a raspberry-red grocery called the People Little Store. On the way to San Pedro Columbia, don't miss **Blue Creek,** a beautiful stretch of river dotted with turquoise swimming holes. Unfortunately, many mature hardwood trees were felled by Hurricane Iris. A path up the riverbank leads to a series of dramatic caves. The Hokeb Ha Cave is fairly easy to explore on your own, but others should be visited only with a local guide. International Zoological Expeditions, a Connecticut-based student travel organization, has established a **jungle lodge** (✉ 210 Washington St., Sherborn, MA 01770 ☎ 508/655–1461, 800/548–5843 in U.S. 📠 508/655–4445) at Blue Creek, with seven rustic cabanas and a restaurant. Don't swim in the river at night—a poisonous snake called the fer-de-lance likes to take nocturnal dips.

Three of Toledo's major Mayan sites have already been excavated: Nim Li Punit, Uxbenka, and Lubaantun. **Nim Li Punit,** a Late Classic site, was discovered in 1976. Twenty-five stelae were unearthed, including one 30 feet tall, the largest ever found in Belize. In 1986 a royal tomb was excavated. Sadly, few of these artifacts remain. There's an informative visitor center on the premises. ✉ *37 km (22 mi) northwest of Punta Gorda* 🎫 *BZ$10.*

Lubaantun, which lies beyond the village of San Pedro Columbia, is also a Late Classic site. It was discovered in 1924 by German archaeologist Thomas Gann, who gave it a name meaning "place of fallen stones." Lubaantun must have been an awe-inspiring sight: on top of a conical hill, with views to the sea in one direction and the Maya Mountains in the other, its stepped layers of white-plaster stone would have towered above the jungle like a wedding cake. No one knows exactly what function the structures served, but the wealth of miniature masks and whistles found suggests it was a center of ceramic production. The trio of ball courts and the central plaza with tiered seating for 10,000 spectators seems like a Maya Madison Square Garden.

In the last century, Lubaantun became the scene of the biggest hoax in modern archaeology. After it was excavated in the 1920s, a British adventurer named F. A. Mitchell-Hedges claimed to have stumbled on what became known as the Crystal Skull. Mitchell-Hedges described the incident in a potboiler, *Danger, My Ally,* in 1951. According to the book, the Crystal Skull was found under an altar at Lubaantun by his daughter Anna. Mitchell-Hedges portrayed himself as a serious archaeologist and explorer: in truth, he was a magazine hack who was later exposed in England as a fraud and a grave robber. The Crystal Skull made good copy. Also known as the Skull of Doom, it was supposedly used by Mayan high priests to zap anyone they didn't care for. Mitchell-Hedges claimed it was 3,600 years old and had taken 150 years to fashion by rubbing a block of pure rock crystal with sand. A similar skull, in the possession of the British Museum, shows signs of having been manufactured with a dentist's drill. Anna Mitchell-Hedges, who today lives in Ontario, has promised to one day reveal the secret. So far, she has adamantly refused to allow the Crystal Skull to be tested and has denied all requests by the Belizean government to return it. ✉ *Northwest of Punta Gorda* 🎫 *BZ$5.*

Where to Stay & Eat

$$ **The Lodge at Big Falls.** You can relax beside a meandering jungle river, listen to otters splashing, and admire colorful butterflies at this small lodge in Toledo. On 30 placid acres beside the Rio Grande River and near the village of Big Falls, there are amazing birding opportunities here: 350 species have been recorded within 5 mi of the lodge. American owners Marta and Rob Hirons built the six thatch cabanas with tile floors and private baths. After dinner (BZ$48) you can read up on naturalist lore in the lodge's Resource Center, where you can use satellite Internet by the light of kerosene lamps. ✉ *Off Mile 79, Southern Hwy.* *Box 103, Punta Gorda* ☎ *No phone* 🌐 *www.thelodgeatbigfalls.com* *6 cabanas* *Restaurant, hiking, bar, bicycles, library, shop, Internet, travel services; no a/c, no room phones, no room TVs* 💳 *MC, V.*

$ **Tranquility Lodge.** Swim in pristine Jacinto Creek or just relax in the gardens at this small and serene lodge on 20 acres near the town of Jacintoville. There aren't even any phones to disturb you. The ground-floor rooms are attractively furnished, and the price (BZ$100) makes peace and quiet affordable. The Verandah restaurant was briefly southern Belize's best restaurant, but now prepares meals only for guests. ✉ *First driveway on right on San Felipe Rd., off Southern Hwy. near Jacintoville, Toledo, 11 ½ km (7 mi) north of Punta Gorda* ☎ *No phone* 🌐 *www.tranquility-lodge.com* *4 rooms* *Dining room, hiking, bar, Internet, travel services; no room phones, no room TVs* 💳 *No credit cards* *CP.*

Toledo & the Deep South A to Z

AIR TRAVEL

Maya Island Air and Tropic Air fly south to Punta Gorda from both the municipal (BZ$152 one-way) and international (BZ$177 one-way) airports. There are about five flights daily on each airline. The Punta Gorda airstrip is on the town's west side from the town square, walk four blocks west on Prince Street.

Maya Island Air ✉ Punta Gorda airstrip ☎ 722/2856. **Tropic Air** ✉ Prince St. ☎ 722/2008.

BOAT & FERRY TRAVEL

Several water taxi services, including Requena's, provide daily boats, usually departing around 9 AM from Punta Gorda, to Puerto Barrios, Guatemala. Fares are BZ$20–BZ$25.

Requena's Charter Service ✉ 12 Front St., Punta Gorda ☎ 722/2070.

BUS TRAVEL

For routes south to Dangriga, Placencia, and Punta Gorda, try Southern Transport. From Belize City to Punta Gorda it's a nine-hour trip that costs around BZ$28. Road conditions are unpredictable in the rainy season, which runs from June to September.

Southern Transport ✉ Main St., Punta Gorda ☎ 522/2160.

CAR TRAVEL

The journey to Punta Gorda via the Hummingbird and Southern highways used to be a chiropractor's nightmare: a bone-shuddering marathon via Belmopan, Dangriga, and Big Creek across some of Belize's worst roads. The paving of the Hummingbird and Southern highways have made the trip much shorter and more pleasant. At this writing, only a short section of the Southern Highway near Golden Stream was unpaved. It's now one of Central America's best roads.

EMERGENCIES

Hospitals **Punta Gorda Hospital** ✉ Main St. at south end of town ☎ 722/2026.

HEALTH

Malaria is a problem in southern Belize. If you are going to spend any time in the bush, discuss with your physician whether to use chloroquine or other malaria prophylaxes. The municipal water supply in Punta Gorda is treated and is safe to drink. In rural areas the water is often from community wells; here you should drink bottled water.

MAIL & SHIPPING

The Punta Gorda post office is on Front Street across from the ferry dock. Hours are 8:30–noon and 1–4:30 weekdays.

Post Offices **Punta Gorda post office** ✉ Front St. ☎ 722/2087.

SAFETY

Punta Gorda is a generally safe, friendly town. With normal precautions, you should have no problem walking around, even after dark. The nearby Mayan villages are also relatively free of crime. Guatemala's Caribbean coast, just a short bus or boat ride away, has a reputation for lawlessness, which can occasionally spill over into Toledo.

TOURS

Operating out of Punta Gorda, Clive Genus is an incredibly pleasant tour operator with whom you'll enjoy jostling around on bumpy roads leading to the ancient ruins.

Clive Genus ✉ 30 Wahima Alley, Punta Gorda ☎ 722/2068.

VISITOR INFORMATION

The office of the Belize Tourism Industry Association on Front Street near the ferry dock, is open Tuesday–Saturday 9–noon and 1–4:30, Sunday 9–noon. It has brochures and information on local hotels, tours, and bus schedules.

Belize Tourism Information Center ✉ Front St. ☎ 722/2531.

BELIZE A TO Z

To research prices, get advice from other travelers, and book travel arrangements, visit www.fodors.com.

AIR TRAVEL

The main airlines serving Belize from the United States are American, with daily flights from Miami and Dallas–Fort Worth; Continental, with daily nonstop flights from Houston and a weekly (Sat.) nonstop flight from Newark; US Airways, with daily nonstops from Charlotte; Delta, with nonstops from Atlanta; and TACA, with nonstops from Houston. It's often cheaper to fly into the Mexican city of Cancún, but the journey by bus to Belize will take nearly a full day away from each end of your Belize vacation. There's no air service from anywhere in Mexico to Belize.

Planes on domestic routes are usually single- or twin-engine island hoppers. Depending on where you depart, you may endure several takeoffs and landings. For example, a flight from Punta Gorda to San Pedro will likely include three stops. Most domestic flights leave from the municipal airport, near the center of Belize City, which is easier to reach than the international airport. Domestic flights tend to be cheaper from the municipal airport than from the international one. The main carriers are Tropic Air and Maya Island Air, both of which fly to Ambergris Caye and Caye Caulker, as well as to Dangriga, Placencia, Corozal, and Punta Gorda, and Santa Elena in Guatemala. Maya Island Air now has service from the international airport to San Ignacio.

Maya Island Air ✉ Belize Municipal Airport, Belize City ☎ 223/1140, 800/225-6732 in U.S. 🌐 www.mayaairways.com. **Tropic Air** ✉ San Pedro ☎ 226/2012, 800/422-3435 in U.S. 🌐 www.tropicair.com.

AIRPORTS & TRANSFERS

Philip S. W. Goldson International Airport is 14 km (9 mi) north of the city. Taxis to town cost BZ$40. The Belize City Municipal Airport has flights to San Pedro and down the coast to Dangriga, Placencia, and Punta Gorda.

Belize City Municipal Airport ✉ North of Belize City. **Philip S. W. Goldson International Airport** ✉ Ladyville.

BUS TRAVEL TO & FROM BELIZE

There is daily bus service from the Guatemalan and Mexican borders. Buses cross from Chetumal, Mexico, and stop in Corozal, Belize, where you can catch another bus to Belize City or a plane to San Pedro. Buses from Guatemala (via Flores) stop in the border town of Melchor de Mencos. Cross the border and take a bus or taxi to San Ignacio, 13 km (8 mi) away, or continue on the bus to Belize City.

BUS TRAVEL WITHIN BELIZE

Although there's no rail system in Belize, there's fairly extensive bus service by private companies. The quality of the buses and the roads on which they travel vary considerably. Novelo's, the country's dominant carrier, especially on the Western and Northern highways, has acquired several competing companies. Because of consolidations in the industry that created Novelo's and other companies, you'll find that schedules are in flux. However, buses are still extremely cheap (about BZ$5–BZ$28 from Belize City to other points in the country) and remain an excellent way to experience Belize as the Belizeans do. Outside the cities you can flag them down like cabs, and the driver will let you off whenever you want. Expect to ride on old U.S. school buses or retired Greyhound buses. On the Northern and Western highways there are a few express buses with air-conditioning and other comforts.

Novelo's buses stop in Corozal, Belmopan, and San Ignacio and go north to Orange Walk and Corozal, while Southern Transport covers Dangriga and Punta Gorda.

Novelo's ✉ W. Collet Canal, Belize City ☎ 227/2025. **Southern Transport** ✉ 3 Havana St., Dangriga ☎ 522/2211.

CAR RENTAL

Belize City has many international car-rental agency branches, as well as several local operators. Prices vary by company, but all are high by U.S. standards (BZ$120–BZ$230 per day). Some cars rented out by local operators—V-8 gas-guzzlers from Texas—will cost you dearly for gas alone, whereas international agencies have modern, dependable fleets. A four-wheel-drive Suzuki with unlimited mileage from Budget costs about BZ$150 per day. A few firms now rent diesel vehicles, which will save you money on fuel, as diesel is about one-third less than unleaded gas in Belize. For serious safaris a four-wheel-drive vehicle (preferably a Land Rover or an Isuzu Trooper) is invaluable. Some major hotels offer all-terrain vehicles with guides for about BZ$400 per day.

CAR TRAVEL

Belize is one of the few countries left in the Americas where off-road conditions are still the norm on some major roads. Getting somewhere is never a question of simply going from A to B; there's always a bit of adventure involved and a few detours to Y and Z.

The Northern Highway (to Orange Walk, Corozal, and the Mexico border), the Western Highway (to Belmopan, San Ignacio, and the Guatemala border), and the Hummingbird Highway (from Belmopan to Dangriga) are all fully paved. But for a few miles near Golden Stream, which are nearly finished, the Southern Highway is almost completely paved as well. Once you get off the main highways, distances don't mean that much—it's time that counts. You might have only 20 km (12½ mi) to go, but it can take you a grueling 90 minutes. If you bring your own car, you'll need to buy insurance in Belize.

GASOLINE Unleaded premium gasoline costs around BZ$7.75 per gallon. There are modern service stations, even a few open 24 hours, in Belize City and in most of the north and west. In remote areas fill up whenever you see a gas station.

EMBASSIES & CONSULATES

There are no Australian or New Zealand embassies or consulates in Central America.

British High Commission ✉ Embassy Sq., Belmopan ☎ 822/2146. **Canadian Consulate** ✉ 29 Southern Foreshore, Belize City ☎ 223/1060. **U.S. Embassy** ✉ 29 Gabourel La., Belize City ☎ 227/7161.

MAIL, SHIPPING & INTERNET

Belize is wired—most hotels have Internet access. Increasingly, Belize hotels provide free Internet access for guests, and some have wireless systems. Internet cafés can be found in San Pedro, Caye Caulker, Belize City, San Ignacio, Placencia, Corozal Town, Punta Gorda, and other areas. Rates are usually around BZ$15 an hour.

MONEY MATTERS

The dollar is accepted everywhere in Belize. Other currencies, including Canadian dollars, aren't generally accepted in Belize. You can exchange currency at one of the five banks operating in Belize: Alliance Bank, Atlantic Bank, ScotiaBank, First Caribbean International Bank (formerly Barclays), and Belize Bank. Most banks have their main offices on Albert Street in Belize City.

Only banks and authorized money changers (Casas de Cambio) are supposed to exchange currency, although private money changers have traditionally operated in Belize, especially at border areas. These entrepreneurs deal for the most part in U.S. and Belize dollars and either Mexican pesos or Guatemalan quetzales, not Canadian or European currencies. They often offer better rates than the usual BZ$2 for each U.S. dollar. In the recent past this gray-market rate has ranged from around BZ$2.05 to BZ$2.30 to the U.S. dollar. Should you exchange U.S. dollars at a bank, expect to be charged a 1%–2% fee. Authorized exchange offices usually pay a slightly better exchange rate than banks.

TOURS

Many tour companies stick to their local area, but several venture farther afield. S&L Travel Services, in Belize City, is one reputable company. Sea Sports Belize, also in Belize City, offers inland and offshore adventure tours as well as dive trips. Amigo Travel, the largest tour company on Ambergris Caye, offers both mainland and island tours and snorkeling excursions.

Amigo Travel ✉ Barrier Reef Dr., San Pedro ☎ 226/2180. **Belize Trips** ✉ Box 1108, Belize City ☎ 223/0376 🌐 www.belize-trips.com. **S&L Travel Services** ✉ 91 N. Front St., Belize City ☎ 227/7593. **Sea Sports Belize** ✉ ☎ 223/5505 🌐 www.seasportsbelize.com.

GUATEMALA

2

MOST HIGH-AND-MIGHTY MONUMENT
The jaw-dropping ruins of Tikal ⇨*p.175*

SAFEST SACRIFICIAL OFFERING
A cigar at Saint Maximón's altar ⇨*p.138*

MOST DRAMATIC VIEW
Three volcanoes *and* Lake Atitlán ⇨*p.132*

BEST T-SHIRT UPGRADE
A colorful highland *huipile* ⇨*p.136*

WORST TIME TO RUN OUT OF FILM
While visiting Semuc Champey,
the most beautiful spot in the country ⇨*p.164*

BEST PRODUCT OF ITS ENVIRONMENT
Ni'tun Ecolodge ⇨*p.179*

BEST CAFFEINE CURATOR
Coffee country's Café El Tirol ⇨*p.163*

BIGGEST SPLASH
Wrangling rapids on Río Coyolate ⇨*p.111*

Updated by Gregory Benchwick

CAPTIVATING TRAVELERS FOR CENTURIES, Guatemala has lost none of its charm. From conquistador Pedro de Alvarado, who stopped between battles to marvel at the beauty of Lago Atitlán, to writer Aldous Huxley, who waxed poetic on the same lake's shores centuries later, this intricate jewel of a country has intrigued and inspired its share of foreigners. In a matter of days you can walk the cobblestone streets of a colonial capital, barter with indigenous people who still worship the gods of the ancient Maya, and explore the meandering trails of a tropical rain forest.

Perched at the top of the Central American isthmus, Guatemala is divided into a number of distinct regions: the Pacific Lowlands, the Western Highlands, the central Verapaces, the Caribbean Lowlands, and the northern jungle region of El Petén. With a territory of just 108,900 square km (42,046 square mi), Guatemala has 19 ecosystems encompassing palm-lined beaches, cloud forests, rugged mountain ranges, scrubby desert valleys, and rain forests chock-full of tropical flora and fauna.

Guatemala's landscape may be fascinating, but its population of more than 12.5 million people is even more compelling. Half are of indigenous descent, and though they have adopted some of the European customs forced on their ancestors, they remain some of the region's most dedicated protectors of ancient culture.

All the indigenous peoples are Maya, but they comprise at least 22 ethnicities, differentiated by sometimes subtle distinctions in language, dress, and customs. The other half of the population is divided among mestizos (Spanish-speaking descendants of Spaniards and Indians), Garífunas (descendents of escaped African slaves), and those of predominantly Spanish ancestry who have maintained their imported bloodline and their lease on power. Though Spanish is Guatemala's official language, it's the mother tongue of only about half the population. Many people in the highlands speak one of the many indigenous languages, while some people along the coast speak Garífuna.

Guatemala's recent history has largely been the story of a struggle for land and political equality in the face of military rule. In 1944 Jorge Ubico, the last of the old-time strongmen, was deposed in a peaceful revolution. Elected in his place was schoolteacher Juan José Arévalo, who promised education and agrarian reform. Arévalo was succeeded by Jacobo Arbenz, who dared to expropriate a small part of the vast holdings of the United Fruit Company. The United States, anxious to protect national interests, sponsored a successful coup in 1954. The move effectively closed the door on democratic elections for nearly 30 years.

By the late 1970s guerrilla groups had begun to tap into the long-held grievances of Guatemala's indigenous peoples. The right-wing government unleashed a brutal campaign not just against the guerrillas, but against civilians. During the worst years of the violence—the "scorched earth" campaigns of the early 1980s—some 100,000 people were tortured and killed as the military razed hundreds of villages in an effort to flush out a handful of guerrillas. Negotiations between the government and the guerrillas, monitored by the United Nations, began in 1990. A peace accord finally put an end to the 36-year civil war in 1996.

Guatemala has entered a period of slow recovery. With peace has come increased international investment, and evidence of this economic growth appears throughout the country in the form of new roads, better communication systems, and more electrical power reaching isolated regions. All these improvements have made the country much more attractive to visitors. There are still problems to overcome, such as a rise in robberies and other violent crimes. Widespread government corruption continues to riddle the country. Guatemala is a land of contrasts. The rich, it seems, keep getting richer, and the poor keep getting poorer. Nevertheless, Guatemalans, both rich and poor, remain optimistic for a brighter future.

Exploring Guatemala

Guatemala is a rugged country where major roads are few and far between and highways are all but nonexistent. But because there are only two airports—one in Guatemala City, the other in Flores—you're forced to do most of your travel by land. All but the hardiest travelers will want to stay in the larger towns and explore the more isolated regions on day trips.

About the Restaurants

The basis of Guatemalan food is corn, usually eaten as a tortilla, as a tamale, or on the cob. Black beans accompany most meals, either whole beans cooked in a broth or mashed and refried. Meats are often served in *caldos* (stews) or cooked in a spicy chili sauce. Thin and tender *lomito,* a popular cut of beef, is on the menu in most restaurants. In rural areas you might also see *venado* (venison) and *tepezcuintle* (a large rodent) on the menu. The most popular fish is the delicious *robálo,* known elsewhere as snook. Along the coast you'll find *tapado,* a coconut stew made with plantains, shrimp, crab, and fish. The *queso fundido* (melted cheese with condiments and tortillas), which is sometimes served as an appetizer, is a good choice for light eaters.

About the Hotels

Guatemala now has a wide range of lodging options, from suites at luxurious high-rises to stark rooms in budget hotels. Guatemala City has the most options, but the much more appealing city of Antigua is a better base for exploring the country. Rooms often fill up on weekends, so make reservations well in advance. Panajachel has the widest selection of accommodations in the highlands, and Chichicastenango and Xelajú can claim some creditable lodgings. Most remote villages offer only spartan lodgings, if any at all.

WHAT IT COSTS In Guatemalan Quetzales

	$$$$	$$$	$$	$	¢
RESTAURANTS	over Q130	Q100–Q130	Q70–Q100	Q40–Q70	under Q40
HOTELS	over Q760	Q560–Q760	Q360–Q560	Q160–Q360	under Q160

Restaurant prices are per person for a main course at dinner. Hotel prices are for two people in a standard double room, including tax and service.

A trip to Guatemala should last no less than five days, during which you can take in the most popular sights and still get off the beaten path. Eight days allow a better look at Tikal and El Petén, and 10 days could add a trip to the Caribbean coast.

If you have 5 days

Fly into **Guatemala City,** departing immediately for the colonial city of **Antigua.** Spend at least two nights here. If you're in Antigua on Thursday or Sunday, plan an early morning excursion to the mountain village of **Chichicastenango,** where the region's best handicrafts are found at a lively market. On your fourth day take an early morning plane to **Flores,** a pastel-painted town in El Petén. Head straight to the ruins at nearby **Tikal.** Depending on your schedule, you may choose to spend the night either here so you can see the ruins in the morning (a must for birders) or in Flores so you'll be closer to the airport for your flight back to Guatemala City.

If you have 7 days

Spend your first day in **Guatemala City,** visiting the museums and dining in Zona Viva. On Day 2 head for **Antigua** so you can tour the remarkable ruins of 16th-, 17th-, and 18th-century monasteries and convents. Spend two nights here, and then head for **Panajachel.** Spend Day 5 visiting the villages surrounding picture-perfect Lago Atitlán or head to the renowned market in the colonial village of **Chichicastenango.** On Day 6 fly north to **Flores,** where you can spend the afternoon shopping, strolling, and sipping cappuccino. Make arrangements for a taxi to pick you up at your hotel the next morning—you'll want to leave before dawn for the breathtaking ruins of **Tikal.** Climb the rustic ladder to the top of the tallest temple, then watch the sun rise over the rain forest that engulfs the ancient city. Spend your last morning hiking the terrific trails of the **Biotopo Cerro Cahuí** before returning to Guatemala City.

If you have 10 days

Those who've come for relaxation should follow the seven-day itinerary, adding additional days to explore the highland markets, tour the villages around Lago Atitlán, or climb Volcán Pacayá. More energetic types should travel east to **Río Dulce,** once an important trading river for the Maya. The next day take an early-morning boat ride to the **Biotopo Chocón Machacas,** then continue onward to the colorful Garífuna community of **Livingston.** On the last morning take a ferry to the banana port of **Puerto Barrios,** where you can swim or explore the waterfront. By early afternoon head back to Guatemala City.

Timing

Most people visit Guatemala from June to August and from January to April. The busiest time of year is *Semana Santa,* the week from Palm Sunday to Easter Sunday. Hotels in Antigua, Panajachel, and Chichicastenango are booked months ahead for this holiday. The rainy season runs from May to November, with a few dry spells in July and August. A typical day in the rainy season is sunny in the morning, cloudy at midday, and pouring throughout the afternoon and evening. Guatemala's climate depends more on altitude than season. The coasts and El Petén are hot, while the mountains enjoy warm days and cool nights.

GUATEMALA CITY

Once hailed as the "jewel of Central America," Guatemala City has certainly lost its luster. The country's capital, a tangle of streets and alleyways, retains little of its colonial charm. As it's the country's transportation hub, you're likely to end up here, but with few of the country's most popular attractions—no ancient ruins, flamboyant markets, or spectacular mountains—there's little reason to linger. To the city's credit, it has some decent restaurants and hotels, as well as several excellent museums and a lively nightlife.

The sprawling metropolis can be intimidating, as it is divided between the Old City and the New City, as well as into 21 different *zonas*. But there's virtually no reason to stray from the four central zones, which makes getting around—and getting your bearings—quite manageable. The Old City covers Zona 1, in the north, and the New City spans Zona 9 and Zona 10, in the south. Between them is Zona 4, notable only because it contains the bus terminals. Otherwise, this seedy section is best avoided.

In the Old and New cities, numbered *avenidas* (avenues) run south to north, while *calles* (streets) run west to east. Addresses are usually given as a numbered avenida or calle followed by two numbers separated by a dash: the first number is a nearby cross street or avenue and the second is a specific building. The building numbers increase as they approach the higher-numbered cross streets and then start over at the next block, so 9 Avenida 5–22 is on 9 Avenida near 5 Calle, and 9 Avenida 5–74 is on the same block, only closer to 6 Calle. A word of warning: make sure you're in the right zone. Different zones often contain identical addresses.

The city's major arteries are 6 and 10 avenidas: 6 Avenida runs from Zona 1 to Zona 4 to Zona 9, passing three series of identically numbered calles; 10 Avenida runs through Zonas 1 and 4 before becoming Avenida La Reforma in Zona 10. Comfort seekers tend to stick to the New City, while those interested in bargain shopping head for the Old City.

Numbers in the text correspond to numbers in the margin and on the Guatemala City map.

The New City

Whereas the Old City is the real Guatemala, the New City's modern look and pace are reminiscent of upscale districts in North American cities. This is especially the case in Zona Viva, the posh center of Zona 10, where dozens of smart restaurants, bars, and clubs stay open long after the rest of the city goes to bed. During the day the New City's museums and cultural sites draw an equally affluent and savvy crowd. While the glitz and glamour of the Zona Viva are a welcome relief for travel-weary visitors, it is a far cry from the rustic enchantment of the real Guatemala to be found in the pueblos and backstreets of the rest of the country.

Archaeological Treasures El Petén, much of which is covered with tropical rain forest, was the heart of the ancient Mayan empire. Only a fraction of the estimated 1,500 ruins have been explored, and even those that have been excavated remain surrounded, if not actually covered, by vegetation. Aside from Tikal, traveling to the archaeological sites often involves maneuvering a four-wheel-drive vehicle down muddy roads. More isolated sites require taking a boat, riding a mule, or hacking your way through the trees. No matter how you get there, it's likely to be an adventure.

Caving An awesome selection of caves awaits subterranean explorers. Aktun Kan, in El Petén, is very easy to reach. In Naj Tunich, near Poptún, you'll find carbon frescoes painted by the ancient Maya. The Candelaria River, in Alta Verapaz, passes through a series of caverns only accessible by water a few months of the year. Many other caves remain largely unexplored.

Shopping Nearly all of Guatemala's handicrafts come from the highlands, so it's no surprise that this region is a shopper's paradise. Most famous are the handwoven fabrics—in every highland village you'll see women weaving traditional patterns. But Guatemala's indigenous population creates countless other kinds of handicrafts; just as each region has its traditional fabrics, Guatemala has other specialties, such as ceramics, baskets, toys, statues, bags, or hats. Don't worry if you forget to buy that souvenir in Sololá, as most of these items are also available in the markets of Antigua and Guatemala City.

Guatemala's markets are a wonderful way to witness the everyday lives of the population. Vendors lining a jumble of narrow passages hawk everything from fruits and vegetables to clothing and toiletries. On Monday markets are held in Antigua, Chimaltenango, and Zunil. Sololá has a market on Tuesday, while Chimaltenango has one on Wednesday. Thursday is a popular day for buying and selling, with markets in Antigua, Chichicastenango, Nebaj, Xelajú, San Juan Atitlán, San Lucas Tolimán, Santa Cruz del Quiché, and Todos Santos Cuchumatán. Friday finds vendors in Chimaltenango, Sololá, and San Francisco El Alto, while Saturday is market day in Antigua and Totonicapán. Sunday markets are everyone's favorite, and some of the most colorful are in Antigua, Chichicastenango, Momostenango, Nebaj, San Lucas Tolimán, Xelajú, and Todos Santos Cuchumatán.

White-Water Rafting Guatemala is filled with raging rivers waiting to be explored. Adding to the adventure, most flow through lush tropical forests where you'll see plenty of wildlife. Some moderately difficult rivers include Río Chiquibul, a smooth ride traversing tall limestone canyons, and Río Naranjo, an exhilarating plunge through the jungle. Adventure of a more challenging nature can be had on Río Los Esclavos, which takes you through a narrow canyon with high waterfalls, and Río Candelaria, which passes through virgin forests and caves. You can also rent *kayukos* (canoes fashioned from tree trunks) at Río Dulce and Río El Boqueron for a more leisurely trip.

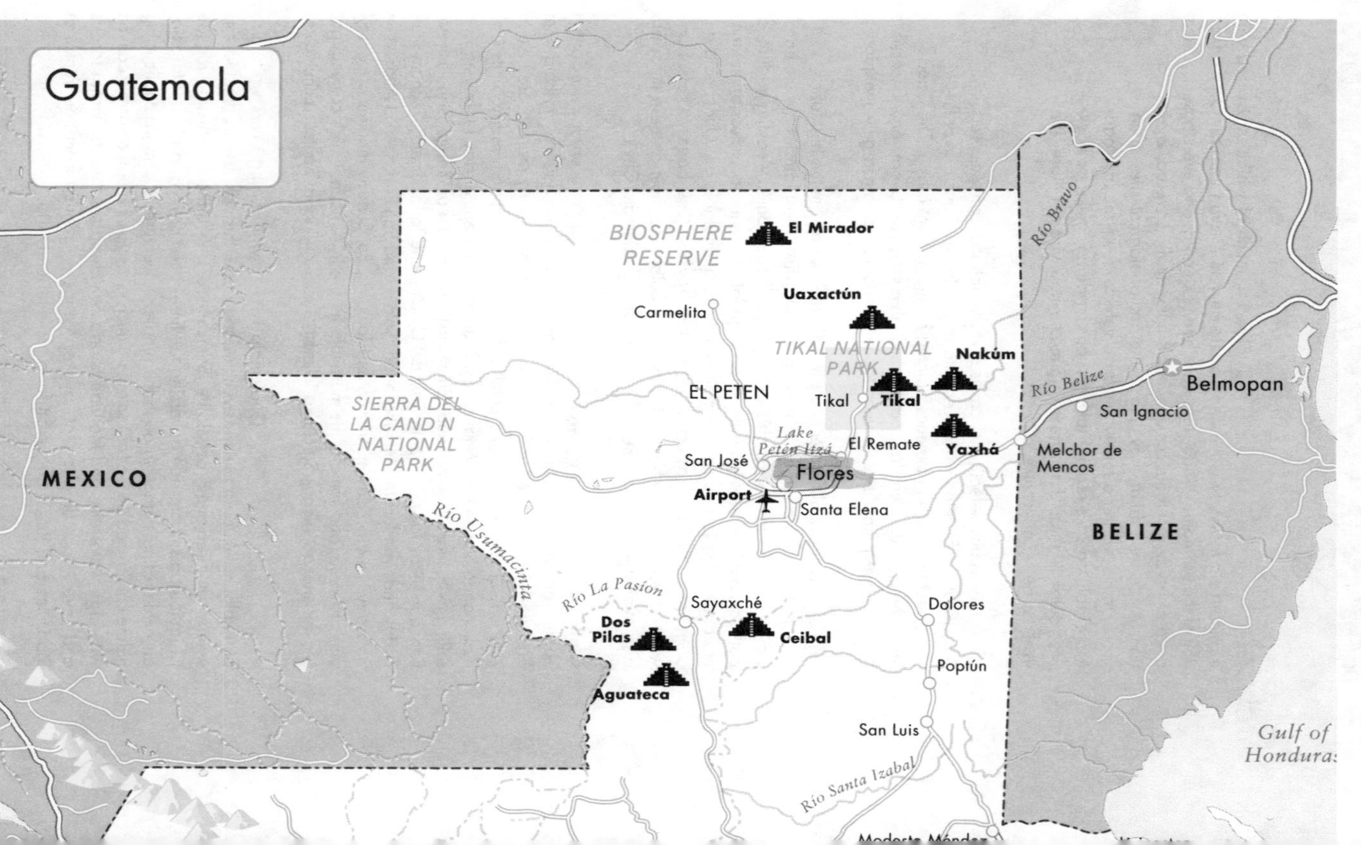

Guatemala
BIOSPHERE RESERVE
El Mirador
Uaxactún
Carmelita
TIKAL NATIONAL PARK
Nakúm
EL PETEN
Tikal
Tikal
SIERRA DEL LA CAND N NATIONAL PARK
Lake Petén Itzá
El Remate
Yaxhá
San José
Flores
MEXICO
Airport
Santa Elena
Río Usumacinta
Río La Pasion
Sayaxché
Dos Pilas
Ceibal
Aguateca
Dolores
Poptún
San Luis
Río Santa Izabal
Río Bravo
Río Belize
Belmopan
San Ignacio
Melchor de Mencos
BELIZE
Gulf of Honduras

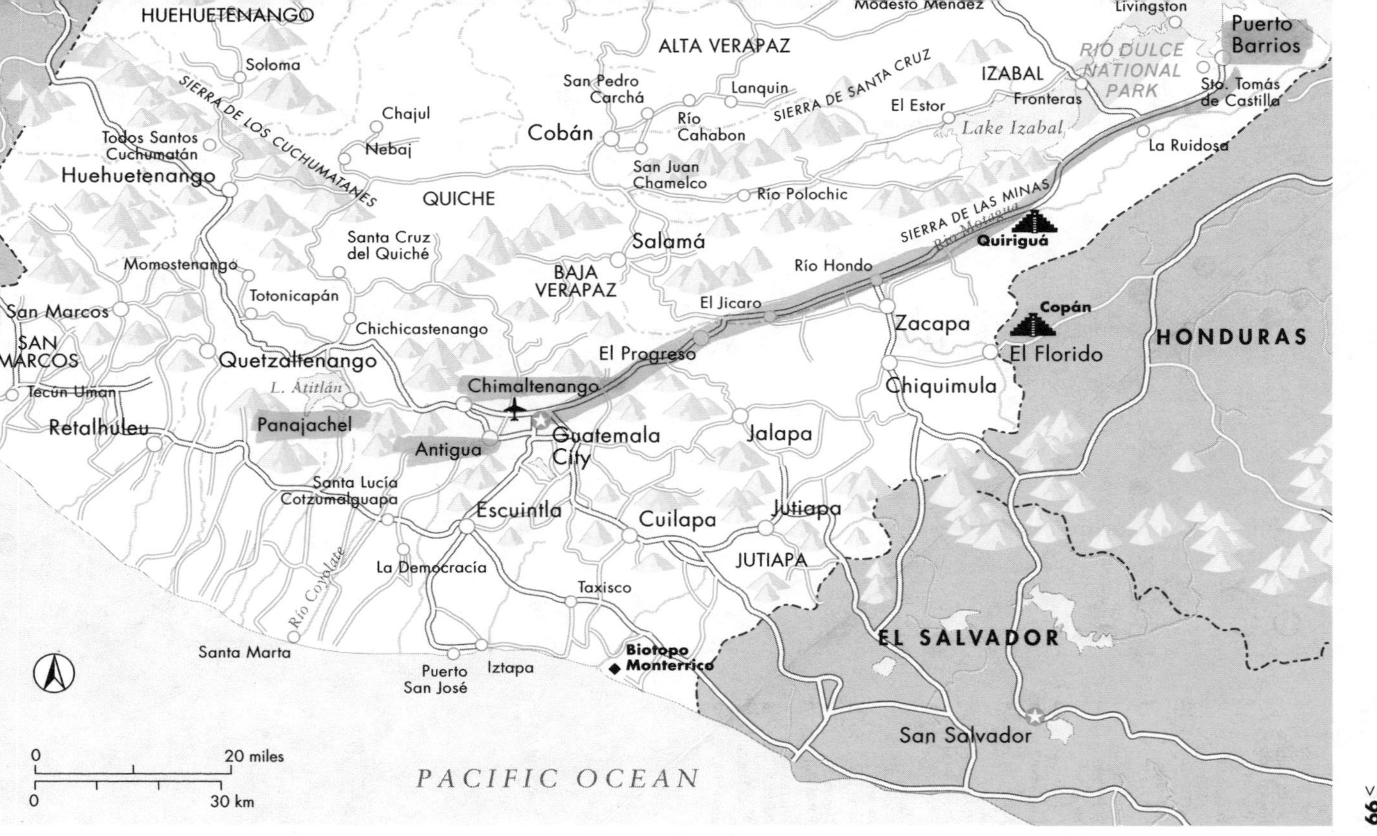
HUEHUETENANGO
Modesto Mendez
Livingston
Puerto Barrios
ALTA VERAPAZ
RÍO DULCE NATIONAL PARK
Soloma
San Pedro Carchá
Lanquin
IZABAL
Sto. Tomás de Castilla
SIERRA DE LOS CUCHUMATANES
SIERRA DE SANTA CRUZ
El Estor
Fronteras
Chajul
Río Cahabon
Lake Izabal
Todos Santos Cuchumatán
Cobán
La Ruidosa
Nebaj
San Juan Chamelco
Huehuetenango
Río Polochic
QUICHE
SIERRA DE LAS MINAS
Río Motagua
Quiriguá
Santa Cruz del Quiché
Salamá
Momostenango
BAJA VERAPAZ
Río Hondo
Totonicapán
El Jicaro
Copán
San Marcos
Chichicastenango
Zacapa
HONDURAS
SAN MARCOS
El Progreso
El Florido
Quetzaltenango
L. Atitlán
Chimaltenango
Chiquimula
Tecún Umán
Panajachel
Guatemala City
Jalapa
Retalhuleu
Antigua
Santa Lucía Cotzumalguapa
Escuintla
Cuilapa
Jutiapa
JUTIAPA
La Democracía
Río Coyolate
Taxisco
EL SALVADOR
Santa Marta
Biotopo Monterrico
Puerto San José
Iztapa
San Salvador
0
20 miles
0
30 km
PACIFIC OCEAN

Catedral Metropolitano . . 9
Centro Cultural Miguel Angel Asturias 14
Edificio de Correos Central 12
Iglesia de San Francisco . . 13
Jardines Botánico 6
Mercado Central 10
La Merced 11
Museo Ixchel . . . 4
Museo Nacional de Arqueología y Etnología 1
Museo Nacional de Arte Moderno 2
Museo Popol Vuh 5
Palacio Nacional 8
Plaza Mayor 7
Zona Viva 3

32-48 Q

Avenida La Reforma splits the New City down the middle, with Zona 9 to the west, and Zona 10 to the east. To save confusion, always check which zone your destination is in before heading there.

a good tour

Begin at the **Museo Nacional de Arqueología y Etnología** 1 for a crash course in Mayan history. Next door, the **Museo Nacional de Arte Moderno** 2 will ricochet you into the present with exhibitions of contemporary Guatemalan art. Take a taxi over to **Zona Viva** 3 for lunch at one of the several terrific restaurants. Afterward, head downhill on 6 Calle past 6 Avenida to the **Museo Ixchel** 4, arguably the city's best museum, where you'll learn about traditional Mayan textiles. Next door is the **Museo Popol Vuh** 5, which holds a collection of remarkable archaeological objects. From here the **Jardines Botánico** 6 is about seven blocks away: walk north on 6 Avenida and turn left on 1 Calle. Strolling here is a great way to wind up your afternoon before heading back to your hotel to rest before dinner.

TIMING If you visit all the museums and stop for lunch, this tour will easily fill a day. Because the Zona 13 museums are somewhat far from the rest of the attractions in the Zona 10 environs, you'll likely want to get a lift. A taxi is about 40 quetzales.

What to See

6 **Jardines Botánico.** The small but lovely Botanical Gardens at the northern end of Zona 10 contain an impressive collection of plants and a little natural history museum. ✉ *Calle Mariscal Cruz, near Av. La Reforma, Zona 10* ☎ *331–0904* *Q10* ⏲ *Weekdays 8–3.*

off the beaten path

KAMINALJUYÚ – From 300 BC to AD 900, an early Mayan city of some 50,000 people flourished in what is now the heart of Zona 7. Though most of this city is buried beneath today's urban sprawl, this impressive site, which includes the bases of several pyramids, offers a glimpse of the area's history. Some of the objects found here are on display at Museo Popol Vuh. Scattered ruins are found creeping up from the urban sprawl throughout Zona 7.

★ 4 **Museo Ixchel.** The city's best museum focuses on textiles of Guatemala's indigenous community, with an impressive array of handwoven fabrics from 120 highland communities, some of which date from the 19th century. You'll also find sculptures, photographs, and paintings, including work by Andres Curruchich, an influential Guatemalan folk painter. Multimedia and interactive weaving displays make the museum engaging for all ages, and there are a café, a bookstore, and a terrific gift shop. The only drawback is its location—at the bottom of a long hill at the Universidad Francisco Marroquín. ✉ *End of 6 Calle at 6 Av., Zona 10* ☎ *331–3739* *Q25* ⏲ *Weekdays 9–5, Sat. 9–1.*

★ 1 **Museo Nacional de Arqueología y Etnología.** Dedicated to the ancient and modern Maya, the National Museum of Archaeology and Ethnology has a large and excellent collection of Mayan pottery, jewelry, masks, and costumes, as well as models of the ancient cities. ✉ *Edificio 5, La Aurora Park, Zona 13* ☎ *472–0478* *Q40* ⏲ *Tues.–Sun. 9–4.*

need a break?

Satisfy your sweet tooth on the porch of **Café Zurich** (⊠ 6 Av. 12–58, Zona 10 ☎ 334–2781), a former colonial home. The menu has specialty coffees as well as chocolate, chocolate, and more chocolate.

❷ **Museo Nacional de Arte Moderno.** Surrealism and multimedia work are among the wide range of styles represented at the National Museum of Modern Art. Many of Guatemala's most distinguished artists are represented here, including Efraín Recinos and Zipacna de León. ⊠ *Edificio 6, La Aurora Park, Zona 13* ☎ *472–0467* 🎫 *Q10* ⊙ *Tues.–Fri. 9–4, weekends 9–noon and 1:30–4.*

★ ❺ **Museo Popol Vuh.** Religious figures, animals, and mythological half-animal–half-man creatures with stolid eyes, hawkish noses, and fierce poses inhabit this museum. Though much smaller than the city's other museums, Popol Vuh has an interesting display of well-preserved stone carvings from the Preclassic period, with the earliest pieces dating from 1500 BC. Some statues are quite big, all the more impressive given that they were each cut from a single stone. Also look for the "painted books," which were historical records kept by the Maya. The most famous is the museum's namesake, the *Popol Vuh,* otherwise known as the Mayan Bible, which was lost (and later recovered) after it was translated into Spanish. ⊠ *Calle 6 at 6 Av., Zona 10* ☎ *361–2301* 🎫 *Q20* ⊙ *Weekdays 9–5, Sat. 9–1.*

❸ **Zona Viva.** Undoubtedly the most cosmopolitan area of town, Zona Viva is filled with well-dressed people flaunting their electronics (cell phones and PDAs are ubiquitous). The daytime crowd is mostly business executives, but at night a livelier bunch takes over. Avenues accommodate pedestrians overflowing from the narrow sidewalks on which restaurants have somehow introduced outdoor seating. Lines extend from popular discos and bars, where the thumping music sometimes gets people dancing in the streets. Although the shopping mall called Los Proceres is nearby, you won't find the boutiques that characterize most upscale neighborhoods. Things seem to be headed in that direction, however. ⊠ *Zona 10.*

The Old City

Older and grittier than the New City, the Old City has the hustle and bustle of many Central American capitals. But walking around the area, especially around the Plaza de las Armas, is quite pleasant. The frenetic colors and sounds of the bustling metropolis can be daunting at first, but with a little patience—and maybe a couple aspirin—the downtown experience can be both memorable and exhilarating.

Start at the **Plaza Mayor** ❼ ⚑, the heart of the Old City. Clustered around the square are some of the city's oldest landmarks, including the **Palacio Nacional** ❽ and **Catedral Metropolitano** ❾. A block east is the **Mercado Central** ❿, an underground maze of stalls selling goods from the highlands. Walk two blocks east to 11 Avenida, then head north until you reach **La Merced** ⓫. The tiny church is worth a look for its ornate interior.

Three blocks south of Plaza Mayor is the **Edificio de Correos Central** 12, a lovely colonial structure that houses the main post office. Two blocks farther is an old church, the **Iglesia de San Francisco** 13. History buffs will want to continue south to the **Centro Cultural Miguel Ángel Asturias** 14.

TIMING A few hours should suffice to see the Old City sights, depending on the time spent in the Mercado Central labyrinth.

What to See

9 **Catedral Metropolitano.** Built between 1782 and 1868, Metropolitan Cathedral is a rare example of colonial architecture in the Old City. Standing steadfast on the eastern end of Plaza Mayor, it is one of the city's most enduring landmarks. The ornate altars hold outstanding examples of colonial religious art, including an image of the Virgen de la Asunción, the city's patron saint. ✉ *8 Calle and 7 Av.* ☎ *No phone* *Free* ⏲ *Daily 8–6.*

14 **Centro Cultural Miguel Ángel Asturias.** The imposing Teatro Nacional and the Teatro del Aire Libre are parts of this cluster of buildings named for Guatemala's Nobel Prize–winning novelist. Asturias opposed the dictatorship and therefore spent much of his life in exile in Argentina. ✉ *24 Calle 3–81, Centro Cívico* ☎ *232–4041* *Free* ⏲ *Weekdays 10–4.*

12 **Edificio de Correos Central.** You can mail packages from your hotel, but it's far more fun to come to the main post office, housed in a cantaloupe-color structure dating from the colonial era. ✉ *7 Av. 12–11* ☎ *332–6101* ⏲ *Weekdays 8–7, Sat. 8–3.*

13 **Iglesia de San Francisco.** The Church of St. Francis, built between 1800 and 1851, is known for its ornate wooden altar. A small museum explains the church's history. ✉ *6 Av. and 13 Calle* ⏲ *Daily 10–4.*

off the beaten path

MAPA EN RELIEVE DE GUATEMALA – This relief map depicting Guatemala's precipitous topography is so immense you have to view it from an observation tower. What makes it even more amazing is that it was built in 1904, before satellite or even aerial topography. ✉ *Minerva Park, at end of Av. Simon Cañas, Zona 2* ☎ *254–1114* *Q16* ⏲ *Daily 9–5.*

10 **Mercado Central.** A seemingly endless maze of underground passages is home to the Mercado Central, where handicrafts from the highlands are hawked from overstocked stalls. It's not as appealing as the open-air markets in Antigua or Chichicastenango, but the leather goods, wooden masks, and woolen blankets found here are often cheaper. There are skilled pickpockets in the market, so keep an eye on your belongings. ✉ *8 Calle and 8 Av.* ☎ *No phone* ⏲ *Mon.–Sat. 9–6, Sun. 9–noon.*

11 **La Merced.** If religious iconography is one of the reasons you're in Guatemala, step inside this lovely church dating from 1813 to see its baroque interior. Many of the elaborate paintings and sculptures originally adorned La Merced in Antigua but were moved here after earthquakes devastated that city. ✉ *5 Calle and 11 Av.* ⏲ *Daily 6 AM–7 PM.*

8 **Palacio Nacional.** The grandiose National Palace was built between 1939 and 1944 to satisfy the monumental ego of President Jorge Ubico Castañeda. It once held the offices of the president and his ministers, but now its 320 rooms house an art museum. The collection of paintings and sculptures by well-known Guatemalan artists was moved here from Antigua after that city's devastating earthquakes. Look for Alfredo Gálvez Suárez's murals illustrating the history of the city above the entry. The palace's ornate stairways and stained-glass windows are a pleasant contrast to the gritty city outside its walls. The guards will lead you to the presidential balcony off the banquet room for a *propina* (tip). ✉ *6 Calle and 7 Av.* ☎ *No phone* *Free* *Daily 9–noon and 2–5:30.*

7 **Plaza Mayor.** Clustered around this historic square are landmarks that survived the 19th century's earthquakes. In the center of the park is a fountain where children sometimes splash, while their parents relax on the nearby benches. ✉ *Between 6 and 8 calles and 6 and 7 avenidas.*

Where to Eat

The New City

Guatemala City has the varied cuisine you'd expect in a major city, with the finer restaurants clustered in the New City. Virtually every street in the Zona Viva has two or more tempting restaurants, making it almost impossible to choose. Some tried-and-true favorites are listed below. Fortunately, the Zona Viva is small enough that you can stroll around until you find that perfect place.

CONTEMPORARY $$–$$$$ Fodor's Choice ★ ✕ **Jake's.** If you only have one meal in Guatemala City, head to Jake Denburg's place. A painter-turned-restaurateur, Jake uses his creative talents on food, producing dishes ranging from handmade smoked-chicken tortellini to *robálo* (snook) in a green-pepper sauce. The crowning achievement is the *vaquero chino* (Chinese cowboy), a tenderloin steak served with a sweet soy, espresso, and star anise sauce. The restaurant is a beautiful converted farmhouse with hardwood ceilings and tile floors. The wine list is quite possibly the best in Central America. ✉ *17 Calle 10–40, Zona 10* ☎ *368–0351* *AE, DC, MC, V* *No dinner Sun.*

$$–$$$$ ✕ **Siriacos.** Modern art adorns the walls of this cheerful bistro, which has a vaguely art deco setting. Take a seat in one of the black high-back chairs and enjoy the excellent pasta and tasty Caesar salad. ✉ *1 Av. 12–12, Zona 10* ☎ *334–6316* *AE, DC, MC, V* *Closed Sun. No lunch Sat.*

★ $$–$$$$ ✕ **Tamarindos.** One of Guatemala City's best restaurants, Tamarindos serves up innovative, decidedly eclectic fare ranging from duck in tamarind sauce to Thai-style curries. Curlicue lamps and whimsical sofas that seem straight out of *Alice in Wonderland* bring a bit of post-modernism to an old city. It's an exhilarating destination for dinner, but the reasonably priced menu also makes this an excellent choice for lunch. The excellent wine list includes choices from around the globe. ✉ *11 Calle 2–19A, Zona 10* ☎ *360–2815* *AE, DC, MC, V* *Closed Sun.*

GUATEMALAN ★ $$$–$$$$ ✕ **Los Ranchos.** A pretty blue colonial facade with picture windows welcomes you to Guatemala's best steak house. Most meats, including the rib eye and chateaubriand, come from the United States, but the specialty of the house, a skirt steak called the *churrasco los ranchos,* is a hearty cut that hails from Argentina. Ask your server to recommend one of the excellent wines from Chile or France. Save room for dessert, which ranges from tiramisu to *tres leches,* a type of cake injected with sweetened condensed milk, evaporated milk, and cream. ✉ *2 Av. 14–06, Zona 10* ☎ *363–5028* 💳 *AE, DC, MC, V.*

★ $$–$$$ ✕ **Hacienda Real.** Small stone pedestals containing hot coals warm the dining room, so even on a chilly day you needn't pass up this charming restaurant serving authentic Guatemalan fare. Choose from platters of robálo, steak, or pork, all served with a variety of savory condiments like fresh salsa, pickled carrots, and jalapeños. The attentive servers bring endless baskets of warm tortillas, but try not to fill up—the truly incomparable caramel flan shouldn't be missed. ✉ *13 Calle 1–10, Zona 10* ☎ *335–5409* 💳 *AE, MC, V.*

$$–$$$ ✕ **Hacienda de los Sanchez.** This Zona Viva steak house is known for its quality cuts of beef, yet the atmosphere has won over more than one vegetarian. The brick-floor dining room calls to mind the American West, with such touches as sturdy wooden tables and old saddles. Eat inside or on the plant-filled patio. Grilled and barbecued meats dominate the menu, but you can also order chicken and seafood. There's a decent wine list. ✉ *12 Calle 2–25, Zona 10* ☎ *334–8448* 💳 *AE, DC, MC, V.*

ITALIAN
★ $$–$$$$ ✕ **Romanello's.** As the name suggests, Italian influences creep into the cooking at this Zona Viva eatery. There's no set menu, but you can usually choose from tenderloin, lobster, and robálo, and there's always a pasta dish that can be prepared with a variety of sauces. The decor is simple but elegant, with a few antiques here and there. One table in the back overlooks a small garden. There is no sign outside; it's next door to the more visible De Mario. ✉ *1 Av. 12–70, Zona 10* ☎ *361–1116* 💳 *AE, DC, MC, V* ⏲ *Closed Sun.*

$ ✕ **Tre Fratelli.** Run by three hip Guatemalans, this bustling restaurant caters to the city's young professionals. The food is definitely Italian, but there are plenty of local touches. Favorites include fettuccine *frutti di mare* (with seafood), ravioli *alla Bolognese* (with a variety of meats), and the *quattro stagione* (four-season) pizza. Top your meal off with chocolate mousse, homemade ice cream, or a cappuccino or espresso brewed in real Italian coffee urns. ✉ *2 Av. 13–25, Zona 10* ☎ *366–2678* 💳 *AE, MC, V* ⏲ *No dinner Sun.*

MIDDLE EASTERN
$–$$ ✕ **Olivadda.** This cozy eatery in the Hotel Santa Clara is an ideal lunch spot. Take a table on the tranquil patio, where a melodic fountain is surrounded by flowers and hummingbirds. Start with traditional Middle Eastern appetizers such as tabbouleh, baba ghanoush, and falafel, then move on to *kafta* (delicately spiced beef patties served in pita bread with tahini). The chicken-breast sandwich with cumin dressing is also delicious. Finish your meal with an orange-and-honey baked apple stuffed with almonds and cinnamon. ✉ *12 Calle 4–21, Zona 10* ☎ *339–1811* 💳 *AE, DC, MC, V.*

SPANISH
$$–$$$$ ✕ **De Mario.** The menu here is one of the country's most original, combining flavors from both sides of the Atlantic: you can enjoy such Spanish traditions as paella and roast suckling pig or more local offerings

like robálo with a mushroom sauce. The restaurant has a much-deserved reputation for impeccable service. ✉ *1 Av. 12–98, Zona 10* ☎ *339–2329* ▭ *AE, DC, MC, V* ⊙ *No dinner Sun.*

The Old City

AMERICAN ¢ ✕ **Europa Bar & Restaurante.** An Oregon native opened this long-standing hangout for American expats. Expect comfort food like hamburgers, mashed potatoes, and chili, as well as diner-style breakfasts of eggs, bacon, and hash browns. In the second-floor bar you can play a game of backgammon or watch football on cable TV. ✉ *11 Calle 5–16, Zona 1* ☎ *253–4929* ▭ *No credit cards* ⊙ *Closed Sun.*

GUATEMALAN $ ✕ **Arrin Cuan.** Ask locals to recommend a place to eat in the Old City, and chances are they will send you to this spirited Guatemalan favorite. The decor couldn't be simpler—wooden masks adorn the walls and soda-bottle flower vases add a touch of color to each table. The flavorful cuisine, typical of the Cobán region, includes *kak-ik* (a spicy turkey stew), *gallo en chicha* (chicken in a slightly sweet sauce), and *sopa de tortuga* (turtle soup). More adventurous types will want to sample the roasted tepezcuintle. On Friday and Saturday nights live marimba music fills the restaurant. ✉ *5 Av. 3–27, Zona 1* ☎ *238–0784 or 238–0242* ▭ *AE, DC, MC, V.*

MEXICAN $–$$$ ✕ **Los Cebollines.** The decor is nothing special, but the attraction here is the delicious Mexican food. Wash down tacos, burritos, fajitas, and, less predictably, *caldo tlalpeño de pollo* (a chicken stew with chickpeas and avocado), with sangria or a cerveza. ✉ *6 Av. 9–75, Zona 1* ☎ *232–7750* ✉ *1 Av. 13–42, Zona 10* ☎ *368–0663* ▭ *AE, DC, MC, V.*

¢–$ ✕ **El Gran Pavo.** You can't miss this restaurant—it's in a pink building with a gaudy neon sign on top. The interior is just as flashy; bright colors dazzle you as you walk past sombreros, blankets, and other Mexican kitsch and a mariachi band holds court most nights. The standard tacos and enchiladas are on the menu, but you'll also run across items like *aujas norteñas* (grilled beef strips covered with a red sauce and surrounded by avocado slices) and *camarones siempre joven* (shrimp in a spicy black chili sauce). The restaurant is open past midnight. ✉ *13 Calle 4–41, Zona 1* ☎ *232–9912* ▭ *AE, DC, MC, V.*

SPANISH ★ $$–$$$ ✕ **Altuna.** Waiters in white jackets and ties move briskly around the covered courtyard that serves as the main dining room. If you want a bit more privacy, ask to be seated in one of several adjacent rooms decorated with Iberian paintings, photographs, and posters. The Spanish and Basque menu is fairly limited; consider the calamari, paella, or filet mignon with mushroom sauce. ✉ *5 Av. 12–31, Zona 1* ☎ *251–7185 or 232–0669* ▭ *AE, DC, MC, V* ⊙ *Closed Mon.*

¢–$ ✕ **El Mesón de Don Quijote.** In the heart of the Old City, this colorful restaurant serves respectable cuisine from northern Spain (Asturias, to be exact). Though popular with old-timers, it's also a favorite late-night spot (it's open until 1 AM). The long bar adjoining several dining rooms hosts live musicians who play under a flashy painting of a flamenco dancer. The extensive menu has such palate pleasers as seafood casserole, sliced Spanish ham, lentils with sausage, and paella big enough for four people. On weekdays people head here for the four-course prix-fixe lunch. ✉ *11 Calle 5–27, Zona 1* ☎ *232–1741* ▭ *AE, DC, MC, V* ⊗ *Closed Sun.*

Where to Stay

Guatemala City has the country's widest range of accommodations. Upscale hotels are found in the New City, while more moderately priced lodgings are clustered in the Old City.

The New City

★ $$$$ **Camino Real.** With every imaginable amenity and a staff that aims to please, it isn't surprising that the immense Camino Real has hosted everyone from rock stars to heads of state. The spacious reception area lies just beyond a long foyer lined with overstuffed leather chairs. Stately rooms are furnished with carved French provincial–style pieces. Executive floors hold spacious suites with room for business travelers to spread out. French doors in the rooms on the executive floors provide views of the nearby volcanoes. ✉ *14 Calle and Av. La Reforma, Zona 10* ☎ *333–3000, 800/228–3000 in U.S.* 🖷 *337–4313* 🌐 *www.westin.com* *388 rooms* *2 restaurants, room service, in-room safes, minibars, cable TV, 2 tennis courts, 2 pools, spa, 3 bars, casino, shops, laundry service, concierge, business services, meeting rooms, travel services, free parking* ▭ *AE, DC, MC, V.*

$$$$ **Guatemala City Marriott.** Although its facade won't win any awards, this hotel does earn points for its excellent location not far from the Zona Viva. The lovely lounge offers rest to the weary; relax with a cocktail in one of the comfortable armchairs as you listen to jazz. You can always head to the Cabaña Club, a spacious spa and sports facility. Rooms are nicely furnished and each has a small balcony with a view of the city. ✉ *7 Av. 15–45, Zona 9* ☎ *339–7777, 800/228–9290 in U.S.* 🖷 *332–1877* 🌐 *www.marriotthotels.com* *385 rooms* *3 restaurants, room service, in-room safes, minibars, cable TV, pool, health club, spa, bar, shop, laundry service, business services, meeting rooms, travel services, free parking* ▭ *AE, DC, MC, V.*

$$$$ **Quinta Real.** The colossal Quinta Real has a neocolonial style—with vaulted ceilings and arabesque arches—and excellent views of the city and the neighboring volcanoes from its hilltop perch. A series of ponds and cascades play out below a covered bridge, which leads to you to the main building. Suites are elegantly appointed with colonial art and sumptuously soft bedding. The only drawback is its location slightly outside the city. ✉ *Prolongación Blvd. Los Próceres, Km. 9, Zona 15* ☎ *365–5050, 800/323–7500 in U.S.* 🖷 *365–5051* 🌐 *www.quintareal.com* *123 suites* *Restaurant, room service, in-room safes, minibars, cable TV, pool, exercise equipment, bar, 2 shops, laundry services, business services, convention center, airport shuttle, helipad, travel services, free parking, no-smoking rooms* ▭ *AE, DC, MC, V.*

$$$–$$$$ **Real Inter-Continental.** A giant statue of bartering Mayas greets you at the entrance of the towering Inter-Continental in the center of the Zona Viva; on either side are sweeping staircases. Despite this nod to the ancient world, the hotel is decidedly modern throughout; comfortable

rooms have modern art on the walls. The very good French restaurant imported its chef from Paris. Other restaurants, as well as shops and boutiques, are within walking distance. ✉ *14 Calle 2–51, Zona 10* ☎ *379–4446* 📠 *379–4447* 🌐 *www.interconti.com* *239 rooms* *2 restaurants, café, room service, in-room safes, minibars, cable TV, pool, spa, bar, shop, laundry service, business services, meeting rooms, travel services, free parking* 💳 *AE, DC, MC, V* 🍴 *BP.*

$$$ **Mansión San Carlos.** Formerly the owner's own home, this modest colonial structure puts a little space between you and the bustling Zona Viva. Floor-to-ceiling windows in the reception area look out onto a sunny courtyard dotted with statues. Sloping stairs lead up to the individually decorated rooms. Other rooms in an annex are newer, but they lack the charm of those in the main house. ✉ *Av. La Reforma 7–89, Zona 10* ☎ *362–9077* 📠 *331–6411* 🌐 *www.hsancarlos.com* *17 rooms, 3 suites* *Restaurant, fans, in-room safes, cable TV, pool, hair salon, bar, business services, free parking; no a/c* 💳 *AE, DC, MC, V* 🍴 *BP.*

$$ **Best Western Stofella.** For those who feel more at home in smaller hotels, Stofella is a real find. A short staircase leads to a flower-filled reception area. Charming rooms have small sitting areas. Ask for one of the original rooms, as those added during a recent renovation lack character. If you're feeling social, join the other guests in the cozy bar. ✉ *2 Av. 12–28, Zona 10* ☎ *334–6191* 📠 *331–0823* 🌐 *www.stofella.com* *102 rooms* *In-room safes, cable TV, gym, bar, laundry service, business services, free parking* 💳 *AE, DC, MC, V* 🍴 *CP.*

$$ **La Casa Grande.** This stately hotel is one of the best options in the New City. You enter through iron gates, then step into a small reception area that leads to a comfortable lounge with a fireplace to keep out the chill. The restaurant spills out into the courtyard; its cast-iron chairs are surrounded by arches covered with dangling philodendrons. Traditional tile floors grace the rooms, which are furnished with antiques. Rooms in the front open onto a balcony, but those in the back are quieter. ✉ *Av. La Reforma 7–67, Zona 10* ☎📠 *332–0914* 🌐 *www.casagrande-gua.com* *28 rooms* *Restaurant, fans, cable TV, bar, free parking; no a/c* 💳 *AE, DC, MC, V.*

$$ **Hotel Santa Clara.** This colonial house has character that most other hotels can't match. Ivy-covered walls give way to a cozy reception area. Some rooms surround a breezy courtyard overflowing with potted plants, while others share a balcony reached by a spiral staircase. The softly lighted rooms have wooden paneling and tile floors, as well as elegant touches like dried flowers. The Middle Eastern restaurant is recommended. ✉ *12 Calle 4–51, Zona 10* ☎📠 *339–1811* 🌐 *www.hotelcasasantaclara.com* *14 rooms* *Restaurant, room service, fans, cable TV, Internet, free parking; no a/c* 💳 *AE, DC, MC, V* 🍴 *BP.*

$$ **Meliá Guatemala.** Giant glass elevators in the atrium-style lobby ascend to a dizzying view of the city. With 22 meeting rooms and 16 ballrooms, the hotel is designed to accommodate large conventions. Rooms on the south side have the most impressive views of the surrounding volcanoes—even the health club overlooks their peaks. The hotel is convenient to the airport, but it's quite a distance from the Zona Viva. ✉ *Av. Las Américas 9–08, Zona 13* ☎ *339–0666* 📠 *339–0690* 🌐 *www.*

lasamericashotel.com ⇆ *177 rooms, 17 suites* ⚐ *2 restaurants, room service, minibars, cable TV, health club, sauna, spa, bar, laundry service, business services, convention center, meeting rooms, car rental, free parking* ▭ *AE, DC, MC, V* 🍽 *BP.*

The Old City

$$ **Hotel Royal Palace.** This diamond-in-the-rough hotel is a welcome retreat from the frantic pace of the streets outside. A tile fountain reminiscent of Andalusia is the centerpiece of the courtyard. The rooms are slightly musty but are nevertheless comfortable and quiet. Ask for one with a view of 6 Avenida—it's a great way to view the action without having to fight the crowds. ✉ *6 Av. 12–66, Zona 1* ☎ *220–8970* 📠 *238–3715* 🌐 *www.hotelroyalpalace.com* ⇆ *74 rooms* ⚐ *Restaurant, cable TV, gym, sauna, concierge, airport shuttle, travel services, parking* ▭ *AE, DC, MC, V.*

★ $$ **Pan American.** The grande dame of downtown hotels, the Pan American was for many years the most luxurious lodging in town. To step into the lobby of this former mansion is to leave the confusion of the city behind. A covered courtyard with attractive wrought-iron chandeliers spills out from the restaurant, whose servers wear traditional highland dress. The rooms are small but attractive, with tile floors, handmade rugs and bedspreads, and walls adorned with traditional paintings. ✉ *9 Calle 5–63, Zona 1* ☎ *232–6807* 📠 *232–6402* 🌐 *www.hotelpanamerican.com* ⇆ *51 rooms* ⚐ *Restaurant, fans, cable TV, laundry services, concierge, Internet, meeting rooms, airport shuttle, travel services, free parking; no a/c* ▭ *AE, DC, MC, V.*

$ **Chalet Suizo.** This quiet hotel has been popular with budget travelers for more than 40 years. An attractive central courtyard behind the reception area is a great place to relax. Facing a series of smaller courtyards, the rooms are all fairly plain. The staff is friendly and will happily store your extra luggage while you travel around the country. ✉ *14 Calle 6–82, Zona 1* ☎ *251–3786* 📠 *232–0429* ⇆ *51 rooms, 15 with bath* ⚐ *Restaurant, travel services; no room TVs, no a/c* ▭ *No credit cards.*

$ **Fortuna Royal.** This hotel has succeeded where few others have by offering stylish accommodations for a reasonable rate. The marble-floor lobby gives way to rooms with plush carpeting and cheery floral wallpaper. To top it off, everything is immaculately clean. ✉ *12 Calle 8–42, Zona 1* ☎ *230–3378* 📠 *251–2215* ⇆ *20 rooms* ⚐ *Restaurant, room service, fans, cable TV, free parking; no a/c* ▭ *AE, DC, MC, V.*

$ **Hotel Colonial.** It occupies a lovely 19th-century house, but this hotel isn't quite as charming inside. However, the reception area overlooks an enclosed patio overflowing with potted plants, and the lounge is furnished with reproductions of antiques. The rooms all have colonial-style furnishings; some of the larger ones have very nice views. ✉ *7 Av. 14–19, Zona 1* ☎ *232–6722 or 232–2955* 📠 *232–8671* 🌐 *www.hotelcolonial.net* ⇆ *42 rooms* ⚐ *Cafeteria, cable TV, free parking; no a/c* ▭ *AE, DC, MC, V.*

★ $ **Posada Belén.** This little bed-and-breakfast on a quiet side street is exceptional, thanks to the couple that runs it. Built in 1873, the family's former home has been renovated just enough to combine old-world charm with modern comfort. Rooms have tile floors, handwoven bedspreads, and walls decorated with Guatemalan paintings and weavings.

A small but impressive collection of Mayan artifacts graces the dining room. Family-style meals are made to order by the owners, who are also a great source of information about the city. ✉ *13 Calle A 10–30, Zona 1* ☎ *232–9226 or 254–4530* 📠 *251–3478* 🌐 *www.guatemalaweb.com* *10 rooms* *Dining room, fans, library, airport shuttle, travel services, free parking; no room TVs, no a/c* 💳 *AE, DC, MC, V.*

¢–$ **Hotel Spring.** Most rooms here face a pleasant courtyard with cast-iron tables and chairs and lots of greenery. Several on the second floor share a balcony that overlooks the avenue. A small café behind the courtyard is a great place to relax after a day of exploring the city. Next door is a refuge for street children, so keep your eyes open for those tempted to pickpocket a less-than-alert tourist. ✉ *8 Av. 12–65, Zona 1* ☎ *232–6637* 📠 *232–0107* *40 rooms, 22 with bath* *Cable TV, free parking; no a/c* 💳 *AE, DC, MC, V.*

¢ **Hotel Ajau.** This slightly faded hotel has an interior courtyard and three floors of balconied rooms. The rooms are clean, and have tile floors and a few pieces of wooden furniture. Rooms facing away from the street are quieter. ✉ *8 Av. 15–62, Zona 1* ☎ *232–0488* 📠 *251–8097* *43 rooms, 23 with bath* *Cable TV, free parking; no a/c* 💳 *No credit cards.*

Nightlife & the Arts

The Zona Viva is the city's nightlife center, offering everything from sedate bars to noisy discos. Strolling the streets is especially entertaining, as people come here to see and be seen. Dress codes have been implemented by many dance clubs, which generally means men must wear dress shoes to be admitted. Expect lines around the block at the most popular places.

Old City nightspots have more character than those in the New City, so they shouldn't be passed up just because the area isn't the greatest. Walking alone at night isn't a good idea, especially south of 15 Calle. At night it's always best to take a cab for any destination more than a few blocks away.

The New City

The **Brass Beer Company** (✉ 3 Av. 12–48, Zona 10) serves a variety of excellent microbrews to a mellow crowd. **Giuseppe Verdi** (✉ 14 Calle at Av. La Reforma, Zona 9) is an upscale bar that caters mostly to tourists. Attracting an international crowd, **Sesto Senso** (✉ 2 Av. 12–81, Zona 10) offers live music ranging from Guatemalan folk to American pop. A longtime favorite, **El Establo** (✉ Av. La Reforma 10–31, Zona 9) has been showcasing rock and roll for more than two decades.

Discos come and go, but the place to be right now is **NYX** (✉ 2 Av. 12–52, Zona 10). **Rich and Famous** (✉ Los Proceres Mall, Av. La Reforma and Blvd. de los Proceres, Zona 9) is a decent club in a mall. A fun crowd heads to **Salambo** (✉ 1 Av. 13–70, Zona 10), where the ambience is decadently campy.

The Old City

Drawing an intellectual crowd, **La Bodeguita del Centro** (✉ 2 Calle 3–55, Zona 1) hosts live music and poetry readings. If you feel like dancing, go to **El Gazabo** (✉ 6 Calle at 3 Av., Zona 1).

Sports & the Outdoors

Fishing

Guatemala's southern coast is one of the best billfishing spots in the world, especially during fall and spring. Several world records have been recorded here. The targets are sailfish that can reach up to 150 pounds, but enormous yellow tuna and blue marlin are often caught in the outer waters. **Artmarina** (✉ Iztapa ☎ 881–4035 🌐 www.artmarina.com) offers outings on well-equipped vessels. **Villas del Pacifico** (✉ Iztapa ☎ 316–1741) is one of the best companies in the area, offering a variety of excursions from the Iztapa area.

White-Water Rafting

On an exhilarating white-water rafting trip down the Río Coyolate, offered June through October, you'll pass iguanas sunning themselves, toucans resting on overhanging branches, and flitting morpho butterflies. Take a break from paddling to enjoy the warm waterfalls. **Clark Tours** (✉ 14 Calle and Av. La Reforma in the Camino Real, Zona 10 ☎ 470–4700 or 470–3850 🌐 www.clarktours.com.gt) offers a range of trips. **Maya Expeditions** (✉ 15 Calle 1–91, Local 104, Zona 10 ☎ 363–4965 🌐 www.mayaexpeditions.com) offers trips that range from easy to challenging.

Shopping

With the exception of the big market in the Old City, shop hours are weekdays 10–1 and 3–7, Saturday 10–1.

Art

Works by contemporary Guatemalan painters are on display at **El Ático** (✉ 4 Av. 15–45, Zona 14). **Galería Ríos** (✉ Calle Montúfar 0–85, Zona 9), in the Centro Comercial Plaza, has a good selection of works by local artists. **Sol de Río** (✉ 5 Av. 10–22, Zona 9) is a small, but well worth a visit.

Books

In the Zona Viva, **Sophos** (✉ Av. La Reforma 13–89, Zona 10) is one of the best places in the city to find books in English (as well as German and French). You can even grab a cup of coffee while you peruse the shelves.

Etc. Ediciones (✉ 6 Av. 13–35, Zona 10) has a decent selection of books. Used English-language paperbacks (including, for some reason, lots of westerns) can be bought or borrowed at **El Establo** (✉ Av. La Reforma 10–31, Zona 9). **Geminis** (✉ 3 Av. 17–05, Zona 14) sells recent titles in English. The **Instituto Guatemalteco Americano** (✉ 1 Ruta 4–05, Zona 4 ☎ 331–0022) has an extensive lending library of English-language titles. The gift shop at **Museo Popol Vuh** (✉ 6 Calle at 6 Av., Zona 10) has an interesting collection of books on art, archaeology, and history.

Handicrafts

If you're in the market for *típica,* a term that roughly translates as "typical goods," head to **Mercado Central** (✉ 8 Calle and 8 Av.). Goods from highland artisans can be found at **Mercado de Artesanías** (✉ 6 Calle in La Aurora Park, Zona 13).

A number of stores east of Avenida La Reforma sell handmade goods. It's small, but **El Gran Jaguar** (✉ 14 Calle 7–49, Zona 9) has a decent selection. The spacious **San Remo** (✉ 14 Calle 7–60, Zona 9) has a wide variety of handcrafted items. **Típicos Reforma Utatlán** (✉ 14 Calle 7–77, Zona 13) has an excellent selection of textiles made in highland villages.

Across Avenida La Reforma is a cluster of souvenir shops. In addition to *artesanía,* **Coleccion 21** (✉ 12 Calle 4–65, Zona 14) has an art gallery featuring works by local painters. The elegant **Casa Solares** (✉ Av. La Reforma 11–07, Zona 10) is pricey, but you can be certain that you are buying the best-quality goods. **In Nola** (✉ 18 Calle 21–31, Zona 10) specializes in textiles, but you'll also find wool and leather items. It's your best bet if you only have time to pop into one shop. **Topis** (✉ Calle 12 and Diagonal 6, Zona 10) has a fine selection of pottery by artists from Antigua.

In the Old City, **Lin Canola** (✉ 5 Calle 9–60, Zona 1) has an excellent selection of típica and other goods. The prices are often inexpensive.

Jewelry

Esmeralda (✉ Hotel Camino Real, 14 Calle and Av. La Reforma, Zona 10) specializes in settings of the precious green stone. **Jades** (✉ Hotel Camino Real, 14 Calle and Av. La Reforma, Zona 10) is a branch of the well-known jewelry shop in Antigua. **Joyería el Sol** (✉ 13 Calle 2–75, Zona 10) is one of the city's best-known jewelers. **L'Elegance** (✉ Camino Real, 14 Calle and Av. La Reforma, Zona 10) sells exquisitely crafted silver trays, vases, jewelry boxes, and place settings by the Italian Camusso family.

Leather

Arpiel (✉ Av. La Reforma 15–54, Zona 9 ✉ Av. Las Américas 7–20, Zona 13) has reasonably priced leather goods. **Principe de Gales** (✉ 2 Calle 16–28, Zona 15) sells clothing, including hand-tailored leather items.

In the Old City, **Piel Kabal** (✉ 10 Av. 16–24) sells custom-made leather jackets.

Side Trips from Guatemala City

Biotopo Monterrico

48 km south of Guatemala City.

The Biotopo Monterrico encompasses 6,916 acres along Guatemala's Pacific coast and includes everything from mangrove swamps to dense tropical forests. This is a haven for ornithologists, as the reserve is home to more than 100 species of migratory and indigenous birds. Turtles swim ashore from July to February, and you can often see them digging nests for their eggs at night. The nearby village of Monterrico even has a decent beach, but be careful about the rough current. Most people choose to go in an organized tour, but heading south from Monterrico by bus will get you within striking distance of the park. From there you'll have to hoof it. ✉ *South of village of Monterrico* ☎ *No phone* *Free.*

Copán

238 km (147½ mi) northeast of Guatemala City.

Lying in the jungles of western Honduras, the ancient city of Copán is considered one of the pinnacles of Mayan achievement. The powerful pyramids, the stately stelae depicting various rulers, and other relics left by this highly advanced civilization make this a must-see. Remarkably well preserved, the ornate ruins are arranged around an expansive, neatly groomed central plaza.

Copán reached its apex during the 8th century, when it controlled much of the southern reaches of the Mayan empire. It was then home to more than 20,000 people. Archaeologists have been excavating the ancient city for more than a century, but significant discoveries have only been made in the last 25 years. What researchers do know comes from hieroglyphics carved when the city was at its peak. The tales still visible today tell of kings, gods, and bloody battles.

The most fascinating artifact here is the Hieroglyphic Stairway, a massive structure that contains the single largest collection of glyphs in the world. Erected by King Smoke Shell, the 63 steps immortalize Copán's kings. The carving pays special attention to King Smoke Jaguar, who ruled over the city at the height of its power. Though once placed chronologically, the history can no longer be read because an earthquake knocked many steps free and archaeologists replaced them out of order. All may not be lost, however, as experts have located an early photograph of the stairway that may prove the key to unlocking the proper sequence. The **Museo de Escultura Maya,** near the entrance, contains facades of a ball court and several temples. Some of the sculptures, such as the leering skulls on the tombs, are amazingly detailed. The main draw is a model of the Rosalila Temple, which archaeologists found buried nearly intact beneath another structure. To get to Copán, head southeast from Guatemala City toward Jalapa. Approximately 50 km from Jalapa, take an unnamed road north toward Zacapa. A sign will indicate the turn-off to Copán and the Honduran border, which is another 50 km east. ✉ *Copán Ruinas, Honduras* ☎ *No phone* 🌐 *www.copanruins.com* 🎫 *$10* ⏲ *Daily 9–5.*

Guatemala City A to Z

AIR TRAVEL

Most international flights into Guatemala head to Aeropuerto Internacional La Aurora, an unusually friendly airport where a marimba band often greets you as you step off the plane. The international airlines serving the airport are American, Aviateca, Continental, Copa, Iberia, KLM, Mexicana, Taca, Tapsa, and United.

Domestic carriers fly between the capital and Flores–Santa Elena, in El Petén; and Puerto Barrios and Río Dulce, on the Atlantic coast. Serving these routes are Aeroquetzal, Aerovias, and Tikal Jets.

Domestic carriers **Aeroquetzal** ☎ 334-7689. **Aerovias** ☎ 332-7470 or 332-5686. **Tikal Jets** ☎ 334-5568.

International carriers **Aerovias** ☎ 332-7470 or 332-5686. **American** ☎ 334-7379. **Continental** ☎ 366-9985. **Copa** ☎ 361-1577. **Iberia** ☎ 332-0911. **KLM** ☎ 367-6179. **Mexicana** ☎ 333-6001. **Taca** ☎ 361-2144. **Tapsa** ☎ 331-9180. **United** ☎ 336-9900.

AIRPORTS & TRANSFERS

Less than a mile from the New City, Aeropuerto Internacional La Aurora is a bit too close for comfort. A taxi to the airport from downtown runs $6–$8, and there is a $3 airport tax.

Aeropuerto Internacional La Aurora ☎ 361-2144 or 332-6085.

BUS TRAVEL TO & FROM GUATEMALA CITY

The *terminal de buses,* or main bus station, is in Zona 4. From here you can catch a bus to almost anywhere in the country. Autobuses de Oriente has service to the Atlantic Lowlands, Las Verapaces, and El Petén. Transgalgos travels to the highlands.

Some companies run small minivans, which are a much more comfortable way to travel. Atitrans, Turansa, and Vision Travel offer shuttle service to most cities.

Atitrans ☎ 832-0644 or 832-3371. **Autobuses de Oriente** ☎ 238-3894. **Transgalgos** ☎ 232-3661 or 220-6018. **Turansa** ☎ 832-2928. **Vision Travel** ☎ 832-3293.

BUS TRAVEL WITHIN GUATEMALA CITY

The bus system can be quite confusing, but locals are usually happy to point you to the one you need. Buses that serve La Reforma say REFORMA on the windshield; likewise, buses that say TERMINAL all pass by the main bus station in Zona 4. Only the buses marked AEROPUERTO go to the airport. Bus service pretty much ends at 8 PM. Watch your belongings at the bus station, as well as while boarding, riding, and exiting the bus.

CAR RENTAL

If you're not intimidated by Guatemala City's winding mountain roads, renting a car is a great way to see the countryside. There are several international agencies at Aeropuerto Internacional La Aurora and dozens in the New City. Reputable local companies include Tabarini and Tikal.

Local Agencies **Avis** ✉ 6 Av. 11-24, Zona 9 ☎ 332-7744. **Budget** ✉ Av. Hincapié 11-01, Zona 13 ☎ 332-2024. **Hertz** ✉ 7 Av. 14-76, Zona 9 ☎ 332-2242. **National** ✉ 12 Calle Montúfar 7-69, Zona 9 ☎ 360-2030 🌐 national@intelnet.net.gt. **Tabarini** ✉ 2 Calle A 7-30, Zona 10 ☎ 331-2643 🌐 www.tabarini.com. **Tikal** ✉ 2 Calle 6-56, Zona 10 ☎ 361-0257.

CAR TRAVEL

Driving in Guatemala City is a headache. You can expect narrow streets jammed with traffic at just about any time of day. Things get better once you move out of the center of the city. Drives to nearby destinations like Antigua, for example, can be quite pleasant.

Break-ins are common in the capital, so it's best to park in a guarded lot. All expensive and most moderate hotels have protected parking areas. Avoid leaving anything of value in the car.

EMERGENCIES

If you're a little out of sorts, there's no reason to leave your hotel because Farmacias Klee delivers 24 hours a day. El Sauce Las Americas, with branches in the Old City and the New City, is open 24 hours a day. Osco and Meykos also have reputable pharmacies in the New City's Zona 10.

Emergency Services **Ambulance** ☎ 128. **Fire** ☎ 122 or 123. **Police** ☎ 110 or 120.

Hospitals **Centro Médico** ✉ 6 Av. 3-47, Zona 10 ☎ 332-3555. **Hospital Herrera Llerandí** ✉ 6 Av. 8-71, Zona 10 ☎ 334-5959 or 332-5455.

Pharmacies **El Sauce Las Americas** ✉ Calle 23 and Av. Las Américas, Zona 13 ☎ 331-5996 ✉ 4 Av. and 16 Calle, Zona 1 ☎ No phone. **Osco** ✉ 16 Calle and 4 Av., Zona 10 ☎ 337-1566. **Meykos** ✉ Blvd. Los Próceres, Zona 10 ☎ 363-5903 ✉ 6 Av. 5-01, Zona 9 ☎ 334-1962. **Farmacias Klee** ☎ 360-8383.

MAIL & SHIPPING

To ship important packages, use Federal Express or United Parcel Service. Both have offices in the New City. You can also send packages from the Correos Central.

Overnight Services **United Parcel Service** ✉ 12 Calle 5-53, Zona 10 ☎ 360-6460. **Federal Express** ✉ Av. 7-12, Bodega 20, Zona 14 ☎ 80/472-2222 in U.S.

Post Offices **Correos Central** ✉ 7 Av. 12-11, Zona 1 ☎ 332-6101.

MONEY MATTERS

You can exchange currency at almost any bank in Guatemala City. Bancared, one of the most popular banks, has 150 ATMs around the city. Many hotels even have ATMs on the premises.

Bancared ✉ 7 Av. 15-45, Zona 9. **Banco Industrial** ✉ 7 Av. 5-10, Zona 4, Guatemala City.

SAFETY

Guatemala City is no more dangerous than any other large city. To avoid being preyed upon by pickpockets and other unsavory characters, leave expensive jewelry and watches at home, carry purses and camera bags close to your body, and take along only as much cash as you need. At night stick to well-lighted areas and take taxis.

TAXIS

Taxis can be found waiting at hotels and intersections or can be flagged down on the street. Most do not have meters, so negotiate a price before getting in. Within a single zone, a ride should cost Q16–Q24; between zones expect to pay Q32–Q48. Taxis Intercontinental is a reputable firm.

Taxis Intercontinental ☎ 336-9624 or 202-0980.

TOURS

Many major tour operators offer half- and full-day tours of the capital as well as day trips outside the city. Area Verde offers white-water rafting and kayaking trips. Other reputable companies are Clark Tours, Jaguar Tours, Tropical Tours, Turansa, and Unitours.

Clark Tours ✉ 14 Calle and Av. La Reforma, in the Camino Real, Zona 10 ☎ 470-4700 or 470-3850 🌐 www.clarktours.com.gt. **Jaguar Tours** ✉ 13 Calle 3-40, Edificio Atlantis, 3rd fl., Zona 10 ☎ 363-2640. **Maya Expeditions** ✉ 15 Calle 1-91, Zona 10 ☎ 363-4955 🌐 www.mayaexpeditions.com. **Tropical Tours** ✉ 3 Calle A 3-22, Zona 10 ☎ 339-3662 🌐 www.tropicaltoursoperador.com. **Turansa** ✉ Km 15, Carretera Roosevelt, Zona 11, locale 69 ☎ 595-3575 🌐 www.turansa.com. **Unitours** ✉ 7 Av. 7-91, Zona 4 ☎ 230-0696.

VISITOR INFORMATION

Inguat, Guatemala's ever-helpful government tourism office, is open weekdays 8–4 and Saturday 8–1.

Inguat ✉ 7 Av. 1-17, Zona 4 ☎ 331-1333 or 331-1334 🌐 www.mayaspirit.com.gt.

ANTIGUA

45 km (28 mi) west of Guatemala City.

Filled with vestiges of its colonial past—cobblestone streets, enchanting squares, and deserted convents—Antigua instantly transports you back hundreds of years to when the Spanish ruled this land. Founded in 1543, the city was initially called Santiago de los Caballeros de Guatemala after the patron saint of the conquistadors. For 200 years it was the capital of a region that included what is now Central America and part of Mexico. Along with Lima and Mexico City, it was one of the greatest cities of the Americas.

By the late 18th century the city had been destroyed by earthquakes several times. Because it was a major political, religious, and intellectual center—it had 32 churches, 18 convents and monasteries, 7 colleges, 5 hospitals, and a university—it was always rebuilt. Powerful tremors struck again in late 1773, reducing much of the city's painstakingly restored elegance to rubble. The government reluctantly relocated to a safer site in the Ermita Valley, 45 km (28 mi) east, where Guatemala City now stands.

Ironically, it is because Antigua was abandoned that it retains so much of its colonial character. Only the poorest inhabitants stayed put after the capital was moved, and being of limited means, they could only repair the old structures, not tear them down or build new ones. In the 1960s laws took effect that limited commercial development and required what development did occur to keep within the city's colonial character. The National Council for the Protection of Antigua Guatemala was formed in 1972 to restore the ruins, maintain the monuments, and rid the city of such modern intrusions as billboards and neon signs. Restoration projects, both private and public, have transformed Antigua into a captivating destination.

Today you'll find a mountainside enclave that is vastly more pleasant than Guatemala City. An ever-increasing influx of visitors has brought in some of the country's finest hotels and restaurants, a collection of boutiques and galleries, and several dozen Spanish-language schools that attract students from all over the world. Antigua is also a favored escape for wealthy Guatemalans. Its higher prices mean that many people cannot afford to live here, so they travel to the city each day to sell their wares.

The most spectacular time to be in Antigua is Semana Santa, which brings a series of vigils, processions, and reenactments of Christ's last days in Jerusalem. You'll see Roman centurions charging through the streets on horseback, boulevards carpeted with colored sawdust and flowers, and immense hand-carried floats wending their way through throngs of onlookers.

Numbers in the text correspond to numbers in the margin and on the Antigua map.

a good walk

Any tour of Antigua must start at **Plaza Mayor** 1, the tree-shaded central park. As in most other Central American communities, this is a place that always buzzes with activity. On the north side of the square stands the **Palacio del Ayuntamiento** 2, an imposing structure that once served as the city hall. Facing it is the **Palacio de los Capitanes Generales** 3. The most impressive building on the square is the **Catedral de San José** 4, one of the loveliest of the city's many churches. Across 5 Calle Oriente from the cathedral is the **Museo de Arte Colonial** 5, where you'll find religious art dating from the 17th century. Between 2 and 4 you can visit **Casa Popenoe** 6, a private residence and a restored and beautifully furnished colonial mansion, two blocks east. Close by are the ruins of **Convento Santa Clara** 7, with hidden passages and mysterious underground rooms, and the **Monasterio San Francisco** 8, where you can knock on the tomb of Friar Pedro de San José de Betancur to have your prayers answered.

Head north on 2 Avenida to reach the labyrinthine ruins of the **Convento de las Capuchinas** 9. Two blocks east, spanning 5 Avenida Norte, is the graceful **Arco de Santa Catalina** 10. Half a block north is the **Nuestra Señora de La Merced** 11, an ornate church painted the same brilliant yellow as the arch. Walk west to walk around the impressive ruins of **La Recolección** 12. Just to the south is a covered market called **Mercado Central** 13. Women from nearby villages come here to sell fruits and vegetables.

TIMING Taken at a leisurely pace, this tour can easily fill a day. Along the way, you'll find plenty of spots with views of the volcanoes in which to take breaks. Remember that most sights close promptly at 5 PM and that some ruins are closed on Sunday and Monday.

What to See

off the beaten path

ANTIGUA SPA RESORT – Massages, facials, and a variety of other treatments are available at this spa, roughly 3 km (2 mi) from Antigua in the village of San Pedro El Panorama. Free transportation to and from Antigua is provided, when you book an appointment. ✉ *3 Av. 8–66, Zona 14* ☎ *832–3960 or 333–4620* 📠 *832–3968.*

★ 10 **Arco de Santa Catalina.** The only remnant of the once-enormous Convent of St. Catherine is this beautiful yellow arch that spans 5 Avenida Norte, a street locals call Calle de Santa Catalina. The convent was founded in 1613 with only four nuns, but by 1693 its growing numbers forced it to expand across the street. The arch was built to allow the sisters to pass from one side to the other unseen. ✉ *5 Av. Norte and 2 Calle Poniente* ☎ *832–0184* *Q30.*

need a break?

Near the Arco de Santa Catalina you'll find the **Posada Don Rodrigo** (✉ 5 Av. Norte 17), a colonial mansion that has been transformed into a hotel. Wander around the courtyards and gardens, listen to the marimba musicians, and indulge in a serving of Antiguan flan, a desert layered with figs and sweet potatoes. You'll want to come back for dinner.

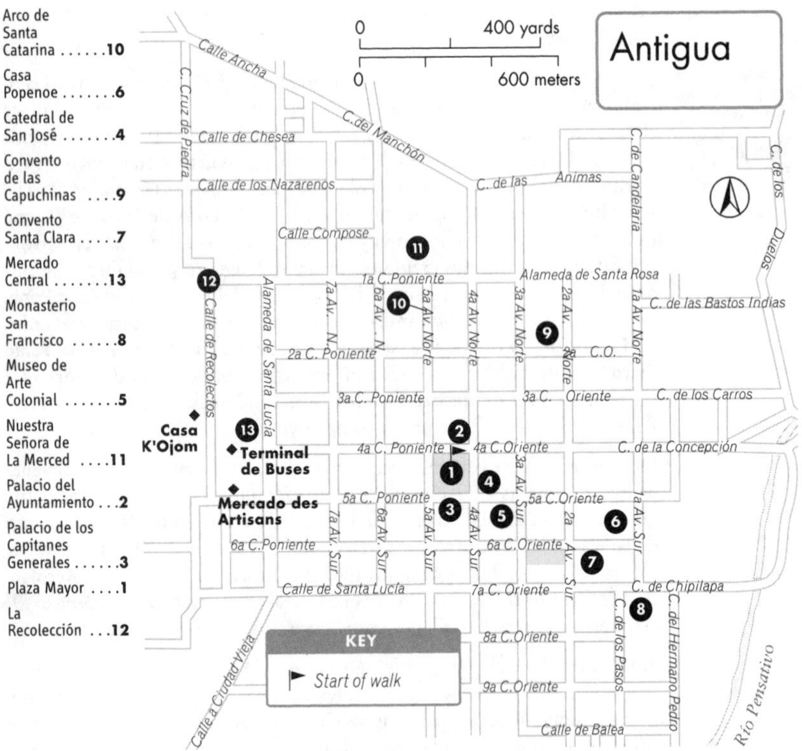

Casa K'Ojom. K'Ojom means "music" in three indigenous languages, and this very modest museum highlights the musical traditions of Guatemala's vastly diverse indigenous population. An interesting 15-minute documentary film is a good introduction for the newcomer touring the collection of musical instruments and other artifacts. A gift shop sells locally made crafts, simple instruments, and recordings of Guatemalan music. While you're here, learn about harvesting and roasting coffee beans at the adjacent coffee plantation, which has a working mill dating from 1883. The museum is in the village of Jocotenango, 4 km (2 mi) from Antigua. Taxis from Antigua run 20–25 quetzales. ✉ *Calle del Cemetario Final, Jocotenango* ☎ *832–0907* *Q25* ⏲ *Weekdays 8:30–4, Sat. 8:30–2.*

❻ **Casa Popenoe.** A short loop through this beautifully restored colonial mansion takes you through courtyards and several rooms containing decorative items, including original oil paintings, fine ceramic dishes, and other items that have been in the house since its original construction in 1636. An English-speaking guide is usually available. Since this is a private home, hours are limited. ✉ *1 Av. Sur at 5 Calle Oriente* ☎ *No phone* *Q10* ⏲ *Mon.–Sat. 2–4.*

❹ **Catedral de San José.** Only two chapels remain in what was once the city's main house of worship. The lovely white cathedral was completed in

1680 but destroyed in an earthquake less than 100 years later. As in most other Latin American churches, the cross and altar are toward the east so that worshippers face the Holy Land. ⊠ *4 Av. Sur, east side of Plaza Mayor* ☎ *No phone* 🎫 *Q3.*

★ 9 **Convento de las Capuchinas.** Antigua's largest convent was built by the Capuchins nuns, whose number had swelled because they, unlike other sisterhoods, did not require young women to pay dowries to undertake the religious life. They constructed the mammoth structure in 1736, just a decade after the first of their order arrived from Madrid. The convent was abandoned after the earthquake of 1773, even though damage to the structure was relatively light. In the 1940s the convent was restored and opened to the public. The ruins, which are quite well preserved, include several lovely courtyards and gardens, the former bathing halls, and a round tower lined with the nuns' cells—two of which illustrate cloistered life with rather eerie mannequins. Climb to the roof for a memorable view of the surrounding landscape. ⊠ *2 Av. Norte at 2 Calle Oriente* ☎ *832–0184* 🎫 *Q30* ⏲ *Daily 9–5.*

7 **Convento Santa Clara.** Shortly after it was founded in 1699, the Convent of St. Clara grew to be a rather elaborate complex housing nearly 50 nuns. When it was destroyed by an earthquake in 1717, the sisters quickly rebuilt it with the intention of having it exceed its former glory. It was struck by violent tremors again in 1773, and the site was finally abandoned. The remaining arches and courtyards make a pleasant place to roam. Keep an eye out for hidden passages and underground rooms. ⊠ *2 Av. Sur at 6 Calle Oriente* ☎ *832–0184* 🎫 *Q30* ⏲ *Daily 9–5.*

13 **Mercado Central.** The smell of fresh fruits and vegetables will lead you to this unassuming market. Women in colorful skirts sell huge piles of produce culled from their own gardens. Their husbands are nearby, chatting with friends or watching a soccer match. ⊠ *Between Amaeda de Santa Lucia and Calle de Recolectos.*

8 **Monasterio San Francisco.** Pedro de San José de Betancur, a friar who lived in the 17th and 18th centuries, was canonized by Pope John Paul II in 2002 for his good works, which has made his tomb at the Monastery of St. Francis an important local landmark. Many miracles are ascribed to Friar Pedro, who until recently answered all the prayers of petitioners, who had only to knock gently on his casket. His remains have since been moved to a more finely rendered receptacle to the left of the main altar, but those in need of his assistance still cover the original tomb with letters, photos, and plaques. The remainder of the ruins, dating from 1579, house a small museum dedicated to Friar Pedro's legacy. You can see his simple clothes and the knotted ropes he used for flagellation. The upper floor is worth a visit for the incredible views of the surrounding hinterland and volcanoes. Enter the ruins through a small path near the rear corner of the church. ⊠ *7 Calle Oriente and 1 Av. Sur* ☎ *No phone* 🎫 *Q3* ⏲ *Daily 9–5.*

5 **Museo de Arte Colonial.** On the former site of the University of San Carlos, the Museum of Colonial Art, its cloisters left largely intact through the shakier centuries, holds a collection of mostly 17th-century religious

paintings and statues commissioned by the Castilians. There's also a display of photographs of Semana Santa celebrations. ✉ *Calle de la Universidad and 4 Av. Sur* ☎ *832–0429* 🎫 *Q25* 🕒 *Tues.–Fri. 9–4, weekends 9–noon and 2–4.*

need a break?

Wander over to **Cookies, Etc.** (✉ 4 Calle Oriente and 3 Av. Norte), a five-table café and pastry shop serving 15 kinds of homemade cookies filled with nuts, chocolate, coconut, oatmeal, and spices.

★ ⓫ **Nuestra Señora de La Merced.** Our Lady of Mercy is one of Antigua's most eye-catching attractions, known far and wide for its fanciful yellow stucco facade. The church was built in 1548, only to be destroyed by an earthquake in 1717. It was finally rebuilt in 1767, six years before a second massive earthquake forced the city to be abandoned. Architect Juan Luis de Dios Estrada wisely designed the church to be earthquake resistant. The squat shape, thick walls, and small, high windows are responsible for La Merced surviving the 1773 quake with barely a crack. The church's unique facade incorporates deities from the Mayan religion, including six squat figures near the top that represent the Mayan equivalent of Atlas. The attached monastery, which has an immense stone fountain in the central courtyard, has excellent views of surrounding volcanoes. There are remnants of unfinished restoration projects here and there, and the fountain never seems to flow, but this doesn't interfere with the church's beauty, particularly when the bougainvillea are in bloom. ✉ *1 Calle Poniente and 6 Av. Norte* ☎ *No phone* 🎫 *Q3* 🕒 *Daily 9–noon and 3–6.*

❷ **Palacio del Ayuntamiento.** As in colonial times, the City Hall continues to serve as the seat of government. Today it also houses two museums, the Museo de Santiago (Museum of St. James) and Museo del Libro Antiguo (Museum of Antique Books). The former, which adjoins what was once the city jail, displays colonial art and artifacts; Central America's first printing press is displayed in the latter, along with a collection of ancient manuscripts. ✉ *4 Calle Poniente, north side of Plaza Mayor* ☎ *832–5511* 🎫 *Q10* 🕒 *Tues.–Fri. 9–4, weekends 9–noon and 2–4.*

❸ **Palacio de los Capitanes Generales.** Although it has not yet been fully restored, the Palace of the Captains General is easily recognized by its stately archways. It houses the city's tourism office and other governmental agencies. ✉ *5 Calle Poniente, south side of Plaza Mayor.*

⚑ ❶ **Plaza Mayor.** Surrounded by old colonial buildings, this tree-lined square is where locals and travelers alike pass quiet afternoons on shady benches listening to the trickling fountain. ✉ *4 Calle Poniente and 5 Av. Norte.*

⓬ **La Recolección.** Despite opposition from the city council, which felt the town already had plenty of monasteries, La Recolección was inaugurated in 1717, the same year it was destroyed by an earthquake. Like many others, it was quickly rebuilt but shaken to the ground again in 1773. A stone arch still graces the church stairway, but the ceiling did not fare so well—it lies in huge jumbled blocks within the nave's crumbling walls. The monastery is in better shape though, with spacious courtyards lined with low arches. Enter by a small path to the left of the church. ✉ *1 Calle Poniente at Calle de Recolectos* ☎ *No phone* 🎫 *Q30* ⏲ *Daily 9–5.*

Where to Stay & Eat

$$–$$$$ Fodor'sChoice ★ ✕ **Welten.** You'll feel like a guest in a private home when you arrive at this restaurant—you even have to knock to get in. Take your pick of tables, which are on a patio with cascading orchid plants, by a small pool in the rear garden, or in one of the elegantly appointed dining rooms. The menu includes homemade pasta dishes, such as *anolini* served with a creamy pepper-and-cognac sauce, as well as fish and meat dishes served with a variety of sauces. All the vegetables are organic, and the bread is baked right on the premises. ✉ *4 Calle Oriente 21* ☎ *832–0630* 💳 *AE, DC, MC, V* ⏲ *Closed Tues.*

$$–$$$ ✕ **La Casserole.** Classic French dishes incorporate subtle Guatemalan influences at La Casserole. Although the menu changes every week or so, there are a few constants—-seafood bouillabaisse cooked in a slightly spicy tomato sauce and steak tenderloin with a salsa made from spicy *chiltepe* peppers are two standouts. The peach-and-gold walls of this restored colonial mansion are lined with rotating painting and photography exhibits. ✉ *Callejón de la Concepción 7* ☎ *832–0219* 💳 *AE, DC, MC, V* ⏲ *Closed Mon. No dinner Sun.*

$–$$ ✕ **Fonda de la Calle Real.** An old Antigua favorite, this place now has three locations serving the same Guatemalan and Mexican fare. The original restaurant, on 5 Avenida Norte near Plaza Mayor, has pleasant views from the second floor. It tends to be a bit cramped, however. A newer space, around the corner on 3 Calle, is in a colonial home spacious enough to offer indoor and outdoor seating. Musicians stroll about on weekends. The menu includes queso fundido and a famous *caldo real* (a hearty chicken soup). ✉ *3 Calle Poniente 7 at 6 Av. Norte* ☎ *832–0507* ✉ *5 Av. Norte 5 at 4 Calle Poniente* ☎ *832–2696* 💳 *AE, DC, MC, V.*

★ **$** ✕ **El Mediterraneo.** This tiny restaurant serves the best Italian food in the city. Northern Italian specialties, delicious antipasti, and delicate homemade pastas are among the favorites. Wash it all down with a selection from the affordable wine list. The atmosphere and decor are low-key, but the service is first rate. ✉ *6 Calle Poniente 6–A* ☎ *832–7180* 💳 *AE, DC, MC, V* ⏲ *Closed Tues.*

¢–$ ✕ **Café Flor.** Once this homey restaurant switched from Mexican to Asian cuisine, it never looked back. The friendly proprietors serve a menu that includes Thai curries, Chinese noodles, and Indian vegetable dishes. Be careful—some of the dishes, especially the curries, are quite spicy. Asian food aficionados will find the food not at all like the real thing, but Antigua is, after all, about as far from the source as you can get. On weekends the restaurant is open until midnight. ✉ *4 Av. Sur 1 at 5 Calle Oriente* ☎ *832–5274* 💳 *AE, DC, MC, V.*

¢–$ ✕ **Frida's.** Looking for a place where you and your friends can knock back a few margaritas? At this festive cantina the whole group can fill up on Mexican fare, including taquitos, enchiladas, and burros, the diminutive siblings of the American-style burrito. Things really get going when the mariachi band shows up. Fans of Frida Kahlo and Diego Rivera will find a great selection of prints from these veritable masters—the menu even bears Frida's signature portrait. ✉ *5 Av. Norte 29, near Arco de Santa Catalina* ☎ *832–0504* ▭ *AE, DC, MC, V.*

¢–$ ✕ **Quesos y Vino.** This small Italian restaurant serves up homemade pastas, pizzas from a wood-burning oven, and a variety of home-baked breads. Choose from an impressive selection of cheeses and wines sold by the bottle. ✉ *5 Av. Norte 32, near Arco de Santa Catalina* ☎ *832–7785* ▭ *V* ⊙ *Closed Tues.*

¢ ✕ **Café Condesa.** Breakfast starts at 6:45 AM and specials such as toast topped with strawberries, papaya, or mango and omelets made with fresh vegetables will give you plenty of sightseeing fuel. For lunch try the quiche or the brie plate; the homemade pies and pastries are also notable. You can eat in the café's airy dining room or grab a cappuccino and a sweet roll at Café Condesa Express next door. ✉ *5 Av. Norte, west side of Plaza Mayor* ☎ *832–0038* ▭ *MC, V.*

¢ ✕ **Café de la Fuente.** This popular eatery takes over the courtyard of La Fuente, a classy collection of shops in a renovated colonial estate. Classical music creates a peaceful atmosphere. The international breakfasts, served until 11 AM, are excellent and the Mexican-style eggs *ranchero* are not to be missed. There are several vegetarian options. La Fuente also makes one of the best desserts in town—a decadently rich chocolate brownie topped with coffee ice cream and chocolate syrup. ✉ *4 Calle Oriente 14, at 2 Av. Norte* ☎ *832–4520* ▭ *AE, DC, MC, V.*

¢ ✕ **La Cuevita de los Urquizá.** With its fixed-price *menu del día,* La Cuevita is a good place for cheap, authentic eats. Mouth-watering aromas from steaming ceramic bowls of authentic Guatemalan food greet you at the restaurant's entrance. There's no guess work at this small eatery, what you see is what you get, and the food is excellent. After choosing your meal, head to the pleasant covered garden in the back. ✉ *2 Calle Oriente 9D* ☎ *No phone* ▭ *V.*

★ ¢ ✕ **Doña Luisa Xicotencatl.** This restaurant—named after the mistress of Spanish conquistador Pedro de Alvarado—is something of a local institution; tables are scattered throughout a dozen rooms, but it's still not easy to get a seat. Early-morning specialties include fruit salad, pancakes, and very fresh bread (the bakery is right downstairs). Sandwiches and other light fare make for ample lunch and dinner options. The service can be slow, but the eclectic decor makes the wait pleasant. The bulletin board downstairs is an excellent source of information for travelers. ✉ *4 Calle Oriente 12, at 3 Av. Norte* ☎ *832–2578* ▭ *DC, MC, V.*

★ $$$–$$$$ ✕🏨 **Mesón Panza Verde.** A beautiful courtyard with a fountain and colorful gardens welcome you to this retreat. The elegant rooms downstairs open onto small gardens, while the romantic suites upstairs have four-poster beds piled high with down comforters and terraces where hammocks swing in the breeze. The rooftop patio is wonderful in late afternoon or early morning, and the restaurant ($–$$$) is one of the best in town. The meat dishes are particularly good, such as the *lomito* (pork) bourguignonne with escargot. ✉ *5 Av. Sur 19* ☎📠 *832–2925* 🌐 *www.panzaverde.com* ⇨ *3 rooms, 9 suites* ☝ *Restaurant, in-room safes, wading pool, bar, shop, laundry service, Internet, free parking; no a/c, no TV in some rooms* ▭ *AE, DC, MC, V* 🍽 *CP.*

★ $$$$ **Casa Santo Domingo.** This elegant hotel was built around the ruins of the ancient Monasterio Santo Domingo, taking advantage of its long passageways and snug little courtyards. Dark carved-wood furniture, yellow stucco walls, and iron sconces preserve the monastic atmosphere, but luxurious amenities abound. Unfortunately, the food at the restaurant is considerably less inspiring than the rest of the package. *3 Calle Oriente 28* *832–0140* *832–4155* *www.casasantodomingo.com.gt* *107 rooms* *Restaurant, room service, in-room safes, cable TV, pool, massage, sauna, spa, bar, shop, laundry service, concierge, airport shuttle, free parking; no a/c* *AE, DC, MC, V.*

$$$$ **Portahotel Antigua.** As a tasteful combination of colonial elegance and modern comfort, Portahotel Antigua is one of the city's most popular lodgings. The sparkling pool, set amid lush gardens, is a treat after a day exploring the dusty city streets. Standard rooms have plenty of space for two, while one- and two-level suites can house a whole family quite comfortably. The oldest part of the hotel is a colonial-style building with a restaurant, bar, and a beautiful sitting room. Weddings are sometimes held in a sunny esplanade overlooking the ruins of Iglesia de San José. *8 Calle Poniente 1, at 5 Av. Sur* *832–0288 or 832–0331* *832–0807* *www.portahotels.com* *77 rooms* *2 restaurants, room service, in-room safes, cable TV, pool, bar, playground, business services, convention center, free parking; no a/c* *AE, DC, MC, V* *BP.*

$$$$ **Posada del Ángel.** You'd never know from the unassuming wooden gate that you're at the threshold of Antigua's most beautiful lodging. It's all part of the ruse at this truly angelic inn. Large corner fireplaces warm the rooms, each of which is decorated with well-chosen antiques. Those on the main floor look out onto a plant-filled courtyard, while the suite on the second floor has a private rooftop terrace. The staff has catered to presidents and prime ministers, but you'll receive the same fine service. *4 Av. Sur 24A* *832–5303, 800/934–0065 in U.S.* *www.posadadelangel.com* *5 rooms* *Dining room, room service, cable TV, bar, library, concierge, airport shuttle, free parking; no a/c* *AE, DC, MC, V.*

Fodor'sChoice ★

$$$ **Casa Azul.** Not many hotels have guest books filled with recommendations for specific rooms, but the ones on the second floor are so good that people want to be sure to share them with others. The upstairs rooms are more expensive, but they're larger and brighter and have views of the volcanoes; all rooms are painted in washes of red and, of course, blue. Communal sitting rooms open onto a pleasant courtyard; breakfast is served beside the small pool. *4 Av. Norte 5* *832–0961 or 832–0962* *832–0944* *www.casazul.guate.com* *10 rooms* *Cable TV, pool, hot tub, sauna, free parking; no a/c* *AE, DC, MC, V* *CP.*

$$$ **La Casa de Los Sueños.** This stunning colonial mansion, recently converted into an elegant bed-and-breakfast, may truly be the house of your dreams, as the name implies. A lovely patio is covered on all sides by hanging plants. A joyful antique hobbyhorse and a square grand piano reside in the sitting room. Tastefully decorated with antiques, the rooms are painted the washed-out hues that typify Antigua. *1 Av. Norte 1* *832–0802 or 832–2177* *www.lacasadelossuenos.com* *8*

rooms ♿ *Restaurant, cable TV, pool, free parking; no a/c* 💳 *AE, DC, MC, V* 🍽 *BP.*

$$$ 🏨 **Hotel Posada de Don Rodrigo.** A night in this restored colonial mansion is a journey back in time. All the rooms have soaring ceilings and gorgeous tile floors and are set around two large courtyards and several smaller gardens. A tile fountain trickles in the dining room, which is on a garden terrace; to the side a woman prepares tortillas on a piping-hot grill. Light sleepers, beware: the lively marimba band can sometimes play long into the night. ✉ *5 Av. Norte 17* ☎ *832–0291* 🌐 *www.hotelposadadonrodrigo.com* *35 rooms* ♿ *Restaurant, cable TV, bar, laundry service, free parking; no a/c* 💳 *AE, DC, MC, V* 🍽 *CP.*

$$ 🏨 **Hotel Aurora.** This genteel inn, still run by the same family that opened it in 1923, has an unbeatable location in the heart of the city. The dimly lighted colonial-style rooms face a beautifully tended garden. You can relax on a tiled portico strewn with plenty of comfortable rattan chairs. Rooms have wooden furniture and old-fashioned armoires. ✉ *4 Calle Oriente 16* ☎📠 *0217/5515* 🌐 *www.hotelauroraantigua.com* *16 rooms* ♿ *Cable TV, free parking; no a/c* 💳 *AE, DC, MC, V* 🍽 *BP.*

★ **$$** 🏨 **Hotel Convento.** This hotel was built among the ruins of an old convent where only the often-photographed Arco de Santa Catalina remains. The spacious rooms, all a bit dimly lighted, are tastefully decorated with handicrafts and handwoven bedspreads. Most face a verdant courtyard where a smattering of tables and chairs encourages you to settle in with a good book. The modern rooms in the annex are brighter and have kitchenettes. ✉ *5 Av. Norte 28, at 2 Calle Poniente* ☎ *832–3080* 📠 *832–3079* 🌐 *www.convento.com* *18 rooms* ♿ *Restaurant, some kitchenettes, cable TV, shop, Internet, free parking; no a/c in some rooms* 💳 *AE, DC, MC, V.*

★ **$$** 🏨 **Quinta de las Flores.** Located southeast of the city, Quinta de las Flores has plenty of peace and quiet along with views of three volcanoes from the well-tended gardens and the open-air dining room. This 19th-century hacienda combines colonial comfort with a sense of whimsy—the decor includes modern takes on traditional crafts. All rooms have fireplaces to keep you cozy on chilly evenings. The quaint bungalows, which sleep as many as five, even have small kitchenettes. ✉ *Calle del Hermano Pedro 6* ☎ *832–3721 or 832–3722* 📠 *832–3726* 🌐 *www.quintadelasflores.com* *9 rooms, 5 bungalows* ♿ *Restaurant, some kitchenettes, minibars, pool, bar, playground, laundry service; no a/c, no TV in some rooms* 💳 *AE, DC, MC, V.*

$ 🏨 **Posada Asjemenou.** There are plenty of charming hotels in colonial mansions, but you won't pay through the nose at this one. The rooms are clean and comfortable, and the staff is friendly and eager. The small café serves breakfast and snacks. If you hanker for more substantial fare, head to the nearby pizzeria run by the same family. ✉ *5 Av. Norte 31, at 1 Calle Poniente* ☎📠 *832–2670* *asjemenou@yahoo.com* *12 rooms, 9 with bath* ♿ *Café; no room TVs, no a/c* 💳 *AE, DC, MC, V* 🍽 *CP.*

$ 🏨 **Posada Los Bucaros.** The pretty fountain that gives this hotel its name, set against a wall in the courtyard, is just one of the little touches that make this hotel special. The rooms have red-tile floors and wrought-iron furnishings. The owner and staff are extremely friendly. ✉ *7 Av. Norte 94* ☎📠 *832–2346* 🌐 *www.hotelosbucaros.com* *12 rooms* *Cable TV, free parking; no a/c* 💳 *No credit cards.*

¢ **Jungle Party.** The cleanest, cheapest, and friendliest budget hostel in Antigua, Jungle Party is the place for backpackers and bargain hunters. The simple, shared rooms with bunkbeds are spotless and the showers have plenty of hot water. The pleasant courtyard restaurant has funky orange and yellow mushroom-shape chairs and swinging hammocks for lounging. The Salvadoran owners Monica and Ricardo are happy to help with travel arrangements. They also serve some of the best smoothies Antigua has to offer. ✉ *6 Av. Norte 20* ☎ *832–0464* *jungleparty2001@yahoo.com* *25 beds in 4 dormitories* *Restaurant, bar, laundry service, travel services; no a/c, no room TVs* 💳 *No credit cards.*

Nightlife & the Arts

You won't have trouble finding a bar in Antigua, as the city is filled with watering holes. Many of those within a few blocks of Plaza Mayor are favored by young people studying Spanish at one of the many language schools. Head a bit farther afield and you can raise a glass with the locals.

Bars

Locals swear that the place to be is **Ricky's** (✉ 4 Av. Norte 4). The conversation is convivial and the cocktails are inexpensive. If you're homesick for a pub head to **Reilly's** (✉ 5 Av. Norte 31), where pub grub is served in a relaxed atmosphere. Jan, the friendly expat owner, serves up a variety of concoctions to help you forget the travails of the day. Upstairs from Frida's is **El Atico** (✉ 5 Av. Norte 29), a popular local hangout. The pool table is free as long as you're drinking.

Guatemalans and foreigners alike enjoy the contempory elegance of **La Sala** (✉ 6 Calle Poniente 9). They close their doors around midnight, but the party continues on inside until the wee hours of the morning. Root for your favorite team at **Monoloco** (✉ 2 Av. Norte 6B), where soccer matches are always on the television. Wash down one of the giant burritos with a pint of one of the microbrews. **Onis** (✉ 7 Av. Norte 2) has a great patio that looks down onto the San Augustine ruins.

Dance Clubs

The ever popular **Chimenea** (✉ 4 Calle Poniente and 7 Av. Sur) caters to students who crowd the small dance floor. If you want to dance the night away, **Casbah** (✉ 5 Av. Norte 45) is Antigua's only real disco. Latin rhythms make the place popular. A packed salsa club with a gin-and-tonic, 1920s speakeasy feel, **La Sin Ventura** (✉ 5 Av. Sur 8) often has live bands on the weekends.

Sports & the Outdoors

From mountain biking to white-water rafting, Antigua has plenty of activities for those who want to explore the great outdoors. Don't head out solo, however. Some of the most popular destinations have been the sites of robberies. Choose a knowledgeable tour operator who will set you up with a guide who knows the area. The most reputable ones will even refund your money if the trip doesn't go as planned. Don't count on having the same luck with the freelance tour operators who approach you in Plaza Mayor.

Biking

The rolling hills that surround Antigua make for great mountain biking. Local agencies rent bikes as well as equipment like helmets and water bottles. **Mayan Bike Tours** (✉ 1 Av. Sur 15 ☎ 832–3383 🌐 www.mayanadventures.com) offers trips ranging from easy rides in a morning or afternoon to more challenging treks lasting several days. **Old Town Outfitters** (✉ 5 Av. Sur 12 ☎ 832–4171 🌐 www.bikeguatemala.com) caters to a backpack crowd, but its trips are suitable for people of all ages.

Hiking

Hikers head to the volcanoes surrounding Antigua. Of the four reachable from Antigua, only Volcán Pacayá is still active (although Volcán Fuego smokes fairly often). Volcán Pacayá erupts with some frequency, so always ask about conditions before you sign up for a tour. The crater is awhirl with sulfur gas emanating from the lava you'll see deep inside. The vapors smell terrible, so bring along a handkerchief to cover your nose. It's also a good idea to bring a sweater, as it gets cold on the summit as the sun begins to set. You'll want to stay a while to enjoy the view. Do not wear sandals to climb any of these monoliths; the volcanic rock can be razor sharp.

Antigua's best volcano expeditions are offered by **Eco-Tours Chejos** (✉ 3 Calle Poniente 24 ☎ 832–2657), whose friendly owner has climbed Volcán Pacaya more than 1,800 times. The prices are higher than most, but there are usually fewer people in each group. **Sin Fronteras** (✉ 5 Av. Norte 15 ☎ 832–1017) will take you on a one-day trip to Pacayá or a two-day trip to Fuego or Acatenango. **Voyageur** (✉ 4 Calle Oriente 14 ☎ 832–4237) is another reputable outfitter.

Shopping

The single largest concentration of shops can be found in the **Mercado de Artisanías** (✉ 4 Calle Poniente and Alameda de Santa Lucía), but stroll down any street and you'll find boutiques selling everything from finely embroidered blouses to beautiful ceramics.

Books

Thanks to its sizable expatriate population, Antigua has Guatemala's best selection of English-language reading material. Facing Plaza Mayor, **Casa del Conde** (✉ 5 Av. Norte 4) has a good selection of books. Along with new and used books, **Hamlin & White** (✉ 4 Calle Oriente 12A) sells newspapers and magazines. **Libreria Pensativo** (✉ 5 Av. Norte 29) has a huge selection of used books. **Un Poco de Todo** (✉ 5 Av. Sur 10) has a decent selection of English titles.

Clothing

A 10-minute drive southwest of Antigua brings you to San Antonio Aguas Calientes, a dusty little village built around a hot springs. It's worth a special trip here to visit **Artesanías Unidas** (✉ San Antonio Aguas Calientes ☎ 831–5950) known for its incomparable selection of handwoven fabrics. In Antigua, **Nim Po't** (✉ 5 Av. Norte 29) is a self-proclaimed *centro de textiles tradicionales.* Here you'll find a large selection of fabrics from a few dozen neighboring villages.

Pues Si Tu (✉ 5 Av. Norte 27A) is a little shop that carries a variety of clothing in traditional patterns.

Galleries

El Sitio (✉ 5 Calle Poniente 15) is a small gallery that also occasionally screens films and hosts concerts. **Galería Estilo de Vida** (✉ 4 Calle Oriente 23) displays art and furniture. An excellent selection of primitivist paintings is on display at **Wer Art Gallery** (✉ 4 Calle Oriente 27).

La Antigua Galería de Arte (✉ 4 Calle Oriente 15) features works from the 19th and 20th centuries. **Mesón Panza Verde** (✉ 5 Av. Sur 19) has a small collection of rotating exhibits.

Handicrafts

With a wide selection of *artisanía,* **Casa de Artes** (✉ 4 Av. Sur 11) is a nice place to browse. **Casa de los Gigantes** (✉ 7 Calle Oriente 18) has a good selection of quality items, including genuine antique festival masks. For hand-painted pottery by local artisans, try **Topis** (✉ 5 Av. Norte 20B).

Menage (✉ 3 Av. Sur 8) carries everything from colorful ceramics to handblown glassware. **Angelina** (✉ 4 Calle Oriente 22) sells surreal items made of carved wood.

Jewelry

Jade is mined all over the country, but it is fashioned into jewelry almost exclusively in Antigua. Most of the jade shops offer free tours of their facilities, so you can see how the stones are selected, cut, and polished. The craftsmanship is beautiful, and many pieces are quite affordable by U.S. standards. **Casa del Jade** (✉ 4 Calle Oriente 10) is small but nice. Perhaps the best place to watch artisans carving the green stone is at **Jades** (✉ 4 Calle Oriente 34 ☎ 832–3841). Former U.S. president Bill Clinton bought a necklace here for daughter Chelsea. With a small in-house workshop, **Jades Imperio Maya** (✉ 5 Calle Oriente 2) has an extremely friendly staff. The **Jade Kingdom** (✉ 5 Av. Norte 28) has tours through its factory.

Tired of green stones? **Joyería del Angel** (✉ 4 Calle Oriente 5A) has a fine selection of 100% jade-free jewelry. **Platería Típica Maya** (✉ 7 Calle Oriente 9) is a top-notch jewelry retailer.

Antigua A to Z

AIR TRAVEL TO & FROM ANTIGUA

The nearest airport is Guatemala City's Aeropuerto Internacional La Aurora, a little less than an hour's drive away. If your hotel does not offer a transfer from the airport, there are plenty of shuttle buses that run this route.

BUS TRAVEL

Several companies run frequent shuttle buses between Guatemala City and Antigua. Transportes Turisticos Atitrans and Turansa are both reputable companies. Buses leave every 15 minutes from 18 Calle and 4 Avenida in Zona 1 in Guatemala City. They depart on a similar schedule from the bus station in Antigua. It's best to call ahead for reservations, but you can also purchase tickets on board.

Transportes Turisticos Atitrans and Turansa also offer service to the Western Highlands, with the cost ranging from 100 quetzales for Chichicastenango and Panajachel to 200 quetzales for Xelajú. You can also catch a public bus at the terminal, which is cheaper but much less comfortable. There are one or two direct buses to Panajachel and Xelajú each day, as well as five or six bound for Chichicastenango. Tickets cost about 16 quetzales.

Bus Companies **Transportes Turisticos Atitrans** ⊠ 6 Av. Sur 8 ☎ 832-0644. **Turansa** ⊠ 5 Calle Poniente 11B ☎ 832-4691.

Bus Stations **Terminal de Buses** ⊠ Alameda Santa Lucía at 4 Calle Poniente, Antigua.

CAR RENTAL

If you want to rent a car to explore Antigua, it's a good idea to do so in Guatemala City's Aeropuerto Internacional La Aurora. In Antigua a reputable local agency is Tabarini Rent-A-Car.

Local Agencies **Tabarini Rent-A-Car** ⊠ 6 Av. Sur 22 ☎📠 832-0107 🌐 www.tabarini.com.

CAR TRAVEL

The roads around Antigua are mostly well paved, so drives through the countryside can be quite pleasant. Keep on your guard, though, as other vehicles may ignore traffic laws and common sense. As one jovial man behind the wheel of a bus recently said, "All drivers in Guatemala are crazy."

To reach Antigua, drive west out of Guatemala City via the Calzada Roosevelt, which becomes the Pan-American Highway. At San Lucas turn right off the highway and drive south to Antigua. If you're coming from the Western Highlands, head south near Chimaltenango.

EMERGENCIES

For all emergencies call the police department. Contact the tourist police for free escorts, information, and minor matters.

Emergencies **Police** ⊠ 5 Calle Poniente, west end of Palacio del Capitán ☎ 832-0251. **Tourist police** ⊠ 4 Av. Norte, Palacio del Ayuntamiento ☎ 832-7290 or 832-0532.

Hospitals **Hospital General de Hermano Pedro de Betancourt** ⊠ Calle de Los Peregrinos and 4 Av. Sur ☎ 831-1319.

Pharmacies **Farmacia Roca** ⊠ 4 Calle Poniente 11 ☎ 832-0612.

INTERNET

With its sizable population of expatriates, Antigua has a good supply of Internet cafés. The competition is fierce, so expect very low prices. Enlaces and Enlinea have conveniently located offices. Antigua Post also has a scanner.

Antigua Post ✉ 6 Av. Sur 12. **Enlaces** ✉ 6 Av. Norte 1. **Enlinea** ✉ 1 Calle Poniente 9 ✉ 1 Av. Sur 17 ✉ 5 Av. Sur 12.

MAIL & SHIPPING

Antigua's main post office is across from the bus station. You can drop off your letters here, or ask the staff at your hotel to mail them for you. For packages try Envios Etc.

Overnight Services **Envios Etc.** ✉ 3 Av. Norte 26.

Post Offices **Correos Central** ✉ 4 Calle Poniente and Alameda Santa Lucía.

MONEY MATTERS

You won't have a problem finding ATMs in Antigua. Bancared, near Plaza Mayor, has one that accepts cards issued in the United States.

Bancared ✉ 4 Calle Poniente 22.

SAFETY

Antigua is one of Guatemala's safest cities and the streets around Plaza Mayor are patrolled by the tourist police. Farther from the square you should walk in groups or take taxis after the sun goes down. Be careful in the countryside, where there have been some robberies. If you plan to tackle one of the nearby volcanoes, hire a reputable guide.

TAXIS

A taxi between Guatemala City and Antigua should cost about 200 quetzales. Many run between Aeropuerto Internacional La Aurora and Antigua. Taxis Antigua has a good reputation.

Taxis Antigua ☎ 832-0479 or 832-7857.

TOURS

There are a number of travel agencies that can book you on trips around the region and throughout the country. Among the better known are Rainbow Travel Center, Vision Travel, and Turansa. One of the best is Antigua Tours, run by independent guide Elizabeth Bell. It offers all sorts of personalized trips, from walking tours of Antigua to excursions to Tikal.

A number of *fincas* (farms) in the hills around Antigua offer tours. Finca Los Nietos, a coffee plantation, and Finca Valhalla, a macadamia farm, are both southwest of the city.

Tour companies **Antigua Tours** ✉ 3 Calle Oriente 28, in the Hotel Casa Santo Domingo ☎ 832-5821 🌐 www.antiguatours.net. **Finca Los Nietos** ✉ 6 km [4 mi] from Antigua ☎ 831-5438. **Finca Valhalla** ✉ 7 km southwest of Antigua ☎ 831-5799. **Rainbow Travel Center** ✉ 7 Av. Sur 8 ☎ 832-0478. **Turansa** ✉ 9 Calle Poniente at Salida a la Ciudad Vieja ☎ 832-4691. **Vision Travel** ✉ 3 Av. Norte 3 ☎ 832-3293 🌐 www.guatemalainfo.com.

VISITOR INFORMATION

Inguat, the national tourism agency, has an office in the Palacio de los Capitanes Generales, on the south side of Plaza Mayor. It is open daily 8–noon and 2–5.

Inguat ✉ 5 Calle Poniente, Palacio de los Capitanes Generales ☎ 832-0763.

THE WESTERN HIGHLANDS

Beginning near the colonial capital of Antigua, the Western Highlands run all the way to the border of Mexico. This is a spectacular stretch where grumbling volcanoes rise above broad alpine lakes and narrow river ravines, tropical valleys and misty cloud forests, pine-draped hillsides and pastoral plains. Many people come to the Western Highlands to experience its natural beauty, and few are disappointed.

This region is home to the majority of Guatemalan's indigenous people, most of whom live in small villages you'll find nestled in the valleys and perched on the hillsides. Most are descendents of the Maya, and they proudly hold onto their heritage. Many of the 23 distinct ethnic groups continue to speak their own languages, such as Cakchiquel, Mam, and Tzutuhil. Some still follow the ancient 260-day Tzolkin Maya calendar, one of the most accurate ever invented. And although Christianity has been practiced here for 500 years, it still has only a tentative hold. In Chichicastenango, Mayan ceremonies unfold on the steps of the local church. Maximón, the saint that likes to smoke and drink, hears prayers and receives symbolic offerings of cigars and whiskey from faithful believers in the lakeside village of Santiago Atitlán.

Village life, for the most part, consists of backbreaking work in the fields. Most survive on subsistence farming, selling what little is left over. Entire families pack fruits, vegetables, and whatever else they have onto their backs and head to market. Market day, held at least once a week in most communities, is as much a social gathering as anything else. Activity starts in the wee hours, when there is still a chill in the air. Bargaining and selling are carried out in hushed, amicable tones. The momentum wanes around late afternoon as the crowds depart, eager to head home before the sun sinks behind the mountains.

Highland markets were once a local affair, but in the past decade or so they have began to attract the attention of the rest of the world. The market for Guatemalan textiles has grown by leaps and bounds, and many villages have benefited. Unfortunately, many of the finer points of the weaving tradition are being left by the wayside to accommodate the frenzied shoppers. The traditional back-strap looms are speedily being replaced with gleaming sewing machines so garments can be churned out faster. Fewer people make the handmade *huipiles,* the embroidered blouses that sometimes take as long as six months to weave. The patterns that once relayed information, such as what village the wearer was from, are now abandoned for those favored by tourists. But you can still witness some symbols that speak volumes about the culture: if a woman's apron is finished with jagged edges, for example, it means she is from the mountains.

Much of the country's 36-year civil war was fought in the Western Highlands. During the "scorched earth" campaigns of the early 1980s, entire towns were burned to the ground and tens of thousands of people were tortured and killed by paramilitary forces. The violence was designed to so terrify the indigenous peoples that they would be afraid to

DANCING WITH THE DEAD

COLORFUL CEMETERIES WITH THEIR *turquoises and pinks, mauves and sky blues play an integral part in the living fabric of contemporary Guatemalan society. It's not uncommon to see entire families visiting their deceased relatives on Sundays. But a visit to the cemetery need not be mournful and they often bring a bottle of alcohol to share amongst themselves, occasionally tipping the bottle to the earth, so that their dead relatives also get their share. Incense is burned and shamanes perform ancient rites alongside Catholic and evangelical priests. Day of the Dead gives family members their greatest chance to celebrate and honor their deceased relatives with music, dance, song, festivals and, yes, much drinking and merriment.*

Celebrating the dead rather than mourning their passing is a Mayan tradition that reaches back to pre-Columbian times. The Popol Vuh *or Mayan Bible as it's sometimes referred to looks toward an active relationship with deceased friends and relatives. "Remember us after we have gone. Don't forget us," reads the* Popul Vuh. *"Conjure up our faces and our words. Our image will be as dew in the hearts of those who want to remember us."*

It is unknown who authored the Popol Vuh, *which was translated into Spanish in the early 18th century by Father Francisco Ximénez, but the practices and myths of the sacred book of the Maya still make their way into the Day of the Dead celebrations across Guatemala. The book has also been integral in understanding the traditions, cosmology, and mythology of the Quiché. According to scholars, it is one of the finest surviving aboriginal American manuscripts.*

The country's two most fascinating Day of the Dead celebrations take place in Santiago Sacatepéquez and Todos Santos Chuchumatán on November 1. In Santiago Sacatepéquez, a Cakchiquel pueblo located 30 km from Antigua, the villagers gather in the early morning hours and have a procession through the narrow streets to the cemetery. Once there, they take part in what is one of Guatemala's most resplendent ceremonies, flying giant kites of up to 2 meters in diameter to communicate with those who have passed away. The villagers tie messages to the kite tails to let the dead know how they are doing and to ask God for special favors. The colorful celebration is finished with a lunch feast of fiambre, *a traditional dish of cold cuts, boiled eggs, vegetables, olives, and other delicacies. The horse races in the remote mountain village of Todos Santos Chuchumatán, near Huehuetenango, are another Day of the Dead celebration not to be missed.*

The color scheme of the cemeteries is more than just decorative: turquoise and green tombs signify an adult member of the family was recently interred in the above-ground crypts, whites and yellows indicating the passing of an elderly family member, and pinks and blues are reserved for deceased children.

Whether or not you are lucky enough to see Guatemala's cemeteries during the Day of the Dead celebrations, they are still worth a visit. While foreigners are welcome in the cemeteries, it's important to respect the traditions and dignity of those visiting deceased relatives—tread softly and leave your camera behind.

— Gregory Benchwick

assist the rebel guerrillas with so much as a loaf of bread. Thousands fled into the mountains or across the border into Mexico or Belize. Although many issues remain unresolved, the people of the Western Highlands are now weary of fighting, and most, regardless of their wartime sympathies, say that they simply want peace.

The heart of the Western Highlands is undoubtedly Lago Atitlán. At the foot of three massive dormant volcanoes—San Pedro (9,920 feet), Tolimán (10,340 feet), and Atitlán (11,560 feet)—the lake is one of the loveliest spots in Guatemala. More than a dozen communities are found along its shores. Early in the morning and on calm nights the lake's water is as smooth as glass, capturing the huge volcanic cones in its reflection. But in the early afternoon a wind known as the *xochomil* blows across the lake, and the surface turns choppy and defiant. Another curiosity of the lake is its lack of outlets—the water drains through underwater fissures. In 1976, when an earthquake broke open a gigantic underwater chamber, the surface level dropped a whopping 6 feet in a matter of hours.

To the north of Lago Atitlán is the charming village of Chichicastenango. Quiet for most of the week, it explodes with activity on Thursday and Sunday, when a sprawling open-air market takes over its main square and the surrounding streets. West of Lago Atitlán lies Xelajú, Guatemala's second-largest city. The Sierra de Chuacús, a string of active and dormant volcanoes just outside the city limits, makes this an ideal place for outdoor activities. It also has a number of Spanish schools, attracting students who want an alternative to the crowded classes in Antigua.

Guatemala has been dubbed the "land of eternal spring," and this region's warm afternoons and cool evenings fit the bill. But Xelajú and other high-altitude towns can get downright cold at night, especially in the winter. There's no need to overpack, but a sweater or jacket is essential.

Numbers in the text correspond to numbers in the margin and on the Lago Atitlán map and the Western Highlands map.

Panajachel

❶ *110 km (68 mi) northwest of Antigua.*

A few decades ago Panajachel was just a quiet Cakchiquel village on the northern shore of Lago Atitlán, but it has since grown into a hangout for foreigners who came here and loved the region so much that they never left. And who can blame them? Bordered by three volcanoes that drop off into the crystalline waters of Lago Atitlán, Panajachel's setting could hardly be more dramatic. In the past few years Panajachel has become an extremely popular destination for international travelers, so it's no surprise that the town has earned the nickname Gringotenango. But the old part of town hasn't lost its charm, and on market day Panajachel looks pretty much like any other highland village.

The **Reserva Natural Atitlán** (✉ 2 km [1 mi] west of Panajachel ☎ 762–2565) has a walking trail that loops through a small river

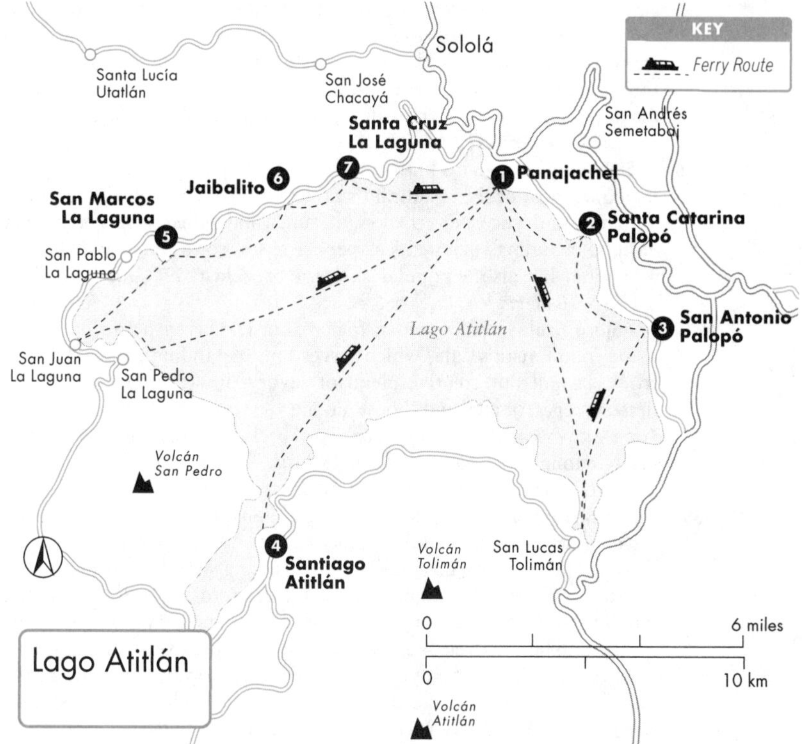

canyon, crossing suspension bridges and passing a butterfly atrium and enclosures of spider monkeys and coatimundis. There's also a private beach for a bit of post-educational relaxation. Campsites are available in the park.

For a brief history of the lake and its people head to the **Museo Lacustre de Atitlán.** Here you'll find a handful of informative displays tracing the history of the region back to precolonial times. ✉ *End of Calle Santander, in the Hotel Posada de Don Rodrigo* ☎ *No phone* 🎫 *Q35* ⏲ *Daily 8–6.*

Where to Stay & Eat

$$–$$$$ ✕ **Casablanca.** Panajachel's most elegant restaurant, Casablanca has a white-walled dining room with windows overlooking the main street. The handful of tables on the upper level is much more intimate. The menu is ample, if a bit overpriced, and includes a few seafood standouts such as lobster. Musicians occasionally entertain. ✉ *Calle Principal 0–93, at Calle Santander* ☎ *762–1015* 📠 *762–2025* 💳 *AE, DC, MC, V.*

¢–$ Fodor'sChoice ★ ✕ **El Bistro.** Hummingbirds dart among flowering vines at this romantic eatery on the shores of Lago Atitlán. Enter through an iron gate that leads into a garden hidden behind a low wall. There are outside tables and a pair of intimate dining rooms. All the delicious Italian food, from the tasty bread to the fresh pasta, is homemade. Two standout specialties are the fettuccine *arrabiata* (with a slightly spicy tomato sauce), and the steak au poivre (cooked in a wine sauce and black pepper) served with fresh vegetables. ✉ *End of Calle Santander* ☎ *762–0508* ▭ *AE, MC, V.*

¢–$ ✕ **El Patio.** Although it's known by the outdoor patio that gives the place its name, most of the restaurant's tables are inside a large dining room with little ambience. Nevertheless, the lunch and dinner menus offer great variety, including such items as pepper steak, roast pork, and chicken à la king. It's also a popular spot for breakfast. ✉ *Calle Santander* ☎ *762–2041* ▭ *V.*

★ ¢ ✕ **Pájaro Azul.** Tired of *frijoles* for breakfast? There isn't a single bean to be found at this café, which serves up outstanding crepes. Choose from a small but creative menu of savory dinner crepes and sweet dessert crepes, or pick and choose among your favorite ingredients. While you wait you can thumb through a pile of back-issue magazines (including, oddly enough, the *New Yorker*). ✉ *Calle Santander, next to the post office* ☎ *762–2596* ▭ *No credit cards.*

★ $$$$ ✕ **Hotel Atitlán.** In a quiet cove east of Panajachel, this Spanish-style inn consists of a main building flanked by two-story wings that surround a pool. The extensive grounds border on a long stretch of shoreline and the Reserva Natural Atitlán, a wooded reserve crossed by footpaths and hanging bridges. The rooms, each with tile floors, carved wooden furniture, and handwoven bedspreads, have balconies overlooking the gardens or the lake. Even if you don't stay here, stop by for views of the lake at sunset. The restaurant ($–$$$) is reliable, if a bit overpriced. ✉ *2 km (1 mi) west of Panajachel* ☎ *762–1441 in Panajachel, 360–8405 in Guatemala City* 📠 *762–0048* 🌐 *www.hotelatitlan.com* *62 rooms, 6 suites* *Restaurant, cable TV, tennis court, pool, beach, boating, bar, shop, laundry service, free parking; no a/c* ▭ *AE, DC, MC, V.*

$$ ✕ **Cacique Inn.** This inn is a collection of little buildings about a block from the main street. Spacious, if sparsely furnished, rooms have sliding-glass doors that open onto the lovely garden. The rooms may seem a bit cool because of the tile floors, but they have fireplaces that warm you up in a snap. The grounds are surrounded by a wall, which makes the terraces by the pool a private place to sunbathe. The restaurant (¢–$$) is one of the best in town, serving a wide selection of Guatemalan dishes. The agreeable chefs will sometimes even prepare dishes to order. ✉ *Calle del Embarcadero, near Calle Principal* ☎📠 *762–1205 or 762–2053* *35 rooms* *Restaurant, room service, cable TV, pool, bar, free parking; no a/c* ▭ *AE, DC, MC, V.*

$$$$ **Hotel San Buenaventura.** The well-manicured gardens of this small complex lead down past a shallow pool, bricked Mayan sauna, and jacuzzi to a private beach. Although many of the condos lack good views of the lake, their barrel-roof brick ceilings and understated Moorish influence more than make up for it. This is a great place for groups or families—each condo has a separate living area, fully outfitted kitchen and private terrace. ✉ *2 km (1 mi) west of Panajachel,* ☎ *762–2559, 337–0461 in Guatemala City* 📠 *337–1961* 🌐 *www.hotelsanbuenaventura.net* *10* *condos* ♨ *Restaurant, kitchens, cable TV, pool, hot tub, sauna, beach, boating, bicycles, playground, free parking; no a/c* ▭ *AE, DC, MC, V.*

$$$ **Hotel Posada de Don Rodrigo.** At the end of Calle Santander, this excellent hotel possesses some of the best views of the lake (they would be even better if the giant waterslide wasn't in the way). The rooms make use of handwoven fabrics from the local communities. Ask for one of the newer rooms, which have better views. Relax by the pool or in one of the hammocks hung along a breezy corridor. There is a small on-site museum that gives insight into the history of the Maya. ✉ *End of Calle Santander* ☎ *762–2326 or 762–2329* 📠 *331–6838* 🌐 *www.posadadonrodrigo.com* *39 rooms* *Restaurant, room service, cable TV, pool, sauna, squash, free parking; no a/c in some rooms* ▭ *AE, DC, MC, V.*

$$$ **Porta Hotel del Lago.** Panajachel's biggest hotel, the Porta Hotel del Lago also has the most amenities. Although it lacks the character of smaller hotels, it's comfortable and convenient and has top-notch service. Rooms have balconies overlooking the public beach on Lago Atitlán. The huge restaurant next door looks out onto the pool. ✉ *End of Calle Rancho Grande at Calle Buenas Nuevas* ☎ *762–1555* 📠 *762–1562* 🌐 *www.portahotels.com* *100 rooms* *Restaurant, room service, cable TV, pool, gym, hot tub, massage, sauna, bar, meeting room, free parking; no a/c* ▭ *AE, DC, MC, V.*

$$ **Hotel Dos Mundos.** Set amid colorful gardens, this hotel gives you comfortable accommodations without the hefty price tag of more deluxe digs. The medium-size rooms are simply and tastefully furnished. Most open onto the pool area, where you can spend your afternoon on a lounge chair with a cocktail. The restaurant has a certain elegance, with tables set beneath a soaring thatch roof. The menu includes well-made pasta dishes and lots of wine. ✉ *Calle Santander 4–72* ☎ *762–2078 or 762–2140* 📠 *762–0127* 🌐 *www.hoteldosmundos.com* *22 rooms* *Restaurant, cable TV, pool, meeting rooms, travel services, free parking; no a/c* ▭ *AE, DC, MC, V.*

$$ **Rancho Grande Inn.** A German immigrant by the name of Milly Schleisier opened this string of bungalows back in the 1940s. In so doing, she created what is still one of the most charming of Panajachel's accommodations, melding the designs of country houses in her homeland with the colorful culture of her adopted country. Each of the bungalows is unique; the largest bungalow, which can sleep up to five, has a fireplace. Breakfast is served family style every morning. ✉ *Calle Rancho Grande* ☎ *762–1554* 📠 *762–2247* 🌐 *www.travellog.com* *11 bungalows, 1 bungalow suite* *Free parking; no a/c, no room TVs* ▭ *AE, DC, MC, V* 🍽 *BP.*

$ **Müllers Guest House.** The rooms of this little inn, on a quiet street parallel to Calle Santander, call to mind a European bed-and-breakfast with their honey-hue wood floors and pastel walls. Breakfast is in the homey sitting room, the same place where you will enjoy wine and cheese in the late afternoon. Reserve well in advance during high season. ✉ *Calle Rancho Grande 1–82* ☎ *762–2442 or 762–2392* 📠 *337–0656* *htmuller@amigo.net.gt* *3 rooms, 1 bungalow* *Cable TV, free parking; no a/c* ▭ *AE, DC, MC, V* 🍽 *BP.*

¢ **Hotel Galindo.** Separate sitting rooms with fireplaces make the suites, which surround a courtyard filled with greenery, worth the extra money. However, if you're on a budget, the standard rooms are also relatively spacious and clean. The restaurant is breezy and attractive. ☒ *Calle Principal* ☎ *762–1168 or 762–2071* *hotelgranvilla@hotmail.com* *14 rooms, 4 suites* *Restaurant, free parking; no a/c, no room TVs* *No credit cards.*

Nightlife & the Arts

Because Panajachel is a resort town, it probably has the liveliest nightlife in the highlands. Most bars are clustered near the intersection of Avenida de los Arboles and Calle Principal. The **Circus Bar** (☒ Av. de los Arboles ☎ 762–2056) is a popular spot for locals and travelers alike. There's often live music. The dimly lighted **Chapiteau Disco** (☒ Av. de los Arboles) plays mostly rock. Up above the fray of Calle Santander, **La Terraza** (☒ Calle Santander, near Av. de Los Arboles) has an open-air, casual elegance perfect for early-evening cocktails. They also have a good menu focusing on continental favorites like rabbit and fondue Bourguignonne. You can enjoy good Mexican food at the aptly named **Sunset Café** (☒ Calle Santander). There's live music almost every night.

Sports & the Outdoors

Water sports are becoming more popular at Lago Atitlán, giving the lake a Club Med feel. You can rent a canoe from **Diversiones Acuáticas Balom** (☒ On the public beach near ferry terminals ☎ 762–2242). It's best to get out early and be back by noon, as the afternoon winds can be fierce. The company also offers tours of the lake.

For exploring the countryside you can rent a mountain bike at **Moto Servicio Quiché** (☒ Av. de los Arboles at Calle Principal) and pedal over to nearby villages.

Shopping

Calle Santander is one long open-air market, lined on both sides with vendors who hang their wares from fences and makeshift stalls. Examine the items carefully, as goods purchased here are often not the best quality. An outdoor market called **Tinimit Maya** (☒ Calle Santander) is easily the best place for reasonably priced artesanía. **El Guipil** (☒ Calle Santander) is a large boutique with a varied selection of handmade items from highland villages. **Ojalá Antiques** (☒ Av. de los Arboles) has a small but excellent selection of antiques.

Santa Catarina Palopó

❷ *4 km (2½ mi) east of Panajachel.*

You'll be surrounded by the brilliant blues and greens of huipiles worn by local women as you walk down the cobblestone streets of this picturesque town. (Interestingly enough, the women used to wear predominantly red huipiles, but an influx of tourists in the 1960s requesting turquoise blouses caused the local women to change their traditional dress and adopt the gringafied turquoise color scheme.) From here you'll be treated to magical views of the trio of volcanoes that loom over the lake. In Santa Catarina you'll see ramshackle homes standing within sight of luxury chalets whose owners arrive as often by helicopter as they do by car.

Where to Stay & Eat

$$$ **Villa Santa Catarina.** Villa Santa Catarina has outstanding views. The long yellow building with an adobe-tile roof has small rooms, each with a private balcony overlooking the lake. The restaurant ($–$$) serves typical Guatemalan dishes such as *pepian de pollo* (chicken in a spicy sauce). You can relax in the pool or head to a series of natural hot springs that are only a few hundred feet away. *Calle de la Playa 334–8136 36 rooms Restaurant, cable TV, pool, waterskiing, bar, free parking; no a/c AE, DC, MC, V.*

$$$$ Fodor'sChoice ★ **Casa Palopó.** By far the best B&B on the lake, luxurious Casa Palopó has an almost mystical atmosphere. Each of the six rooms, decorated with religious-theme artworks from around the world, offer incredible views of the volcanoes. Muted blues run throughout this former villa, mirroring the colors of the lake. Most baths have giant tubs perfect for prolonged soaks. *South of Santa Catarina Palopó 762–2270 762–2721 www.casapalopo.com 4 rooms, 2 suites Restaurant, minibars, pool, hot tub, massage, sauna, bar, library, Internet, free parking; no room TVs, no a/c, no kids under 15 AE, DC, MC, V.*

San Antonio Palopó

3 *6½ km (4 mi) east of Santa Catarina Palopó.*

San Antonio Palopó is a quiet farming village, slightly larger than neighboring Santa Catarina Palopó. Most people have tiny plots of land where they grow green onions, which you may see them cleaning down by the lake. This is one of only a handful of regions in Latin America where men still dress in traditional costumes on a daily basis. Their pants have geometric motifs and calf-length woolen wraparounds fastened by leather belts or red sashes. Women go about their business wearing white blouses with red stripes. The Cakchiquel people still hold many of their Maya beliefs. For instance, infants here don't see the light of day for the first year of life; their faces are kept covered to ward off evil spirits.

The beautiful adobe **Iglesia de San Antonio Palopó** stands in a stone plaza that marks the center of town. The interior is particularly peaceful. During the day the steps are a meeting place where all passersby are sure to stop for a while.

Where to Stay

$ **Terrazas del Lago.** This charming hotel overlooking the lake is notable for its floral-pattern stone tiles. Simply decorated rooms have wooden tables and iron candlesticks. Those in front have patios with great vistas. A small restaurant serves simple meals, while several terraces are perfect for a quiet cup of afternoon tea. *Calle de la Playa 762–0037 762–0157 12 rooms Restaurant, boating, free parking; no a/c, no room TVs No credit cards.*

Shopping

On the main street, not far from the church, is an excellent women's textile cooperative, where you see master weavers in action. The process is fascinating to watch, and the finished fabrics are stunning. There's a small shop on-site where the proceeds help sustain the cooperative.

Santiago Atitlán

★ ❹ *21 km (13 mi) west of San Antonio Palopó.*

Across the lake from Panajachel, Santiago Atitlán has a fascinating history. With a population of about 48,000, this capital of the proud and independent Tzutuhil people is one of the largest indigenous communities in Guatemala. They resisted political domination during the country's civil war, which meant that many residents were murdered by the military. After a 1990 massacre in which 12 people were killed, the villagers protested the presence of the army in their town. To everyone's surprise, the army actually left, and Santiago Atitlán became a model for other highland towns fighting governmental oppression.

A road that leads up from the dock is lined on both sides with shops selling artesanía—take a good look at the huipiles embroidered with elaborate depictions of fruits, birds, and spirits. Many local women wear a "halo," which is a 12-yard-long band wrapped around their forehead. Older men also wear traditional dress, sporting black-and-white-stripe calf-length pants with detailed embroidery below the knee.

The main road leads to the squat white **Iglesia de Santiago Atitlán,** the church where Tzutuhil deities can be seen in the woodwork around the pulpit. It was on this very pulpit that Father Stanley Francis Rother was assassinated by right-wing death squads in July 1981 for his outspoken support of the Tzutuhil cause. Beloved by the local parishioners, he is remembered with a plaque near the door.

As you get off the boat, small children may offer to lead you to the **Casa de Maximón** in exchange for a few quetzales. Santiago Atitlán is one of the few places where people actively worship Guatemala's cigar-smoking Maximón, a local deity who also goes by the name San Simón. Every year a different member of the local *cofrade* (religious society) houses the wooden idol and accommodates his many faithful followers. When the children bring you to the house, you'll be ushered inside to see the shrine. If you haven't brought a cigar to leave is his collection plate, a few quetzales will do just fine. Maximón has been known to offer myriad favors, from curing illnesses to helping the faithful get a bigger house.

On the road west to San Pedro, **Parque de la Paz** commemorates a dozen Tzutuhil people, including several children, who were killed when the army open fired on a peaceful demonstration that protested the military presence here. The massacre drew national outrage, and President Serrano Elías himself apologized and withdrew military forces from Santiago. The memorial is a sober reminder of Guatemala's tortured past.

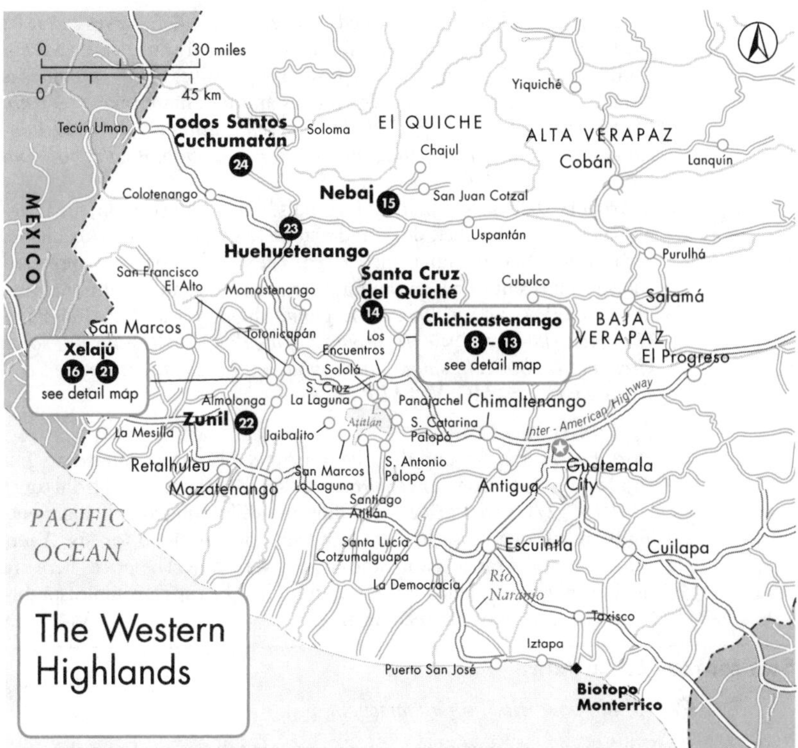

off the beaten path

SAN JUAN LA LAGUNA – Not many people stop in the Tzutuhil village of San Juan La Laguna, making it a great place to get away from the crowds and get a more authentic look at indigenous life on the lake. There are several artisan collectives in the town's center. The town is located 3 km north of San Pedro. To get here, take a water taxi from Santiago Atitlán and ask the driver to drop you at the *Muelle Uxlabil.*

Where to Stay & Eat

$$ **Bambú.** Run by a Spanish expatriate, Bambú is known for its excellent restaurant, an A-frame dining room warmed by a crackling stone fireplace. On the beautifully tended grounds are a string of thatch-roof bungalows with private patios overlooking the lake. Stone pathways loop through a series of taxonomically arranged gardens (cacti in one, flowers in the next, and so on)—most of the restaurant's fruits, vegetables, and herbs are cultivated out back. Canoes are available for paddling around the lake. *1 km (½ mi) east of town* 721–7332 721–7197 *5 bungalows* *Restaurant, boating, bar; no a/c, no room TVs* *AE, DC, MC, V.*

$$ Fodor'sChoice ★ **Posada de Santiago.** This longtime favorite has deluxe accommodations in private stone-wall bungalows with volcano views. Pass through the carved-wood doors of your bungalow and you'll find a fireplace and thick

wool blankets piled high on the bed. The restaurant (¢–$) serves exquisite food, such as smoked chicken píbil in a tangy red sauce and Thai coconut shrimp. The wine list is surprisingly extensive. On the premises is a small store where you can rent canoes and mountain bikes. ✉ *1 km (½ mi) south of town* ☎📠 *721–7167* 🌐 *www.atitlan.com* *12 bungalows* *Restaurant, boating, mountain bikes, shop; no a/c, no room TVs* 💳 *AE, DC, MC, V.*

$$ **Ecohotel Uxlabil.** San Juan La Laguna's best lodging option, the Uxlabil has its own thatched dock and extensive grounds with a medicinal herb garden, Mayan sauna, and jacuzzi. The simple rooms have textured walls reminiscent of beach sand, rather hard beds, and traditional textile bedclothes. ✉ *San Juan La Laguna, Muelle Uxlabil* ☎ *366–9555* 🌐 *www.uxlabil.com* *10 rooms, 2 bungalows* *Restaurant, some kitchenettes, hot tub, sauna, dock, boating, horseback riding; no a/c, no room TVs* 💳 *MC, V* *BP.*

Sports & the Outdoors

Horseback riding around the lake is arranged by American expats Jim and Nancy Mattisson at **Aventura en Atitlán** (✉ 10 km [6 mi] from town ☎ 201–5527). Various rides, including an exhilarating torchlit night outing, wind through lush lowlands and spectacular cloud forests. A terrific meal at the ranch awaits the end of every ride. The prices here are significantly higher than at other outfitters, but the trips are immeasurably better. Reservations are recommended.

San Marcos La Laguna

5 *15-min boat trip from Panajachel.*

San Marcos is a tiny village catering mostly to tourists. From the dock you can reach the center of the village by walking uphill along a narrow cobblestone path. The village itself has one or two stores and a restaurant around the central square. If you plan on staying in San Marcos you should remember to bring a flashlight, as most of the town does not have electricity.

Where to Stay

¢ ✕ **Il Giardino.** An open-air restaurant centered around a bamboo hut and a firepit, this little Italian eatery offers continental favorites like fondue and spaghetti, and also has a good selection of vegetarian entrées. There's live music from time to time, making this one of San Marcos' social hubs. Be sure to leave room for the delicious tiramisu. ✉ *San Marcos La Laguna* ☎ *891–0482* 💳 *No credit cards.*

$–$$ **Posada Schumann.** Full of old-fashioned charm, this little inn has bungalows set along a narrow swath of garden stretching down to the lake. Exposed stonework and unfinished wood paneling lend the place a slightly rustic feel, but the rooms are enlivened by the festive colors from local textiles. The hot water can be unreliable. ✉ *San Marcos La Laguna* ☎ *202–2216* *6 rooms, 2 rooms without bath, 4 bungalows* *Restaurant, in-room safes, some minibars, sauna, boating, laundry service; no a/c, no room TVs* 💳 *No credit cards.*

$ **Las Pirámides.** The tranquillity of the lake provides the perfect setting for this yoga retreat, which offers day-, week-, and monthlong courses.

Pyramid-shape cabins concentrate energies for spiritualists seeking that elusive "Om." The price includes accommodations, classes, and use of the sauna and other facilities. ✉ *San Marcos La Laguna* ☎ *205–7151 or 205–7302* 🌐 *www.laspiramides.com.gt* *5 rooms* *Restaurant, sauna, library; no a/c, no room TVs* *No credit cards.*

¢ **Hotel Jinava.** This small hotel is in a secluded cove and each of its bungalows is shaded by avocado and papaya trees. Ask the friendly German owner to make you a tropical drink, one of his favorite pastimes. If piña coladas are not your thing, then request a massage—he is rumored to be the best masseur on the lake. The restaurant serves up great curries and other international dishes. ✉ *San Marcos La Laguna* ☎ *705–6035 or 406–5986* 🌐 *www.jinava.de* *5 bungalows* *Restaurant, massage; no a/c, no room TVs* *No credit cards.*

2

Jaibalito

6 *10-min boat trip west of Panajachel.*

So small that it rarely appears on maps of the region, Jaibalito is the most undisturbed of the villages surrounding Lago Atitlán. Santa Cruz La Laguna is a short walk away, but otherwise Jaibalito is quite isolated. There is no boat service after 6 PM, so this village is only for those seeking peace and quiet.

Where to Stay & Eat

¢–$ **Casa del Mundo.** Built atop a cliff overlooking the azure waters, this gorgeous inn has unquestionably the best vantage point for gazing at Lago Atitlán. All the rooms have views, but those from Number 1 and Number 3 are the most breathtaking. If you can tear yourself away from the windows you'll notice the beautifully decorated rooms have wood-beam ceilings, red-tile floors, and stucco-and-stone walls hung with local handicrafts. If you want to get a closer look at the lake, kayaks are available. Meals are served family style in the cozy restaurant (¢–$). ✉ *Jaibalito dock* ☎ *204–5558 or 218–5332* 🌐 *www.lacasadelmundo.com* *12 rooms, 8 with bath* *Restaurant, boating; no room TVs, no a/c* *No credit cards.*

¢–$ **Vulcano Lodge.** This lodge amidst a coffee plantation has well-tended gardens strung with hammocks for afternoon naps. The tastefully decorated rooms are on the small side, but they all have private terraces. Alas, there are no views of the lake. The restaurant (¢-$) serves up international favorites. ✉ *Jaibalito* ☎ *410–2237* 🌐 *www.atitlan.com/vulcano* *4 rooms, 1 suite* *Restaurant; no a/c, no room TVs* *AE, DC, MC, V.*

Santa Cruz La Laguna

7 *10-min boat ride west of Panajachel.*

It's a steep walk to the hillside village of Santa Cruz La Laguna, but the hale and hearty are rewarded with a stroll through a community that most travelers overlook. The square adobe houses are positioned precariously on the slopes, looking as if they might be washed away by the next heavy rain. A highlight of this little village is a squat adobe church in the main plaza. Make sure to look inside at where the walls are lined with carved wooden saints.

Where to Stay & Eat

¢–$ **Arca de Noé.** Magnificent views are the big draw at this rustic retreat. Rooms, in several wood-and-stone bungalows, are small but neat. The delicious home cooking is served family style in the main building, which resembles a New England farmhouse. The menu changes constantly, but each meal comes with fresh vegetables, and bread hot out of the oven. Electricity is solar-generated, so there is no hot water. ✉ *Santa Cruz La Laguna* ☎ *515–3712* 🌐 *www.atitlan.com/arcadenoe.htm* *10 rooms, 5 with bath* *Restaurant, boating; no a/c, no room TVs* *No credit cards.*

¢ **La Iguana Perdida.** The Lost Iguana is part hotel and part summer camp. There is no electricity and no hot water, and the toilets are about as basic as they come. The restaurant serves up good family-style meals, and the dormitory rooms can hold up to eight of your traveling companions. For a bit more privacy choose one of the thatch-roof bungalows lit with kerosene lamps. Guests tend to be fairly young—most come for scuba-diving courses. ✉ *Santa Cruz La Laguna* ☎ *762–2621* *14 rooms, 3 cabins, 2 dormitory rooms* *Restaurant, sauna, dive shop, boating; no a/c, no room TVs* *No credit cards.*

Sports & the Outdoors

There are plenty of opportunities for hiking in the hills around Santa Cruz. It is the starting point of a scenic four-hour walk to San Marcos de La Laguna. The trail passes through several tiny villages and over gusty bluffs overlooking the lake.

Lago Atitlán's wealth of underwater wonders draws divers from around the world. **ATI Divers** (✉ Iguana Perdida ☎ 762–2621) is a certified diving school that offers courses for all levels, from basic certification to dive master.

Chichicastenango

★ *37 km (23 mi) north of Panajachel, 108 km (67 mi) northwest of Antigua.*

Perched on a hillside, Chichicastenango is in many ways a typical highland town. The narrow cobblestone streets converge on a wide plaza where most days you'll find a few old men passing the time. You'd hardly recognize the place Thursday and Sunday, when row after row of colorful stalls fill the square and overflow into the adjoining alleys. There's a dizzying array of handmade items, from wooden masks to woolen blankets to woven baskets. Much of the artesanía is produced for tourists, but walk a few blocks in any direction and you'll find where the locals do their shopping. South of the square you'll see a narrow street where women sell chickens. To the east you might run across a family trying to coax a just-purchased pig up a rather steep hill.

Try to get to Chichicastenango at dawn, when the early morning mist swirls around the vendors as they set up shop. Better yet, come late in the day on Wednesday or Saturday. Not only will you get better deals before the tourists arrive, but you'll witness the town's amazing transformation. Arriving by bus or by foot, the people of the surrounding villages come with whatever they have to sell strapped to their backs. Men balance heavy wooden tables across their shoulders, while old women bend over under the weight of wrought-iron machines for making shaved ice. Even little children help, balancing bundles bigger than they are.

With a little luck you'll visit Chichicastenango during an elaborate procession marking a saint's day for one of the equally elaborate Mayan rituals. The biggest celebration is Día de Santo Tomás, when the city explodes with parades and dances. During the festivities, held December 13–21, the *cofrades* (city leaders) wear elegant silver costumes and carry staffs topped by magnificent sun medallions.

a good walk

Any tour of Chichicastenango begins in the tranquil **Parque Central** 8, which is transformed twice each week when hundreds of vendors arrive from villages near and far. Don't forget to wander along the neighboring streets, as the market outgrew the square long ago. Presiding over Parque Central is the gleaming white **Iglesia de Santo Tomás** 9, where Christian ceremonies and Mayan mysticism intertwine. Across the square is the smaller, but no less lovely, **Capilla de Calvario** 10. On the south side of the square is **Museo Regional** 11, which provides a look at the culture of the region before the arrival of the Spanish. Head west down a street hill to the colorful **cementerio** 12, just outside town. You'll be treated to wonderful views of the city's red rooftops. If you're intrigued by the evidence of ancient rituals found in the cemetery, head south of town to the Mayan shrine of **Pascual Abaj** 13, which is still used today. If you're lucky, you might see locals praying before the stone head.

TIMING After a morning wandering around the market, you can see the rest of the sights in this little town in the course of an afternoon. Wear comfortable shoes, as the walk uphill to Pascual Abaj can be challenging.

What to See

10 **Capilla de Calvario.** Across from the Iglesia de Santo Tomás is this squat little chapel. It doesn't attract the attention that its much larger neighbor does, but from its steep steps you'll have a nice view of the market. ✉ *West end of Plaza Mayor.*

12 **Cementerio.** Filled with mausoleums painted brilliant shades of teal, yellow, and orange, the town's cemetery is one of the most colorful in the Western Highlands. In the midst of headstones topped with crosses you'll doubtless find candles and incense—evidence of Mayan rituals. ✉ *West end of 8 Calle.*

9 **Iglesia de Santo Tomás.** Standing watch over the square is this gleaming white church, busy with worshippers all day and late into the night. Enter through a door on the right side. The church was built in 1540 on the site of an ancient temple, and locals say a block of stone near the massive front doors is all that remains of the altar. The Quiché people still consider Chichicastenango their holy city. Church officials look the other way as Mayan ceremonies are still practiced here today. Some worshippers wave around pungent incense during the day, while at night

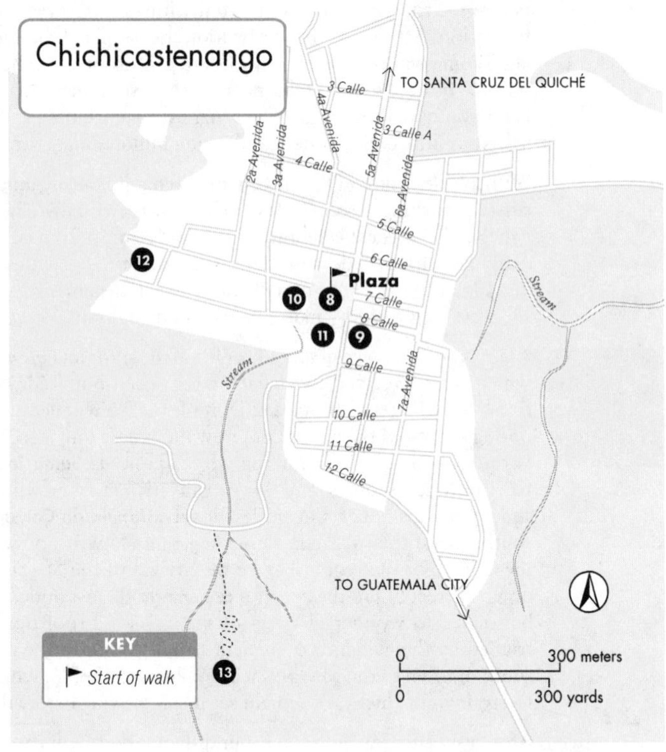

others toss rose petals and pine needles into a raging fire right on the steps of the church. ✉ *East end of Plaza Mayor.*

11 **Museo Regional.** If you want to learn more about the history of Chichicastenango, check out this little colonial-era building, which displays pre-Columbian artifacts that came from the private collection of a local priest. ✉ *Next to Iglesia de Santo Tomás* 🎫 *Donation suggested.*

8 **Parque Central.** As in most colonial villages, the heart of Chichicastenango is its central square. All the major sights are either here or on the nearby streets. Three blocks north is Arco Gucumatz, an arch over 5 Avenida where you watch vendors heading to the square. ✉ *5 Av. and 7 Calle.*

13 **Pascual Abaj.** This ancient Mayan shrine, perched on a hilltop south of town, is often vandalized by overzealous Christians. The elongated stone face of the waist-high idol is always restored so that believers can return to their daily prayers. *Shamanes,* the local shamans, lead villagers in special rites that occasionally include slaughtered chickens. Because it's one of the most accessible of the highland shrines, Pascual Abaj often attracts travelers eager to see these rituals firsthand. Try to be as unobtrusive as possible and always ask permission before taking photos. To see the shrine, follow 9 Calle until you see the signs for the narrow

footpath up the hill. Boys hanging around Plaza Mayor will guide you to the shrine for a small fee and can tell you when the rituals will take place. There is a mask factory on-site. ✉ *South of Chichicastenango.*

Where to Stay & Eat

¢–$ ✕ **Las Brasas.** An eclectic collection of local handicrafts brightens the walls of this excellent second-floor steak house. The chef, formerly of Hotel Santo Tomás, grills up a great steak, but there are plenty of other options, including a delicious *longaniza* (a spicy sausage similar to chorizo). Music and a full bar keep things lively, but not intrusively so. ✉ *6 Calle 4–52, 2nd level* ☎ *756–2226* ▭ *AE, DC, MC, V.*

¢–$ ✕ **La Fonda del Tzijolaj.** This restaurant's second-story balcony overlooking Plaza Mayor is a great place to watch the vendors set up on the eve of the market. The *pollo chimichurri* (chicken in an herb sauce) is one of the best choices from the mostly traditional menu. There are also a few surprises, such as pizza and pasta. ✉ *7 Calle and 4 Av.* ☎ *756–1013* ▭ *AE, DC, MC, V.*

¢–$ ✕ **La Villa de los Cofrades.** With two locations within a block of each other, it's hard to miss this longtime favorite. The smaller of the two has patio seating right on Plaza Mayor, where you can watch the vendors setting up their stalls while you feast on Belgian waffles or sip one of the finest cappuccinos in the country. If you're in a hurry to get to the market, remember that the service here can be miserably slow. The other location, a block away on 5 Calle, has a less hectic atmosphere. ✉ *6 Calle and 5 Av.* ✉ *Centro Comercial Santo Tomas 11* ☎ *756–1643* ▭ *AE, DC, MC, V* ⏲ *Closed Tues.*

$$$ ✕ **Hotel Santo Tomás.** Built in the Spanish style around a central courtyard, Hotel Santo Tomás is one of the town's best lodgings. Breezy passageways in which hundreds of plants spring from rustic clay pots lead past two trickling fountains. Spacious rooms are decorated with traditional textiles and antique reproductions. Each has a fireplace to warm you when the sun goes down. The back of the hotel is quieter and has views of the surrounding countryside. The large restaurant serves an excellent lunch buffet on market days. ✉ *7 Av. 5–32* ☎ *756–1316 or 756–1061* 🖷 *756–1306* ✉ *hst@itelguat.com* *70 rooms* *Restaurant, pool, gym, hot tub, sauna, bar, free parking; no a/c, no room TVs* ▭ *AE, DC, MC, V.*

$$$ Fodor'sChoice ★ ✕ **Mayan Inn.** Intricate woodwork and solid adobe construction make the luxurious Mayan Inn one of the country's loveliest hotels. It's regarded by locals as a town treasure. A tour is highly recommended, even if you're staying elsewhere. Rooms with corner fireplaces surround a series of beautifully maintained garden courtyards. Most have wide windows overlooking the pine-covered hills. The service is excellent—an attendant in traditional costume is assigned to each room. ✉ *3 Av. at 8 Calle, 1 block west of plaza* ☎ *470–4700* 🖷 *470–4701* 🌐 *www.mayaninn.com.gt* *30 rooms* *Restaurant, bar, laundry service, free parking; no a/c, no room TVs* ▭ *AE, DC, MC, V.*

★ $ **Posada El Arco.** This great little hotel has a distinctly homey feel. The spacious rooms are clean and tastefully decorated with *típica*. All rooms have fireplaces for the chilly evenings. To get here, climb up the stairs to the top of the arch that crosses 5 Avenida and turn left. ✉ *4 Calle*

4–36 ☎ *756–1255* *7 rooms* *Laundry facilities; no a/c, no room TVs* *No credit cards.*

¢–$ **Hotel Chugüila.** This hotel, in an older building a few blocks north of the plaza, has a variety of rooms facing a nice cobblestone courtyard. The plant-filled portico leading to most rooms is scattered with inviting chairs and tables. Rooms are simply furnished, and a few have fireplaces. ✉ *5 Av. 5–24* ☎ *756–1134* *luzmarielarodas@hotmail.com* *13 rooms* *No a/c, no room TVs* *AE, DC, MC, V.*

¢ **Hospedaje Salvador.** Looking like something out of the game Chutes and Ladders, this colorful mishmash of a hotel is a favorite among budget travelers. Rooms are aligned along three and four levels of incongruously curved breezeways, with steep stairs zigzagging all about. In the middle of it all is a cobblestone courtyard decorated with statues. Facing the entrance is a small shrine shared by the Virgin Mary and a Mayan deity. Though the rooms are a bit musty, the beds a bit lumpy, and the hot water sporadic at best (usually available only for a couple of hours in the morning), what the hotel lacks in comfort it compensates for with lots of character. ✉ *10 Calle at 5 Av., 3 blocks south of the plaza* ☎ *756–1329* *46 rooms, 10 with bath* *No credit cards.*

¢ **Hotel Chalet.** The Alps are nowhere to be seen, but at the very least, the sun-splashed breakfast room at this cozy little hotel does the name justice. The rooms are smallish but not cramped. Wooden masks and other handicrafts adorn the walls. A pleasant terrace is a great place for relaxing after a taxing day of roaming the markets. The hotel is down a small unpaved road near 7 Avenida. ✉ *3 Calle C 7–44* ☎ *756–1793* *756–2286* *9 rooms* *Café, travel services; no a/c, no room TVs* *AE, DC, MC, V.*

Nightlife & the Arts

Nightlife is limited in hard-working Chichicastenango, although there are many tiny bars along the streets surrounding the plaza where you can join the locals for a beer. Do not stray from the city center at night as there have been numerous attacks by *maras* (gangs). **Las Brasas** (✉ 6 Calle 4–52 ☎ 756–2226) occasionally has live music. **Café San Juan** (✉ 4 Av. San Juan 6–58 ☎ 756–2086) has a refreshing neocolonial feel and live music on the weekends. The light fare is also quite good.

Santa Cruz del Quiché

14 *19 km (12 mi) north of Chichicastenango.*

Adventurous travelers may want to continue north from Chichicastenango for further glimpses of the region called El Quiché, where you'll find traditional villages on pine-covered hills. A half-hour north of Chichicastenango lies the provincial capital of Santa Cruz del Quiché, which serves as a base for exploring the area. Quiché, as the town is commonly called, is known for its pretty white church on the east side of the Parque Central. It was built from the stones taken from a Mayan temple destroyed by the Spanish.

North of town is **K'umarcaaj,** the ancient capital of the Quiché kingdom. This once-magnificent site was destroyed by Spanish conquistadors in 1524. The ruins haven't been restored, but they are frequently used for Mayan rituals. A taxi to and from the ruins should cost less than 60

I, RIGOBERTA MENCHÚ. . . MOSTLY

In 1992 the Nobel Peace Prize was awarded to Guatemalan writer Rigoberta Menchú, raised in the tiny highland village of San Miguel Uspantán. Menchú was born in 1959, just before a string of military dictators usurped control of Guatemala for 43 war-filled years. She grew up as dozens of opposition and guerrilla groups rose to resist them. Along with many of her family members, Menchú opposed the dictatorship with peaceful demonstrations that included peasants from various regions. When she was eventually forced into exile, she continued her opposition to Guatemala's military rule by drawing international attention to the repressive regime.

In 1983 she published her testimonial, I, Rigoberta Menchú: An Indian Woman in Guatemala, *and the plight of Guatemala's indigenous people—and the brutality of the military regime—was revealed in wrenching detail. In her book Menchú described losing two brothers to malnutrition on a coffee plantation and the razing of her village by wealthy land prospectors. Most disturbingly, Menchú related the story of a third brother, who was kidnapped by the army, tortured, and then burned alive.*

In 1999 American anthropologist David Stoll challenged Menchú's account with the publication of Rigoberta Menchú and the Story of All Poor Guatemalans. *His research suggested that the conflict over the lands of Menchú's village was actually a long-running dispute between her father and his in-laws and that although Menchú's brother was unquestionably kidnapped, tortured, and murdered by the military, it was probably not carried out in the manner that Menchú had suggested. Although still a potent symbol of indigenous rights, Menchú is now viewed by some with incredulity. More than a few have called for her Nobel Prize to be revoked.*

Whether or not Menchú personally witnessed the events she describes, it is indisputable that hundreds of indigenous workers, particularly children, died of disease, malnutrition, or outright abuse on the plantations. It is also clear that the military committed innumerable acts of brutality, including public executions, in villages all across the country. In 1998 the Guatemalan Truth Commission sponsored by the United Nations denounced the military's actions during the civil war as genocide. Some argue that if Menchú's account wasn't wholly her own, but included incidents suffered by other indigenous men and women, that it doesn't detract from the horror of what occurred. If she included the experiences of others to draw attention to a conflict the international community had ignored for more than 20 years, they argue, can anyone really blame her?

Stoll himself admits Menchú is fundamentally right about the army's brutality, though he downplays it considerably, no doubt to bolster his own book's more dubious claim: that it was the guerrillas, not the ruling generals, who were responsible for igniting political violence in the highlands. But it is the debunking of Rigoberta Menchú that he will be remembered for and that will forever endear him to Guatemala's war criminals, many of whom remain in public life. Stoll may claim he's playing the devil's advocate, but in this case, the devil really doesn't need his help.

— Gary Chandler

quetzales. You can also walk the pleasant 3-km (2-mi) route without much difficulty. Follow 10 Calle out of town, where it becomes a dirt road. A tight S curve is the halfway point. The road forks at the bottom of a hill; take the road to the right.

Where to Stay & Eat

¢ ✕ **Comedor Flipper.** A cage of lively birds lends a cheerful atmosphere to this small eatery, which serves good Guatemalan fare. The *avena* (a warm wheat beverage) is delicious, especially on a cold morning. There is no sign of the restaurant's trusty namesake, though a ceramic sailfish atop the refrigerator comes close. ✉ *1 Av. 7–31, around the corner from Hotel San Pasqual* ☎ *No phone* ▭ *No credit cards.*

¢ **Hotel San Pasqual.** This little hotel has a definite charm, most of it emanating from the engaging couple that runs it. The simple rooms, with handwoven bedspreads, surround a sunny courtyard. Clotheslines full of the day's laundry stretch to the roof next door. The shared baths are clean, but hot water is available only in the morning. ✉ *7 Calle 0–43, Zona 1* ☎ *755–1107* *37 rooms, 11 with bath* ▭ *No credit cards.*

Nebaj

⓯ *95 km (59 mi) north of Santa Cruz del Quiché.*

An interesting although somewhat inaccessible part of the Western Highlands is a region called the Ixil Triangle. The Ixil Triangle is home to the indigenous Ixiles, who speak a unique language and preserve a rich culture.

The main town in this region is Nebaj, where cobblestone streets lead to a central plaza with a large colonial church. On Thursday and Sunday the town swells with people who come from the surrounding villages to sell their distinctive weavings. Besides shopping, hiking in the surrounding mountains is the main draw for tourists.

Where to Stay

¢ **Hotel Ixil.** Nebaj doesn't have much in the way of lodging; the best bet is this friendly hotel set around two courtyards. Some of the spacious rooms overlook the garden. ✉ *Nebaj* ☎ *No phone* *12 rooms* ▭ *No credit cards.*

Xelajú

91 km (56 mi) southwest of Chichicastenango.

Originally part of the Mayan empire, Xelajú was captured in the 14th century by the Quiché people. It remained part of the Quiché kingdom until 1524, when Spaniard Pedro de Alvarado defeated the great warrior Tecún Umán at a battle here in 1524. The conquistador destroyed the city and used the stones for a new city called Quetzaltenango, which means "place of many quetzals." Locals have never gotten used to the name and still refer to Quetzaltenango as Xelajú, or simply Xela.

In a valley guarded by Volcán Santa María, Xelajú has long had an economy based on agriculture. The rolling hills are particularly good for growing coffee. More recently, it has begun to attract travelers, who come

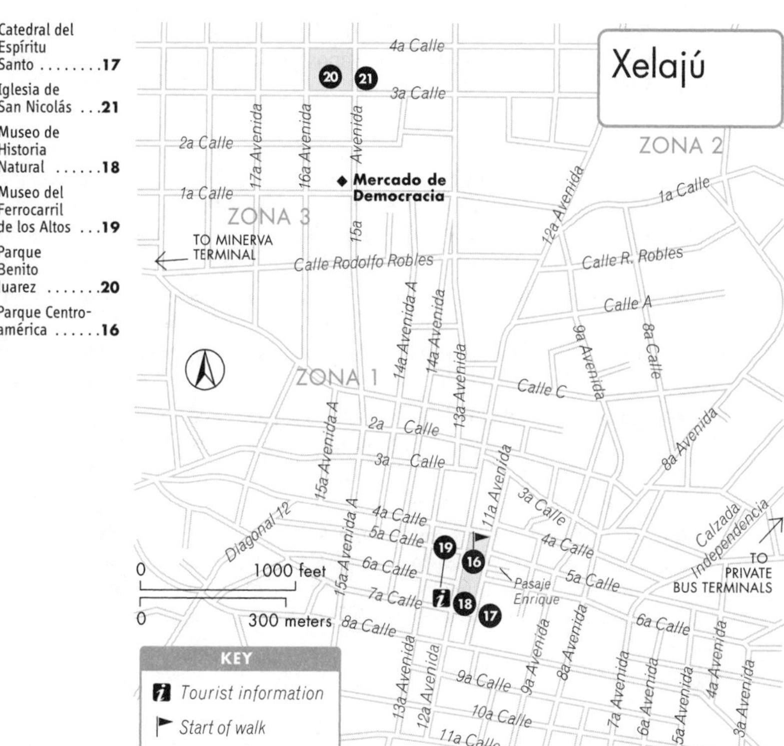

here to purchase the intricate weavings from the surrounding villages. The first Sunday of each month is the main market day, and the central square is filled with women selling their wares. The neighboring village of San Francisco El Alto plays host to one of Central America's largest markets on Friday. Less popular with tourists than Chichicastenango's Sunday market, the hillside San Francisco market with its myriad handicrafts and huge animal market is a must see.

Xelajú is also a choice place to study Spanish, as here you'll find several excellent programs widely considered more rigorous than those in Antigua. Word spreads fast, however, and the city has recently seen a sharp rise in the number of students. Xelajú is no longer the place to visit if you really want to avoid speaking English.

a good walk

Begin your stroll in the beautiful **Parque Centroamérica** 16, pausing to admire the facade of the colonial-era **Catedral del Espíritu Santo** 17. Be sure to visit the **Museo de Historia Natural** 18. Save your ticket stub for an afternoon visit to the **Museo del Ferrocarril de los Altos** 19. From the central plaza head north, stopping along the way at Mercado La Democracia for a little shopping. Two blocks north is the shady **Parque Benito Juarez** 20. Enjoy an ice cream cone in this lovely park, then check out the **Iglesia de San Nicolás** 21.

TIMING Xelajú is fairly compact, so it's possible to see the major sights in a sunny afternoon. Remember that while most sights are in Zona 1, Parque Benito Juarez is to the north in Zona 3.

What to See

Almolonga. In this charming village you'll find women wearing bright orange huipiles and beautiful headbands. At the busy Wednesday and Saturday markets you can buy fruits cultivated in the area. A few kilometers beyond the town are several hot springs where you can relax for a few quetzales. ✉ *5 km (3 mi) south of Xelajú.*

17 **Catedral del Espíritu Santo.** On the southeastern corner of Parque Centroamérica, this cathedral dates from 1535. The crumbling facade, which features life-size saints that look down upon those headed here to pray, is currently undergoing reconstruction. ✉ *11 Av. and 7 Calle, Zona 1.*

21 **Iglesia de San Nicolás.** This bluish church, on the east side of Parque Benito Juarez, is known for its unusual baroque design. Although lovely, it looks a bit out of place in the town's mix of Greek and colonial structures. ✉ *15 Av. and 3 Calle, Zona 3.*

18 **Museo de Historia Natural.** To the south of Parque Centroamérica, the Museum of Natural History is interesting mainly for its neoclassic flourishes. Inside are some examples of pre-Columbian pottery. ✉ *7 Calle and 11 Av., Zona 1* ☎ *761–6427* *Q6.*

need a break?

The inexpensive **Café Baviera** (✉ 5 Calle and 12 Av.), just off Parque Centroamérica, has an ample selection of excellent coffees and fresh pastries.

★ 19 **Museo del Ferrocarril de Los Altos.** In the same building that houses the Museum of Art, the Los Altos Railroad Museum tells the history of the railroad that once connected Xelajú with other towns in the Western Highlands. ✉ *12 Av. and 7 Calle, Zona 1* ☎ *No phone.*

20 **Parque Benito Juarez.** About 10 blocks north of Parque Centroamérica is this palm-lined park where many families spend their Sunday afternoons. Ice cream stands are in glorious abundance. ✉ *15 Av. and 3 Calle, Zona 3* *Q6.*

16 **Parque Centroamérica.** The central plaza is one of the most beautiful in Central America. It's surrounded by architectural masterpieces, such as the magnificent building called Pasaje Enríquez. ✉ *12 Av. and 4 Calle, Zona 1.*

San Miguel Totonicapán. This traditional highland village is famous for its wooden toys. The community is full of workshops where a wide variety of handicrafts are actually produced. Come on Saturday for the market day, when you can find hand-loomed textiles, wax figures, and painted and glazed ceramics. ✉ *5 km (3 mi) south of Xelajú.*

Where to Stay & Eat

$–$$$ ✕ **Il Cardinali.** For a homestyle southern Italian atmosphere with checked tablecloths, opera music, and basketed Chianti bottles hanging from the rafters, head to Il Cardinali. The extensive, pasta-heavy menu also includes pizza and a decent wine selection. The service is friendly and quick. ✉ *14 Av. 3–25, Zona 1* ☎ *761–0924* ▭ *AE, DC, MC, V.*

¢–$$ ✕ **Royal Paris.** This bistro caters to foreign students, so the menu covers a lot of bases. Some dishes aren't the least bit Parisian, such as the succulent chicken curry kebab. It's all prepared with flair, however. The ambience is definitely imported, and slightly bohemian, courtesy of the paintings of cabaret scenes. There's also a bar with an extensive wine list. ✉ *Calle 14A 3–06, Zona 1* ☎ *761–1942* ▭ *AE, DC, MC, V* ⊙ *No lunch Mon.*

$ ✕ **Da Valentino.** White walls sparsely adorned with watercolor paintings provide a subdued setting for this Italian eatery. This lets the food do all the talking, and the handmade egg noodles and delicious gnocchi covered with rich sauces speak volumes. Da Valentino advertises "high-quality slow food," and for good reason: expect to wait a while for the steaming platters of pasta to arrive. ✉ *14 Av. A 1–37, Zona 1* ☎ *761–4494* ▭ *No credit cards* ⊙ *Closed Mon.*

¢–$ ✕ **El Kopetín.** Good food, attentive service, and reasonable prices make this place popular with the locals, so it can be tough to get a table later in the evening. It couldn't be described as fancy, but this restaurant's long polished bar and wood paneling raise it above the usual neighborhood dive. The menu has a number of delicious appetizers, including traditional queso fundido and a selection of meat and seafood dishes that are smothered in rich sauces. ✉ *14 Av. 3–51, Zona 1* ☎ *761–8381* ▭ *AE, DC, MC, V.*

$$ ✕ **Hotel Villa Real Plaza.** Surrounding a covered courtyard illuminated by skylights, the spacious rooms at Hotel Villa Real Plaza all have fireplaces that you'll appreciate on cool evenings. Those in a newer wing are superior to those in the dimly lit older section. The restaurant (**¢**–$$) has an interesting menu whose offerings range from chicken cordon bleu to a variety of meaty stews. ✉ *4 Calle 12–22, Zona 1* ☎ *761–6270* 📠 *761–6780* *villareal@xelaenlinia.com* *58 rooms* *Restaurant, room service, cable TV, free parking; no a/c* ▭ *AE, DC, MC, V.*

$$ ✕ **Pensión Bonifáz.** Don't let the name fool you into thinking this is a modest establishment—Pensión Bonifáz is Xelajú's most upscale hotel. Though housed in a stately old building at the central plaza's northeast corner, it has a modern interior that doesn't quite live up to its exterior. Still, it is a comfortable, well-run establishment. The nicest rooms are in the older building, where small balconies offer nice views of the plaza. A small café serves light fare for lunch, while the larger restaurant has a continental menu. ✉ *4 Calle 10–50, Zona 1* ☎ *765–1111* 📠 *763–0671* *penbonifaz@hotmail.com* *74 rooms* *Restaurant, café, room service, cable TV, pool, bar, laundry service, free parking; no a/c* ▭ *AE, DC, MC, V.*

★ $$ **Casa Mañen.** This romantic little B&B, west of the central plaza, blends colonial comforts with modern conveniences. The rooms are spacious and homey, with handmade wall hangings and throw rugs and the occasional rocking chair. On the roof is a two-level terrace with a fantastic view of the city. Breakfast is served in a small dining room downstairs. The staff is incredibly friendly and will be happy to help you with travel plans. ✉ *9 Av. 4–11, Zona 1* ☎ *765–0786* 📠 *765–0678* 🌐 *www.*

comeseeit.com 7 rooms, 2 suites Restaurant, in-room safes, cable TV, laundry service; no a/c AE, DC, MC, V BP.

$ **Hotel Modelo.** Founded in 1892, this family-run establishment is run by a wizened man who was actually born on the premises. Over the years the distinguished hotel has maintained its tradition of good service. The wood-floor rooms, furnished with antiques, surround a few small courtyards leading off the lobby. Dinner is served in a fine colonial-style restaurant. *14 Av. A 2–31, Zona 1 761–2529 763–1376 24 rooms Restaurant, in-room safes, cable TV, bar, free parking; no a/c AE, DC, MC, V.*

¢ **Casa Kaehler.** This slightly ramshackle hotel, a few blocks off the plaza, is a popular spot with travelers on a budget. Rooms on two floors of a converted residence face a small courtyard overflowing with plants. Though simple, they're clean and comfortable. There's a separate lounge where you can chat with other guests. *13 Av. 3–33, Zona 1 761–2091 7 rooms, 1 with bath No credit cards.*

Nightlife

Aside from the lounges in the big hotels, there are only a few nightspots in Xela. Catering to the university crowd, **El Duende** (14 Av., between 1 Calle and 2 Calle, Zona 1) is the place to go dancing on the weekends. **Casa Babylon** (5 Calle 12–54, Zona 1) attracts foreign students and Guatemalans alike. They have an extensive mixed drink list. Right off the central square, **Salon Tecún** (Pasaje Enrique, Zona 1) is a small pub that is popular with students.

For a taste of Xela's bohemian scene, head to the oh-so-funky **La Luna** (8 Av. 4–1, Zona 1). Though they don't serve alcohol, the extensive hot drink menu is enough to satisfy any espresso addict or chocophile. **Cinema Paraíso** (1 Calle and 2 Av., Zona 1) is a small café that screens artsy films.

Sports & the Outdoors

BICYCLING There's great mountain biking through the hills and villages surrounding Xela. **Vrisa Bicicletas** (15 Av. 3–64, Zona 1 761–3237) rents both on-road and off-road bikes by the day or week and has maps so you can take self-guided tours of the countryside.

HIKING **Quetzaltrekkers** (Casa Argentina, 12 Diagonal 8–67, Zona 1 761–2470 beef.brownrice.com/streetschool) is a nonprofit company that supports three major social-service programs by coordinating truly unforgettable hiking trips. The three-day trek to Lago Atitlán and the two-day ascent of Volcán Tajamulco both pass through spectacular countryside and several remote villages.

Shopping

The bustling **Mercado Minerva** (6 Calle, Zona 3), next to the main bus terminal, is the best of the city's markets. There are plenty of interesting handicrafts to be found here. But watch your pockets—groups of skillful thieves prey on tourists coming to and from the buses. Artisanía from most of the villages in the region can be found in the **Mercado La Democracia** (1 Calle and 15 Av., Zona 3). Since there are relatively few shoppers, prices tend to be lower than elsewhere in the city. Near Parque Centroamérica, the **Centro Comercial Municipal** (✉ 7 Calle and 11 Av., Zona 1) has a more limited selection of souvenirs.

Brilliant views and unbelievable buys are to be found at the Friday market in **San Francisco El Alto** (✉ 16 km east of Xelajú). Many say this market is more colorful and larger than the over-visited market in Chichicastenango. Make sure to leave time to visit the open-field animal market where everything from pigs to parrots are sold. This is pickpocket heaven, so be aware of your belongings and bring only the cash you'll need for the day.

Xelajú is famous for its beautiful glass. **Vitra** (✉ 13 Av. 5–27 ☎ 763–5091) is one of the most noted stores. You'll find excellent hand-blown glass at affordable prices.

Zunil

★ 22 *9 km (5½ mi) south of Xelajú.*

At the base of an extinct volcano, the radiant village of Zunil is one of the prettiest in the highlands. Mud and adobe houses are clustered around the whitewashed church that marks the center of town. On the outskirts of the village you'll find the local cemetery, which is lined with tombstones painted in soft shades of pink and blue.

Zunil is surrounded by the most fertile land in the valley, so it's no surprise most people make their living off the land. The best day to visit Zunil is Monday, when women wearing vivid purple shawls crowd the covered market hawking fruits and vegetables grown in their own gardens.

Zunil is a good place to pay your respects to a cigar-smoking deity called San Simón. You can ask anyone in town where his likeness is, as almost everyone asks a favor of him at some time or another. The idol has become a tourist attraction, and foreigners are charged a few quetzales to see him. Be sure to bring a small gift, preferably a cigar.

High in the hills above Zunil are the wonderful hot springs of **Fuentes Georginas.** There are four pools, two of which remain in their natural basins. Unfortunately, the spring has been losing its potency over the years and is now only tepid throughout. Lounging near the rocky source in the natural pool will give you the most warmth. The springs are tucked in a lush ravine in the middle of a cloud forest, so hikers should take advantage of the beautiful trails that begin here. To get here, take the first left off the main road after passing Zunil. The entrance is open from dawn until dusk; admission is 10 quetzales.

Where to Stay

¢ **Fuentes Georginas.** Although they're a bit rundown, these dozen bungalows are adequate and have fireplaces that keep you cozy at night. The best part of staying here is having round-the-clock access to the hot springs, which close to the public at 5 PM. ✉ *8 km (5 mi) from main road* ☎ *No phone* *8 bungalows* *Restaurant, pool, free parking; no a/c, no room TVs* *No credit cards.*

Huehuetenango

23 *94 km (58 mi) north of Xelajú.*

At the foot of a mountain range called Los Cuchumatanes, Huehuetenango was once part of the powerful Mam Empire, which dominated most of the highland area. It wasn't until much later that the Guatemalan Quiché came into the area to stir things up, pushing the Mam up into the mountains.

Today Huehuetenango is a quiet town, serving mostly a gateway to the magnificent Cuchumatanes and the isolated villages scattered across them. The town surrounds **Parque Central,** where you'll find a pretty fountain and shell-shaped bandstand. The butter yellow **Catedral de la Immaculada Concepción** stands guard over the main square.

The ancient city of **Zaculeu,** 4 km (2 mi) from Huehuetenango, was built around AD 600 by the Mam tribe. The site was chosen for its strategic location, as it has natural barriers on three sides. The defenses worked all too well against the Spanish. Realizing they could not take the Zaculeu people by force, the Spaniards chose instead to starve them out. Within two months they surrendered. Today the ruins consist of a few pyramids, a ball court, and a two-room museum that gives a few insights into the world of the Mam. The site's restoration is said to be the worst in all of Guatemala, as the original archaeologists simply covered the pyramids with concrete, which was not a common building material in pre-Colombian Central America. Admission is 25 quetzales.

A short drive north of Huehuetenango, the dirt road begins to wind its way up into the mountains where traditional villages are set between massive rocky peaks. There's a **mirador,** or scenic view, about 6 km (4 mi) from Huehuetenango.

Where to Stay & Eat

¢–$$ ✕ **Las Brasas.** Grilled meats are the specialty at Huehuetenango's most elegant restaurant. Simple típica tablecloths are the only nod toward decor, actually making it the sole place in town with any atmosphere. The menu has a surprisingly broad range of options. There are even Chinese entrées, which you won't find anywhere else in town. ✉ *4 Av. 1–55* ☎ *764–2339* ▭ *AE, DC, MC, V.*

¢–$ ✕ **Lekaf.** Definitely one of Huehue's better eateries, offering everything from filet mignon to pizza, which is reputed by many locals to be the best in town. All can be washed down with a nice selection of liquados (fruit or yogurt smoothies). With live music on the weekends, this is also a good place for after-dinner drinks. ✉ *6 Calle 6–40* ☎ *764–3202* ▭ *AE, DC, MC, V.*

¢ ✕ **Jardín Café.** This colorful little corner restaurant is friendly and popular among the locals. Come early for the excellent pancakes served at breakfast, or stop by for beef and chicken dishes at lunch or dinner. The menu includes a few Mexican favorites as well. ✉ *4 Calle and 6 Av.* ☎ *769–0769* ▭ *No credit cards.*

$ **Hotel California.** There's plenty of room to live it up at this large, high-rise travelodge at the entrance to town. The entire hotel is bathed in pink, giving it a clean, though rather sterilized, feel. That said, the small rooms are pleasant enough, with televisions and tiny balconies. It's a bit from the city center. *3 Av. 4–25, Zona 5* *769–0600 or 769–0698* *769–0999* *35 rooms* *Restaurant, room service, cable TV, laundry service, free parking; no a/c* *AE, DC, MC, V.*

$ **Hotel Casa Blanca.** Who would've thought that little Huehuetenango would have such a top-notch hotel? Spacious rooms, excellent service, and a central location make it the town's best lodging option. Third-floor rooms have great views, especially when the bougainvillea are in full bloom. At the restaurant you can choose between a table in the shady courtyard or in the cozy dining room warmed by a fireplace. *7 Av. 3–41* *769–0777* *15 rooms* *Restaurant, cable TV, meeting rooms, free parking; no a/c* *AE, DC, MC, V.*

$ **Hotel Zaculeu.** When you pass through the front doors of this hotel, north of the main square, you enter a courtyard overflowing with greenery. The older rooms, set around a portico, are brightened by locally made fabrics. They can be a bit noisy, however, especially those facing the street. The newer ones in the back are quieter, but lack character. *5 Av. 1–14* *764–1086* *764–1575* *39 rooms* *Restaurant, cable TV, free parking; no a/c* *V.*

¢ **Hotel Mary.** This four-story hotel in the heart of town offers clean, if spartan, accommodations. Ask to see a few rooms, as some are much better than others. *2 Calle 3–52* *764–1618* *764–7412* *27 rooms* *Restaurant, cable TV, free parking; no a/c* *No credit cards.*

Shopping

A few blocks to the east is the **Mercado Central,** where you can purchase local handicrafts.

Todos Santos Cuchumatán

24 *40 km (24 mi) north of Huehuetenango.*

Although it takes about three hours to cover the short distance from Huehuetenango to Todos Santos Cuchumatán, the bumpy ride is probably the best way to experience the tremendous height of Los Cuchumatanes. The drive can be anxiety-provoking when one side of the winding dirt road drops off into a deep ravine. Despite the arduous journey, Todos Santos Cuchumatán is the most frequently visited mountain village. Many people come between October 21 and November 1, when the villagers celebrate the Festival de Todos Santos. The highpoint of the celebration is a horse race in which the competitors ride bareback.

Market day is Thursday. Men wear the traditional candy-cane-stripe pants and shirts with long embroidered collars. The women wear stunning red, pink, and purple huipiles with indigo skirts.

The Western Highlands A to Z

AIR TRAVEL

There is no air service to the Western Highlands.

BOAT & FERRY TRAVEL

With the exception of the service between Panajachel and Santiago Atitlán, Lago Atitlán's public ferries have been replaced by private water taxis. Although they don't follow a schedule, the private boats are much faster and cost about the same. Panajachel has two primary docks, one at the end of Calle del Embarcadero and one at the end of Calle Rancho Grande. The first is for private boats on the San Pedro route, stopping at Santa Cruz, Jaibalito, San Marcos, Santa Clara, and San Pedro. It's about 15 quetzales, no matter where you get off.

The other dock is for hour-long journeys to Santiago, with departures at 6 AM, 8:30 AM, 9 AM, 9:30 AM, 10:30 AM, 1 PM, 3 PM, 4:30 PM, and 5 PM, and return trips at 6 AM, 7 AM, 11:45 AM, 12:30 PM, 1:30 PM, and 4:30 PM. The cost is about 10 quetzales. Private boats occasionally take passengers to Santiago in about half the time.

BUS TRAVEL

Transportes Rebuli travels from Guatemala City to Panajachel hourly from 5 AM to 4 PM daily. Buses bound for Guatemala City leave Panajachel hourly from 6 AM to 3 PM daily. The 6 AM and 3 PM buses are more expensive, but they're also much more comfortable. Count on a four-hour trip.

To get to Chichicastenango and Santa Cruz del Quiché, take Veloz Quichelense, which departs from the capital on the half hour between 5 AM and 6 PM and returns on a similar schedule. For Xelajú, take Galgos buses, which leave Guatemala City at 5:30 AM, 8:30 AM, 11 AM, 12:45 PM, 2:30 PM, 5 PM, 6:30 PM, and 7 PM. They depart from Xelajú at 4, 5, 8:15, 9:45, 11:45, 2:45, and 4:45. The trip takes four hours.

To travel to Huehuetenango, you can choose from several companies for the five-hour run from Guatemala City. Los Halcones has departures at 7 AM and 2 PM. Rápidos Zaculeu runs buses at 6 AM and 3 PM. Transportes Velasquez also has daily departures at the same time.

Transportes Turisticos Atitrans and Turansa have buses that travel from Antigua to towns in the Western Highlands. You can also catch a public bus at the terminal, which is cheaper but much less comfortable. The one or two direct buses to Panajachel and Xelajú each day, as well as five or six bound for Chichicastenango.

Galgos ✉ 7 Av. 19-44, Zona 1, Guatemala City ☎ 232-3661. **Los Halcones** ✉ 7 Av. 15-27, Zona 1 ☎ 238-1979. **Rápidos Zaculeu** ✉ 9 Calle 11-42, Zona 1 ☎ 232-2858. **Transportes Rebuli** ✉ 21 Calle 1-34, Zona 1, Guatemala City ☎ 251-3521. **Transportes Velasquez** ✉ 20 Calle 1-37, Zona 1 ☎ 221-1084. **Veloz Quichelense** ✉ Terminal de Buses, Zona 4, Guatemala City ☎ No phone.

CAR RENTAL

There is only one national car rental agency in the Western Highlands, Tabarini Rent-A-Car. It might be easier to rent a car in Guatemala City instead.

Local Agencies **Tabarini Rent-A-Car** ✉ 9 Calle 9-21, Zona 1, Xelajú ☎ 763-0418 ✉ Hotel Los Cuchumatanes, Sector Brasil Zona 7, Huehuetenango ☎ 764-1951.

CAR TRAVEL

The Pan-American Highway—more country road than highway, really—heads northwest out of Guatemala City, where it is called the Calzada Roosevelt. It passes through Chimaltenango before reaching a crossroads called Los Encuentros. Here you can head north to Chichicastenango, Santa Cruz del Quiché, and Nebaj. Continue on the Pan-American Highway, and you'll pass a turnoff to Panajachel and then another for San Marcos La Laguna and other towns on Lago Atitlán. The Pan-American Highway continues over some impressive ridges and then descends to a crossroads called Cuatro Caminos, about 200 km (124 mi) from the capital. Here the road to Xelajú heads off to the south. About 60 km (37 mi) north of Cuatro Caminos, the road to Huehuetenango cuts off to the right. Many roads to the north of Huehuetenango and Santa Cruz del Quiché are unpaved and pretty rough—this is nerve-racking mountain driving relieved intermittently by memorable views.

EMERGENCIES

In Panajachel, Panamedic Centro Clínico Familiar offers 24-hour medical attention. The doctors, Francisco Ordoñez and his wife, Zulma Ordoñez, both speak English.

Emergency Services **Ambulance** ☎ 762-4121 in Panajachel, 761-2956 in Xelajú. **Police** ☎ 761-5805 in Xelajú.

Hospitals **Panamedic Centro Clínico Familiar** ✉ Calle Principal 0-72, Panajachel ☎ 762-2174.

Pharmacies **Farmacia Nueva Unión** ✉ Calle Santander near Calle Principal, Panajacel. **Farmacia Nueva** ✉ 6 Calle and 10 Av., Zona 1, Xelajú ☎ 762-4531.

INTERNET

MayaNet is the best Internet café in Panajachel. It is open daily until 9 PM and charges about 20 quetzales per hour.

Internet Cafés **MayaNet** ✉ Calle Santander, Panajachel.

MAIL & SHIPPING

All the villages in the Western Highlands have post offices, but you are probably better off posting your letters from the larger towns. If you are sending something valuable, go with DHL or one of the local companies that will ship packages. Alternativas is in Xelajú, while Get Guated Out is in Panajachel.

Overnight Services **Alternativas** ✉ 16 Av. 3-35, Zona 3, Xelajú. **Get Guated Out** ✉ Comercial Pueblito, upstairs, Panajachel. **DHL** ✉ Calle Santander, Panajachel ☎ 762-1474 ✉ 12 Av. C-35 Local 2, Zona 1 Xelajú ☎ 763-1209.

Post Offices **Chichicastenango** ✉ 7 Av. 8-47. **Panajachel** ✉ Calle Santander and Calle 5 de Febrero. **Xelajú** ✉ 15 Av. and 4 Calle, Zona 1.

MONEY MATTERS

All the larger towns in the Western Highlands have ATMs where you can use your bank card. Bancared has branches in Panajachel, Chichicastenango, Xelajú, and Huehuetenango.

Banks **Bancared** ✉ 5 Av. and 6 Calle, Chichicastenango ✉ 4 Calle 6-81, Zona 1, Huehuetenango ✉ Calle Principal 0-78, Zona 2, Panajachel ✉ 4 Av. 17-40, Zona 3, Xelajú.

SAFETY

Several groups of travelers have been robbed while hiking around the Lago Atitlán area. It is always a good idea to hire a guide, especially when you are not familiar with your destination. In Xelajú and Chichicastenango it is best to avoid the areas outside the city center at night as gang activity is reportedly on the rise.

TOURS

In Panajachel, Atitrans and Centroamericana Tourist Service are both reputable companies. Chichicastenango's only tour company, Chichi Turkaj–Tours, is well-regarded. In Xelajú, Quetzaltrekkers supports social-service programs in the area. Union Travel in Xelajú also offers tours to just about everywhere in the region.

Atitrans ✉ 3 Av. 1–30, Zona 2, Panajachel ☎ 762–2336. **Centroamericana Tourist Service** ✉ 3 Av. 4–70, Zona 2, Panajachel ☎ 762–1569. **Chichi Turkaj–Tours** ✉ 5 Calle 4–42, Zona 1, Chichicastenango ☎ 756–2111. **Quetzaltrekkers** ✉ Casa Argentina, Diagonal 12 8–67, Zona 1, Xelajú ☎ 761–2470. **Union Travel** ✉ In Los Pinos Av. Santander, Zona 2, Xelajú ☎ 762–2426.

VISITOR INFORMATION

The Guatemala tourism agency Inguat has offices in Panajachel, Xelajú, and San Miguel Totonicapán. The staff at the office in Panajachel is particularly helpful.

Inguat ✉ Calle de la Playa Publica, Panajachel ☎ 762–1392 ✉ Parque Centro América, Xelajú ☎ 761–4931 ✉ Casa de Cultura, 8 Av. 2–17, next to Hospedaje San Miguel, Zona 1, San Miguel Totonicapán ☎ 766–1575.

LAS VERAPACES

Northeast of Guatemala City you'll find heavily forested mountains drained by wild rivers running through deep caverns. This region of central Guatemala, known collectively as Las Verapaces, is split between Baja Verapaz, to the south, and Alta Verapaz, to the north. The smaller Baja Verapaz is much drier than Alta Verapaz, where mist-covered mountains are the norm. The area's humid climate, which often comes in the form of a drizzly rain called *chipi-chipi,* has made it the cradle of Guatemala's cardamom and coffee production.

Las Verapaces was once the home of the Rabinal Maya, one of the most feared tribes of the Americas. When the Spanish arrived in the early 1500s, the Rabinal fought back so fiercely that the region became known as Tezulutlán, the "Land of War." Although the Spaniards failed to overcome this tribe with brute force, they finally succeeded with ideology. In 1537 Bartolomé de Las Casas, a Jesuit who crusaded against the maltreatment of indigenous peoples, struck an unusual bargain with his compatriots: if the military stayed away for five years, Las Casas would deliver the land without spilling a single drop of blood. Spain agreed, and Las Casas began translating religious hymns into local languages. The Rabinal chief, realizing the Spanish weren't going to go away, agreed to be baptized. His people followed suit, and the "conquest" of the region meant that the area was soon dotted with orderly Spanish-style villages. It became known as Las Verapaces, "The Lands of True Peace."

Las Verapaces retains a mystical air, particularly because of the presence of the resplendent quetzal, a bird found only in the region's cloud forests. The male has a spectacularly long tail and shiny blue-green feathers, the inspiration for weaving designs and paintings all over Guatemala, as the Maya royalty wore the feathers in their crowns. The pride Guatemalans feel for this bird is reflected in the name of the country's currency, the quetzal.

The region's inhabitants are predominantly Pokomchí and Q'eqchí people, who over the years have lost much of their territory to expanding coffee plantations. As a result, they have abandoned some of their traditional ways of sustaining themselves. The region's largest city is Cobán, which has an almost completely indigenous population. Here you'll find a handful of businesses catering to visitors, making it a good base for exploring the region.

Numbers in the text correspond to numbers in the margin and on the Las Verapaces & the Atlantic Lowlands map.

Biotopo del Quetzal

★ ❶ *50 km (31 mi) south of Cobán; 164 km (102 mi) northeast of Guatemala City.*

A 2,849-acre tract of cloud forest along the road to Cobán, the Biotopo del Quetzal was created to protect Guatemala's national bird. The resplendent quetzal, known for its brilliant plumage, is endangered because of the indiscriminate destruction of the country's forests. The reserve is also known as the Biotopo de Mario Dary Rivera in honor of the Guatemalan ecologist who fought for its creation.

The elusive quetzal has been revered since the days of the ancient Maya, who called it the winged serpent. Though the Maya often captured quetzals to remove their tail feathers, killing one was a capital offense. The quetzal has long symbolized freedom because it is said the bird cannot live in captivity. Although the female quetzal is attractive, the male is as spectacular a creature as ever took to the air, with a crimson belly, blue-green back, and flowing tail feathers. Its unforgettable appearance notwithstanding, the quetzal remains difficult to spot in the lush foliage of the cloud forest. The reserve offers the chance to see the quetzal in its natural habitat during its mating season, between April and June. The best place to see the birds is not in the park itself, oddly enough, but in the parking lot of the Ranchito del Quetzal, 1½ km (1 mi) north. Since it is easier to spot quetzals around dawn or dusk, it's worth spending a night in the area. Even if you don't catch a glimpse of the legendary bird, there are plenty of other species to spot, and the luxuriant greenery of the cloud forest is gorgeous in its own right.

One of the last remaining cloud forests in Guatemala, the Biotopo del Quetzal is a vital source of water for the region's rivers. Moisture that evaporated from Lago Izabal settles here as fog, which provides sustenance for the towering old-growth trees. Plants like lichens, hepaticas, bromeliads, and orchids abound. If you're lucky, you can see howler mon-

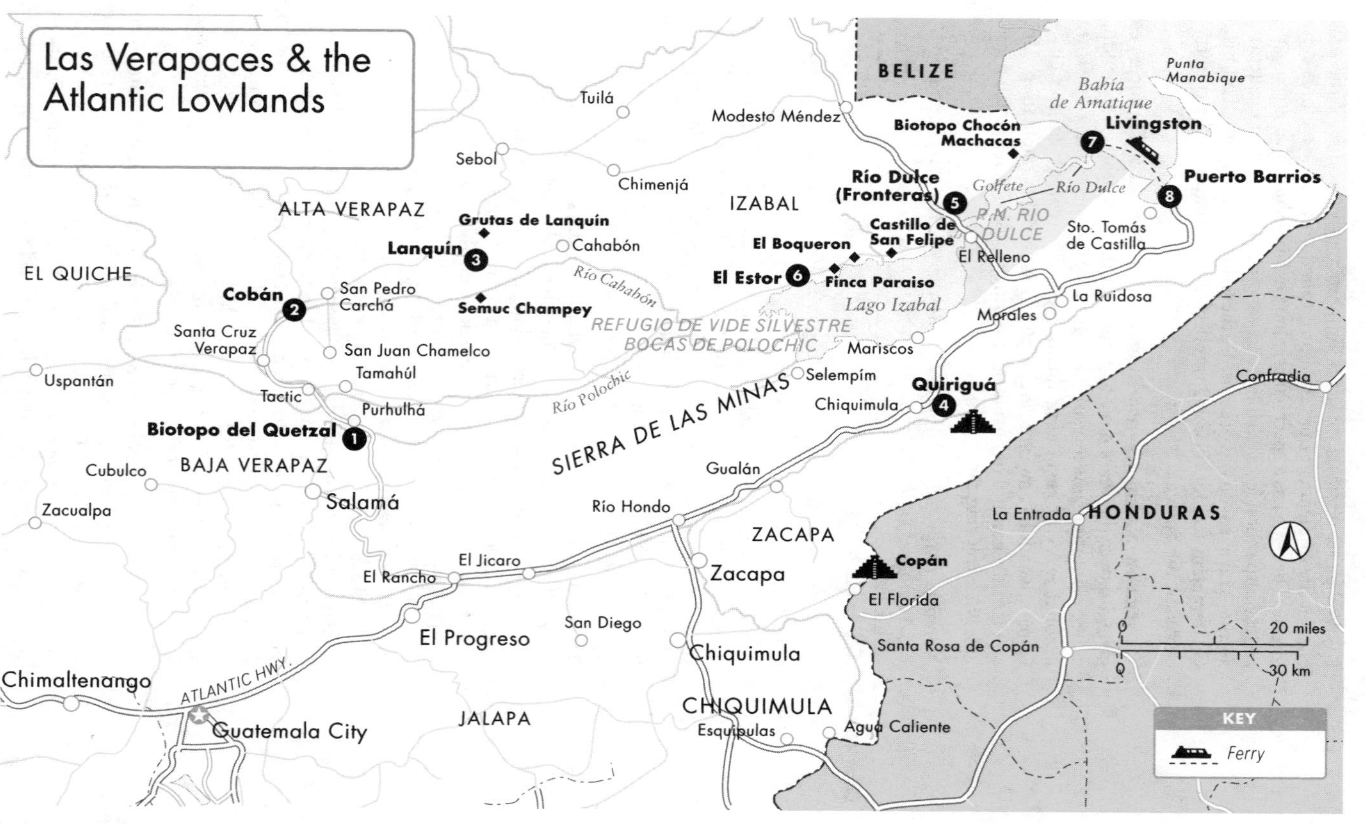
Las Verapaces & the Atlantic Lowlands
BELIZE
HONDURAS
KEY
Ferry
20 miles
30 km
Punta Manabique
Bahía de Amatique
Livingston
Puerto Barrios
Río Dulce
Golfete
P.N. RIO DULCE
Biotopo Chocón Machacas
Río Dulce (Fronteras)
Castillo de San Felipe
El Relleno
Sto. Tomás de Castilla
La Ruidosa
Morales
Quiriguá
Confradia
La Entrada
Santa Rosa de Copán
Copán
El Florida
Agua Caliente
Modesto Méndez
IZABAL
El Boqueron
Finca Paraiso
El Estor
Lago Izabal
Mariscos
Selempím
Chiquimula
REFUGIO DE VIDE SILVESTRE BOCAS DE POLOCHIC
SIERRA DE LAS MINAS
Gualán
ZACAPA
Zacapa
CHIQUIMULA
Chiquimula
Esquipulas
Río Hondo
San Diego
El Jicaro
El Progreso
JALAPA
El Rancho
Tuilá
Chimenjá
Sebol
Cahabón
Río Cahabón
Río Polochic
Grutas de Lanquín
Lanquín
Semuc Champey
ALTA VERAPAZ
San Pedro Carchá
San Juan Chamelco
Tamahúl
Purhulhá
Cobán
Santa Cruz Verapaz
Tactic
Biotopo del Quetzal
Salamá
BAJA VERAPAZ
Cubulco
Zacualpa
Uspantán
EL QUICHE
Chimaltenango
Guatemala City
ATLANTIC HWY.
1
2
3
4
5
6
7
8

keys swinging above the two well-maintained trails, the 2-km (1-mi) Los Helechos (The Ferns) and the 4-km (2-mi) Los Musgos (The Mosses). The latter takes a short detour past a series of beautiful waterfalls. Both trails cross a river with concrete bathing pools where you can swim if you don't mind the cold. An interpretive guide is available at the stand at the trailheads. ☎ *No phone* 🎫 *Free.*

Where to Stay & Eat

★ $ ✕🏨 **Ram Tzul.** Like little tree house temples, the Ram Tzul's funky cabins have rustic log-stump floors, and pitched pine and cedar ceilings—and terrific views of the surrounding private nature reserve. The octagonal stained glass windows are a little incongruous, but the bamboo furniture and studied rusticity more than make up for it. The hotel has its own trail that leads to a magnificent 196.9-foot waterfall, which is worth the visit even if you're not a guest. ✉ *Km 158.5, Carretera a Cobán,* ☎ *908–4066* 🖷 *335–1802* ✍ *ramtzul@intelnet.net.gt* 🛏 *12 rooms* 🛎 *Restaurant, free parking; no a/c, no room TVs* 💳 *AE, MC, V.*

Cobán

❷ *214 km (133 mi) northeast of Guatemala City.*

Cobán exists because of the worldwide demand for a morning cup of coffee. German immigrants flooded into Cobán in the 1880s to establish the vast coffee fincas that still cover the surrounding hillsides. They transformed the city of Cobán from a sleepy village into a wealthy enclave. This period of European high society was short-lived, however. With the onset of World War II, the U.S. government pressured Guatemala to expel the Germans. Traces of their influence remain, however.

The longtime residents of Cobán are the Q'eqchí Maya. Though they are seldom featured in the tourism brochures, many still wear traditional clothing in a style quite different from those of the highlands. *Cortes* (woven skirts), each made of 9 yards of fabric, are gathered and usually worn to just below the knees. They are paired with embroidered huipiles fashioned from a rectangular piece of fabric, with a hole cut out for the neck and the sides sewn up.

Following in the traditions of the ancient Maya, the Q'eqchí are religious people mixing modern theologies with older rituals and beliefs. Many caves around the region are used for religious ceremonies involving candle and incense burning.

A short walk from the prosperous modern markets of central Cobán, **Templo El Calvario** is at the top of a cobblestone path bordered by a series of small shrines, each sheltering a cross darkened with ash. The offerings inside include feathers, hair, and coins stuck to the crosses with gobs of wax. If you sit a while, you might see families muttering prayers in Q'eqchí. The view from the top of the hill is one of the best in the city. ✉ *3 Calle and 7 Av.* ☎ *No phone* 🎫 *Free* 🕓 *Daily 7–7.*

The **Catedral de Santo Domingo,** bordering the main square, is worth peeking into. It's one of the more understated churches you'll see. Near the altar is an Englishman's account of his travels to Cobán. To the right of the cathedral is the convent. Built in the late 1500s, it is one of Cobán's oldest surviving buildings. ✉ *1 Av. and 1 Calle.*

Parque National Las Victorias, near Templo El Calvario, sits on what used to be a privately owned plantation. Today the park is filled with winding paths with great views of the town. ✉ *9 Av. and 3 Calle.*

The **Museo El Principe Maya,** a 10-minute walk from the plaza, has a collection of ancient Mayan artifacts, mostly recovered from El Petén. Though the exhibit is relatively small, the variety of pieces is impressive. See fearsome masks, giant sacrificial pots, a reconstructed tomb, jade jewelry, and weapons. ✉ *6 Av. 4–26, Zona 3* ☎ *952–1541.*

At the **Finca Santa Margarita,** three blocks west of Parque Central, you can take a 45-minute tour of an operating coffee farm and witness the process of planting, growing, harvesting, and processing coffee beans. Owned by the Dieseldorff family, which has lived in Cobán for more than a century, the slatted wooden buildings have a distinct old-world feel. ✉ *3 Calle 4–12, Zona 2* ☎ *952–1286* ⏲ *Weekdays 8–12:30 and 1:30–5, Sat. 8–noon.*

Run by the friendly Concha de Mittelstaedt, the magnificent orchid farm called **Viveros Verapaz** is a good place for an afternoon jaunt. Mittelstaedt clearly enjoys sharing her passion with visitors, pointing out breathtaking blossoms and describing the painstaking process of coaxing the temperamental ornamentals to bloom. Typically, orchids bloom in late November and early December, the height of the season, culminating in Cobán's International Orchid Festival held annually in early December. Orchid cultivators from as far as Japan come to show off their flowers. ✉ *Carretera Antigua, 2 km south of Cobán* ☎ *952–1133* 🎫 *Q90* ⏲ *Closed Sun.*

off the beaten path

SAN PEDRO CARCHÁ – An interesting daily market is the highlight of this traditional little town 6 km (4 mi) east of Cobán. Nearby Las Islas, with a waterfall and pool, is a popular spot for picnics.

Where to Stay & Eat

¢–$ ✕ **Kikoe's Tasca.** Kikoe, the owner, makes newcomers feel welcome with his eagerness to chat about anything from his career as a mineralogist to his expertise in all types of beer. With a wraparound bar warmed by a fireplace, Kikoe's is the only real watering hole in Cobán, serving 150 kinds of liquor. The place doesn't get hopping until late and stays open until 1 in the morning. It also has a small but savory menu that will please meat lovers, featuring smoked leg of pork, goulash, and cheese fondue. ✉ *2 Av. 4–33, Zona 2* ☎ *952–1248* 💳 *V* ⏲ *Closed Sun. and Mon.*

¢–$ ✕ **Restaurante El Chino.** For an authentic taste of Cobán's gastronomic offerings, head to El Chino, which serves up the town's best *caldo de chunto,* a greasy turkey stew. They also have excellent grilled meats and game dishes like *venado* (venison) and *tepescuintle,* a rain forest rodent. On game day the requisite TV becomes the focal point for both servers and customers. ✉ *4 Av. 3–34, Zona 4* ☎ *951–3211* 💳 *No credit cards.*

¢ **Café El Tirol.** The owner of this popular café grew up on a coffee plantation near Cobán. Duly qualified, she serves the largest selection of caffeinated beverages in this coffee-growing region. Hot coffee, cold coffee, coffee with liquor, coffee with chocolate, and a wide assortment of teas make up most of the six-page menu. She also whips up the best breakfasts in town. The café is opposite the church. *1 Calle 3–13, Zona 1 951–4042 No credit cards Closed Sun.*

$ **Hotel La Posada.** True charm pervades La Posada, an attractive colonial inn overlooking Cobán's central plaza. Rooms have wood floors and exposed beams and are furnished with antiques. Some have special touches like wardrobes and writing desks. Blue chairs and cloth hammocks fill the porch overlooking the small garden. A cozy restaurant (**¢**–$) with a fireplace serves international as well as Guatemalan favorites. *1 Calle 4–12, Zona 2 952–1495 951–0646 laposada@c.net.gt 16 rooms Restaurant, café, Ping-Pong, Internet, free parking; no a/c, no TV in some rooms AE, DC, MC, V.*

Fodor's Choice ★

¢ **Casa D'Acuña.** The Restaurante Casa D'Acuña (**¢**) is a necessary stop when you're in Cobán, regardless of whether you're a guest at the hotel. Take a seat in the dining room or out in the garden and enjoy a variety of Italian dishes. Homemade carrot cake and a cup of locally grown coffee make a great dessert or midday snack. A small and clean hostel is adjacent to the restaurant. One room has a double bed; the rest have bunk beds. The proprietors—a lovely Guatemalan–American family—are an invaluable resource of information about the region. They run excellent two- to five-day ecoadventures to the Biotopo del Quetzal and other sights. *4 Calle 3–11, Zona 2 951–0482 951–0482 hacuna@itelgua.com 7 rooms without bath Restaurant, café, travel services, free parking; no a/c, no room TVs AE, DC, MC, V.*

$ **Hostal Doña Victoria.** The colonial-style Doña Victoria was built as a convent more than 400 years ago. It's filled with gorgeous antiques; rocking chairs and overstuffed couches line the stone porch encircling the gardens. Rooms are spacious and have beds piled high with blankets for the cold Cobán nights. *3 Calle 2–38, Zona 3 951–4214 952–1389 www.aventurasturisticas.com 8 rooms Restaurant, cable TV, travel services, free parking; no a/c AE, DC, MC, V.*

Sports & the Outdoors

CAVING The Cuevas de Rey Marco, near the village of San Juan Chamelco, are relatively untouched caves. Tours take you into the caves only a few hundred yards, but the potential for further exploring is limitless, as the caverns stretch for many miles beneath the mountains of the Sierra Yalijux. Getting inside is difficult; expect to crawl through the entrance and cross a waist-high river. Tours can be arranged through **Access Computación** (1 Calle 3–13, Zona 1 951–4040).

SOCCER Cobán's more-than-respectable national soccer team, Cobán Imperial, plays regularly in the hilltop **Estadio Verapaz,** five blocks northwest of the bus station. Sit in the bleachers or on the grassy hillside. Look for the sandwich board in the main square for information. Tickets are about 20 quetzales.

Lanquín

3 *63 km (39 mi) east of Cobán.*

This pretty village is on the doorstep of some impressive natural wonders. The **Grutas de Lanquín,** a system of caves cut through by underground rivers, are easy to explore. A trail with iron railings will help you keep your footing among the huge stalactites and stalagmites. Visit toward sunset and you'll see thousands of bats leave their dark dwellings and head for the starry night sky. The Q20 entrance is worth it, despite the garish labels painted on the formations.

Fodor'sChoice ★ Often praised as the most beautiful spot in Guatemala, **Semuc Champey** appears to be a series of emerald pools surrounded by dense forest. On further investigation you'll notice that the pools are actually the top of a natural arch through which the raging Río Cahabón flows. Local legend has it that various explorers have tried to enter the underground passage by lowering themselves over the lip of the arch; many turned back right away, while some were swallowed up, their bodies never recovered. There's a short 2-km nature trail here so be sure to bring decent shoes. Semuc Champey is only 10 km (6 mi) south of Lanquín on a dirt road, but you'll need a four-wheel-drive vehicle to reach it.

Where to Stay & Eat

$ **Hotel El Recreo Lanquín Champey.** This concrete-block hotel at the mouth of the Grutas is a good choice for budget travelers. There are single and double rooms in the main building and several bungalows out back. The hot water only runs sporadically. The restaurant (¢–$) was built with the expectation of more diners than it typically garners; it serves decent Guatemalan fare. ✉ *Near Grutas de Lanquín* ☎ *983–0056 or 983–0057* *38 rooms, 4 bungalows* *Restaurant, free parking; no a/c, no room TVs* *AE, DC, MC, V.*

¢ **Hostal Las Marias.** A stone's throw from Semuc Champey, Las Marias has shared, dorm-style accommodations. The simple rooms are immaculately clean, with thin mattresses and very little else. Travelers young and old trade tales over cold beers and sandwiches at the decent restaurant. ✉ *9 km south of Lanquín on the road to Semuc Champey* ☎ *951–3407* *erickalba7@hotmail.com* *5 rooms, 6 dormitories all with shared bath* *Restaurant, free parking; no a/c, no room TVs* *No credit cards.*

Sports & the Outdoors

WHITE-WATER RAFTING Rafting expeditions on the Río Cahabón, a challenging river near Lanquín, usually last from one to three days. The Guatemala City–based **Maya Expeditions** (✉ 15 Calle 1–91, Zona 10, Guatemala City ☎ 363–4965) arranges trips down the raging river.

Las Verapaces A to Z

AIR TRAVEL

There are no airports in Las Verapaces. Most people headed for this region fly into Guatemala City's Aeropuerto Internacional La Aurora.

BUS TRAVEL

Transportes Escobar runs comfortable buses between Guatemala City and Cobán, passing the Biotopo del Quetzal. The driver will let you off if you ask. Buses depart every hour or so from 4 to 4 at both ends of the route, and the trip takes four hours.

Transportes Escobar ✉ 8 Av. 15–16, Zona 1, Guatemala City ☎ 238-1409 ✉ 2 Calle 3-77, Zona 4, Cobán ☎ 952-1536.

CAR RENTAL

Several agencies in Cobán rent cars for about 400 quetzales a day, which is a great deal if you want to spend some time exploring the area on your own. Companies with good reputations include Geo, Inque, Sears, and Tabarini. Reserve ahead of time, especially on the weekends.

Local Agencies **Geo Rental** ✉ 1 Calle 3-13, Zona 1, Cobán ☎ 952-2059. **Inque** ✉ 3 Av. 1-18, Zona 4, Cobán ☎ 952-1994. **Sears** ✉ 8 Av. 2-36, Zona 4, Cobán ☎ 952-1530. **Tabarini** ✉ Av. 227, Cobán ☎ 952-1504.

CAR TRAVEL

To get to Las Verapaces from Guatemala City, take the Carretera Atlántica to El Rancho, where you'll take Route 17 north to reach Cobán and Lanquín. There are not many gas stations before you reach Cobán, so make sure you fill up before you leave the capital.

EMERGENCIES

Emergency Services **Police** ☎ 951-1306 in Cobán.
Hospital **Hospital Regional de Cobán** ✉ 8 Calle 1-24, Zona 4, Cobán ☎ 952-1315.
Pharmacies **Farmacia Central** ✉ 1 Calle, Zona 1, Cobán ☎ 951-0581.

MAIL & SHIPPING

Letters and packages can be shipped from the post office in Cobán, but you're better off bringing them back to Guatemala City and mailing them from there.

Post Offices **Cobán** ✉ 3 Calle 2-02, Zona 3.

MONEY MATTERS

Currency can be exchanged in Cobán's hotels and banks, but there are very few ATMs, so make sure to bring enough cash. Some banks will give you cash advances on credit cards.

Bancared ✉ 1 Av. 2-66, Zona 1, Cobán.

TOURS

Proyecto Ecológico Quetzal specializes in tours of the Biotopo del Quetzal. This nonprofit organization benefits the indigenous Q'eqchí people. Ultimate Flying Tours offers custom-designed private tours of the region, including flights to hard-to-access places.

Proyecto Ecológico Quetzal ✉ 2 Calle 14-36, Zona 1, Cobán ☎ 952-1047. **Ultimate Flying Tours** ✉ 1 Calle 3-13, Zona 1, Cobán ☎ 814-0452.

VISITOR INFORMATION

There are no tourist offices in Las Verapaces, but a good place for information is a cybercafé called Access Computación. It provides not only Internet access, but also information on tours to Semuc Champey and other points of interest.

Access Computación ✉ 1 Calle 3-13, Zona 1 ☎ 951-4040.

THE ATLANTIC LOWLANDS

Hot and humid, Guatemala's eastern coast was immortalized by Nobel Prize–winning writer Miguel Ángel Asturias in *Viento Fuerte* (1950), *El Papa Verde* (1954), and *Los Ojos de los Enterrados* (1960). Known as the Banana Trilogy, these books chronicle the pain inflicted on the country by the United Fruit Company. Bananas are still big business here, and Dole and Chiquita remain owners of huge plantations in the region's lowlands. From the docks in Puerto Barrios gigantic freight liners leave daily with enormous crates of bananas stacked like children's blocks. Groups of farmworkers can be spotted along the roadside, each carrying nothing more than a small knit bag. Men from one village often seek work as a group to increase their chances of being hired. Although the minimum wage is about $3.50 a day, some will work for half that amount. They usually return home on Sunday, the one day of the week they don't live on the farms.

Although the indigenous culture here is not as striking as that in the highlands, you'll run across many people who speak only their native Q'eqchí. Living in remote mountain villages, they sometimes must walk a full day or more to get to the market towns. The coastal towns of Livingston and Puerto Barrios are home to the Garífuna, Afro-Caribbean peoples who speak a language all their own.

Traces of the Mayan empire, such as the impressive city of Quiriguá, mark the movement of this ancient people through the lowlands. But even with sights like Quiriguá you won't run into many fellow travelers. The region is practically untouched by tourism, even though it contains treasures such as stunning Lago Izabal. The largest lake in Guatemala, Lago Izabal is in a tropical valley bordered by two mountain ranges, the Sierra de las Minas, to the south, and the Sierra Santa Cruz, to the north.

You'll enjoy your trip to the Atlantic Lowlands much more if you adapt to the local rhythm of life. Wake at sunrise and do most of your activities in the morning. With a good book in hand, find a hammock in which to relax during the steamy midday hours. Hit the street again in the late afternoon and evening, when the temperatures are a bit cooler. The best time to visit is November and December—the end of the rainy season, when temperatures are tolerable. It is best to avoid the region during March, when the heat is dizzying and farmers are burning their fields, leaving the skies thick with smoke that obliterates the views.

Numbers in the text correspond to numbers in the margin and on the Verapaces and Atlantic Lowlands map.

Quiriguá

4 Fodor'sChoice ★ *186 km (115 mi) northeast of Guatemala City, 96 km (60 mi) southwest of Puerto Barrios.*

Unlike the hazy remnants of chiseled images you see at most other archaeological sites in Central America, Quiriguá has some that are seemingly untouched by winds and rain. They emerge from the rock faces in breathtaking detail. Quiriguá is famous for the amazingly well-preserved stelae, or carved pillars, that are the largest yet discovered. They depict Quiriguá's ruling dynasty, especially the powerful Cauac Chan (Jade Sky). Several monuments, covered with interesting zoomorphic figures, still stand, and the remains of an acropolis and other structures have been partially restored.

In ancient times Quiriguá was an important Mayan trading center that stood on the banks of the Río Motagua (the river has since changed its course). The ruins are surrounded by a stand of rain forest—an untouched wilderness in the heart of banana country. There is a small museum on site that gives insight into the history of Cauac Chan and his contemporaries. ✉ *Near Chiquimula* ☎ *No phone* 🎫 *Q25* ⏲ *Daily 7:30–5.*

Río Dulce

5 *30 km (19 mi) northwest of La Ruidosa, where the road to El Petén leaves the Carretera Atlántica.*

Fodor'sChoice ★

Although it sits on the shore of a beautiful waterway, the town of Río Dulce falls sadly short of its potential. A major transportation hub, it's where you'll find the country's longest bridge, which crosses the river that gave this town its name. Drive south, and you'll hit the road leading to the Central Highlands; head north, and you'll eventually reach El Petén. Río Dulce has little to keep you here, although unexpectedly good restaurants and hotels in nearby communities are easily reached by boat. The *launcheros* (captains) who congregate on the river will take you anywhere in the area for under 40 quetzales.

Once an important stop along the Mayan trade route, the Río Dulce later became the route over which the conquistadors sent the gold and silver they plundered back to Spain. All this wealth attracted pirates, who attacked both the ships and the warehouses on shore. In hopes of curtailing these buccaneers, colonists built a series of fortresses on the river's northern banks. In the 1950s the Guatemalan government reconstructed the ruined fortress of **Castillo de San Felipe** (✉ Southwest of Río Dulce, ☎ No phone 🎫 Q10), named after King Philip II of Spain. From 1655 to 1660 it was used as a prison. You can reach it by the road leading west from Río Dulce or by a short boat ride.

The northern banks of the Golfete, an expansive body of water between Lago Izabal and Río Dulce, are covered by the 17,790-acre **Biotopo Chocón Machacas.** Among the stretches of virgin rain forest and the extensive mangrove swamp here are gentle manatees—shy marine mammals also known as sea cows because of their enormous size. Manatees are as elusive as quetzals, so as you boat through the reserve you're more likely to see other animals such as sea otters. Some of the creeks go through thick forests where giant mahogany, ceiba, and mangrove trees hang over the water to form tunnels so thick they block out the sun. A tiny island surrounded by the park's dozens of creeks and lagoons has a well-maintained nature trail of a half mile or so that is easily walked by those with stiff boating legs. The trail has such interesting examples of old-growth trees as the San Juan, a tall, straight tree with yellow blossoms, and such exotic plants as orchids and bromeliads.

The only way to get to the reserve is a 45-minute boat trip from Río Dulce or Livingston. Most launches up and down the river will stop at the park entrance if requested, but they rarely enter the park. Most major hotels on the Río Dulce rent boats with guides for individual or group tours. ✉ *Northeast of Río Dulce* ☎ *No phone.*

Where to Stay & Eat

★ $$ **Catamaran Island Hotel.** On the north bank of the Río Dulce, this lovely resort takes advantage of its location with a restaurant (¢–$$) built right over the water. The specialties are grilled steaks and fresh fish, including the delicious robálo plucked from the river. A string of spacious bungalows is cooled by river breezes, the nicest feature of which are the porches, perfect for watching boats. The staff can arrange boat trips along the river and to Livingston. ✉ *5 km (3 mi) east of Río Dulce* ☎ *930–5494* 📠 *930–5492* *35 rooms* *Restaurant, fans, pool, boating, marina, bar, travel services; no a/c in some rooms, no room TVs* 💳 *AE, DC, MC, V.*

$ **Bruno's.** At this popular hangout for the yachting crowd, many of the regular patrons arrive by boat. Bruno's is best known for its lively restaurant (¢–$), featuring a great international menu. Expats enjoy sandwiches and other light fare as they watch football on the big-screen TV. The rooms, next to a pool, are spacious and clean. ✉ *Under bridge, on north side* ☎ *219–2799* ☎📠 *930–5174* 🌐 *www.mayaparadise.com* *10 rooms, 7 with bath, 1 dormitory* *Restaurant, fans, cable TV, pool, boating, marina, bar, laundry service, free parking; no a/c in some rooms* 💳 *AE, MC, V.*

$ **Planeta Río.** Although Planeta Río has less character than the competition, it's quite close to town. Rooms surround a large pool, and a three-story complex holding a restaurant ($–$$$) and bar overlooks the water. Each of the well-maintained buildings has several modern rooms, but the slightly bedraggled bungalows have much better views. Try an exhilarating canopy tour, which whisks you through the hotel's small nature reserve on high-tension ziplines. ✉ *1½ km (1 mi) east of El Relleno, Km 275, Carretera á Peten* ☎ *473–0317* ☎📠 *930–5230* 🌐 *www.planetario.com* *38 rooms* *Restaurant, pool, jet skiing, marina, bar, travel services, free parking; no a/c, no room TVs* 💳 *AE, DC, MC, V* *BP.*

¢–$$ **Hacienda Tijax.** Built out over the water, this jungle lodge offers a number of types of accommodations, from cozy birdhouse-shape cabañas to large two-story bungalows with kitchens and dining rooms. A series of swinging bridges over a mangrove swamp lets you stroll to the adjacent nature reserve. Also nearby is a plantation where you can learn how rubber is extracted from trees. The lodge is also well known for its restaurant (¢–$), which serves a variety of Italian dishes including homemade pesto. There are also plenty of vegetarian dishes. ✉ *Near Río Dulce* ☎ *930–5196* 📠 *902–7523* 🌐 *www.tijax.com* *9 rooms* *Restaurant, fans, some kitchenettes, pool, marina; no a/c, no room TVs* 💳 *No credit cards.*

¢ **Finca Tatin.** A rustic bed-and-breakfast run by a friendly Argentine family, Finca Tatin is far off the beaten path. The inn, which doubles as a Spanish school, rents canoes, which are a great way to see the river without the roar of a motor. ✉ *8 km (5 mi) south of Livingston* ☎ *902–0831* *fincatatin@hotmail.com* *3 bungalows, 4 rooms without bath* *Restaurant, dock; no a/c, no room TVs* *No credit cards.*

Nightlife

Head to **Hotel Backpackers** (✉Under bridge on southern end ☎930–5168) for a beer at the waterfront bar. All the proceeds go to benefit Casa Guatemala Orphanage, so drink up. They also offer Río Dulce's most affordable accommodation.

Sports & the Outdoors

One of the most beautiful boat trips in the country is the two- to three-hour ride on the river between the town of Río Dulce and Livingston. The *collectivos* (public boats) leave from Río Bravo Restaurant when they have at least eight passengers (the launcheros will keep you waiting all afternoon if the boat is not full). The rate is usually about 75 quetzales per person. Private boats can also be hired, but they cost between 600 and 750 quetzales depending on how well you negotiate the price. All public launches stop at Bird Island, a roosting place for several hundred cormorants, and Flower Lagoon, a small inlet covered in bobbing water lilies. There's also a stop at a hot springs that tumbles into a shallow river. Definitely bring your bathing suit.

Planeta Río (✉ 1½ km (1 mi) east of El Relleno, Km 275, Carretera á Peten ☎ 473–0317) has the area's only zip line canopy tour. You may see monkeys or lizards on the tour, which costs Q200.

El Estor

6 *40 km (24 mi) west of Río Dulce.*

Although the vast majority of this little town's population is Q'eqchí, there's also a decidedly Caribbean influence. Locals describe El Estor as *tranquilo,* which means easygoing or laid-back, and this becomes evident as you stroll around the brick streets. The town, which grew up around the nickel mine to the west, seems to have drifted to sleep after the facility was shut down. There's a waterfront walk where you can look for birds along the banks of Lago Izabel. El Estor is on a migratory path, so hundreds of species can be spotted here.

The hour-long drive here from Río Dulce takes you past expansive banana plantations as well as cattle ranches. Look for the massive ceiba trees along the road. They are sacred to the Maya—the only reason they were left standing when the rest of the forest was cleared. Also try to spot strangler figs, which wrap themselves around the trunks of palms. Eventually they overcome the palms, which die from lack of sunlight.

Fodor's Choice ★ Perhaps the most beautiful of Guatemala's natural wonders, **El Boqueron** is a narrow limestone canyon whose 590-foot walls are covered in foliage heavy with hanging moss. Hummingbirds dance around lavish blooms, blue morpho butterflies flutter between branches, and kingfishers dive at minnows. Sometimes howler monkeys visit the trees nearby—listen for their thunderous cries in the late afternoon. All along the canyon you can climb rocks and explore caves filled with clinging bats. Close to the entrance is a turnoff past a giant ceiba tree that leads to several thatch huts along the river; the proprietors, Antonio and Miguel, provide roughly fashioned *kayukos* (canoes) that you can rent for a ride through the canyon. The water is clean and cool and great for swimming except after a heavy rain, when all the local rivers turn a muddy brown. ✉ *3 mi (2 mi) east of El Estor.*

Known for its steaming waterfall, think of **Finca Paraíso** as a natural spa for the tired traveler. Don't be dissuaded from a trip here even if the weather is hot and humid, as the falls descend into an icy cold river. A trail from the front gate leads to a short yet somewhat bumpy climb to the falls—be careful, as the rocks can be slippery. Around the falls are small indentations in the rock that serve as natural saunas. You can also hike upstream to the narrow cave at the source of the river. The rock formations here are otherworldly. About 2 km (1 mi) downstream from the hot springs is a simple restaurant that serves hearty meals. From here you can also rent horses and ride to the springs. ✉ *10 mi east of El Estor* ☎ *949–7122* 🎫 *Q10.*

Declared a protected area in 1996, **Refugio de Vida Silvestre Bocas del Polochic** is home to more than 250 species of birds, including blue herons, kingfishers, and snowy egrets. If you're lucky, you'll spot the blue-throated motmot. On the western end of Lago Izabal, the country's largest wetland encompasses more than 51,000 acres. An organization called Defensores de la Naturaleza manages the reserve. From the office in El Estor you can arrange a guided boat trip to the reserve and a visit to the Q'eqchí village of Selempím, with meals prepared by local women. The organization also runs a remote ecolodge at the base of the Sierra de las Minas. The thatch-roof lodge has rooms with bunk beds and a full kitchen. A midnight thunderstorm is magical, but regardless of the weather you'll hear the roar of howler monkeys long into the night. Rates are $25. *Defensores de la Naturaleza* ✉ *El Estor* ☎ *369–7777.*

Where to Stay & Eat

¢–$ ✕ **Restaurante Chaabil.** The name means "beautiful" in the language of the Q'eqchí, and that's an apt description for the best eatery in El Estor. Built over the water, the palm-thatched building is the perfect place for a breakfast with a view of the majestic Sierra de las Minas or for a dinner accompanied by a spectacular sunset over Lago Izabal. You may even get a chance to snap a photo of a fisherman delivering the catch of the day. Call ahead of time to enjoy a bowl of seafood tapado, or stop by anytime for lake perch or river robálo. For dessert try a pineapple or papaya smoothie. ✉ *West of main square* ☎ *949–7272* ▭ *No credit cards.*

$ ✕🏨 **Hotel Marisabela.** This hotel has clean, simply furnished rooms overlooking the lake. A third-floor balcony with wooden lounge chairs is the best place in town for an afternoon siesta. Although the restaurant (**¢**–$) always looks closed, it's open for business. Just call out "*¡Buenas tardes!*" until one of the workers appears. The Italian dishes are authentic and filling. ✉ *2 blocks east of the main square* ☎ *949–7206* *12 rooms* *Restaurant, fans, free parking; no a/c, no room TVs* *No credit cards.*

¢ **Hotel Vista al Lago.** This hotel was once the general store that gave El Estor its name. Now run by the loquacious Oscar Paz, it has clean, cozy rooms. The wide wooden balcony is a great place to observe the town's waterfront. Before checking in, make sure the town hall next door has no plans for a dance; otherwise the thumping music will keep you awake until 4 AM. ✉ *Next to town hall* ☎ *949–7205* *21 rooms* *Fans, free parking; no a/c, no room TVs* *AE, DC, MC, V.*

2

Shopping

You can watch how the beautiful weavings of Guatemala are made at the **Q'eqchí Women's Weaving Workshop** (✉ North of main square ☎ No phone ⏲ Mon.–Sat. 8–noon and 3–5). Every year small numbers of women come from their villages to live at the workshop, where they spend a year learning the age-old crafts of loom and belt weaving. Every woman who successfully completes the course is given a loom to take back to her village and is encouraged to teach other women how to weave.

Livingston

★ 7 *37 km (23 mi) northeast of Río Dulce.*

At the mouth of the Río Dulce, Livingston is known as La Buga, or "the Mouth," by the Garífuna people. Although it's on the mainland, Livingston might as well be a Caribbean island—the only way to get to or from the town is by boat, and the culture is closer to that of Jamaica than to the rest of Guatemala. Once you arrive here, shed your worries and settle under a coconut palm.

Livingston is home to the Garífuna people, who came here from the Lesser Antilles. After two decades of resisting British encroachment, the Garífuna were forcibly removed from their homeland and deposited on Roatán, an island off the coast of Honduras. Most of the Garífuna migrated to the mainland, settling all along the coast from Belize to Nicaragua. Each year from November 24 to 26, Livingston hosts a festival to celebrate the arrival of the Garífuna. The town rejoices with traditional music and dancing. The Feast of St. Isidore, held May 13–15, is a huge celebration dedicated to the patron saint of corn. The best time to visit Livingston is during these energetic holidays.

Livingston's single paved road is the only evidence left of its heyday as a major port for coffee and other crops during the late 19th century. Livingston's population now makes its living mostly from fishing. By day the soft lick of waves on the shore measures out the slow pace that makes this laid-back community so attractive. At night roving bands of musicians take to the streets. The Garífuna are famous for their *punta* dancing—they may grab you from the crowd and teach you some moves you didn't know your body could make.

Anyone expecting white sandy beaches and azure waters is bound to be disappointed. The narrow beach that stretches north from the river mouth is not especially attractive. It is, however, a great place to explore, as it is home to several bars and a little shop where Pablo Marino sells handmade drums, shakers, and wood carvings. Afternoon breezes off the ocean make resting on the beach a good place to pass the torrid afternoons.

Where to Stay & Eat

Be aware that young men wait on the town dock to "escort" you to your hotel. You can accept their offer or refuse; either way, they will follow you and ask for money. "Tipping" them to leave you alone is your prerogative.

¢–$ ✕ **Restaurante Bahía Azul.** The walls are literally covered with travel information at Bahía Azul, the most popular tourist restaurant in town. If you're thinking about a trip, you can probably arrange it here. At the curve on the main street, its porch is a great place to watch people stroll past. The large menu includes everything from sandwiches to lobster. Most nights include live drumming by a local band. ✉ *On the main street* ☎ *947–0151* 🖷 *947–0136* 💳 *AE, DC, MC, V.*

¢–$ ✕ **Restaurante Margoth.** Presided over by the well-respected Doña Margoth, this longtime favorite serves the usual fish dishes. It's famous, however, for its delicious seafood tapado with plantains. The stew is a challenge to eat, so tuck your napkin into your collar. The doña keeps a sharp eye on her workers, so the service in this bright and bustling café is speedy. ✉ *North of the main street* ☎ *947–0019* 💳 *AE, MC, V* ⏲ *Closed 3 PM–7 PM.*

¢–$ ✕ **Tilindo Lindo.** For the best curry this side of the Darien Gap head to this small bistro, which sits near the beach. The menu features such international favorites as Israeli *shockshuka* (an egg soup), chow mein, and chicken a l'orange. Meals all come with tasty salads and garlic bread. The intimate, rustic feel will keep you content while you wait for your meal, which takes awhile to arrive. ✉ *North end of Main St. at the beach* ☎ *No phone* 💳 *No credit cards.*

★ **$$$$** ✕🏨 **Hotel Villa Caribe.** Livingston's finest hotel, the Villa Caribe has some great views of the Caribbean from its hilltop perch. The extensive grounds overflow with foliage. Spacious rooms, in a thatch-roof building, all have ocean views. Palm trees surround the large pool, where you can relax in one of the lounge chairs or order a drink at the bar. The restaurant ($–$$$) serves seafood dishes, such as coconut shrimp and robálo, but is almost always empty. The staff can arrange trips up the Río Dulce and to spots around the Bahía de Amatique. ✉ *On the main street* ☎ *334–1818 in Guatemala City* 🖷 *334–8134 in Guatemala City* 🌐 *www.villasdeguatemala.com* *44 rooms, 4 bungalows* *Restaurant, pool, beach, dock, bar, travel services, laundry service; no a/c, no room TVs* 💳 *AE, DC, MC, V.*

¢ ✕🏨 **Casa Rosada.** This string of waterfront bungalows can best be described as Guatemala's most luxurious way of roughing it. Each is furnished with bright highland furniture and a pair of beds draped with mosquito nets. Don't be scared off by the shared baths; they're clean and comfortable, and the showers have hot water. The main building houses a restaurant (**¢**–$) serving excellent meals on a pretty patio overlooking the water. The dinner menu changes daily but always includes

Fodor's Choice ★

lobster and other favorites. Dinner, at 7 sharp, is by candlelight. ✉ *Near public dock* ☎ *947–0303 or 334–8136 in Guatemala City* 📠 *947–0304* 🌐 *www.hotelcasarosada.com* ⇨ *10 bungalows without bath* ♖ *Restaurant, fans, boating, laundry service, travel services; no a/c, no room TVs* ▭ *AE, DC, MC, V.*

¢ **Hotel Garífuna.** Run by the cordial Livingston family, Hotel Garífuna puts you in the heart of a lively neighborhood. The rooms in this two-story building open onto a porch overlooking the street or a tree-filled backyard. ✉ *Off the main street* ☎ *947–0183* 📠 *947–0184* ⇨ *8 rooms* ♖ *Fans, laundry service; no a/c, no room TVs* ▭ *No credit cards.*

Nightlife

Residents of Livingston are famous for their weekend bashes, mostly centering around several beachfront discos. **Barique's Place** is a lively spot at the end of the main street, but it's also a good idea to ask around town. Punta music pulls everyone out onto the dance floor. The **Ubafu,** a Rasta-inspired shack (note the Bob Marley posters) on the main street is sometimes open for a late-night jam if there are enough beer-drinking customers.

Sports & the Outdoors

A short boat ride to the north takes you to a gorgeous little jungle river called Siete Altares, a series of deep pools that are ideal for swimming. Arrange for a guided tour with the friendly folks at **Bahía Azul** (☎ 947–0151). Tours are about 60 quetzales; a bag lunch is included. There have been numerous attacks on tourists on the way to Siete Altares, so be sure to go with a guide and never walk in the countryside around Livingstone after dark.

Puerto Barrios

❽ *295 km (183 mi) from Guatemala City, 2 hrs by ferry from Livingston.*

Once a thriving port for the United Fruit Company, the commercial boom has long since subsided for Puerto Barrios, leaving behind paint-chipped wooden buildings. Some old stilt houses built in the traditional Caribbean style line many of the streets. The people are as warm as the tropical air, and a simple "buenas noches" will make even the most hard-hearted dock worker smile.

Where to Stay & Eat

¢–$ ✕ **Restaurante Safary.** A longtime favorite in Puerto Barrios, this grass-roof restaurant is one of the few right on the water. On a hot afternoon or steamy night the ocean breezes are a tremendous relief. ✉ *End of 5 Av. at water* ☎ *948–0563* ▭ *AE, DC, MC, V.*

$$$$ **Amatique Bay Resort & Marina.** Sprawling resorts like this waterfront complex are the newest trend in Guatemala. The beautiful natural surroundings are somewhat diminished by all the effort to make things luxurious. The impressive pool, complete with a replica of a Spanish galleon that shoots water from its cannons, has slides for children and an island bar for adults. Few of the sunny suites have views of the ocean, but they are equipped with everything you would find in a well-furnished apartment, including washers and dryers. ✉ *North of Puerto Barrios*

948–1800 or 366–2717 Ext. 576 in Guatemala City 363–5359 www.amatiquebay.com 57 rooms 2 restaurants, kitchens, cable TV, 2 pools, boating, jet skiing, marina, bicycles, bar, dance club AE, DC, MC, V FAP.

$$–$$$ **Cayos del Diablo.** Set amid a tropical garden, this string of thatch bungalows faces the expansive waters of the Bahía de Amatique. The grounds are adjacent to a forest-draped hill with a small waterfall. You can relax by the pool or the private beach, or arrange a cruise on the bay and up the Río Dulce. Boats pick up guests at the dock in Puerto Barrios each hour. *13 km (8 mi) west of Puerto Barrios 948–2361, 800/528–1234 in U.S. 948–2361 50 rooms Restaurant, cable TV, pool, beach, waterskiing, bar, meeting room, travel services AE, DC, MC, V.*

¢–$ **Finca Ixobel.** On your way up to El Petén from the Atlantic Lowlands you'll run across the Finca Ixobel, a great place to stop for the night. This large nature reserve has a summer camp atmosphere, with an animal rescue center, horseback riding, private lake, cave trips, and jungle treks. You can choose to stay in either funky treehouses or in well-appointed cabins, complete with mosquito nets and private bathrooms. *Km 376, Carretera a Santa Elena, 100 km. south of Flores, just before town of Poptún 410–4306 or 892–3188 927–8590 www.fincaixobel.com 6 rooms, 3 bungalows, treehouses, 2 dormitories Restaurant, lake, bicycles, horseback riding, bar, shop, free parking; no a/c, no room TVs No credit cards.*

The Atlantic Lowlands A to Z

AIR TRAVEL

There are no flights to the Atlantic Lowlands.

BOAT TRAVEL

Daily ferry service leaves Puerto Barrios at 10:30 AM and 5 PM and Livingston at 5 AM and 2 PM. The trip takes about two hours. Launches that connect the two cities take about 34 minutes, but they don't depart until they are full. This can really dent your plans, especially if you are leaving late in the day.

BUS TRAVEL

Bound for Puerto Barrios, comfortable buses leave Guatemala City hourly from 6 to 5. Be sure to ask for the *especial* service operated by Litegua. Trips to the capital from Puerto Barrios also leave hourly.

Litegua also has direct service to Río Dulce from the capital. Linea Dorada runs between Guatemala City and Flores, but it passes through Río Dulce. Buses leave the capital every day at 10. The trip takes about six hours.

Linea Dorada 16 Calle 10-03, Zona 1, Guatemala City 232-9658. **Litegua** 15 Calle 10-40, Zona 1, Guatemala City 232-7578 6 Av. 9-10, Puerto Barrios 948-1002.

CAR TRAVEL

From Guatemala City most people drive to the Atlantic Lowlands via the Carretera Atlántica. The journey to Río Dulce or Puerto Barrios is about five hours on a good day. Descending the curving roads through the mountains you can feel the temperature and humidity rising.

EMERGENCIES

Emergency Services **Police** ✉ Puerto Barrios ☎ 948-0120.
Hospital **Hospital Nacional** ✉ Puerto Barrios ☎ 948-3077.

HEALTH

The heat and sun in the Atlantic Lowlands can be intense. Be prepared with a good sun hat and lightweight clothing that covers your arms and legs. Shorts don't protect legs from the sun, tall grass, insects, and dust. Also pack plenty of sunscreen and insect repellent.

2

MAIL & SHIPPING

Most towns in the Atlantic Lowlands have post offices, but you should wait to post letters in Puerto Barrios. The main post office here is about four blocks from the bay.
Post Office **Puerto Barrios** ✉ 6 Calle and 6 Av.

MONEY MATTERS

If you need to exchange cash in the Atlantic Lowlands, the place to do it is Puerto Barrios. There are several banks that will be happy to help you, including Banco Industril.
Banco Industril ✉ 7 Av. Norte 73, Puerto Barrios.

SAFETY

Robberies have been known to occur in Puerto Barrios and Livingstone, so be on your guard. Use the same precautions you would anywhere else—don't wear flashy jewelry and watches, keep your camera in a secure bag, and don't handle money in public. Remain alert for pickpockets, especially in crowded markets. Only hike in the countryside with a reputable guide. Women should never hike alone.

VISITOR INFORMATION

There are no visitor information kiosks in the area, but heading to a restaurant, tour operator or hotel will certainly get you on the right path.

TIKAL & THE MAYAN RUINS

The jungles of El Petén were once the heartland of the Mayan civilization. The sprawling empire—including parts of present-day Mexico, Belize, Honduras, and El Salvador—was once made up of a network of cities that held hundreds of thousands of people, but a millennium ago this fascinating civilization suddenly vanished without a trace. The temples that dominated the horizon were swallowed up by the jungle.

The first major Mayan society dates to 2000 BC, based largely on the traditions of the Olmecs, a people living in what is now Mexico. Over the next 2,000 years the Maya proved to be an intellectually curious people. They developed a type of writing (one of the earliest) and a sophisticated system of mathematics (the first to use a zero). The Maya were particularly adept astronomers, mapping the orbits of the sun, moon,

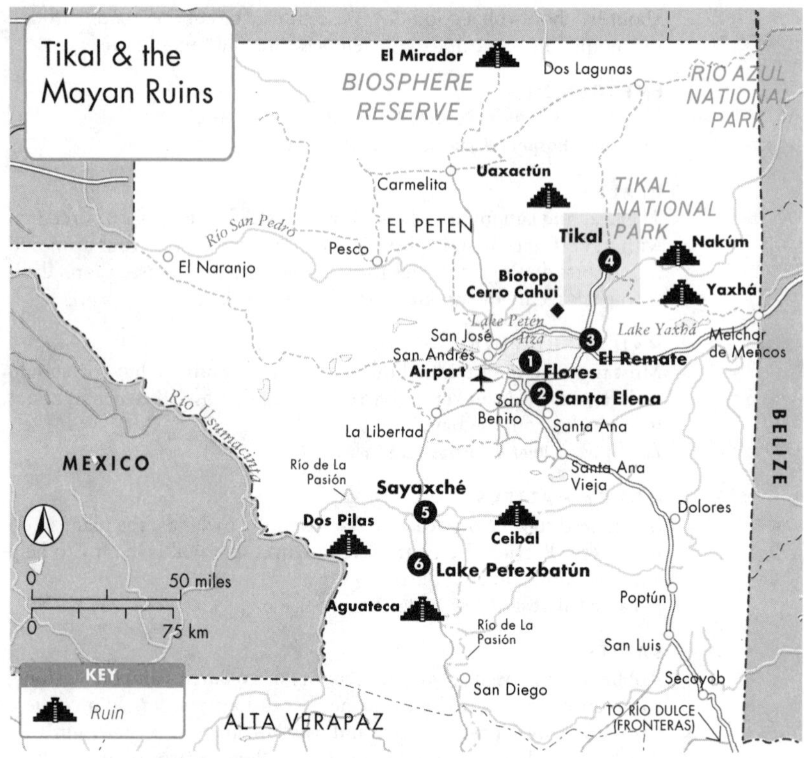

and planets with incredible accuracy—the Mayan lunar cycle differs from today's calculations by only seven minutes.

From about 250 BC to AD 900 the Maya developed complex social systems, agricultural practices, and religious beliefs, reaching their zenith with the construction of temples like Tikal in El Petén. Around AD 1000, the Maya suffered repeated attacks from rival civilizations, followed by a sudden and mysterious period of decline. The arrival of conquistadors like Hernán Cortés and Pedro de Alvarado in the early 1500s marked the beginning of the subjugation of what was left of the Maya people.

Today El Petén is a sparsely populated backwater where ancient ruins just seem to crop up from the landscape. Nature reigns supreme, with vines and other plants quickly covering everything that stands still a little too long. Whatever your primary interest—archaeology, history, birding, biking—you'll find plenty to do and see in this remote region.

It wasn't until 1970 that a dirt road linking the region to the rest of the country finally appeared. It wasn't paved, however, until 1999. Four-wheel-drive vehicles are still required to get to many of the sites, while others are reachable only by boat or on foot. The difficulty doesn't just enhance the adventure, it gives you time to take in the exotic scenery and rare tropical flora and fauna that's with you all the way.

Numbers in the text correspond to numbers in the margin and on the Tikal & the Mayan Ruins map.

Flores

★ 1 *206 km (133 mi) north of Río Dulce, 61 km (38 mi) northeast of Sayaxché.*

The red-roof town of Flores, on an island surrounded by the waters of Lago Petén Itzá, is on the site of the ancient city of Tatyasal. This was the region's last unconquered outpost of Mayan civilization, until finally falling to the Spanish in 1697. The conquerors destroyed the city's huge pyramids.

Today the provincial capital is a pleasant place to explore, with its narrow streets lined with thick-walled buildings painted pink, blue, and purple. Flowering plants droop over balconies, giving the town a tropical flavor. There's a central square presided over by a colonial church. Connected to the mainland by a bridge, it serves as a base for travelers to El Petén. It is also the center of many nongovernmental organizations working for the preservation of the Mayan Biosphere, an endangered area covering nearly all of northern Petén. Flores is also one of the last remaining vestiges of the Itzá, the people who built Mexico's monumental Chichén Itzá.

In the 1800s, before it was a departure point for travelers headed for the ruins, Flores was called Devil's Island because of the prison on top of the hill (a church stands there now). Since 1994 the building has been home to the **Centro de Información sobre la Naturaleza, Cultura, y Artesanía de Petén** (☒ North side of Parque Central ☎ 926–0718). This center has a small museum with photographs of the region and information about local resources, such as allspice, chicle (a chewing-gum base made from tree sap), and *xate* (a shade palm used in floral decorations). A gift shop sells wood carvings, woven baskets, cornhusk dolls, and even locally made peanut butter.

Where to Stay & Eat

¢–$$ ✕ **Capitán Tortuga.** The large, cartoonlike Capitán Tortuga sign may fool you into thinking this restaurant is just for kids, but the excellent grilled steak and seafood options make this one of Flores' best restaurants. The *pinchos* (grilled kebabs) are cooked on an open barbecue, sending enticing aromas throughout the restaurant. There's a nice patio out back, which offers tremendous sunset views of the lake. ☒ *Av. 30 de Julio and Callejón San Pedrito* ☎ *926–0247* ▭ *AE, DC, MC, V.*

¢–$$ ✕ **La Luna.** With its homemade paper lamp shades illuminating lovely blue walls, La Luna inspires romance on any moonlit night. But you can just as easily fall in love with the place when you stop in for a delicious lunch. Choose from inventive dishes, including wonderful vegetarian options like the stuffed squash in white sauce. Many people drop by for a drink at the bar. ☒ *Calle 30 de Junio* ☎ *926–3346* ▭ *AE, DC, MC, V* ⊙ *Closed Mon.*

¢–$$ ✕ **El Tucán.** Toucans and parrots, part of the menagerie belonging to the owner, share the breezy terrace with diners. The small dining room, dec-

Restaurants ▼

Capitán Tortuga 5

La Luna 1

Pizzeria Picasso 3

Las Puertas 2

El Tucán 4

Hotels ▼

Hospedaje Doña Goya 2

Hotel Petén 4

Hotel Sabana 1

Hotel Santana 3

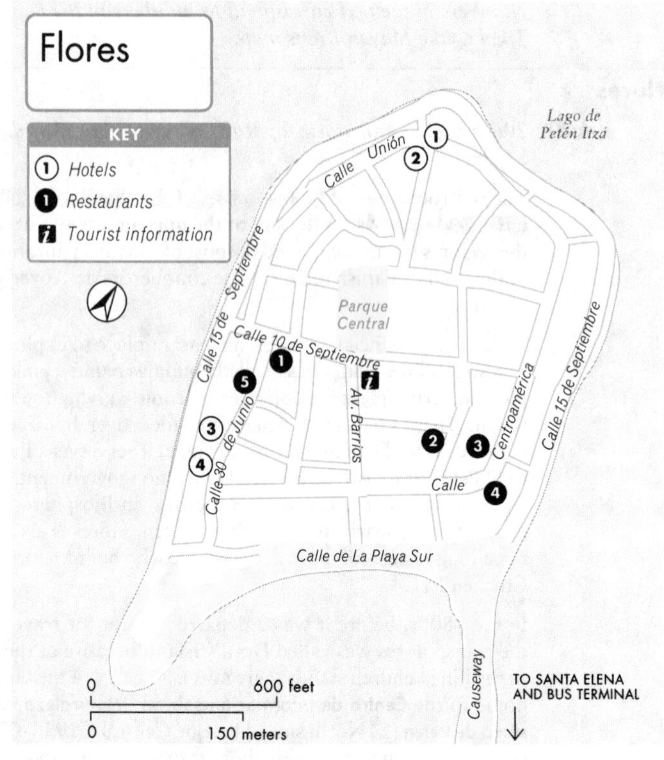

orated with highland weavings, also has good views of one of Flores's cobblestone streets. The menu includes a variety of traditional meals, though Mexican cuisine is the specialty here. The bread is baked on the premises. ✉ *Av. 15 de Septiembre and Calle Centroamérica* ☎ *926–0536* 💳 *AE, DC, MC, V.*

★ ¢–$ ✕ **Las Puertas.** On a quiet side street, Las Puertas was named for its six screened doors. It's a favorite hangout for locals and travelers alike. The friendly couple who run the place take great pride in serving only the freshest foods. Notable are the delicious sandwiches made with homemade bread and mozzarella cheese and the giant goblets of incredible iced coffee. In the afternoon you can relax with a fruit drink as you play one of the many board games. Don't forget to stop back at night for a hearty dinner and live music. ✉ *Calle Central at Av. Santa Ana* ☎ *926–1061* 💳 *AE, DC, MC, V* ⊗ *Closed Sun.*

¢ ✕ **Pizzeria Picasso.** If you find yourself returning to Pizzeria Picasso, it's because the brick-oven pizza is incomparably hot and delicious. The decor, featuring a print of Picasso's *Guernica,* is another draw. If you're not in the mood for pizza, there are a variety of pastas as well. Save room for cheesecake or tiramisu and a cup of steaming cappuccino. ✉ *Calle Centroamérica* ☎ *926–0673* 💳 *AE, DC, MC, V* ⊗ *Closed Mon.*

$$$ **Ni'tun Ecolodge.** After hiking through the jungle, you'll love returning to this charming cluster of cabins. The point is to disturb the environment as little as possible, so the buildings are constructed of stone and wood left behind by farmers clearing land for fields. The common areas, including a massive kitchen downstairs and an airy bar and reading room upstairs are delightful. The owners also run Monkey Eco Tours, so you can choose from itineraries ranging from one-day trips to nearby villages to a seven-day journey to El Mirador. *2 km (1 mi) west of San Andres 201–0759 www.nitun.com 4 cabins Restaurant, fans, travel services, free parking; no kids, no a/c, no room TVs AE, DC, MC, V.*

Fodor's Choice ★

$ **Hotel Sabana.** This small hotel offers simple rooms that open onto a terrace overlooking the pool. A sundeck has nice views of the lake. This is a good choice if you require a few creature comforts like air-conditioning and television. *Calle Union and Av. Libertad 926–1248 www.hotelsabana.com 28 rooms Restaurant, cable TV, pool, bar AE, DC, MC, V.*

$ **Hotel Santana.** Sitting right on the water, this bright pink hotel is the best lodging on the island. All the rooms open up onto wide balconies with wicker chairs where you can enjoy the view. The sunny central courtyard surrounds a pleasant pool. *Calle 30 de Junio 926–0662 www.santanapeten.com 32 rooms Restaurant, in-room safes, cable TV, pool, Internet AE, DC, MC, V.*

¢ **Hospedaje Doña Goya.** A rooftop terrace with hammocks swinging in the breeze is the best part of this budget lodging. If you prefer, grab a good book and sink into one of the comfortable lounge chairs. The hotel is clean and well run, which explains why it is so popular. Arrive early in the day to secure a room. *Calle Union 926–3538 6 rooms, 3 with bath, dormitory Fans; no a/c, no room TVs No credit cards.*

$ **Hotel Petén.** An arabesque plunge pool graces the central courtyard of this lovely lodging. Taking a dip to escape the midday heat is a treat not to be missed. The rooms are simply furnished. Ask for one facing the lake, as the views are incredible. *Off Calle 30 de Junio 926–0593 www.corpetur.com 21 rooms Restaurant, fans, cable TV, pool, bar, Internet, travel services AE, DC, MC, V BP.*

Nightlife

Discoteca Raices (Av. Periferico) is the island's only true disco. The bar at the **Mayan Princess** (Av. La Reforma and Av. 14 de Noviembre) shows nightly movies on a big-screen TV.

Las Puertas (Calle Central at Av. Santa Ana 926–1061) has live music every night. The artsy **La Luna** (Calle 30 de Junio 926–3346) has a pleasant atmosphere.

Sports & the Outdoors

BOATING Boat trips on Lake Petén Itzá can be arranged through most hotels in Flores or by haggling with boat owners who congregate behind the Hotel Santana. Tours often include a stop at Paraíso Escondido, a small mainland park northwest of Flores.

Santa Elena

❷ *½ km (¼ mi) south of Flores.*

Although it lacks the charms of neighboring Flores, gritty Santa Elena is pretty much unavoidable. Most services that you'll need for your trip to El Petén, from currency exchange to travel planning, are usually offered here. There are also nicer hotels here than in Flores.

Where to Stay & Eat

★ $$$$ **Villa Maya.** You could lie in bed and count the birds flying by your window at these modern villas on beautiful Lago Petén Itzá. Some 50 species have been spotted in the region. If you're more interested in wildlife, ask an attendant where to find the troop of spider monkeys that roams the grounds and the adjacent rain forest. All the rooms, tastefully decorated with colorful weavings and mahogany accents, have terrific views. Vans shuttle you to and from Tikal. ✉ *12 km (7 mi) east of Santa Elena* ☎ *926–0086 or 415–1592, 334–8136 in Guatemala City* 📠 *334–8134 in Guatemala City* 🌐 *www.villasdeguatemala.com* *36 rooms* *Restaurant, pool, boating, bicycles, horseback riding, laundry service, travel services, free parking; no a/c, no room TVs* 💳 *AE, DC, MC, V.*

$$$ **Maya International.** This string of thatch bungalows built over Lago Petén Itzá has lost a bit of its former grandeur. The simple accommodations are surrounded by water speckled with water lillies, which were sacred to the Maya. From the private balconies you can watch the waterfowl who forage here for their dinner. For your own meals there's the moderately priced restaurant, housed in a round building set out over the water. The set menu changes daily. ✉ *3 blocks east of bridge to Flores* ☎ *926–2083, 334–8136 in Guatemala City* 📠 *334–8134* 🌐 *www.villasdeguatemala.com* *20 bungalows* *Restaurant, cable TV, laundry service, free parking* 💳 *AE, DC, MC, V.*

$$$ **Petén Espléndido.** You're not on Flores, but the views of that pretty island from your private balcony are the next best thing. The pool, surrounded by palm trees, is a great place to spend an afternoon sunbathing. Sit at one of the shaded tables on the terrace or in the pretty dining room and enjoy the *especial del día* (daily special). The hotel is popular among business travelers, who appreciate the fully equipped convention center. Families enjoy the paddleboats on the lake. ✉ *At foot of bridge leading to Flores* ☎ *926–0880* 📠 *926–0866* 🌐 *www.petenesplendido.com* *62 rooms* *Restaurant, in-room safes, cable TV, pool, bar, convention center, airport shuttle, free parking* 💳 *AE, DC, MC, V.*

$$ **Casa Elena Hotel.** An attractive lobby paneled with lots of dark wood welcomes you to this centrally located hotel. Just beyond the entrance is a pretty restaurant that lets the breeze in through lace curtains. There's a wide range of dinner options, from fresh fish to grilled steak. The rooms lack the charm of others in the area, but they are clean and comfortable. There are no balconies—for a view, head to the meeting room on the top floor. The pool has a small waterslide that kids seem to love. ✉ *6 Av.* ☎ *926–2239* 📠 *926–0097* 🌐 *www.casaelena.com* *28*

rooms ♿ *Restaurant, cable TV, pool, laundry service, meeting room, free parking* ▭ *AE, DC, MC, V.*

$$$ 🏨 **Hotel del Patio-Tikal.** Built in traditional Spanish style, this modern hotel is known by its barrel-tile roof. Rooms face a small patio with a trickling fountain. Ask for a room on the first floor, as these have much larger windows. The patio restaurant sits under big arches leading to a grassy courtyard, making it a much more pleasant place to relax than the musty bar. ✉ *2 Calle and 8 Av., Santa Elena* ☎ *926–0104* 📠 *926–3030* *21 rooms* ♿ *Restaurant, cable TV, pool, gym, free parking; no a/c* ▭ *AE, DC, MC, V* 🍽 *BP.*

Sports & the Outdoors

There are several caves in the hills behind Santa Elena with interesting stalactite and stalagmite formations and subterranean rivers. The easiest to visit is Aktun Kan, just south of town. The bilingual guides of the **Tourist Guide Association of Santa Elena** (✉ Hotel Tayasal, St. Elena and San Benito ☎ 926–3133) can take you to Aktun Kan and other sites.

Ixpanpajul Parque Natural (✉ Km 468, Ruta a Santa Elena ☎ 336–0576 🌐 www.ixpanpajul.com) is a private nature reserve sitting on a large stand of primary rain forest. Hiking the suspended bridges of the skyway will give you a bird's-eye view of the indigenous flora and fauna that make the rain forest the most biodiverse ecosystem on the planet. The park also offers myriad adventure opportunities from night-time ATV tours to horseback rides to mountain bike excursions. The entrance to the reserve is 10 km south of Santa Elena.

El Remate

❸ *30 km (18½ mi) northeast of Flores.*

A mellow little town on the eastern shore of Lago Petén Itzá, El Remate is known mostly for its wood carvings, made by families that have dedicated themselves to this craft for generations. Because it's less than one hour from both Tikal and Yaxhá, El Remate makes a good base for exploring the area.

With more than 1,500 acres of rain forest, **Biotopo Cerro Cahuí** (✉ West of El Remate 🎫 Q20) is one of the most accessible wildlife reserves in El Petén. It protects a portion of a mountain that extends to the eastern edge of Lago Petén Itzá, so there are plenty of opportunities for hiking. Two well-maintained trails put you in proximity of birds like oscillated turkeys, toucans, and parrots. As for mammals, look up to spot the long-armed spider monkeys or down to see squat rodents called *tepezcuintles*. Tzu'unte, a 6-km (4-mi) trail, leads to two lookouts with views of nearby lakes. The upper lookout, Mirador Moreletii, is known by locals as Crocodile Hill because, from the other side of the lake, it looks like the eye of a half-submerged crocodile. Los Ujuxtes, a 5-km (3-mi) trail, offers a panoramic view of three lakes. Both hikes begin at a ranger station, where English-speaking guides are sporadically available.

Where to Stay & Eat

¢–$ ✕ **La Estancia Cafetería.** Owner Victor Morales's specialty is an exquisite whitefish served with vegetables sautéed in butter on a wooden platter.

Every once in a while he cooks up some fresh venison. Even though the driveway is usually filled with cars, this eatery is easy to miss—look for the Orange Crush sign. ✉ *2 km (1¼ mi) south of El Remate* ☎ *No phone* ▭ *No credit cards.*

★ **$$$$** ✕ **Camino Real Tikal.** To experience the natural beauty of the jungles surrounding Lago Petén Itzá without sacrificing creature comforts, many people head to Camino Real Tikal. It's possible to spend several days at the hotel without exhausting the possibilities—kayaking on the lake, hiking in a private reserve, swimming in the pool, lounging in the lakeside hammocks, and experiencing a traditional Mayan sauna. A dozen thatch-roof villas set high on the hillside hold the rooms, all of which have porches with views of the sparkling lake. ✉ *5 km (3 mi) west of El Remate* ☎ *926–0204, 800/722–6466 in U.S.* *926–0222* *www.caminoreal.com* *72 rooms* *Restaurant, coffee shop, cable TV, pool, gym, boating, bar, shop, airport shuttle, car rental, travel services, free parking* ▭ *AE, DC, MC, V* *BP.*

$$ ✕ **La Mansión del Pajaro Serpiente.** Perched high on the hillside, La Mansión del Pajaro Serpiente has what are perhaps the prettiest accommodations in El Petén. Canopy beds grace the bedrooms, which are furnished in dark tropical woods and have big windows that let in lots of light. You can throw open the windows to catch the lake breezes, so sleeping is comfortable. Up a nearby hill is a swimming pool, and farther up you'll find a covered terrace with several hammocks. The open-air restaurant serves local and international dishes. ✉ *On main hwy. south of El Remate* ☎ *926–4246* *10 rooms* *Restaurant, pool, travel services, free parking; no a/c, no room TVs* ▭ *No credit cards.*

¢–$ ✕ **La Casa de Don David.** As you chat with David Kuhn, the owner of this cluster of bungalows, keep an eye out for his pet parrot. The little fellow sometimes gets jealous. But talking with Kuhn is worth it, as he and his wife, Rosa, have lived in the area for more than 25 years and are a great source of travel tips. Rooms are simple and clean, with private baths. Perhaps La Casa is most famous for its second-story restaurant (**¢**), which has good home cooking. Have dinner for two in a booth, or eat at the "friendship table" and make some new acquaintances. ✉ *On road to Biotopo Cerro Cahuí* ☎ *306–2190 or 928–8469* *www.lacasadedondavid.com* *15 rooms* *Restaurant, fans, free parking; no a/c, no room TVs* ▭ *No credit cards* *FAP.*

Sports & the Outdoors

The fun folks at **Tikal Canopy Tour** (✉ Near entrance to Tikal ☎ 708–0674) have expeditions that take you to the true heart of the rain forest—not on ground level, but more than 100 feet up in the air. In the canopy you'll see monkeys and maybe even a sloth. The tour ends with an exhilarating 300-foot-long ride down a zip line.

Shopping

Although most souvenirs here are similar to those found elsewhere in Guatemala, the beautiful wood carvings are unique to El Petén. More than 70 families in this small town dedicate themselves to this craft. Their wares are on display on the side of the highway right before the turnoff for the Camino Real hotel on the road to Tikal.

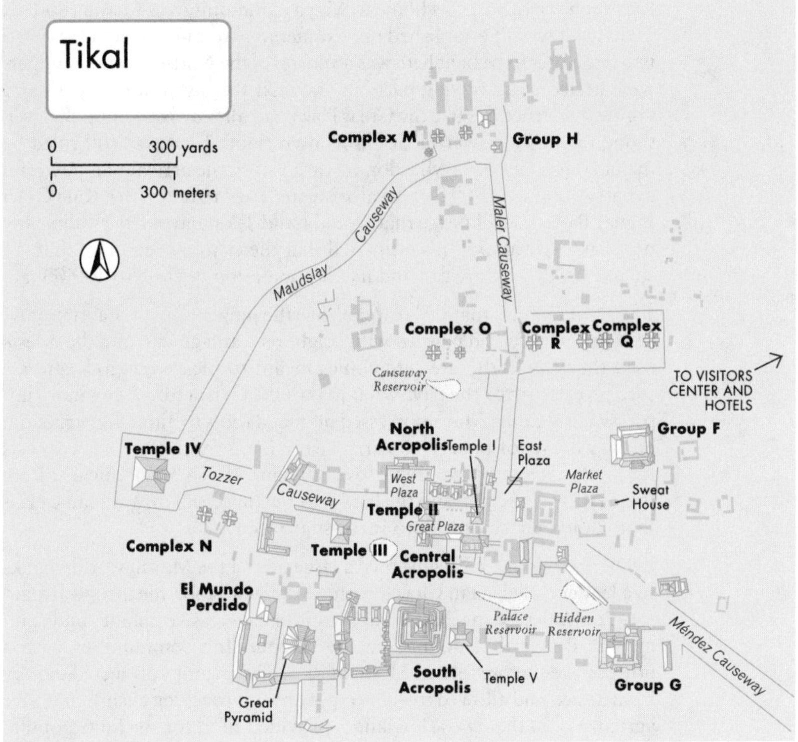

Tikal

4 35 km (22 mi) north of El Remate, 68 km (42 mi) northeast
Fodor'sChoice ★ *of Flores.*

You rise shortly before dawn. It isn't long before you hear the muffled roars of howler monkeys in the distance. After a quick cup of coffee you and your fellow adventurers follow your guide through the deserted plazas toward the pyramid that towers over everything else. The climb up the side is difficult in the dark, but after scrambling up rickety ladders and over roots and vines you find yourself at the top. You glance to the east, past the endless expanse of jungle, just as the sun starts to rise.

The high point of any trip to Guatemala is a visit to Central America's most impressive ruins. Tikal is one of the most popular tourist attractions in Central America—and with good reason. Smack in the middle of the 575-square-km (222-square-mi) Parque Nacional Tikal, the towering temples are ringed on all sides by miles of virgin forest. The area around the ruins is great for checking out creatures that spend their entire lives hundreds of feet above the forest floor in the dense canopy of trees. Colorful birds like yellow toucans and scarlet macaws are common sights.

Although the region was home to Maya communities as early as 600 BC, Tikal itself wasn't established until sometime around 200 BC. One of the first structures to be built here was a version of the North Acropolis. Others were added at a dizzying pace for the next three centuries. By AD 100 impressive structures like the Great Plaza had already been built. But even though it was a powerful city in its own right, Tikal was still ruled by the northern city of El Mirador. It wasn't until the arrival of a powerful dynasty around AD 300 that Tikal arrogated itself to full power. King Great Jaguar Paw sired a lineage that would build Tikal into a city rivaling any of its time. By AD 500 it's estimated that the city covered more than 47 square km (18 square mi) and had a population of close to 100,000.

The great temples that still tower above the jungle were at that time covered with stucco and painted with bright reds and greens, and the priests used them for elaborate ceremonies meant to please the gods and assure prosperity for the city. What makes these structures even more impressive is that the Maya possessed no metal tools to aid in construction, had no beasts of burden to carry heavy loads, and never used wheels for anything except children's toys. Of course, as a hierarchical culture they had a slave class, and the land was rich in obsidian, a volcanic glass that could be fashioned into razor-sharp tools.

By the 6th century Tikal governed a large part of the Mayan world, thanks to a leader called Caan Chac (Stormy Sky), who took the throne around AD 426. Under Caan Chac, Tikal became an aggressive military and commercial center that dominated the surrounding communities with a power never before seen in Mesoamerica. The swamps protected the city from attack and allowed troops to spot any approaching enemy. Intensive agriculture in the *bajos* (lowlands) provided food for the huge population. A valuable obsidian trade sprang up, aided by the city's strategic position near two rivers.

Tikal thrived for more than a millennium, forming strong ties with two powerful centers: Kaminal Juyu, in the Guatemalan highlands, and Teotihuacán, in Mexico City. The city entered a golden age when Ah-Cacao (Lord Chocolate) acscended the throne in AD 682. It was Ah-Cacao and his successors who commissioned the construction of most of the city's most important temples. Continuing the tradition of great structures, Ah-Cacao's son commissioned Temple I, which he dedicated to his father, who is buried beneath it. He also ordered the construction of Temple IV, the tallest temple at Tikal. By the time of his death in 768, Tikal was at the peak of its power. It would remain so until its mysterious abandonment around AD 900.

For almost 1,000 years Tikal remained engulfed by the jungle. The conquistadors who came here searching for gold and silver must have passed right by the overgrown ruins, mistaking them for rocky hills. The native Peténeros certainly knew of the ancient city's existence, but no one else ventured near until 1848, when the Guatemalan government dispatched archaeologists to the region. Tikal started to receive international attention in 1877, when Dr. Gustav Bernoulli commissioned locals to remove the carved wooden lintels from across the doorways of Temples I and IV. These items were sent to a museum in Basel, Switzerland.

HISTORY OF THE MAYA

The immense stone structures at Tikal and other archaeological sites in Guatemala are certainly impressive, but they barely suggest the culture that once existed here. The first thing you must remember is that these streets and plazas were once full of people. Archaeologists estimate that nearly 100,000 people lived in the region surrounding Tikal. Many lived in the city itself, while some lived beyond its borders on farms. When you consider that Tikal is but one of the region's dozens of cities, it's clear that this was a major metropolitan area.

The pyramids were not always the faded gray you see today. In ancient times this was a vibrant city, with facades covered in stucco painted vivid shades of red and green. If you wonder what a temple might have looked like, head to the ruins of Copán in Honduras. You can see the remains of the Rosalila Temple, then head to the nearby museum to see a re-creation of that structure.

The buildings might have been colorful, but the people also adorned themselves in bright clothing. Especially fine were the rulers, who decorated themselves with quetzal feathers and jade jewelry.

Besides the ruins of the great cities, other traces of the Maya survive. Their pottery and jade work are unmatched in the ancient world. The Museo Popol Vuh, in Guatemala City, has fascinating examples of the artistic sensibilities of the Maya, from religious figurines of mythological creatures to skull-covered burial urns.

Traditionally, Western anthropologists have divided Mayan history into the following periods: the Preclassic, Late Preclassic, Classic, Late Classic, and Postclassic.

The ***Preclassic*** *(2,000 BC–AD 100) period is characterized by the influence of the Olmec, a civilization in what is present-day Mexico. The Maya adopted many of the customs of that culture. During this period cities began to sprout up here and there, especially in the southern highlands of Guatemala and El Salvador. The Maya language also began to take shape.*

By the ***Late Preclassic*** *(400 BC–AD 100) period, the Maya experienced a burst of creativity. They developed an advanced mathematical system, an impressively precise calendar, and one of the world's first writing systems. It was during this time that some of the great Mayan cities of the north, including Tikal, were founded.*

During the ***Classic*** *(AD 100–AD 1000) period, Maya artistic, intellectual, and architectural achievements literally reached for the stars. Vast city-states were crisscrossed by numerous paved roadways, some of which still exist today.*

The single largest unsolved mystery about the Maya is their rapid decline during the ***Late Classic*** *(800–1000) period. The current theory is that siege warfare caused rural people to seek shelter in the cities. The growing urban populations drained the agricultural potential of the land around the cities. As crops failed, famine ensued, causing a mass exodus out of the cities and into smaller, sustainable populations.*

The Maya of the ***Postclassic*** *(1000–1521) period were heavily affected by growing powers in central Mexico. Architecture, ceramics, and carvings from this period show considerable outside influence. Although still dramatic, Postclassic cities such as Mayapán, Chichén Itzá, and Uxmal pale in comparison to their Classic predecessors.*

— Mark Sullivan and Melisse Gelula

In 1881 and 1882 English archaeologist Alfred Percival Maudslay made the first map showing the architectural features of this vast city. As he began to unearth the major temples, he recorded his work in dramatic photographs—you can see copies in the museum at Tikal. His work was continued by Teobert Maler, who came in 1895 and 1904. Both Maler and Maudsley have causeways named in their honor. In 1951 the Guatemalan air force cleared an airstrip near the ruins to improve access for large-scale archaeological work. Today, after more than 150 years of digging, researchers say that Tikal includes some 3,000 buildings. Countless more are still covered by the jungle. ✉ *Parque Nacional Tikal* ☎ *No phone* 🎫 *Q50* ⏲ *Daily 6–6.*

The Tikal Ruins

As you enter the Tikal, keep to the middle trail. You'll soon arrive at the ancient city's center, filled with awe-inspiring temples and intricate acropolises. The pyramid that you approach from behind is **Temple I,** known as the Temple of the Great Jaguar because of the feline represented on one of its carved lintels. It's in what is referred to as the **Great Plaza,** one of the most beautiful and dramatic in Tikal. The Great Plaza was built around AD 700 by Ah-Cacao, one of the wealthiest rulers of his time. His tomb, comparable in magnitude to that of Pa Cal at the ruins of Palenque in southern Mexico, was discovered beneath the Temple of the Great Jaguar in the 1960s. The theory is that his queen is buried beneath **Temple II,** called the Temple of the Masks for the decorations on its facade. It's a twin of the Temple of the Great Jaguar. In fact, construction of matching pyramids distinguishes Tikal from other Mayan sites.

The **North Acropolis,** to the west of Ah-Cacao's temple, is a mind-boggling conglomeration of temples built over layers and layers of previous construction. Excavations have revealed that the base of this structure is more than 2,000 years old. Be sure to see the stone mask of the rain god at Temple 33. The **Central Acropolis,** south of the Great Plaza, is an immense series of structures assumed to have served as administrative centers.

If you climb to the top of one of the pyramids, you'll see the gray roof combs of others rising above the rain forest's canopy but still trapped within it. **Temple V,** to the south, underwent a $3 million restoration project and is now open to the public. **Temple IV,** to the west, is the tallest-known structure built by the Maya. Although the climb to the top is difficult, the view is unforgettable.

To the southwest of the plaza lies the **South Acropolis,** which hasn't been reconstructed, and a 105-foot-high pyramid, similar in construction to those at Teotihuacán. A few jungle trails, including the marked Interpretative Benil-ha Trail, offer a chance to see spider monkeys and other wildlife. Outside the park, a somewhat overgrown trail halfway down the old airplane runway on the left leads to the remnants of old rubber-tappers' camps and is a good spot for bird-watching.

At park headquarters you'll find two archaeological museums that display Mayan artifacts. They are a good resource for information on the enigmatic rise and fall of the Maya people.

Other Nearby Ruins

Although Tikal is the most famous, El Petén has hundreds of archaeological sites, ranging from modest burial chambers to sprawling cities. The vast majority have not been explored, let alone restored. Within a few miles of Tikal are several sites that are relatively easy to reach. Because they are in isolated areas, it's a good idea to go with a guide.

Nakúm lies deep within the forest, connected to Tikal via jungle trails that are sometimes used for horseback expeditions. You cannot visit during the rainy season, as you'll sink into mud up to your ankles. Two building complexes and some stelae are visible. ✉ *26 km (16 mi) east of Tikal.*

The 4,000-year-old city of **Uaxactún** was once a rival to Tikal's supremacy in the region. It was conquered by Tikal in the 4th century and lived in the shadow of that great city for centuries. Inscriptions show that Uaxactun existed longer than any other Mayan city, which may account for the wide variety of structures. Here you'll find a Maya observatory.

Uaxactún is surrounded by thick rain forest, so the trip can be arduous, but as it is difficult to get here, you most likely won't have to fight the crowds as you do at neighboring Tikal, leaving you free to enjoy the quiet and mystic air of the ruins. The rock-and-dirt road is passable during the drier seasons and nearly impossible at other times without a four-wheel-drive vehicle. You'll need to secure a permit to visit Uaxactún. The administration building in Tikal is on the road between the Jaguar Inn and the Jungle Lodge. Obtaining a permit is sometimes easier said than done, but with a little persistence and perhaps a small *mordida* (bribe), you should be able to get past the guards into the administration area where they grant the free permits. Sometimes police will ask to accompany you on the trip, which is helpful for two reasons: it prevents potential robberies and, most important, will give you an extra person to push if your vehicle gets stuck. The police may ask you for some money; a Q20 tip goes a long way toward making your trip smooth. ✉ *24 km (16 mi) north of Tikal.*

Overlooking a beautiful lake of the same name, the ruins of **Yaxhá** are divided into two sections of rectangular structures that form plazas and streets. The city was probably inhabited between the Preclassic and Classic periods. The ruins are currently being restored by a German organization. Lake Yaxhá, surrounded by virgin rain forest, is a good bird-watching spot. During the rainy season only a four-wheel-drive vehicle—or setting out on horseback, motorcycle or on foot—will get you to Yaxhá; the rest of the year the road is passable. ✉ *48 km south of Flores, 30 km (19 mi) east of Tikal.*

A popular ecotourism destination, **El Zotz** is where you'll find the remnants of a Mayan city. On a clear day you can see the tallest of the ruins at Tikal from these unexcavated ruins. The odd name, which means "the bat" in Q'eqchí, refers to a cave from which thousands of bats make a nightly exodus. Troops of hyperactive spider monkeys seem to have claimed this place for themselves, swinging through the treetops and scrambling after each other like children playing a game of tag. Unlike those in Tikal, however, these long-limbed creatures are not used to people and will shake branches and throw twigs and fruit to try to scare you away. During the rainy season the mosquitoes can be fierce, so bring your strongest repellent. ✉ *24 km (15 mi) west of Tikal.*

Where to Stay & Eat

★ **$$$$** **Tikal Inn.** This cluster of comfortable bungalows wraps around a well-manicured garden and a pool. It's set apart from the other lodgings, affording a bit of privacy. The rooms have a modern feel, yet they have thatch roofs and stucco walls decorated with traditional fabrics. A small restaurant has a menu that changes daily. ✉ *Parque Nacional Tikal* ☎ *926–1917* ☎ *926–0065* *hoteltikalinn@itelgua.com* *24 rooms* *Restaurant, pool, free parking; no a/c, no room TVs* *AE, DC, MC, V* *MAP.*

$$$ **Jungle Lodge.** Built to house archaeologists working at Tikal, this hotel has cute duplexes, with a noticable lack of privacy—the dividing wall between the rooms does not meet the ceiling. The rooms are clean, though the furnishings are dated. ✉ *Parque Nacional Tikal* ☎ *477–0570* *476–0294* *www.junglelodge.guate.com* *46 rooms, 34 with bath* *Restaurant, pool, free parking; no a/c, no room TVs* *V* *MAP.*

$ **El Campamento del Sombrero.** This cluster of wooden cabins is a restful place to spend the night. There's only three hours of electricity a day, but the lakefront views and ample opportunities for bird-watching more than make up for it. The friendly Italian owner Gabriella Moretti goes out of her way to arrange trips for her guests. There are rooms with shared bathrooms for very reasonable rates. ✉ *Yaxká* ☎ *861–1687 or 861–1688* *www.ecosombrero.com* *6 rooms, 7 without bath* *Restaurant, boating, horseback riding, bar, free parking; no a/c, no room TVs* *No credit cards.*

Sayaxché

5 *61 km (38 mi) southwest of Flores.*

Down a newly paved road from Flores, this muddy frontier town on the southern bank of the Río de La Pasión is a good base for exploring the southern reaches of El Petén. This is river country, and the La Pasión and Petexbatún lead to a number of important yet largely unvisited ruins in various stages of excavation.

★ Upriver from Sayaxché are the impressive ruins of a city called **Ceibal,** which served as a tollgate, if you will, for barges plying the river. Its archaeological attractions are several restored temples, including the only circular one known to exist. Here you will also find intricately carved stelae. Interestingly, a number of anomalies were found in these monuments, which hint at a foreign influence, most likely from the Toltecs of central Mexico. Though it can be reached via a dirt road that floods during the rainy season, Ceibal is best accessed by boat on the Río de la Pasión, followed by a half-hour ascent through the forest. ✉ *On the Río de la Pasión.*

Where to Stay & Eat

$ **La Montaña.** On the Río Petexbatún, this jungle lodge was built in a clearing hacked out of the rain forest. Rustic bungalows have cement floors and bamboo walls, but they do have private baths. Family-style meals are served in an open-air dining hall. The staff can book tours of local archaeological sites. For reservations contact Viajes Turísticos La Montaña. ✉ *Sayaxché* ☎ *928–6114* 📠 *928–6169* *8 rooms* *Dining room, travel services, free parking; no a/c, no room TVs* 💳 *MC, V.*

¢ **Hotel Guayacan.** By the south bank of the Río de La Pasión, this place looks run-down but has clean, comfortable rooms on the second floor. It even has air-conditioning, a rarity in these parts. The owner can arrange boat trips to nearby Mayan ruins. ✉ *Sayaxché* ☎ *928–6111* *25 rooms, 19 with bath* *Travel services, free parking; no room TVs* 💳 *No credit cards.*

2

Sports & the Outdoors

The lowland Río de la Pasión flows into the Usumacinta, which winds for countless miles through the rain forest. Both rivers were important Mayan trade routes and thus pass numerous archaeological sites. Local agencies book expeditions to the sites that can last from a day to more than a week. Along the way you can catch a glimpse of the area's many animal inhabitants, including turtles, crocodiles, and a vast array of birds.

A day trip to one of the ruins costs Q240–Q480, depending on the number of passengers. The rate is not set in stone, so feel free to bargain. A reputable company in Sayaxché is **Viajes Don Pedro** (☎ 928–6109). **Viajes Turísticos La Montaña** (☎ 928–6114) also offers trips on the river.

Lake Petexbatún

6 *2 hrs by boat from Ceibal.*

This impressive rain-forest lagoon was the site of a 6th-century kingdom that was likely ruled by a power-hungry prince who fled Tikal and engaged in battles for territory from two twin capitals, Dos Pilas and Aguateca. A three-hour hike from Sayaxché brings you to **Dos Pilas.** Recent archaeological finds here indicate that continual warfare may have caused an ecological imbalance that led to the collapse of the Mayan civilization. Most spectacular of the ancient structures found here is a limestone staircase covered with carvings that recount the battles the upstart ruler waged against his brother at Tikal. Unlike most other Mayan cities, this one was surrounded by a defensive wall.

On the southern shore of the lake lies **Aguateca,** a small site by a 200-foot escarpment. It was likely the final capital after Dos Pilas was subsumed by Tikal. Few of the ruins have been excavated, but the trip here is a wonderful adventure.

The fortress of **Punta de Chimino,** 2½ mi north of Aguateca, was the last residence of the area's besieged royal family. The defenders dug several moats into the peninsula where the fort stood, turning it into an island.

Where to Stay & Eat

$$$ **Chiminos Island Lodge.** Archaeologists speculate that Punta de Chimino was once the retreat of Maya nobility. Beautiful cabins are scattered along the peninsula's edges, with private views of the lake and the jungle beyond. Rooms have hardwood floors and screened walls that

keep the jungle near and the insects at bay. Delicious meals using local ingredients are served in an open-air restaurant. Tours of nearby archaeological sites for both the hearty or the delicate are included. Transportation (a 1½-hour boat ride) is arranged from Sayaxché. ✉ *Punta de Chimino* ☎ *337–0009* 🌐 *www.ecotourism-adventure.com* *5 bungalows* *Restaurant, pool, horseback riding, travel services; no a/c, no room TVs* *No credit cards* *FAP.*

Tikal & the Mayan Ruins A to Z

AIR TRAVEL

Grupo Taca, Racsa, and Tikal Jets operate flights from Guatemala City to Santa Elena that take less than an hour and cost about $60 each way. Several daily flights leave the capital around 7 AM and return around 4 PM. Air service between Santa Elena and the Mexican resort of Cancún is offered by Aviateca and Aerocaribe. Aerocaribe also offers flights to the ruins of Pelenque.

Aeropuerto Internacional Santa Elena is less than 1 km (½ mi) outside town. Taxis and shuttles meet every plane and charge about 20 quetzales to take you into town. Plans to build a new runway are on the drawing boards. This would allow direct international flights from the United States to land in Santa Elena.

Aerocaribe ☎ 926-0923. **Grupo Taca** ☎ 926-1238, 332-6034 in Guatemala City 🌐 www.grupotaca.com. **Racsa** ☎ 926-1477, 332-7470 in Guatemala City. **Tikal Jets** ☎ 926-0386, 332-5070 in Guatemala City 🌐 www.tikaljets.com.

BUS TRAVEL

Linea Dorada offers direct bus service between Guatemala City and Santa Elena and Flores. The 10-hour trip on air-conditioned buses with comfortable reclining seats, TVs, and bathrooms costs $30–$50 round-trip. Call at least one day ahead for reservations. Inexpensive local service is available, but those buses stop in every village along the way, which adds hours to the trip.

Linea Dorada ✉ Calle Principal, Santa Elena ☎ 926-0528 ✉ Calle de la Playa, Flores ☎ 232-9658.

BUS TRAVEL WITHIN EL PETÉN

In Santa Elena the San Juan Hotel serves as the local bus terminal. Here you can catch a bus operated by San Juan Travel that makes the two-hour trip to Tikal at 6, 8, 10 AM and return trips at 2, 4 and 5 PM. Local buses serving other destinations like Sayaxché depart from the market in Santa Elena. They are inexpensive but very slow.

San Juan Travel ✉ San Juan Hotel, Santa Elena ☎ 926-0041.

CAR RENTAL

If you're not booked on a tour, the best way to get around El Petén is by renting a four-wheel-drive vehicle. The major rental agencies, including Budget and Hertz, have offices at Aeropuerto Internacional Santa Elena. Koka, a local company, rents four-wheel-drive vehicles from an office in the Camino Real Tikal near El Remate. San Juan Travel, at the San Juan Hotel in Santa Elena, rents four-wheel-drive vehicles and passenger vans.

Local Agencies **Budget** ✉ Aeropuerto Internacional Santa Elena ☎ 950-0741. **Koka** ✉ Camino Real Tikal, El Remate ☎ 926-1233. **Hertz** ✉ Aeropuerto Internacional Santa Elena ☎ 950-0204. **San Juan Travel** ✉ San Juan Hotel, Santa Elena ☎ 926-2013.

CAR TRAVEL

Roads in El Petén are often in poor repair and not very well marked. Some roads are impassable during the rainy season, so check with the tourist office before heading out on seldom traveled roads, such as those to the more-remote ruins surrounding Tikal. A four-wheel-drive vehicle is highly recommended.

To be on the safe side, never travel at night. If you come upon a fallen tree across the road, do not get out of your car to remove the debris. Robbers have been known to fell trees to get tourists to stop. Turn around as quickly as possible.

EMERGENCIES

Medical facilities in El Petén are not as modern as in the rest of the country. If you're really sick, consider getting on the next plane back to Guatemala City.

Emergency Services **Police** ☎ 926-1365.

Hospitals **Hospital del Instituto Guatemalteco de Seguridad Social** ✉ Santa Elena ☎ 926-0619.

Pharmacies **Farmacia Nueva** ✉ Av. Santa Ana, Flores ☎ 926-1387. **Farmacia San Carlos** ✉ 4 Calle 1-92, Zona 1, Santa Elena ☎ 926-0753.

MAIL & SHIPPING

The main post office in Flores is a half block east of the main square. In Santa Elena the post office is a block east of the bridge leading to Flores. Mail service is slow, so expect to get back home before your letter does.

Post Offices **Flores** ✉ Calle 10 de Noviembre, Flores. **Santa Elena** ✉ 2 Calle and 7 Av., Flores.

MONEY MATTERS

There are several banks in Santa Elena, but none anywhere else in the region. Make sure to exchange your money before heading off on your jungle adventure. Some high-end hotels will exchange dollars for a small commission.

Banco Industrial ✉ Calle Principal, Santa Elena ☎ 926-0281.

TOURS

Flores-based Martsam Travel, run by Lileana and Benedicto Grijalva, offers many different types of tours in the area. The El Petén environmental group ProPetén offers adventure trips led by rubber-tappers who once worked at plantations in the forest.

Guatemala City–based Adventuras Naturales and Flores-based Expedition Panamundo specialize in tours of the Mayan world and bird-watching expeditions. Guatemala City–based Maya Expeditions has trips down Sayaxché area rivers and the nearby archaeological sites. From Antigua, Inter Quetzal, Sin Fronteras, and Vision Travel all offer tours of El Petén.

Adventuras Naturales ✉ 9 Calle 18-17, Zona 14, Guatemala City ☎/fax 333-6051 or 832-3328 🌐 www.aventurasnaturales.tripod.com. **Expedition Panamundo** ✉ Av. Reforma, Flores ☎ 926-0501 or 331-7588. **Inter Quetzal** ✉ 7 Av. 1-20, Zona 4, Guatemala City ☎ 331-9282 or 360-1422. **Martsam Travel** ✉ Calle Centroamérica and Av. 30 de Junio, Flores ☎ 926-0346 ☎/fax 926-3225. **Maya Expeditions** ✉ 15 Calle 1-91, Zona 10, Guatemala City ☎ 363-4965. **Sin Fronteras** ✉ 5 Av. Norte 15, Antigua ☎ 832-1226. **Vision Travel** ✉ 3 Av. Norte 3, Antigua ☎ 832-3293 🌐 www.guatemalainfo.com.

VISITOR INFORMATION

Arcas, which returns illegally captured animals to the wild, is a great resource on the flora and fauna of El Petén. Inguat has two offices in El Petén, one in Flores and one at Aeropuerto Internacional Santa Elena.

Arcas ✉ 10 km (6 mi) east of Santa Elena fax 591-4731. **Inguat** ✉ On Parque Central, Flores ☎ 926-0669 ✉ Aeropuerto Internacional Santa Elena ☎ 926-0533 at the airport.

GUATEMALA A TO Z

To research prices, get advice from other travelers, and book travel arrangements, visit www.fodors.com.

AIR TRAVEL

Guatemala has two international airports: Aeropuerto Internacional La Aurora, at the edge of Guatemala City, and the smaller Aeropuerto Internacional Santa Elena, in El Petén.

Domestic carriers fly between Guatemala City and Santa Elena.

BUS TRAVEL

There is bus service from Guatemala City to cities on the Mexican and Honduran borders, as well as to destinations in Belize and El Salvador. To La Mesilla, on the Mexican border, El Condor departs at 4, 8, 10, 1, and 5 for the seven-hour trip. To Tecún Umán, on the Mexican border, Fortaleza has hourly departures from 1 AM to 6 PM; the journey takes five hours. For service to El Carmen–Talismán, also on the Mexican border, contact Galgos. Departures for the five-hour ride are at 5:30, 10, 1:30, and 5. Maya Mundo runs buses to Quintana Roo, Mexico.

Melva International has service to San Salvador. Eight buses a day depart between 4 AM and 6 PM for the five-hour journey. For service to Esquipulas, on the border of Honduras, try Rutas Orientales. Buses run almost hourly from 5 AM to 6 PM and take four hours. For El Florido take the bus to Chiquimula at 7 AM, 10 AM, or 12:30 PM and change there. Linea Dorada operates from Santa Elena to destinations in Belize.

El Condor ✉ 19 Calle 2-01, Zona 1, Guatemala City ☎ 232-8504. **Fortaleza** ✉ 19 Calle 8-70, Zona 1, Guatemala City ☎ 220-6730. **Galgos** ✉ 7 Av. 19-44, Zona 1, Guatemala City ☎ 232-3661 or 220-6018 🌐 www.transgalgosinter.com. **Melva International** ✉ 3 Av. 1-38, Zona 9, Guatemala City ☎ 331-0874. **Rutas Orientales** ✉ 19 Calle 8-18, Zona 1, Guatemala City ☎ 238-3894. **Mundo Maya** ✉ Calle de la Playa, Edificio Hotel Itza 1, Flores ☎ 926-0070.

CAR TRAVEL TO & FROM GUATEMALA

It's possible to enter Guatemala by land from Mexico, Belize, El Salvador, and Honduras. The Pan-American Highway, which passes through most major cities, connects the country with Mexico at La Mesilla and with El Salvador at San Cristobal Frontera. It's also possible to travel to El Salvador via the coastal highway, crossing at Ciudad Pedro de Alvarado, or Valle Nuevo. Pacific routes to Mexico pass through Tecún Umán and El Carmen–Talismán.

To reach Belize, take the highway east from Flores, passing El Cruce before reaching the border town of Melchor de Mencos. There are also two routes into Honduras, through El Florido or Esquipulas.

Travelers often get harassed or swindled at border towns. There is no entry fee, although you may be asked for a bribe. Crossing the border in a rental car can be troublesome; if you need to do so, ask your rental agency for advice. When in a border town, always watch your belongings carefully.

CAR TRAVEL WITHIN GUATEMALA

You need a valid driver's license from your own country to drive in Guatemala. Most roads leading to larger towns and cities are paved; those leading to small towns and villages are generally dirt roads. *Doble-tracción,* or four-wheel drive, is a necessity in many remote areas, especially at the height of the rainy season. Gas stations can also be scarce, so be sure to fill up before heading into rural areas. Consider bringing some extra fuel along with you. Don't count on finding repair shops outside the major towns.

Many locals ignore traffic laws, so you should be on your guard. *Alto* means "stop" and *Frene con motor* ("use engine to break" or downshift) means that a steep descent lies ahead. Travel only by day, especially if you are driving alone. Keep your eyes peeled for children or animals on the road. If you arrive at a roadblock such as a downed tree, do not attempt to remove the roadblock, simply turn around. Highway robbers often deliberately fell trees to ensnare drivers.

DISABILITIES & ACCESSIBILITY

People with disabilities will find Guatemala's cobbled streets and lack of wheel-chair access nearly impossible to negotiate. This said, most high-end hotels and tour providers are able to accommodate people with disabilities.

EMBASSIES

Canada ✉ Edificio Edyma Plaza, 8th fl., 13 Calle 8-44, Zona 10, Guatemala City ☎ 333-6102. **United Kingdom** ✉ Centro Financiero Torre II, 7th fl., 7 Av. 5-10, Zona 4, Guatemala City ☎ 332-1601. **United States** ✉ Av. La Reforma 7-01, Zona 10, Guatemala City ☎ 331-1541.

HEALTH

The most common health hazard for visitors to Guatemala is traveler's diarrhea. To avoid this problem, drink only bottled water. Remember to avoid raw vegetables unless you know they've been thoroughly washed and disinfected with *agua pura* (purified water). Be wary of strawberries and other unpeeled fruits for the same reason. Heat stroke is another risk, but one that can easily be avoided. The best way to avoid it is to do as the locals do (wake early and retire at midday for a siesta) and drink lots of water.

MAIL & SHIPPING

There are post offices in most communities, but the best way to mail letters and packages is often through your hotel. If at all possible, bring the items home with you, as Guatemala brings new meaning to the concept of "snail mail."

MONEY MATTERS

You can exchange U.S. dollars at any bank and in most hotels. It's far more difficult to exchange other currencies. If you are traveling with currency other than U.S. dollars, it would be wise to change the money into dollars or quetzales before you arrive. Traveler's checks are accepted only in larger hotels.

ATMS There are ATMs that work on the Cirrus and Plus systems in most major cities. In smaller cities you will be hard pressed to find an ATM, but you should be able to go to the bank to withdraw money from your account using your ATM card. Make sure you only have a four-digit pin number, as many ATMs only take four digits.

CURRENCY Guatemalan currency is called the quetzal, after the resplendent national bird. There are 1-, 5-, 10-, and 25-centavo coins. Bills come in denominations of one-half, 1, 5, 10, 20, 50, and 100 quetzales. At this writing, $1 was worth roughly Q8.

SAFETY

Most crimes directed at tourists have been pickpocketings and muggings, as well as thefts from cars. In the cities you should do the same as you would in any metropolitan area—leave flashy jewelry and watches at home, keep your camera in a secure bag, and don't handle money in public. Hire taxis only from official stands at the airport, outside hotels, and at major intersections. When traveling outside the cities, it's a good idea to hire a guide. Some of the volcanoes near Antigua and Lago Atitlán have been frequented by muggers.

If you can avoid it, don't drive after sunset. Watch out on the roads, as one common ploy used by highway robbers is to construct a roadblock, such as logs strewn across the road, and then hide nearby. When unsuspecting motorists get out of their cars to remove the obstruction, they are waylaid. If you come upon a deserted roadblock, don't stop; turn around.

Avoid participating in local rallies, as protesters are not always treated well. Several Guatemalans were killed protesting a bus fare increase in spring 2000.

The increase in adoption of Guatemalan children has provoked the fear by many here, particularly rural villagers, that children will be abducted by foreigners. In April 2000 two Japanese tourists suspected of this were killed in a market area of Todos Santos Cuchumatán. Limit your interaction with children you do not know, and be discreet when taking photographs.

TELEPHONES

Public phones are few and far between in Guatemala, but most towns have offices where you can place both national and international calls. The easiest way to place a call is from your hotel.

Guatemala's country code is 502; there are no local area codes.

TIPPING

A tip of about 10% is standard at most Guatemalan restaurants. Bellhops and maids expect tips only in the more expensive hotels. Tip tour guides about 10% of the tour price.

VISITOR INFORMATION

The staff at Inguat is courteous, professional, and knowledgeable. There are offices in Guatemala City, Antigua, Xelajú, Panajachel, Flores, and Santa Elena.

Inguat ✉ 7 Av. 1–17, Zona 4, Guatemala City ☎ 331–1333 🌐 www.guatemala.travel.com.gt ✉ Palacio de los Capitanes, Antigua ☎ 832–0763 ✉ 7 Calle 11–35, Zona 1, Xelajú ☎ 761–4931 ✉ Calle de la Playa Publica, Zona 2, Panajachel ☎ 762–1392 ✉ Parque Central, Flores ☎ 926–0669 ✉ Santa Elena Airport, Santa Elena ☎ 926–0533.

UNDERSTANDING BELIZE & GUATEMALA

BELIZE AT A GLANCE

Fast Facts

Name: Officially changed from British Honduras to Belize in 1973
Capital: Belmopan
Type of government: Parliamentary democracy
National anthem: *Land of the Free*
Administrative divisions: 6 districts (similar to U.S. states)—Corozal, Orange Walk, Belize, Cayo, Stann Creek, and Toledo
Independence: September 21, 1981; Belize remains a member of the British Commonwealth
Constitution: September 21, 1981
Legal system: Based on English Common Law
Suffrage: 18 years of age; universal
Legislature: An elected House of Representatives and an appointed Senate
Population: 266,000
Population density: 30 people per square mi, the lowest population density in Central America and one of the lowest population densities in the Americas
Median age: Male 18.8, female 19
Life expectancy: Male 65, female 70
Infant mortality: 27.07 deaths per 1,000 live births
Literacy: 94%
Language: English (official). Spanish is widely spoken. Creole, Garifuna, and several Mayan languages also spoken
Ethnic groups: Mestizo, 49%; Creole, 25%; Maya, 11%; Garifuna, 6%
Religion: Roman Catholic, 50%; Pentecostal, 7%; Seventh Day Adventist, 7%; Anglican 5%; Methodist, 4%; Mennonite, 4%
Discoveries & inventions: When Western Europe was still in the Dark Ages, the ancient Maya in Belize and elsewhere in Mesoamerica created astronomical, mathematical, agricultural, calendrical, medical, and hieroglyphic writing systems of extraordinary complexity.

Geography & Environment

Land area: 22,966 square km (8,866 square mi); about the size of Massachusetts
Coastline: 386 km (240 mi), bordered on the east by the Caribbean
Terrain: Low-lying coastal plains that give way to low mountains in the south
Islands: More than 400 islands offshore in the Caribbean, the largest of which is Ambergris Caye
Natural resources: Farm land, timber, fish
Natural hazards: Hurricanes (June–November) and coastal flooding
Environmental issues: Deforestation, water pollution from sewage and agricultural runoff, deterioration of coral reefs

If the world had any ends, British Honduras would certainly be one of them.

—Aldous Huxley

The Macal River Valley is sacred land. It's worth fighting for. Everything is connected in the biological world. We have lost too much of the planet, bit by bit, piece by piece. And that is exactly how we have to save it, piece by piece.

—Sharon Matola, director of the Belize Zoo, on the fight against building a hydropower dam on the Macal River, a fight apparently lost, as construction of the dam continues

Economy

Currency: Belize dollar
Exchange rate: BZ$2 = $1
GDP: US$1.3 billion
Per capita income: BZ$9,653 ($4,900)
Inflation: 1.9%
Unemployment: 9%
Work force: 90,000 (services 55%, agriculture 27%, industry 18%)
Debt: US$475 million
Major industries: Tourism, agriculture, fishing
Agricultural products: Sugar cane, citrus fruit, bananas
Exports: US$290 million
Major export products: Sugar, bananas, citrus, clothing, fish, molasses, wood
Export partners: U.S. 54%, U.K. 23%, Caricom 6%, Mexico 1%
Imports: US$430 million
Major import products: Machinery, manufactured goods, fuels, chemicals, pharmaceuticals, food, beverages
Import partners: U.S. 47%, Mexico 11%, other Central America 5%, U.K., 3%

No wait till de man ded, fu tell am y good (Creole for "Don't wait until a man is dead to tell him that he is good.")
—Lucio Alcocer, Belizean songwriter

Political Climate

In an ongoing dispute, Guatemala claims Belize territory in the south and north; at this writing an agreement reached in late 2002 to resolve the issue has not yet been brought to a referendum in either country.

Our two countries (Belize and the United States) share the same side of planet Earth. We can draw wisdom and strength from the basic values of a common heritage, the same language and common law, a kindred parliamentary democracy, and a mixed economy.
—George Cadle Price, prime minister of Belize, 1983, to President Ronald Reagan

Did You Know?

- More than 40% of Belize's land is protected as national parks or reserves.
- Belize has the longest barrier reef in the Western and Northern hemispheres.
- The two tallest buildings in Belize, one at Caracol and one at Xunantunich, date back some 1,000 years.
- Belize is thought to have the largest population of manatees in the world.
- Belize has less than 400 mi of paved roads.
- The expanse of *Selva Maya* (Maya Forest), which Belize shares with Guatemala and Mexico, covers some 25,000 square km, the largest block of tropical forest north of the Amazon Basin.
- At the height of the Mayan empire, Belize may have had a population approaching 1 million people, four times the population of the country today.

GUATEMALA AT A GLANCE

Fast Facts

Capital: Guatemala City
National anthem: *Guatemala Feliz* (*Fortunate Guatemala*), by José JoaquÌn Palma and music by Rafael Alvarez Ovalle
Type of government: Constitutional democratic republic
Administrative divisions: 22 departments
Independence: September 15, 1821 (from Spain)
Constitution: May 31, 1985
Legal system: Civil law system
Suffrage: 18 years of age; universal (active duty members of the armed forces can't vote)
Legislature: Unicameral congress; 140 members are elected by popular vote to serve four-year terms
Population: 13.9 million
Population density: 294 people per square mi
Median age: Male 18.1, female 18.5
Life expectancy: Male 64.3, female 66.2
Infant mortality rate: 37.92 deaths per 1,000 live births
Literacy: 70.6%
Language: Spanish 60%, Amerindian languages 40%
Ethnic groups: Mestizo (Ladino), 55%; Amerindian, 43%; other, 2%
Religion: Roman Catholic, Protestant, indigenous Mayan religions
Discoveries & inventions: At the period when Western Europe was in the Dark Ages, the ancient Maya in Guatemala and elsewhere in Mesoamerica created astronomical, mathematical, agricultural, calendrical, medical, and hieroglyphic writing systems of extraordinary complexity.

As I was to discover in the years to come, things would be much easier to understand if our black-and-white picture of a country like Guatemala held true once we got to know the place. But of course things are never so simple.

—Stephen Connely Benz, *Guatemalan Journey*

Geography & Environment

Land area: 108,890 square km (42,043 square mi), slightly smaller than Tennessee
Coastline: 400 km (249 mi), along the Pacific and Atlantic oceans and the Caribbean
Terrain: Mostly mountainous, with narrow coastal plains and rolling limestone plateaus
Natural resources: Petroleum, nickel, rare woods, fish, chicle
Natural hazards: Volcanoes, occasional violent earthquakes, hurricanes on the Caribbean Coast
Environmental issues: Deforestation in the Petén; soil erosion; water pollution

This is the first account, the first narrative. There was neither man, nor animal, birds, fishes, crabs, trees, stones, caves, ravines, grasses, nor forest; there was only the sky.

—Popul Vuh (Book of the Mat)

Economy

Currency: Quetzal
Exchange rate: Q8.17 = $1
GDP: US$53.2 billion
Per capita income: Q31,874 ($3,900)
Inflation: 8.1%
Unemployment: 7.5%
Work force: 4.2 million (services 35%, agriculture 50%, industry 15%)
Debt: US$4.9 billion
Economic aid: US$250 million
Major industries: Sugar, textiles, furniture, chemicals, petroleum, metals, rubber, tourism
Agricultural products: Coffee, sugar, bananas
Exports: US$2.7 billion
Major export products: Coffee, sugar, bananas, fruits and vegetables, cardamom, meat, apparel, petroleum, electricity
Export partners: U.S. 58.7%, El Salvador, 9.3%, Nicaragua, 3.1%
Imports: US$5.6 billion
Major import products: Fuels, machinery, construction materials, grain, fertilizers, electricity
Import partners: U.S. 33.2%, Mexico 9.9%, South Korea 8.2%, El Salvador 5.7%, China 4%

My story is the story of all poor Guatemalans. My personal experience is the reality of a whole people.
—Rigoberta Menchu, in *I, Rigoberta Menchu: An Indian Woman in Guatemala*

Political Climate

In an ongoing dispute, Guatemala claims Belize territory in the south and north; at this writing an agreement reached in late 2002 to resolve the issue has not been brought to a referendum in either country. Guatemalan squatters continue to settle in Belize border region.

If you write novels merely to entertain—then burn them!
—Miguel Angel Asturias, from his Nobel prize lecture, 1967

Poor Guatemala! So far from God, so close to the United States.
—Folk saying (said of Guatemala and many other Latin American countries)

Did You Know?

- Guatemala has 19 different ecosystems ranging from the tropical lowlands of the Rio Dulce to the semitropical and temperate cloud forests of the Western Highlands to desert thorn forests.
- Guatemala has 487 FM and 130 AM radio stations and 26 television stations.
- The highest mountain in Guatemala is Volcan Tajumulco, at 13,816 feet.
- Guatemalans speak at least 24 different languages.
- Guatemala has 3,027 mi (4,871 km) of paved roads and 551 mi (886 km) of railroads.
- The expanse of *Selva Maya* (Maya Forest), which Guatemala shares with Belize and Mexico, covers some 25,000 square km, the largest block of tropical forest north of the Amazon Basin.
- Almost two-thirds of Guatemalan children live in poverty.

BUSING IT IN GUATEMALA

THE SUN IS RISING in the highlands of Guatemala. Along bumpy back roads, a school bus bounces over rocks and ruts to the whine of *ranchero* drinking music akin to country, declaring the woes of lost loves and long days of working the fields. Outside, villages show the first signs of waking—men carrying machetes walk to their *milpa* or cornfields; girls carrying plastic bowls full of corn dough return from the neighborhood grinder ready to make the day's tortillas; women stoke the cooking fires. Inside the restyled Virginia Public School Bus #121, young students aren't aboard, but a wide range of travelers, from newborns swaddled in hand-woven cloth, toothless grandmas with unflinching stares, cowboy-hat-wearing men in bright patchwork pants and wool skirts, to a European couple reading travel guides.

The driver uses the windshield as a tableau of personal expression: stickers of the Virgin Mary, the Tasmanian Devil, a winking Jesus, the Playboy bunny, and a baby wearing a leather jacket and sunglasses are juxtaposed here, a cast of characters assembled nowhere else, it would seem. Highlighting the driver's more sensitive side is a small menagerie of stuffed animals dangling from the rear-view mirror. As he passes a jalopy on a blind, cliff-side curve, the early morning passengers appear unconcerned. Maybe that's because the sticker above the NO SMOKING sign declares in red glistening letters, *Yo manejo, pero Jesus me guia* (I drive, but Jesus guides me.)

The driver's helper, his *ayudante,* is busy carrying 100-pound bags of beans up the ladder to the bus's rooftop. It's difficult to keep an eye fixed on him: one minute he's squeezing down the aisle selling tickets, the next, he's swinging out the emergency exit used as the back door and climbing along the outside of the speeding bus. He leans out the front door, pointing at the people on the roadside and flipping his hand upward. "*¿Donde?*" Where do you want to go? He jumps off the bus and helps a woman toting a little baby to climb aboard. "*¡Dále!*" he then yells. Then in English, "Put the pedal to the metal!" Young boys look on with admiration as the ayudante runs alongside and jumps aboard just when it seems the bus has picked up too much speed. With his spare moments he pulls up a turned-over bucket and from his perch keeps the driver company by leaning close and telling him any number of fables or rumors or jokes; so animated his face and so attentive is the driver, you wish you could listen in for a while over the din.

The bus roars off leaving a group of colorfully dressed women and their children on the roadside. It is almost noon in a small Guatemalan town on market day. With the children grabbing at their skirts, the women wander off, silently entering a mass of crowded stalls packed with everything from *típica,* traditional clothes, to superglue. They pass by a little girl concentrating on balancing a bowl of hot beef soup in her hands, carrying it to her parents who are busy peddling a dozen different varieties of hot peppers. A little old woman clutches two chickens by the feet and haggles with a man over their price, yanking them up and down in the air as she bargains. Behind her, a peddler is enticing some tourists into a sale by showing them an impressive selection of thick wool blankets, even though it's 95°. There are no price tags or cash registers or express aisles; shopping on market day is not an expedient experience—it's a social transaction, in which every purchase requires a discussion or at least a certain amount of feigned indecision.

Being Sunday, the market is filled with churchgoers as well as shoppers. A procession leaves the church and descends into the market led by elderly men wearing black robes, swinging golden globes of incense. One man beats a small drum while another blows into a wooden reed instrument with a ducklike honk. Boys stride ahead and, unconcerned, with long poles, raise the electrical wires to make room for an 18-foot statue of the Virgin Mary to pass. When the procession is gone, the market swings back to its regular affairs and is once again quiet and *tranquilo*. Only a few noises rise above the pitch of hushed talking. Ice-cream vendors ring small bells. A young girl drags a snorting pig along on a leash. Several young boys playing marbles on a dirt patch behind the market argue about the ownership of a shooter. And off in the distance is the ubiquitous cry of ranchero music rising from the radios of the townspeople who peek out of their houses inspired by the passing of strangers and buses.

The sun is setting on the Central American isthmus. The ayudante hoses down the bus while the driver counts the day's take. The peddlers in the market load their wares into woven baskets and boxes and haul them away. The young children drag their feet home for dinner. The bus driver heads off and greets a circle of friends gathered around a domino game at a local drinking house. He orders a round of beers and raises the bottle for a toast, "For a day well done."

—Joanna Kosowsky

BOOKS & MOVIES

Belize

Two histories stand out: *The Making of Modern Belize,* by C. H. Grant, and *A Profile of the New Nation of Belize,* by W. D. Setzekorn. *Jaguar,* by Alan Rabinowitz, an interesting book about the creation of the Cockscomb Basin Wildlife Sanctuary, unfortunately tells you too much about the man and too little about the cat. Aldous Huxley, who wrote *Beyond the Mexique Bay,* is always hard to beat. If you're interested in the Maya, Ronald Wright's *Time Among the Maya* ties past and present together in one perceptive whole. Classic works on the Maya include *The Maya* by Michael Coe, a compendious introduction to the world of the Maya, and *The Rise and Fall of the Maya Civilization,* by one of the grand old men of Maya archaeology, J. Eric S. Thompson.

For natural history enthusiasts, four books belong in your suitcase: *A Field Guide to the Birds of Mexico* by E. P. Edwards; *Guide to Corals and Fishes of Florida, the Bahamas and the Caribbean* by I. Greenberg; *The Ecotravellers' Wildlife Guide, Belize and Northern Guatemala* by Les Belesky; and *An Introduction to Tropical Rainforests* by T. C. Whitmore. *Our Man in Belize* is a fascinating memoir of life in British Honduras in the 1950s and '60s. For beach reading, *Belize, a Novel* by Carlos Ledson Miller is a fast-paced saga of a Belizean family over four decades.

Paul Theroux's novel, *The Mosquito Coast,* about an obsessed American who drags his family to Central America, was actually set in Honduras, but the movie by the same name, starring Harrison Ford, was filmed in Belize in 1986. The rip-roaring *The Dogs of War,* 1981, starring Christopher Walken, about soldiers of fortune in Africa, has wonderful scenes of Belize City, especially the lobby of the Chateau Caribbean Hotel, and Emory King, now film commissioner for the Belize government, has a bit part (as indeed he has in nearly all the TV shows and movies shot in Belize).

Heart of Darkness (1994, starring John Malkovich), and 2001's *After the Storm,* directed by Guy Ferland, were also filmed in Belize. One of the first reality TV shows, *Temptation Island,* was shot mostly on Ambergris Caye, at Mata Chica and Captain Morgan's resorts, in 2000–2001. He hasn't filmed anything in Belize, but Francis Ford Coppola (*The Godfather, Apocalypse Now*) owns two resorts in Belize, Turtle Inn in Placencia and Blancaneaux in the Mountain Pine Ridge, along with a third in Flores, Guatemala.

Guatemala

For travel literature, try Ronald Wright's *Time Among the Maya* or Aldous Huxley's *Beyond the Mexique Bay,* which describes his travels in 1934. Nobel laureate Miguel Angel Asturias is the country's most famous author, and his *Men of Maize* is full of history and cultural insight. Francisco Goldman's *The Long Night of White Chickens* is a lyrical novel that touches on some contemporary social issues. Michael Coe's *The Maya* is an authoritative book on the lost societies of the region's prehistory, as is J. Eric S. Thompson's *The Rise and Fall of the Maya Civilization.* Tour Tikal with a copy of Coe's *Tikal: A Handbook of the Ancient Maya Ruins.* It can often be purchased in the airport, at the area's larger hotels, and sometimes at the park entrance. For a guide to Guatemala's flora and fauna, try John C. Kricher's *A Neotropical Companion.*

For historical and political background, try James Painter's *Guatemala: False Hope, False Freedom,* or Jean-Marie Simon's

Guatemala: Eternal Spring, Eternal Tyranny, which has excellent photographs. Victor Perera's *Unfinished Conquest* is a thorough and fascinating account of Guatemala's guerilla war, while Rigoberta Menchú's memoir, *I, Rigoberta Menchú; An Indian Woman in Guatemala,* opened the world's eyes to the human-rights abuses perpetrated during the country's 36-year "dirty war," and earned the author a Nobel Prize.

WILDLIFE GLOSSARY

An amazing array of creatures make their homes in Belize and Guatemala. Many are not terribly difficult to see, thanks to their brilliant coloring. Others are likely to elude you completely. A rundown of some of the region's most attention-grabbing mammals, birds, reptiles, amphibians—even a few insects—are listed below. Common names are given, so you can understand the local wildlife lingo.

Agouti (*guanta, paca, tepezcuintle*): A 20-inch-long tailless rodent with small ears and a large muzzle, the agouti is known locally as the gibnut. It's reddish brown on Guatemala's Pacific coast, more tawny orange on Belize's Caribbean slope. You might spot one sitting on its haunches and eating large seeds and fruit. Largely nocturnal, the agouti is more likely to be seen on a menu than in the wild. Known as the royal rat, it was served to Queen Elizabeth on her last visit to Belize.

Anteater (*oso hormiguero*): Three species—giant, silky, and collared—are found in this region. Only the collared, or vested, anteater is commonly seen (and too often as a roadkill). This medium-size anteater (30 inches long with an 18-inch tail) has long sharp claws for ripping into insect nests. You may spot one lapping up ants and termites with its long sticky tongue.

Aracari (*cusingo*): These slender toucans, known for their strikingly colored bills, eat ripe fruit. They often travel in groups of six or more. Collared aracaris on the Caribbean coast have a chalky upper mandible.

Armadillo (*cusuco*): These are the same animals that are found in southern U.S. Mostly nocturnal and solitary, this edentate roots in the soil with its long muzzle for a varied diet of roots, insects, and small animals. They are sometimes found on the menu in local restaurants.

Basilisk (*gallego*): Flaps of skin on their long toes enable the "Jesus Christ lizard" to run across water. The emerald basilisk in the Caribbean lowlands is marked with turquoise and black on its green body. Adult males grow to 3 feet and have crests on their heads, backs, and tails.

Booby: This red-footed bird received its unflattering name because it was unafraid of humans. Because of this it became the easy prey of hungry sailors landing at Belize's Half Moon Caye, where 4,000 now live in a protected nature reserve. Look for nests with fuzzy white chicks.

Caiman (*cocodrilo*): The spectacled caiman is a small crocodile that subsists mainly on fish. It's most active at night (its eyes glow red when illuminated by a flashlight), basking in the sun by day. It's distinguished from its American cousin by its sloping brow and smooth back scales.

Capuchin monkey (*mono carablanca*): With black fur and pink faces surrounded by wisps of white, capuchin monkeys are found singly or in groups of up to 20. They are extremely active foragers, sometimes even coming to the ground to search for food.

Coati (*pizote*): A long-nose relative of the raccoon, the coati has a slender, ringed tail it often holds straight up. Lone males or groups of females with young are active during the day, either on the ground or in the trees. Omnivorous, they feed on fruit and seeds as well as mice and rats. In Belize, they are known as Quash.

Cougar (*puma*): Growing to 5 feet in length, mountain lions are the largest unspotted cats in Central America. Rarely seen, they live in most habitats in the region and feed on vertebrates ranging from snakes to deer.

Crocodile (*lagarto*): Although often referred to as alligators, crocodiles reign supreme in this region. They are distinguished from the smaller caiman by their flat heads, narrow snouts, and spiky scales. The American crocodile can reach 16 feet in length, while the smaller Morelet's crocodile only grows to 8 feet. The territories of both species overlap in estuaries and brackish coastal waters, but only the American crocodile is able to filter excess salt from its system, allowing it to venture to the more distant cayes. Crocodiles seldom attack humans, preferring fish, birds, and the occasional small mammal. Both species are endangered and protected by international law.

Ctenosaur (*garrobo*): Known in Creole as the wish willy, this 36-inch-long lizard is mostly tan with four dark bands on its body and a tail ringed with rows of sharp, curved spines. This cousin of the iguana sleeps in burrows or tree hollows and is most commonly seen along the coast of Belize. Though largely vegetarian, it won't turn its nose up to a meal of a small creature.

Dolphin (*delfin*): Several species are frequently spotted off the Pacific shores. They often travel in groups of 20 or more and play around vessels. Look for spotted dolphins, which are 6 feet long and have pale markings on their posterior.

Eagle Ray: One of the Caribbean's most graceful swimmers, these flat-bodied rays range in size from 6 to 8 feet. They have a white underside and numerous white spots and circular markings over their darker backs. Their pronounced heads have flattened, tapered snouts, and their long, thin tails have one to five venomous spines at the base. They prefer cruising sandy areas, occasionally stopping to dig for mollusks.

Fer-de-lance (*barba amarilla*): One of the most dangerous of all pit vipers, the fer-de-lance has a host of names, such as tommygoff in Belize and tomagasse in Guatemala. This aggressive snake grows up to 8 feet in length and is distinguished by the bright yellow patches on its head.

Frigate Bird (*tijereta del mar*): These black birds with slender wings and forked tails are some of the most effortless and agile fliers of the avian world. Coastal dwellers, they are more common on the Pacific than on the Atlantic. When mating season approaches, males inflate a scarlet pouch beneath their beaks in an effort to attract females.

Frog (*rana*): Some 120 species of frogs can be found in Belize and Guatemala. Most are nocturnal in an effort to avoid being eaten, but the brightly colored poison dart frogs—whose brilliant red, blue and green coloration warns predators that they don't make a good meal—can be spotted during the day. Red-eyed leaf frogs are among the showiest of nocturnal species. They firmly attach themselves to plants with neon-orange legs, scarlet eyes bulging out from a metallic green body splashed with white dots and blue patches. Large brown marine toads are also common at night.

Howler monkey (*mono congo*): These chunky-bodied monkeys travel in troops of up to 20. A bit on the lethargic side, they eat leaves, fruits, and flowers. The deep, resounding howls of the males serve as communication among and between troops. Erroneously termed "baboons" by Belizeans, these dark-faced monkeys travel only from tree to tree, limiting their presence to dense jungle canopy. They are increasingly difficult to spot in the wild.

Iguana (*iguana*): The largest lizards in Central America, these scaly creatures can can grow to 10 feet. They are good swimmers, and will often plop into a body of water when threatened by a predator. Only young green iguanas are brightly colored; adult females are grayish, while adult males are olive (with orangish heads during mating season). They are considered a delicacy among Belizeans, who call them "bamboo chicken."

Jacana (*gallito de agua*): These birds are sometimes referred to as "lily trotters" because their long toes allow them to walk on floating vegetation. They eat aquatic plants and animals and are found at almost any body of water. They expose their yellow wing feathers when in flight. The liberated females lay eggs in several floating nests tended by males.

Jaguar (*tigre*): The largest feline in the western hemisphere grows up to 6 feet long and can weigh up to 250 pounds. Exceedingly rare, this nocturnal predator is most often spotted near the Cockscomb Basin Wildlife Sanctuary in Belize.

Kinkajou (*martilla*): A nocturnal relative of the raccoon, kinkajous are known for their 20-inch-long prehensile tails. They actively and often noisily forage for fruit, insects, and the occasional sip of nectar. (If you aren't sure what you have spotted is a kinkajou, simply look at the picture on Belize's $20 note.)

Leaf-cutter ant (*zompopa*): Called wee wee ants in Creole, leaf-cutter ants are the region's most commonly noticed ants. They are found in all lowland habitats. Columns of these industrious little guys, all carrying clippings of leaves, sometimes extend for several hundred yards from plants to the underground nest. The leaves are used to cultivate the fungus that they eat.

Macaw (*lapas*): The beautiful scarlet macaw is the only species of this bird found in Belize and Guatemala. Huge, raucous birds with long tails, they use their immense bills to rip apart fruits to get to the seeds. Their nests are in hollow trees. They are endangered because of poachers and deforestation.

Magpie jay (*urraca*): A southern relative of the blue jay, magpie jays have long tails and distinctive crests of forwardly curved feathers. They are residents of Guatemala's Pacific slope. Omnivorous, bold, and inquisitive, with amazingly varied vocalizations, these birds travel in noisy groups of four or more.

Manatee: An immense and gentle mammal, the manatee is often called the sea cow. Living exclusively in the water, particularly in shallow and sheltered areas, manatees are said to be the basis of myths about mermaids. Scarce today, these vegetarians have been hunted for thousands of years for their tasty flesh; their image frequently appears in ancient Maya art.

Margay (*caucel*): This nocturnal, spotted cat is similar to the somewhat larger ocelot, but has a longer tail. Mobile ankle joints allow it to climb down trunks head first. The margay eats small vertebrates.

Morpho (*morfo*): This spectacular butterfly doesn't fail to astound first-time viewers. Easy to overlook when resting, their color is only apparent when they take flight. One species has brilliant-blue wings, while another is distinguished by its intense violet color. Adults feed on fallen fruit, never flowers.

Motmot (*pajaro bobo*): Handsome birds of the forest, motmots sit patiently while scanning for large insects and small vertebrates. The four species found in Belize and Guatemala make their nests in burrows.

Ocelot (*manigordo*): These medium-size spotted cats have shorter tails than their cousins the margays. They are active night and day, feeding on rodents and other small animals. Their forepaws are rather large in relation to their bodies, hence the Creole name that translates as "fat hand."

Oropéndola (*oropéndola*): These crow-size birds, members of the oriole family, have bright yellow tails. They nest in colonies with the female building pendulous nests in isolated trees. Males make unmistakable gurgling calls. They are fairly omnivorous, but subsist mostly on fruit.

Parrot (*loro*): A prerequisite of any tropical setting, there are five species of parrot in Central America. All are clad in green, which means they virtually disappear upon landing in the trees. Most have a splash of color or two on their head or wings.

Pelican (*pelícano*): Their large size, big bills, and flapping throat pouches make brown pelicans unmistakable inhabitants of both coasts (although they are far more abundant on the Pacific side). A white American variety prefers freshwater locations. They often fly in V formations and dive for fish.

Quetzal (*quetzal*): One of the world's most exquisite and elusive birds, resplendent quetzals were revered as sacred by the Mayas. The glittering green plumage and long tail feathers of the males were used in Maya ceremonial costumes. No longer found in Belize, they can be seen in and around Guatemala's Biotopo del Quetzal from February to April.

Roseate spoonbill (*garza rosada*): Pink plumage and distinctive bills set this wader apart from all other wetland birds. They feed by swishing their bills back and forth in the water while using their feet to stir up bottom-dwelling creatures.

Sea turtle: Sea turtles on the coasts of Belize and Guatemala come in three varieties: green, hawksbill, and loggerhead. All have paddlelike flippers and have to surface to breathe.

Spider monkey (*mono colorado, mono araña*): These lanky, long-tailed monkeys hang out in groups of two to four. Their diet consists of ripe fruit, leaves, and flowers. These incredible aerialists can swing effortlessly through the trees using their long arms and legs and prehensile tails. Caribbean and southern Pacific populations are dark reddish brown, while their cousins in the northwest are blond.

Tapir (*danta*): The national animal of Belize is also known as the mountain cow. Something like a small rhinoceros without the armor, it has a stout body, short legs, and small eyes. Completely vegetarian, it uses its prehensile snout for harvesting vegetation. The shy creature lives in forested areas near streams and lakes, where it can sometimes be spotted bathing.

Toucan (*tucán, tucancillo*): Recognizable to all who have ever seen a box of Fruit Loops, the toucan is common in Belize and Guatemala. The largest are the keel-billed and chestnut-mandibled toucans, growing to 22 inches long. The much smaller and stouter emerald toucanet and yellow-ear toucanet are among the most colorful. All eat fruit with their curved, multihued beaks.

— Elbert Greer

VOCABULARY

	English	Spanish	Pronunciation
Basics			
	Yes/no	Sí/no	see/no
	Please	Por favor	pore fah-*vore*
	May I?	¿Me permite?	may pair-*mee*-tay
	Thank you (very much)	(Muchas) gracias	(*moo*-chas) *grah*-see-as
	You're welcome	De nada	day *nah*-dah
	Excuse me	Con permiso	con pair-*mee*-so
	Pardon me/what did you say?	¿Como?/Mánde?	ko-mo/mahn-dey
	Could you tell me?	¿Podría decirme?	po-*dree*-ah deh-*seer*-meh
	I'm sorry	Lo siento	lo see-*en*-toe
	Hello	Hola	*oh*-lah
	Good morning!	¡Buenos días!	*bway*-nohs *dee*-ahs
	Good afternoon!	¡Buenas tardes!	*bway*-nahs *tar*-dess
	Good evening!	¡Buenas noches!	*bway*-nahs *no*-chess
	Goodbye!	¡Adiós!/¡Hasta luego!	ah-dee-*ohss*/ *ah*-stah-*lwe*-go
	Mr./Mrs.	Señor/Señora	sen-*yor*/sen-*yore*-ah
	Miss	Señorita	sen-yo-*ree*-tah
	Pleased to meet you	Mucho gusto	*moo*-cho *goose*-to
	How are you?	¿Cómo está usted?	*ko*-mo es-*tah* oo-*sted*
	Very well, thank you.	Muy bien, gracias.	*moo*-ee bee-*en*, grah-see-as
	And you?	¿Y usted?	ee oos-*ted*
	Hello (on the telephone)	Bueno	*bwen*-oh
Numbers			
	1	un, uno	oon, *oo*-no
	2	dos	dos
	3	tres	trace
	4	cuatro	*kwah*-tro
	5	cinco	*sink*-oh
	6	seis	sace
	7	siete	see-*et*-ey
	8	ocho	*o*-cho

9	nueve	new-*ev*-ay
10	diez	dee-*es*
11	once	*own*-sey
12	doce	*doe*-sey
13	trece	*tray*-sey
14	catorce	kah-*tor*-sey
15	quince	*keen*-sey
16	dieciséis	dee-es-ee-*sace*
17	diecisiete	dee-*es*-ee-see-*et*-ay
18	dieciocho	dee-*es*-ee-*o*-cho
19	diecinueve	*dee-es*-ee-new-*ev*-ay
20	veinte	*bain*-tay
21	veinte y uno/ veintiuno	*bain*-te-oo-no
30	treinta	*train*-tah
32	treinta y dos	train-tay-*dose*
40	cuarenta	kwah-*ren*-tah
43	cuarenta y tres	kwah-*ren*-tay-*trace*
50	cincuenta	seen-*kwen*-tah
54	cincuenta y cuatro	seen-*kwen*-tay *kwah*-tro
60	sesenta	sess-*en*-tah
65	sesenta y cinco	sess-*en*-tay *seen*-ko
70	setenta	set-*en*-tah
76	setenta y seis	set-*en*-tay *sace*
80	ochenta	oh-*chen*-tah
87	ochenta y siete	oh-*chen*-tay see-*yet*-ay
90	noventa	no-*ven*-tah
98	noventa y ocho	no-*ven*-tah *o*-cho
100	cien	see-*en*
101	ciento uno	see-en-toe *oo*-no
200	doscientos	doe-see-*en*-tohss
500	quinientos	keen-*yen*-tohss
700	setecientos	set-eh-see-*en*-tohss
900	novecientos	no-veh-see-*en*-tohss
1,000	mil	meel
2,000	dos mil	dose meel
1,000,000	un millón	oon meel-*yohn*

Colors

black	negro	*neh*-grow
blue	azul	ah-*sool*
brown	café	kah-*feh*
green	verde	*vair*-day
pink	rosa	*ro*-sah
purple	morado	mo-*rah*-doe
orange	naranja	na-*rahn*-hah
red	rojo	*roe*-hoe
white	blanco	*blahn*-koh
yellow	amarillo	ah-mah-*ree*-yoh

Days of the Week

Sunday	domingo	doe-*meen*-goh
Monday	lunes	*loo*-ness
Tuesday	martes	*mahr*-tess
Wednesday	miércoles	me-*air*-koh-less
Thursday	jueves	who-*ev*-ess
Friday	viernes	vee-*air*-ness
Saturday	sábado	*sah*-bah-doe

Months

January	enero	eh-*neh*-ro
February	febrero	feh-*brair*-oh
March	marzo	*mahr*-so
April	abril	ah-*breel*
May	mayo	*my*-oh
June	junio	*hoo*-nee-oh
July	julio	*who*-lee-yoh
August	agosto	ah-*ghost*-toe
September	septiembre	sep-tee-*em*-breh
October	octubre	oak-*too*-breh
November	noviembre	no-vee-*em*-breh
December	diciembre	dee-see-*em*-breh

Useful Phrases

Do you speak English?	¿Habla usted inglés?	*ah*-blah oos-*ted* in-*glehs*
I don't speak Spanish	No hablo español	no *ah*-blow es-pahn-*yol*

I don't understand (you)	No entiendo	no en-tee-*en*-doe
I understand (you)	Entiendo	en-tee-*en*-doe
I don't know	No sé	no *say*
I am from the United States/ British	Soy de los Estados Unidos/ inglés(a)	soy deh lohs ehs-*tah*-dohs oo-*nee*-dohs/ in-*glace*(ah)
What's your name?	¿Cómo se llama usted?	*koh*-mo say *yah*-mah oos-*ted*
My name is . . .	Me llamo . . .	may *yah*-moh
What time is it?	¿Qué hora es?	keh *o*-rah es
It is one, two, three . . . o'clock.	Es la una; son las dos, tres	es la *oo*-nah/sone lahs dose, trace
How?	¿Cómo?	*koh*-mo
When?	¿Cuándo?	*kwahn*-doe
This/Next week	Esta semana/ la semana que entra	*es*-tah seh-*mah*-nah/ lah say-*mah*-nah keh *en*-trah
This/Next month	Este mes/el próximo mes	*es*-tay mehs/el *proke*-see-mo mehs
This/Next year	Este año/el año que viene	*es*-tay *ahn*-yo/el *ahn*-yo keh vee-*yen*-ay
Yesterday/today/ tomorrow	Ayer/hoy/mañana	ah-*yair*/oy/mahn-*yah*-nah
This morning/ afternoon	Esta mañana/tarde	*es*-tah mahn-*yah*-nah/*tar*-day
Tonight	Esta noche	*es*-tah *no*-cheh
What?	¿Qué?	keh
What is this?	¿Qué es esto?	keh es *es*-toe
Why?	¿Por qué?	pore *keh*
Who?	¿Quién?	kee-*yen*
Where is . . . ?	¿Dónde está . . . ?	*dohn*-day es-*tah*
the train station?	la estación del tren?	la es-tah-see-*on* del *train*
the subway station?	la estación del Metro?	la es-ta-see-*on* del *meh*-tro
the bus stop?	la parada del autobús?	la pah-*rah*-dah del oh-toe-*boos*
the bank?	el banco?	el *bahn*-koh
the ATM?	el cajero automática?	el *kah*-hehr-oh oh-toe-*mah*-tee-kah
the . . . hotel?	el hotel . . . ?	el oh-*tel*
the store?	la tienda . . . ?	la tee-*en*-dah
the cashier?	la caja?	la *kah*-hah

the . . . museum?	el museo . . . ?	el moo-*seh*-oh
the hospital?	el hospital?	el ohss-pea-*tal*
the elevator?	el ascensor?	el ah-*sen*-sore
the bathroom?	el baño?	el *bahn*-yoh
Here/there	Aquí/allá	ah-*key*/ah-*yah*
Open/closed	Abierto/cerrado	ah-be-*er*-toe/ ser-*ah*-doe
Left/right	Izquierda/derecha	iss-key-*er*-dah/ dare-*eh*-chah
Straight ahead	Derecho	der-*eh*-choh
Is it near/far?	¿Está cerca/lejos?	es-*tah sair*-kah/ *leh*-hoss
I'd like . . .	Quisiera . . .	kee-see-air-ah
a room	un cuarto/una habitación	oon *kwahr*-toe/ *oo*-nah ah-bee-tah-see-*on*
the key	la llave	lah *yah*-vay
a newspaper	un periódico	oon pear-ee-*oh*-dee-koh
I'd like to buy . . .	Quisiera comprar . . .	kee-see-*air*-ah kohm-*prahr*
cigarettes	cigarrillo	ce-gar-*reel*-oh
matches	cerillos	ser-*ee*-ohs
a dictionary	un diccionario	oon deek-see-oh-*nah*-ree-oh
soap	jabón	hah-*bone*
a map	un mapa	oon *mah*-pah
a magazine	una revista	*oon*-ah reh-*veess*-tah
paper	papel	pah-*pel*
envelopes	sobres	*so*-brace
a postcard	una tarjeta postal	*oon*-ah tar-*het*-ah post-*ahl*
How much is it?	¿Cuánto cuesta?	*kwahn*-toe *kwes*-tah
Do you accept credit cards?	¿Aceptan tarjetas de crédito?	ah-*sehp*-than tahr-*heh*-tahs deh *creh*-dee-toh?
A little/a lot	Un poquito/ mucho . . .	oon poh-*kee*-toe/ *moo*-choh
More/less	Más/menos	mahss/*men*-ohss
Enough/too much/too little	Suficiente/de-masiado/muy poco	soo-fee-see-*en*-tay/ day-mah-see-*ah*-doe/*moo*-ee *poh*-koh
Telephone	Teléfono	tel-*ef*-oh-no
Telegram	Telegrama	teh-leh-*grah*-mah
I am ill/sick	Estoy enfermo(a)	es-*toy* en-*fair*-moh(ah)

Please call a doctor	Por favor llame un médico	pore fa-*vor ya*-may oon *med*-ee-koh
Help!	¡Auxilio! ¡Ayuda!	owk-*see*-lee-oh/ ah-*yoo*-dah
Fire!	¡Encendio!	en-*sen*-dee-oo
Caution!/Look out!	¡Cuidado!	kwee-*dah*-doh

On the Road

Highway	Carretera	car-ray-*ter*-ah
Causeway, paved highway	Calzada	cal-*za*-dah
Speed bump	Tope	*toh*-pay
Toll highway	Carretera de cuota	car-ray-*ter*-ha day dwoh-tah
Toll booth	Caseta	kah-*set*-ah
Route	Ruta	*roo*-tah
Road	Camino	cah-*mee*-no
Street	Calle	*cah*-yeh
Avenue	Avenida	ah-ven-*ee*-dah
Broad, tree-lined boulevard	Paseo	pah-*seh*-oh
Waterfront promenade	Malecón	mal-lay-*cone*
Wharf	Embarcadero	em-bar-cah-*day*-ro

In Town

Church	Templo/Iglesia	*tem*-plo/e-*gles*-se-*ah*
Cathedral	Catedral	cah-tay-*dral*
Neighborhood	Barrio	*bar*-re-o
Foreign exchange shop	Casa de cambio	*cas*-sah day *cam*-be-o
City hall	Ayuntamiento	ah-yoon-tah-mee *en*-toe
Main square	Zócalo	*zo*-cal-o
Traffic circle	Glorieta	glor-e-*ay*-tah
Market	Mercado (Spanish)/ Tianguis (Indian)	mer-*cah*-doe/ tee-*an*-geese
Inn	Posada	pos-*sah*-dah
Group taxi	Colectivo	co-lec-*tee*-vo
Mini-bus along fixed route	Pesero	pi-*seh*-ro

Dining Out

I'd like to reserve a table	Quisiera reservar una mesa.	kee-*syeh*-rah rreh-sehr-*vahr* oo-nah *meh*-sah
A bottle of . . .	Una botella de . . .	*oo*-nah bo-*tay*-yah deh
A cup of . . .	Una taza de . . .	*oo*-nah *tah*-sah deh
A glass of . . .	Un vaso de . . .	oon *vah*-so deh
Ashtray	Un cenicero	oon sen-ee-*seh*-roh
Bill/check	La cuenta	lah *kwen*-tah
Bread	El pan	el pahn
Breakfast	El desayuno	el day-sigh-*oon*-oh
Butter	La mantequilla	lah mahn-tay-*key*-yah
Cheers!	¡Salud!	sah-*lood*
Cocktail	Un aperitivo	oon ah-pair-ee-*tee*-voh
Mineral water	Agua mineral	*ah*-gwah mee-neh-*rahl*
Beer	Cerveza	sehr-*veh*-sah
Dinner	La cena	lah *seh*-nah
Dish	Un plato	oon *plah*-toe
Dish of the day	El platillo de hoy	el plah-*tee*-yo day oy
Enjoy!	¡Buen provecho!	bwen pro-*veh*-cho
Fixed-price menu	La comida corrida	lah koh-*me*-dah co-*ree*-dah
Is the tip included?	¿Está incluida la propina?	es-*tah* in-clue-*ee*-dah lah pro-*pea*-nah
Fork	El tenedor	el ten-eh-*door*
Knife	El cuchillo	el koo-*chee*-yo
Spoon	Una cuchara	*oo*-nah koo-*chah*-rah
Lunch	La comida	lah koh-*me*-dah
Menu	La carta	lah *cart*-ah
Napkin	La servilleta	lah sair-vee-*yet*-uh
Please give me	Por favor déme	pore fah-*vor* *day*-may
Pepper	La pimienta	lah pea-me-*en*-tah
Salt	La sal	lah sahl
Sugar	El azúcar	el ah-*sue*-car
Waiter!/Waitress!	¡Por favor Señor/Señorita!	pore fah-*vor* sen-*yor*/sen-yor-*ee*-tah

INDEX

D

E

F

G